Case Studies in
Abnormal Psychology

SECOND EDITION

Ethan E. Gorenstein
Behavioral Medicine Program
Columbia-Presbyterian Medical Center

Ronald J. Comer
Princeton University

WORTH PUBLISHERS
A Macmillan Higher Education Company

Vice President, Editing, Design, and Media Production: Catherine Woods
Publisher: Kevin Feyen
Senior Acquisitions Editor: Rachel Losh
Senior Developmental Editor: Mimi Melek
Assistant Editor: Katie Garrett
Marketing Manager: Lindsay Johnson
Marketing Assistant: Tess Sanders
Art Director: Diana Blume
Director of Editing, Design, and Media Production: Tracey Kuehn
Managing Editor: Lisa Kinne
Project Editor: Edgar Bonilla
Production Manager: Sarah Segal
Composition: Northeastern Graphic
Printing and Binding: RR Donnelley
Cover image: Gary Waters/Illustration Source

Library of Congress Control Number: 2014937988

ISBN-13: 978-0-7167-7273-6
ISBN-10: 0-7167-7273-6

Printed in the United States of America
Fourth printing

Worth Publishers
41 Madison Avenue
New York, NY 10010
www.worthpublishers.com

For Margee, Eleazer, and Julian
—E. E. G.

For Delia and Emmett
—R. J. C.

CONTENTS

Several fine case study books available today provide in-depth descriptions of psychological disorders and treatments. In writing *Case Studies in Abnormal Psychology,* Second Edition, we wanted to maintain the clinical richness of such books and in addition offer a number of important and unique features that truly help bring clinical material to life. In both the previous edition and this one, our approach helps readers to appreciate the different perspectives of clients, friends, relatives, and therapists; reveals the nitty-gritty details of treatment programs; and challenges readers to apply their clinical insights, think critically, and make clinical decisions. We believe that *Case Studies in Abnormal Psychology,* Second Edition, can stimulate a deeper understanding of abnormal psychology by use of the following features that set it apart from other clinical case books:

1. **Multiple perspectives:** As with other case books, our cases offer in-depth descriptions of clinical symptoms, histories, and treatments. In addition, however, each case looks at a disorder from the point of view of the client, the therapist, and a friend or relative. These different points of view demonstrate that a given disorder typically affects multiple persons and help readers to empathize with the concerns and dilemmas of both clients and those with whom they interact.

2. **In-depth treatment presentations:** Extra attention is paid to treatment in this book, particularly to the interaction between client and therapist. Our detailed treatment discussions help readers to fully appreciate how theories of treatment are translated into actual procedures and how individuals with particular problems respond to a clinician's efforts to change those problems.

3. **Research-based treatments, integrated approaches:** The treatments described throughout the book represent approaches that are well supported by empirical research. In most of the cases, the treatment is actually an

integration of several approaches, again reflecting current trends and findings in the clinical research.

4. **Balanced, complete, accurate presentation:** Overall, a very balanced view of current practices is offered, with cases presented free of bias. Readers will find each of the major models of abnormal psychology—behavioral, cognitive, psychodynamic, humanistic, biological, and sociocultural—represented repeatedly and respectfully throughout the book, with particular selections guided strictly by current research and applications.

5. **Stimulating pedagogical tools:** An array of special pedagogical tools helps students process and retain the material, appreciate subtle clinical issues, and apply critical thinking. For example, every page of the book features marginal notes that contain important clinical and research points as well as other food for thought, each introduced at precisely the right moment. Testing shows that readers greatly enjoy this exciting technique and that it helps them to learn and retain material more completely.

6. **Readers' interaction and application:** The final three cases in the book are presented without diagnosis or treatment so that readers can be challenged to identify disorders, suggest appropriate therapies, and consider provocative questions (stated in the margins). By taking the perspective of the therapist, readers learn to think actively about the cases and apply their clinical knowledge and insights. These three special cases, each entitled "You Decide," are followed by corresponding sections in the appendix that reveal probable diagnosis, treatment approaches, and important clinical information about the disorder under discussion.

7. **Diagnostic checklists:** Each case is accompanied by a diagnostic checklist, a detailed presentation of the key DSM-5 criteria for arriving at the diagnosis in question.

8. **Real clinical material:** The cases presented in this book are based on real cases, as are the treatments and outcomes. They are taken from our own clinical experiences and from those of respected colleagues who have shared their clinical cases with us.

9. **Interwoven clinical material, theory, and research:** Each case weaves together clinical material, theoretical perspectives, and empirical findings so that readers can appreciate not only the fascinating clinical details and events but also what they mean. Similarly, they can recognize not only what and how treatment techniques are applied but why such techniques are chosen.

10. **Current material and references:** The theories and treatment approaches that are described reflect current writings and research literature. Indeed, we are proud to note that several exciting new cases have been added to this

second edition of *Case Studies in Abnormal Psychology*. In addition, the cases retained from the first edition have been carefully updated to reflect the clinical field's growing insights, new research findings, and DSM-5-based diagnostic changes. Similarly, the second edition's numerous margin notes are fully up to date, and like the cases themselves, they truly capture the state of affairs in the clinical field and world today.

II. **Readability:** Of course, every book tries to be interesting, readable, and widely appealing. But case books provide a unique opportunity to bring material to life in a manner that deeply engages and stimulates the reader. We have worked diligently to make sure that this opportunity is not missed, not only showing the diversity of our clients and therapists but making sure that readers walk away from the book with the same feelings of deep concern, passion, fascination, wonder, and even frustration that we experience in our work every day.

It is our fervent hope that the cases in this edition, like those in the first edition, will inspire empathy for clients, their relatives, their friends, and their therapists. The practitioners described in these pages struggle mightily to maintain both their humanity and their scientific integrity, and we believe that humanity is indeed served best when scientific integrity is maintained.

A number of people helped to bring this project to fruition. Foremost are the clinicians and patients who dedicated themselves to the efforts described in these pages. We are particularly grateful to Danae Hudson and Brooke Whisenhunt, professors of psychology at Missouri State University. These wonderfully talented individuals wrote the cases on somatic symptom disorder (Danae), and gender dysphoria (Brooke) for this edition. In addition, they helped revise and update the rest of the book. Throughout all of this work, their outstanding writing, teaching, clinical, and research skills are constantly on display.

Finally, we are indebted to the extraordinary people at Worth Publishers, whose superior talents, expertise, and commitment to the education of readers guided us at every turn both in this edition and the first edition of *Case Studies in Abnormal Psychology*. They include Kevin Feyen, Rachel Losh, Katie Garrett, Tracey Kuehn, Sarah Segal, Diana Blume, Edgar Bonilla, and developmental editor extraordinaire Mimi Melek. They have all been superb, and we deeply appreciate their invaluable contributions.

Ethan E. Gorenstein
Ronald J. Comer
April 2014

CASE 1

Panic Disorder

Table 1-1

Dx Checklist

Panic Attack

1. Persons experience a sudden outburst of profound fear or discomfort that rises and peaks within minutes.

2. The attack includes at least 4 of the following:

   (a) Increased heart rate or palpitations.

   (b) Perspiration.

   (c) Trembling.

   (d) Shortness of breath.

   (e) Choking sensations.

   (f) Discomfort or pain in the chest.

   (g) Nausea or other abdominal upset.

   (h) Dizziness or lightheadedness.

   (i) Feeling significantly chilled or hot.

   (j) Sensations of tingling or numbness.

   (k) Sense of unreality or separation from the self or others.

   (l) Dread of losing control.

   (m) Dread of dying.

(Based on APA, 2013.)

Table 1-2

Dx Checklist

Panic Disorder

1. Unforeseen panic attacks occur repeatedly.

2. One or more of the attacks precedes either of the following symptoms:

   (a) At least a month of continual concern about having additional attacks.

   (b) At least a month of dysfunctional behavior changes associated with the attacks (for example, avoiding new experiences).

(Based on APA, 2013.)

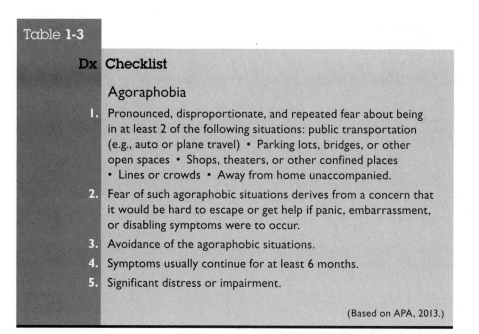

Table 1-3

Dx Checklist

Agoraphobia

1. Pronounced, disproportionate, and repeated fear about being in at least 2 of the following situations: public transportation (e.g., auto or plane travel) • Parking lots, bridges, or other open spaces • Shops, theaters, or other confined places • Lines or crowds • Away from home unaccompanied.

2. Fear of such agoraphobic situations derives from a concern that it would be hard to escape or get help if panic, embarrassment, or disabling symptoms were to occur.

3. Avoidance of the agoraphobic situations.

4. Symptoms usually continue for at least 6 months.

5. Significant distress or impairment.

(Based on APA, 2013.)

Joe's childhood was a basically happy one. At the same time, it was steeped in financial hardship, as his Hungarian immigrant parents struggled to keep the family afloat in the United States during World War II. Joe's father, after a series of jobs as a laborer, ultimately scraped together enough money to start a small hardware store, which survived, but Joe had to quit school in the ninth grade to help run the business. He put in 9 years at the store before being drafted for the Vietnam War at age 23.

> Panic disorder is twice as common among women as men.

Joe An American Success Story

When Joe returned from the army, he took more of an interest in the store, and with some far-sighted marketing strategies turned it into a successful enterprise that ultimately employed 6 full-time workers. Joe was proud of what he had accomplished but harbored lifelong shame and regret over his shortened education, especially as he had been an outstanding student. The store was thus both the boon and the bane of his existence.

Joe met Florence at age 45, after he took over the store from his father and established himself as a respectable neighborhood businessman. Before meeting Florence, the energetic businessman's social life was spare; his goal of making a success of himself was his overriding concern. Florence was a 40-year-old college-educated administrator for an insurance company when they met. She was impressed with Joe's intelligence and wisdom and would never have suspected that his education stopped at the ninth grade. As their relationship progressed, Joe revealed his lack of education to her as though making a grave confession. Far from being repelled, Florence was all the more impressed with Joe's accomplishments. The couple married within a year.

Joe and Florence worked hard, raised a daughter, saved what they earned, and eventually enjoyed the fruits of their labor in the form of a comfortable retirement when he was 70. The couple continued to live in the neighborhood where Joe grew up and had his business. They spent much of their time with friends at a public country club that was popular among local retirees. Joe also enjoyed tinkering daily with the couple's modest investments.

Six years into Joe's retirement, when he was 76, Joe and Florence were returning from a Florida vacation when catastrophe struck. The catastrophe was not an airplane accident or anything like that. It was a more private event, not apparent to anyone but Joe. Nevertheless, it had a profound and expanding effect on the retired veteran, and it began a journey that Joe feared would never end.

> Unlike Joe's case, panic disorder usually begins between late adolescence and the mid-30s, with the median age of onset being 20 to 24 years (APA, 2013).

Joe The Attack

After their plane took off from the Miami airport and Joe settled back in his seat, he noticed that it was getting difficult to breathe. It felt as if all the air had been sucked out of the plane. As Joe's breathing became increasingly labored, he began staring at the plane's sealed door, contemplating the fresh air on the other side. Then, suddenly, he had another thought, which frightened him. He wondered if he might feel so deprived of oxygen that he would be tempted to make a mad dash for the door and open it in midflight. He struggled to banish this vision from his brain, but soon he became aware of his heart racing furiously in his chest cavity. The pounding became almost unbearable. He could feel every beat. The beating grew so strong that he thought he could actually hear it.

Joe looked over at his wife, Florence, in the seat next to his. She was peacefully immersed in a magazine, oblivious to his condition. He stared at her, wondering what he must look like in such a state. His spouse glanced up for a moment, gave Joe the briefest of smiles, and went back to her reading. She obviously hadn't a clue as to what he was going through. Joe felt as if he were about to die or lose his mind—he couldn't tell which at this point—and she continued reading as if nothing were happening. Finally Joe had to say something. He asked Florence if the air in the plane felt stuffy to her. She said it seemed fine but suggested that her husband open the valve overhead if he felt uncomfortable. He did so and felt only slightly better.

The rest of the plane ride was sheer torture. Joe spent the entire time trying to get the cool air to flow directly onto his face from the valve above. This activity sustained him until the plane landed. When the passengers were finally permitted to disembark, Joe couldn't get to the door fast enough. As he emerged from the plane, he felt released from a horrible confinement.

After arriving home at his apartment in the city, the retired store owner felt better. He was still shaky, but he said nothing to Florence, who remained unaware of what had happened. Joe slept well that night and by the next morning felt like his old self. He decided to put the whole episode behind him.

Joe continued to feel fine for the next few days. Then one night he awoke at 2:00 A.M. in a cold sweat. His heart felt as though it were about to leap out of his chest; his lungs seemed incapable of drawing any oxygen from the air. His first thought was to open the bedroom window to make it easier for him to breathe. But as Joe got out of bed, he suddenly drew back in alarm. He recalled the airplane door and what had seemed like an almost uncontrollable urge to force it open in midflight. He wondered if this meant he had an unconscious desire to commit suicide. Joe concluded he should stay away from the window. Instead, he sat motionless on the edge of the bed while his thoughts raced along with his heart toward some unreachable finish line. The man was frightened and confused. He was also gasping loudly enough to awaken Florence. She asked him what was wrong, and he told her his physical symptoms: he couldn't breathe and his heart was pounding so hard that his chest ached. Florence immediately concluded that her husband was having a heart attack and called an ambulance.

> Many people (and their physicians) mistake their first panic attack for a general medical problem.

The ambulance workers arrived, administered oxygen, and rushed Joe to the emergency room. By the time the patient got there, however, he was feeling much better. A cardiologist examined him, performed a battery of tests, and eventually informed Joe that he had not had a heart attack. In fact, there was nothing obviously wrong with him. The doctor told Joe he could go home, that the episodes were probably "just anxiety attacks."

Joe felt relieved that his heart seemed to be okay but was confused as to exactly what was wrong with him. He wanted nothing more than to forget the whole matter. However, as time passed, that became increasingly difficult. In fact, over the course of the next few weeks, he had 2 more attacks in the middle of the night. In both cases, he just lay in bed motionless, praying that the symptoms would go away.

Then there was a new development. One morning, Joe was walking down a busy street in his neighborhood, on a routine trip to the store, when he was overcome by the same symptoms he had previously had at night. Out of the blue, his heart started pounding, his breathing became labored, and he felt dizzy; also, he couldn't stop trembling. He looked around for a safe haven—a store or restaurant where he could sit down—but he felt as if he were in a kind of dream world. Everything around him—the people, the traffic, the stores—seemed unreal. He felt bombarded by sights and sounds and found it impossible to focus on anything. The overwhelmed man then recalled the cardiologist's mention of the term *anxiety attack* and came to the sickening realization that the doctor must have detected that he had mental problems. Joe feared that he was on the verge of a nervous breakdown.

He was several blocks from home but discovered, to his relief, that he could make his way back to the apartment with less difficulty than he anticipated. Once inside, Joe sat down on the living room sofa and closed his eyes. He felt certain he was losing his mind; it was just a matter of time before the next attack sent him off the deep end. As he became caught up in his private terror, he heard a sound at the front door. It was Florence returning home from her shopping.

Once again, Florence appeared to have no inkling that anything was amiss. She cheerfully related the details of her shopping trip: the neighbors she met at the store, the things she bought, and the like. Joe could barely follow what she was saying, further proof, in his mind, that he was rapidly losing his grip. Finally, his wife suggested that they go out for a walk. At this, Joe realized that the very thought of leaving the apartment was terrifying to him. What if he had an attack in the middle of the street and could no longer function, physically or mentally? He felt as if he had a time bomb inside him. In response to Florence's suggestion, he simply broke down in tears.

Florence begged her husband to tell her what was wrong. Joe confessed that he had just had another one of his attacks, this time on the way to the store, and that this one was so bad he was forced to return home. Now he dreaded going outside.

Florence could see that Joe was extremely upset, but at the same time she was puzzled. There didn't seem to be anything wrong with him. He was in no obvious physical pain, and he appeared vigorous and alert. She insisted they make an appointment with their primary care physician.

In the week before the appointment, Joe made a few tentative forays onto the street in Florence's company. He felt some symptoms while outside but did not have as intense an attack as he had that one time when he was alone. His nighttime episodes increased in frequency, however—to the point that he could count on waking up with an attack almost every time he went to bed.

The Family Doctor Armed with New Knowledge

At the doctor's office, Joe recounted his repeated attacks of racing heart, breathlessness, and tremulousness. He didn't know quite how to describe his fear of losing his mind, nor did he really want to, so he left that part out. He did convey, however, that he had now become so apprehensive about the attacks that he was reluctant to venture outside for fear of being overwhelmed. In describing his symptoms, Joe noticed that he was actually starting to have some of them.

As he continued, his physician became increasingly confident that the patient had panic disorder. The doctor marveled to himself at how far medicine had come

Around 2.8 percent of people in the United States have panic disorder in a given year; 5 percent develop the disorder at some point in their lives (Kessler et al., 2010).

since he started practicing. Years ago, a patient like Joe would have been hospitalized for weeks with a suspected heart problem and subjected to dozens of tests. If no major disease turned up, he would be released, but even then the suspicion would linger that he was on the verge of a major cardiac problem, and the patient would be advised to cut back on his activities and keep on the lookout for further symptoms. Far from being reassured, the person would feel like a ticking time bomb.

Now physicians were very aware of the power of panic attacks and of how their symptoms mimicked those of a heart attack. As soon as cardiac and other physical conditions were ruled out, practitioners usually turned their attention to the possibility of panic attacks. Indeed, Joe's was the fourth case of probable panic disorder that the doctor had seen this month alone. Even more gratifying, very effective treatments for panic disorder were available, with many patients benefiting from only 5 therapy sessions (Otto et al., 2012). Now he could offer patients 2 forms of good news: one, that their heart was fine; and 2, that their condition was fully treatable.

After examining Joe, the doctor informed him that other than a slightly elevated heart rate, everything seemed normal. He told his patient that his symptoms were by no means imaginary; rather, he had a well-known condition known as panic disorder. He suggested that Joe see Dr. Barbara Geller, a professor of clinical psychology at the nearby university, who also saw clients 2 evenings each week in private practice. Dr. Geller specialized in panic-related problems.

Joe was encouraged by his doctor's pronouncement that his condition could be helped, but he was leery of the idea of seeing a "shrink." He had never had any psychological treatment of any kind, and the whole idea fueled his secret fear, not yet expressed to anyone, that he was on the brink of insanity.

When they returned home, Florence urged Joe to call Dr. Geller, but he continued to put it off for a few more days. Florence, growing increasingly impatient, said she would call the psychologist herself to arrange the appointment, and Joe reluctantly agreed.

Joe in Treatment *Regaining Control over His Mind and Body*

After Joe recounted his experiences of the past few weeks in minute and animated detail, Dr. Geller asked him if he could recall ever having had similar attacks or sensations prior to these. Upon reflection, Joe realized that he had had these sensations before, during the Florida vacation itself. He recalled that the day after arriving in Florida he fell as he was walking down some steps toward the outdoor pool. His injuries were not serious, but a cut on his chin was deep enough to require a couple of stitches from the house physician. For the remainder of the vacation, Joe had momentary jolts of anxiety—including heart palpitations and mild

Today's physicians must also be careful to consider possible medical explanations before making a diagnosis of panic disorder. Certain medical problems, such as thyroid disease, seizure disorders, cardiac arrhythmias, and mitral valve prolapse (a cardiac malfunction marked by periodic episodes of palpitations) can cause panic attacks. Medical tests can rule out such causes.

According to research, people who are prone to panic attacks typically have a high degree of anxiety sensitivity. That is, they generally are preoccupied with their bodily sensations and interpret them as potentially harmful. Research has shown that cognitive-behavioral therapy can decrease anxiety sensitivity, which leads to a decrease in symptoms of panic disorder (Gallagher et al., 2013).

dizziness—at the slightest indication of physical imbalance. He also realized now that since falling, he had been very tentative in his walking.

Joe strained his memory to recall whether he had ever had similar attacks or sensations before the Florida incident. The only thing he recalled in this connection was an extremely upsetting experience he had had more than 50 years ago, when he was in his 20s. It was something that he had never discussed with anyone.

When he was in Vietnam, he and some buddies were driving a jeep back to base when they passed a local man walking along the side of the road. To demonstrate goodwill, Joe offered him a ride. The man was grateful for this kindness and took a seat in the open vehicle. After traveling only a few hundred yards, however, the jeep hit an enormous pothole, throwing the man onto the road, where his leg fell under the jeep's wheel. The soldiers quickly loaded him carefully back onto the jeep and raced to the nearest civilian hospital. They had to leave the injured man there and depart, however, as they were already close to being AWOL.

When Joe visited the hospital the next day to assure himself that their passenger would recover satisfactorily, he was shocked at what he saw. Due to lack of staffing or supplies, or some such difficulty, the hospital had done nothing more than provide a bed for the injured man. As Joe tried to talk to him, the man just lay there, obviously traumatized, gazing absently into space. Joe left the hospital even more shaken than when he had witnessed the actual accident. He was certain he had ruined the life of another human being. He drove back to the base in a trancelike state, with his heart pounding and his eyes barely able to focus on the road. That intensity of feeling was the closest he had ever experienced to what he was going through now.

After interviewing Joe and reviewing his medical reports, Dr. Geller concluded that his condition met the DSM-5 criteria for a diagnosis of both panic disorder and agoraphobia. His panic attacks typically included several of the defining symptoms: breathlessness, heart palpitations, chest discomfort, tremulousness, sweating, and fear of losing control or going crazy. Moreover, he was almost constantly apprehensive about the possibility of further attacks. He was also diagnosed with agoraphobia, because he was beginning to avoid leaving the house except in Florence's company.

Dr. Geller's reading of psychological literature and her own research on panic disorders had convinced her, along with many other clinicians, that panic attacks and disorders can best be explained by a combination of biological and cognitive factors. On the biological side, she believed that panic attacks are similar to the so-called fight-or-flight response, the normal physiological arousal of humans and other animals in response to danger. The difference is that with a panic attack there is no external triggering event. From this standpoint, a panic attack can be considered a false alarm of sorts. The body produces its reaction to danger in

The *fight-or-flight response* is so named because it prepares an organism to cope with a dangerous predicament either by fighting or fleeing. It primes the organism for a rapid use of energy by increasing heart rate, breathing rate, perspiration, blood flow to large muscles, and mental alertness.

the absence of any objectively dangerous event. People whose bodies repeatedly have such false alarms are candidates for panic disorder.

On the cognitive side, Dr. Geller believed that a full-blown disorder affects those who repeatedly interpret their attacks as something more than false alarms. They typically identify the physiological reactions as a real source of danger. They may conclude that they are suffocating or having a heart attack or stroke; or they may believe they are going crazy or out of control. Such interpretations produce still more alarm and further arousal of the sympathetic nervous system. As the nervous system becomes further aroused, the person's sense of alarm increases, and a vicious cycle unfolds in which anxious thoughts and the sympathetic nervous system feed on each other.

For many people with panic disorder, the panic experience is aggravated by hyperventilation. As part of their sympathetic nervous system arousal, they breathe more rapidly and deeply, ultimately causing a significant drop in their blood's level of carbon dioxide. This physiological change results in feelings of breathlessness, light-headedness, blurred vision, dizziness, or faintness—sensations that lead many people to conclude there is something physically or mentally wrong with them.

Even if people with panic disorder eventually come to recognize that their attacks are false alarms set off by their nervous system, they may live in a heightened state of anxiety over what their sympathetic nervous system might do. Many also develop anxieties about situations in which they feel a panic attack would be especially unwelcome (in crowds, closed spaces, airplanes, trains, or the like). Because of such anticipatory anxiety, their sympathetic nervous system becomes aroused whenever those situations are approached, and the likelihood of a panic attack in such situations is increased.

Given this integrated view of panic attacks, panic disorder, and agoraphobia, Dr. Geller used a combination of cognitive and behavioral techniques, each chosen to help eliminate the client's anxiety reaction to his or her sympathetic nervous system arousal. The cognitive techniques were designed to change the individual's faulty interpretations of sympathetic arousal. The behavioral component of treatment involved repeated exposure to both internal (bodily sensations) and external triggers of the person's panic attacks.

Session 1 To begin treatment, Dr. Geller showed Joe a list of typical symptoms associated with panic attacks, including the mental symptoms "sense of unreality" and "fear of going crazy or losing control." She asked the client which symptoms he had personally had. Joe was astonished to see his most feared symptoms actually listed on paper, and he seized the opportunity to discuss them openly at long last.

Dr. Geller explained to Joe that fears of going crazy were very common among panic sufferers; indeed, many people found them to be the most disturbing aspect

> Panic disorder is similar to a phobia. However, rather than fearing an external object or situation, those who have it come to distrust and fear the power and arousal of their own autonomic nervous system.

> About 80 percent of those who receive cognitive-behavioral treatment for their panic disorder fully overcome their disorder (Clark & Wells, 1997).

of the disorder. She emphasized, however, that the fear of losing one's mind on account of the panic disorder, although common, was completely unfounded. There was no chance of Joe's going insane. Although visibly relieved to hear this, he wondered aloud why it seemed as if he were coming apart mentally.

The psychologist gave him a quick sketch of the workings of the autonomic nervous system and the fight-or-flight response. She explained that Joe's disorientation on the street was due to extreme arousal of his central nervous system, a useful feature in an actual emergency but confusing when there is no concrete danger. This hyperarousal, Dr. Geller indicated, made it hard—but not impossible—for Joe to focus his thoughts, leading to the feeling of disorientation. As for Joe's thoughts about rushing for the door of the airplane (and, later, the window at home), the psychologist emphasized that these were simply ideas: fleeting thoughts associated with the fight-or-flight response, but not actions that he was ever close to carrying out. And as far as Joe's disorientation on the street was concerned, she noted that in spite of it all, he had made it home satisfactorily and was in complete command of his faculties at all times. Increasingly, Joe seemed ready to entertain the possibility that his condition was not as dire as he originally believed.

Dr. Geller further outlined for him the steps that would be taken to treat his panic disorder and the rationale behind them. There would be 4 basic components of treatment: (a) training in relaxation and breathing techniques, (b) changing his cognitive misinterpretations of panic sensations, (c) repeated exposure to sensations of panic under controlled conditions, and (d) repeated practice in situations that Joe was avoiding or apprehensive about. For the coming week though, he was instructed only to monitor his anxiety and panic attacks.

Session 2   At the next session, the psychologist reviewed the records Joe had kept during the week. It turned out that he had not had any panic attacks during the day—he was still avoiding going out except with Florence—but that he was waking up almost every night with breathlessness, palpitations, a feeling of unreality, and fear of losing control. Dr. Geller asked Joe what he did when these symptoms occurred, and the client explained that he simply lay in bed, fervently hoping that the symptoms would subside. To help him recognize some of his cognitive misinterpretations and to begin changing them, Dr. Geller had the following exchange with Joe:

Dr. Geller:	You said that when you got those attacks in the middle of night, you just lay in bed. Why is that?
Joe:	Well, it could be dangerous if I got up.
Dr. Geller:	Why would it be dangerous?
Joe:	I might have a heart attack, or something else serious might happen.
Dr. Geller:	What did the cardiologist say about your heart?

Panic disorder can also be treated by medications that lower the arousal of a person's sympathetic nervous system. About 40 percent to 60 percent of those who receive the antianxiety drug alprazolam or certain antidepressant medications fully overcome their disorder (Cuijpers et al., 2013; Lecrubier et al., 1997). Selective serotonin reuptake inhibitors (SSRIs) are now the first line of defense, and regular use of benzodiazepines is discouraged because of the risks associated with their chronic use (Bystritsky, Khalsa, Camerson, & Schiffman, 2013).

Joe: He said it was fine; all the tests were normal. But my heart is pound-
            ing so hard, and it's so hard to breathe, I can't think of any other
            explanation.

Dr. Geller: Let's review what we discussed last time about the physiology of
            panic attacks and why people get certain symptoms with these
            attacks.

Dr. Geller described in greater detail the fight-or-flight response, the physiological changes it produces in various organ systems, and the role of hyperventilation. In addition, she gave Joe a written summary of this material for him
to study at his leisure. She explained that the most important conclusion to be
drawn from this material was that his panic attacks, although extremely unpleasant, were ultimately harmless, to both his physical and his mental well-being. Then
the psychologist resumed the discussion with Joe about his nightly panic attacks.

Dr. Geller: In light of what we just discussed, how might you respond differently
            to the attacks you're getting at night?

Joe: Well, according to what you say, there would be no danger in my get-
            ting up. After all, the cardiologist did say my heart was fine. But I won-
            der if I might keel over just from the panic attack.

Dr. Geller: What has happened on other occasions when you had panic attacks
            and were sitting or standing up?

Joe: I certainly never keeled over. In fact, when I had the big one out in the
            street, I even managed to walk several blocks to get back home.

Dr. Geller: So it seems that your fear of keeling over might be unfounded. Do you
            think you would prefer to get up for a while when you wake up with
            an attack, rather than lie in bed?

Joe: I suppose it would make more sense. When I have trouble falling
            asleep under normal conditions I certainly don't just lie in bed doing
            nothing. I usually get up and putter around or do a little paperwork at
            my desk.

Dr. Geller: From now on, why don't you try getting up when you awaken with
            a panic attack and do the things you would normally do. We'll dis-
            cuss how this works out next time.

In the remainder of the session, the psychologist had Joe carry out a standard
progressive muscle relaxation exercise. Under her direction, he alternately tensed
and relaxed various muscle groups, with the goal of achieving complete relaxation
in all muscle groups by the end of a 20-minute training session. This widely used
exercise teaches clients to recognize excess muscle tension and to relax the tension at will. Dr. Geller felt that Joe could benefit from the relaxed feelings that the
exercise produces and that the relaxation training might also lay the groundwork
for an additional exercise in breathing control.

> The close biological rela-
> tives of people with panic
> disorder are up to 8
> times more likely than
> the general population to
> develop the disorder.

The breathing control exercise trains clients both to prevent hyperventilation and to cope effectively when hyperventilation occurs. For this exercise, patients practice breathing using the diaphragm as opposed to the chest. Use of the chest is discouraged because it fosters pressured breathing, promotes hyperventilation, and can produce chest pain or discomfort when employed regularly. With diaphragm breathing (the so-called natural way to breathe), the chest is almost immobile; only the abdomen moves, ballooning out as the person inhales and collapsing as the person exhales. Use of the diaphragm promotes slow, unpressured breathing of the sort necessary to prevent or counteract hyperventilation.

Dr. Geller recommended an app that Joe could put on his phone or tablet that had progressive muscle relaxation and breathing control exercises. He was to practice his relaxation and breathing once a day and record his level of physical and mental stress before and after his practice session.

Session 3 Joe and Dr. Geller again reviewed the records he kept during the preceding week. As advised, Joe had changed his response during the nightly panic attacks. Rather than lying in bed, he got up and did minor chores, reminding himself as he did so that the sensations he was experiencing were not dangerous. After following this practice every night, Joe noted that the nightly attacks were getting shorter; one attack subsided after only 5 minutes, as opposed to the 20 minutes or so that the attacks used to last.

Dr. Geller took this result as an opportunity to point out the cognitive component of panic, specifically how overestimating the danger of panic sensations fuels the attacks, whereas assessing the sensations realistically allows the sensations to subside. Joe's more realistic mind-set about the nightly attacks this past week had resulted in shorter and less intense attacks by the end of the week.

Session 4 When Joe returned the following week, he reported that he still was waking every night with his panic symptoms; but as instructed, he was trying to appraise the sensations realistically and function normally, regardless. As a result, the symptoms seemed to be getting weaker and not lasting as long; in most cases now, it was only a matter of minutes before they subsided, aided, he felt, by his use of slow diaphragm breathing. Still, he was leery of venturing outside on his own.

Dr. Geller gave Joe several instructions for the coming week. First, he was to continue with his current strategy for handling the nightly attacks and to continue practicing the diaphragm breathing exercise daily. In addition, he was to venture out at least 3 times on his own, if only to walk to the end of the block and back. If he had any panic sensations, he was to handle them as he did the nightly sensations: breathe slowly and with his diaphragm, appraise the sensations rationally, and behave normally.

At least 10 percent of people with panic disorder also experience major depressive disorder. In one-third of such cases, the panic disorder precedes the onset of depression (APA, 2013).

Panic disorder frequently precedes the onset of agoraphobia. According to the DSM-5, agoraphobia is diagnosed separately (APA, 2013).

Session 5 Joe reported that he had slept through the night 3 times this week, and on the nights when he was awakened, his symptoms had subsided within a few minutes. As instructed, he had gone out 3 times to the end of his block and back. In so doing, he had typical panic symptoms: heart palpitations, breathlessness, light-headedness, and unreality. The first time he did this exercise, Joe felt so fearful he almost returned home before completing it. However, he followed the psychologist's instruction to complete the assignment regardless of any symptoms. The second and third times, Joe also had symptoms but was better prepared for them and carried out the assignment without any thoughts of abandoning it.

Next, Dr. Geller proceeded with the interoceptive exposure exercises—repeated exposures to panic sensations under controlled conditions. She explained that he would do several exercises designed to produce sensations similar to those arising from autonomic arousal and that therefore might trigger panic symptoms. The goal was to progressively extinguish his anxiety reactions to these sensations, to give Joe opportunities to practice more accurate cognitive appraisals of such sensations, and to help him develop behavioral coping skills. The specific exercises that were carried out are listed in Table 1-4.

Procedures that are used by researchers or therapists to induce hyperventilation or other panic sensations are called biological challenge tests.

After each exercise, Joe reported his specific physical symptoms and rated the symptoms with respect to (a) intensity, (b) resemblance to panic, and (c) level of anxiety provoked. Dr. Geller instructed Joe to practice the mildest of the 3

Table 1-4 Interoceptive Exposure Exercises and Individual Reactions*				
Activity	Duration (seconds)	Intensity of Symptoms	Resemblance to Panic	Anxiety Level
1. Whole body tension	60	3	0	0
2. Breathe through straw	120	1	0	0
3. Shake head from side to side	30	6	1	1
4. Place head between legs and then lift	30	3	2	2
5. Stare at spot on wall	90	2	2	0
6. Hold breath	30	5	5	3
7. Run in place	60	6	6	4
8. Hyperventilate	60	7	7	5

Joe's ratings on a 0–10 scale. Exercises were derived from Craske & Barlow (1993).

panic-producing exercises—holding his breath for 30 seconds—3 times a day in the coming week. In addition, Joe was to continue taking short trips on his own, this week to a nearby store at least 3 times.

Sessions 6 to 9 Joe continued to progress over the next few weeks. By Session 9, he was carrying out on a daily basis 3 interoceptive exposure exercises—shaking his head from side to side for 30 seconds, staring at a spot on the wall for 90 seconds, and hyperventilating for 60 seconds—and getting minimal panic effects. In addition, his nightly awakenings were becoming infrequent, and he was traveling farther and farther from home without Florence. For Session 9, he traveled to see Dr. Geller alone by subway for the first time. Although Joe arrived at that session with stronger panic sensations than he had had in weeks, he simply mentioned his symptoms to the psychologist and proceeded to describe the other details of his week as if the symptoms themselves were a minor annoyance. Within a few minutes, they subsided.

Joe's instructions for the coming week were to continue practicing the interoceptive exposure exercises 3 times a day, and to travel freely, without allowing fear of a panic attack to restrict his behavior. The next session was scheduled for 2 weeks away.

Session 10 Joe reported that he had been panic-free for the entire 2 weeks. In addition, he was going wherever he needed to go on his own and without apprehension. He continued to perform the interoceptive exposure exercises, but at this stage they evoked no reaction; they mainly bored him.

Now he had a new concern. Florence was determined that they take a trip to Europe in the next couple of months. They would have to fly, of course, and the very idea revived painful memories of his experience on the plane from Florida, where his problem began. Joe had visions of reliving that terrible episode. Dr. Geller outlined a program of progressive exposure over the next couple of weeks to images and situations involving airplanes. This would include multiple viewings of movies involving airplanes and trips to the airport twice each week.

> Around half of people with panic disorder receive treatment for it (Narrow et al., 1993).

Sessions 11 and 12 When Joe returned 2 weeks later for Session 11, he had spent the intervening time immersing himself in airplane-related images and situations. As anticipated, initially he was anxious while watching the airplane movies, but by the 2nd week he was watching them without emotional reaction; he and Florence had also made it out to the airport 3 times, and each time Joe felt more at ease. Two weeks later, Joe and Dr. Geller met for the last time before the trip to Europe. At this meeting, he was panic free but still apprehensive about the trip. His parting words were, "I'll see you in a month—if I survive."

Epilogue The Final Conquest

Joe returned triumphant from his trip to Europe. He had had no problems on the plane or anywhere else. He felt his problem was behind him now. Dr. Geller chatted with him for a while about the trip and said she was glad that things had turned out so well. She and Joe reviewed the treatment program, including strategies he would follow should he have any symptoms in the future. Joe was feeling better—enormously better than he had for many months. Most of all, he felt that he had regained control over his body and his mind.

Assessment Questions

1. In the case of "Joe," what event precipitated his panic attack?

2. Why is Joe's case different from most panic attacks?

3. What are the symptoms of most panic attacks?

4. Why do individuals first suspect a general medical condition?

5. Why was Dr. Geller convinced that panic disorders are "best explained by a combination of biological and cognitive factors"?

6. Describe the 4 steps Dr. Geller decided to take to help Joe overcome his panic attacks. List each of the interoceptive exposure exercises that were part of Joe's treatment.

7. How did Joe's avoidance of going outside by himself contribute to his panic disorder?

8. What was the outcome for Joe?

CASE 2

Obsessive-Compulsive Disorder

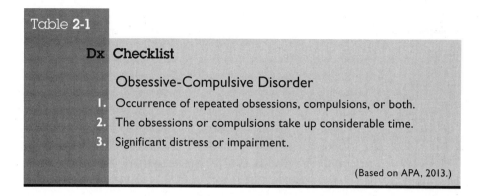

Table 2-1

Dx Checklist

Obsessive-Compulsive Disorder

1. Occurrence of repeated obsessions, compulsions, or both.
2. The obsessions or compulsions take up considerable time.
3. Significant distress or impairment.

(Based on APA, 2013.)

Sarah, a 26-year-old accountant, recalled her childhood as basically happy and care-free. She and her younger brother grew up in a comfortable middle-class environment in an ethnically diverse suburb. Although she had never personally been subject to any discrimination, as an African American she felt some pressure both to perform well in school and to conduct herself in a manner that was beyond reproach, as though the slightest misstep might increase her vulnerability to prejudice.

Sarah was in fact an excellent student and was considered a model for other children to follow. By junior high school, it was apparent that she excelled in mathematics, and even at that early age she had set her sights on a career in accountancy. Her seriousness as a student continued through high school, where she described her social life as conservative. In college, where she majored in mathematics and accounting, her commitment to academics continued. She also became more involved with boys and developed a serious relationship with a boyfriend in her senior year.

Sarah Early Worries and Odd Behaviors

Despite her generally happy youth, Sarah had been a worrier for as long as she could remember. For example, she always seemed more concerned about safety than other people did. She recalled that in college she had to check the lock on her door 3 or 4 times before she could walk away from her dormitory room. And even then, she was often left with a feeling of doubt, as though the door still hadn't been locked properly and someone would break in because of her negligence. She dreaded the losses her roommate might sustain if there was a theft. Curiously, her own losses didn't seem to matter so much; it was more the idea of being responsible for another person's misfortune that troubled her.

Similarly, other areas of anxiety had produced some difficulties for Sarah over the years. For example, paying her bills online often posed problems. Although

Obsessive-compulsive disorder usually begins in adolescence or early adulthood, although it may begin in childhood. The average age of onset is 19.5 years (APA, 2013).

she always carefully checked her bills and made sure she entered the correct amount online, when it came time to click submit, she doubted that everything had been done properly. Thus, she would stare at the computer, rereading the numbers 3 or 4 times and checking the due date as well, before actually submitting the payment. After receiving her confirmation number, she always felt a sense of unease, as though something irrevocable had just taken place. Occasionally Sarah's doubts were so strong that she would have to call the company to see if it had received the payment.

Sarah Beyond Worrying

Around 4 years back, soon after graduating from college, Sarah's worries and excessive behaviors began to take an extreme form. This change first occurred on the heels of a traumatic experience. Specifically, Sarah was the target of an attempted sexual assault. About to enter her car after seeing a movie with some friends, she was accosted from behind by a stranger who tried to talk her into letting him into the vehicle with her. When Sarah refused, the man tried physically to force his way in, with the clear intention of sexually assaulting her. Sarah struggled and screamed for help, and the attacker was scared off. Hearing her cries, 2 ushers ran to the scene and apprehended the man as he was fleeing.

Eventually, the man was sentenced to 4 years in prison. Nevertheless, as time passed, Sarah began to have increasing feelings of insecurity. She started to check her door lock several times before going to bed at night. Gradually this practice extended to the checking of windows, faucets, appliances, and the like.

Sarah's feelings of insecurity and her accompanying rituals continued to increase during the next several years, to the point that they were making it impossible for her to lead a fully normal life. Mornings were a particular problem: she was finding it more and more difficult to leave her apartment and get to work. Each morning, Sarah felt compelled to perform a large number of rituals to verify that everything in the apartment was being left in a safe condition. She was concerned that her negligence might bring about some terrible event (a fire or flood) that would damage both her apartment and—more important, it seemed—her neighbors' apartments.

Thus, Sarah would check that the stove had been turned off, the faucets turned off, and the windows closed and that various appliances were unplugged, including the hair dryer, the microwave, her laptop, and the television, among others. Just checking all the items once would have been a chore, but Sarah typically felt compelled to check each item several times. Often, after checking one item, she would lose track of what she had already checked and so would have to go back and check everything all over again.

Sometimes she would go back to check an item even having checked it seconds before. It seemed she could never be reassured completely. Sometimes she would

Studies reveal that many people with obsessive-compulsive disorder have unusually high standards of conduct and morality that are coupled with an inflated sense of responsibility (Rachman, 1993; Salkovskis, 2000).

stand and stare at an item for a full 5 minutes, hoping that this would be enough to persuade her that the item had been properly checked. However, even this was often not enough, and within a few minutes, she would find herself checking the item all over again.

On a bad morning, it could take Sarah up to 2 hours to get out of the apartment. Occasionally, after completing all of her checking behaviors and getting out of her apartment building, she was suddenly seized with doubt about a particular item—had she really checked the stove satisfactorily or did she just think she had?—and she would have to return to her apartment to end her suspense. A few times, she missed work altogether due to this checking. More often, she was able to break away after a certain point and would arrive at work late.

Fortunately, she had a flexible schedule and it didn't matter when she showed up at the office, only that she got her work done. This she was able to accomplish by staying late. Indeed, she was highly valued for her abilities and had been promoted several times since beginning work at her firm 2 years before. However, her life in the morning had become, in her mind, a "living hell."

When Sarah returned home in the evening, the urge to check would be revived; she felt compelled to make sure that all was in order before going to bed. This nighttime checking was not as severe as the morning routine, however. She was somehow able to tell herself that everything had been checked earlier that day and if she avoided using the stove or appliances before going to bed, a less thorough inspection would suffice. The next morning, however, the urge to carry out the complete checking routine would start anew.

Sarah also had another set of symptoms, which would manifest as she was driving to work. These other symptoms had begun a while back, after she drove past a minor accident one day. Soon after passing the accident, she ran over a bump of some kind. She looked in the rearview mirror to see what she might have hit but observed nothing. After driving for another 15 minutes, Sarah was suddenly seized by the thought that she had struck another car or person. In the throes of this anxiety, she got off the highway and doubled back to where she had felt the bump. She was trying to determine if there was any evidence of an accident there—a disabled car or a body in the road—to confirm or disconfirm her fears. She discovered nothing, however, so she went on to work, still in a state of anxiety that she might have been responsible for an accident.

The next morning, similar doubts arose on the way to work, and the problem continued thereafter. Now, almost every day while driving, she would wonder if she had accidentally hit a person or another car. Any irregularity in the feel of the car could set her off: a bump, a swerve, or even just the realization that she hadn't been concentrating very hard on her driving. To reassure herself, Sarah would scrutinize the road through the rearview mirror. Most of the time she could reassure herself enough to keep on driving. Occasionally, though, she

Neuroimaging techniques have been used to map specific areas of the brain that show distinct activation during different compulsive behaviors (e.g., checking versus washing versus hoarding) (Mataix-Cols et al., 2004).

would feel compelled to double back on her route to confirm that no accident had occurred.

Since these driving doubts had arisen, Sarah had also been experiencing other intrusive images of havoc and destruction. The slightest thing could provoke them. For example, if she saw a book of matches on a desk at work, she would get an image of setting fire to her office building. Sometimes, after walking away from the matches, she would half wonder if she actually had set fire to the building; she would then review in her mind the sequence of events to reassure herself that no such thing had occurred. Occasionally, she would go back to obtain visual proof that the matches were still resting safely on the desk. In another case, she might see a knife on a table in a restaurant and get an image of stabbing somebody. Again, as she walked away, she would half wonder if she actually had stabbed someone; and then, as with the matches, she would review the sequence of events in her mind or return to the scene to establish that the knife was still there and she had not in fact carried out the imagined act. At other times, she would imagine less catastrophic events, insulting someone, for example, or neglecting to leave her car keys with the parking lot attendant.

> The 12-month prevalence of OCD is 1.2 percent, which is similar to prevalence rates in other countries (APA, 2013).

James Trying to Understand

Sarah and James met during their senior year at college. They were in an accounting class together, and as James would tell friends, "The numbers added up quickly." He was totally taken with Sarah. He found her to be beautiful, effervescent, and caring. She took herself seriously, in a good way he thought—always wanting to be of service to others and to do the right thing in the right way. And as a bonus, they had similar interests, particularly in the business world: she wanted to be an accountant and he was determined to make it as a stockbroker. He felt that she was perfect and that their relationship was perfect.

Well, as it turned out, things were not perfect. In fact, perfection was part of the problem. As James and Sarah grew closer, he became aware that she had some very odd habits—behaviors that she would repeat again and again according to certain rules until she was certain that everything was okay. At first he found her behaviors—checking locks again and again, meticulously making lists, and the like—to be kind of funny, like a personality quirk. But over time they became less funny. He saw that Sarah was a prisoner of her rituals. They made her very unhappy, they made her late for everything, and they prevented her from living a spontaneous life; but she could not stop them. When James pushed her for explanations, Sarah was clearly embarrassed. She would say she just felt that she had to do these things and that she felt very anxious otherwise, but she didn't offer much more.

Concerned (and often annoyed) as he was, James believed that Sarah's behaviors were more or less tolerable—a price that he had to pay to have a relationship

> Compulsive acts are often a response to obsessive concerns. People who repeatedly perform cleaning rituals may be reacting to obsessive fears of contamination. Similarly, individuals who repeatedly check to make sure doors are locked and that they have their cell phone may be reacting to obsessive fears that their life is unsafe.

with an otherwise great woman. The two of them continued to grow close, and in fact they had gotten engaged 2 years before.

Unfortunately, his fiancée's strange habits had grown stranger still since the start of their engagement. The behaviors that he himself witnessed—constant checking, no longer just of locks, but of windows, faucets, appliances, and more—were certainly odd; but even more disturbing were the rituals that a desperate Sarah told him about one evening: the endless morning rituals in her apartment and the doubt-ridden drives to work. And then there were those mystery areas, the way she would go cold and freeze with apparent fear whenever she saw matches or came into contact with a knife. What was going through her head at these times? What was she worried about? These reactions she would not discuss with James at all, as close as they were and as much as she trusted him. She confided only that it was too dark to discuss and that if he loved her, he would let it go and let her be.

James did love her, and so, after much thought and heartfelt talks with a close friend, he decided to stay in the relationship with Sarah. Their wedding date was now 6 months away, and he decided to focus on all the positive things about Sarah and go full-steam ahead with the marriage plans. He asked one thing of her, however—that she seek treatment for her problem, whatever it was. His request was not an ultimatum or condition of marriage, but rather, he explained, a plea from the man who loved her greatly and who worried that all of their wonderful plans could unravel if she continued as she was doing. Sarah more than understood the request. She knew, even better than James, how disturbed she was and how much worse she had been getting. And although James was not threatening to end the relationship, she knew that there was probably only so much that he could take. She loved him and didn't want to lose him. Even more, she was tired of living this way. Within a few days, she made an appointment with Dr. Marlene Laslow, a psychologist whose treatment of obsessive-compulsive disorders had received some attention in a recent news feed online.

Treatment for Sarah Eliminating Obsessions and Compulsions

Sarah recognized that her fears and rituals were in some sense absurd but also acknowledged that she found them too compelling to resist. As she put it during her first visit with Dr. Laslow, "When I describe it to you here, I can practically laugh about it, because I know it's so dumb. But when I'm in the situation, I just can't stop myself, the feeling is so overpowering."

After hearing Sarah's description of her thoughts and rituals, Dr. Laslow concluded that the client did indeed have obsessive-compulsive disorder. Like most people with this disorder, the client exhibited both obsessions and compulsions. Her obsessions consisted of thoughts that some disaster (fire, flood, burglary)

Obsessive-compulsive disorder is equally common in men and women, although men are more affected in childhood and women have a slightly higher prevalence rate in adulthood (APA, 2013).

might be visited upon her apartment or her neighbors' if she did not take special precautions; thoughts that she might have caused a serious road accident; and thoughts and images of setting fires, stabbing people, or carrying out other more minor antisocial or negligent acts. Sarah's compulsions included her morning and evening checking routines, her unusual driving habits, and her repeated mental reviews of events to reassure herself that she had not run anyone over, burned down the house, or stabbed someone.

Research indicates that antidepressant drugs, particularly the selective serotonin reuptake inhibitors, significantly reduce the obsessions and compulsions of many people with this disorder. But so does cognitive-behavioral therapy, including exposure and response prevention. Dr. Laslow's usual practice was to try the cognitive-behavioral approach first, referring clients to a psychiatrist for medication only if they failed to improve with this approach.

In exposure and response prevention, clients are repeatedly exposed to anxiety-provoking stimuli, typically stimuli that are the subjects of their obsessive fears and thoughts. Then they are prevented from performing the anxiety-reducing compulsions that they would usually feel compelled to follow. The repeated prevention of compulsive behaviors eventually shows clients that the compulsions serve no useful purpose. The rituals are not needed to prevent or undo the clients' obsessive concerns, nor are they needed to reduce anxiety. In short, clients learn that nothing bad will happen if they fail to perform compulsive behaviors. At the same time, this approach helps them increasingly learn that their obsessive concerns are groundless and harmless, and so their anxious reactions to the obsessions lessen. In addition to exposure and response prevention, Dr. Laslow also used a cognitive approach. The cognitive approach to treatment involved helping Sarah to recognize that intrusive thoughts are a very common occurrence in most people and that the problem was not the thoughts themselves but the way Sarah was interpreting them. She helped Sarah to recognize that having an intrusive thought or image didn't mean that she was more likely to act on that thought. Dr. Laslow also helped Sarah realistically assess the amount of responsibility she held in a variety of situations in an effort to reduce Sarah's beliefs in her excessive responsibility for herself and others.

Session 1   In the first session, after Sarah described her symptoms and their background, Dr. Laslow spent some time discussing Sarah's views on the danger posed by the objects of her obsessions. Sarah could see objectively that her morning efforts were excessive. She acknowledged that the danger from plugged-in appliances or dripping faucets was minuscule, but she felt compelled to take repeated measures "just in case, because if anything did go wrong, it would be horrible." Sarah was also aware that it was extremely unlikely that she could hit someone on the road, set a fire, or stab someone and not know it. "It just seems that I want to know for certain that it isn't true; if I review it in my mind or go back to check that the person is okay, I feel relieved."

In the past, only repetitive behaviors were considered compulsions. Today, however, repetitive mental acts (such as Sarah's frequent review of events to make sure that she had not run anyone over) can also be considered compulsions.

Thought-action fusion (TAF) is a cognitive bias characteristic of individuals with obsessive-compulsive disorder. The construct of TAF has 2 components: (a) the belief that having the thought makes the event more likely to happen and (b) the belief that having the thought is as bad as engaging in the behavior (Abramowitz, Whiteside, Lynam, & Kalsy, 2003; Shafran, Thordarson, & Rachman, 1996).

Sarah was less confident about her violent thoughts and intrusive images. Occasionally, when talking to someone, she would get an image of a knife in the person's chest; or on seeing a book of matches, she might get the thought of setting fire to the building. Sarah was frightened by these images and thoughts because she assumed they indicated she was capable of committing such acts, even though all her life she had conscientiously obeyed every rule and regulation.

Dr. Laslow explained that these images should be viewed in the same spirit as the dripping faucet or the plugged-in hair dryer: They provoked anxiety, but they posed no objective danger. The psychologist pointed out that most people occasionally experience a bizarre image or a thought of doing something outlandish or destructive; however, they just dismiss these thoughts as meaningless or unimportant. Sarah, on the other hand, kept reading disproportionate significance into such images; thus, she kept monitoring them closely and becoming extremely anxious in their presence.

Sarah: But isn't there a problem with these thoughts? I mean, if I am thinking such things, doesn't it mean I'm capable of doing such things or want to do such things?

Dr. Laslow: Do you have any conscious desire to do these things?

Sarah: Of course not. They are the last things I would ever want to do.

Dr. Laslow: I think the reason the thoughts scare you so much is that you've been assuming that their very existence means that you are in danger of carrying them out. The fact that you think something doesn't mean you want to carry it out or would ever carry it out. In fact, in spite of having the thoughts hundreds of times, you've never once made even the smallest gesture implied by the thoughts.

Sarah: True. But sometimes I feel so close, like I have to put away the knives if anyone comes over, or if I were to touch a knife in someone's presence I would lose control.

Dr. Laslow: Again, these are just assumptions on your part. The problem is not the thoughts or images themselves; it's your incorrect assumptions about them and your excessively anxious reaction. During this treatment, you will learn through experience that these assumptions are not valid. When you are ready, we will do certain exercises in which you start coming into contact with knives more frequently, in fact more frequently than the average person. In doing this, you will learn that your fears are unfounded, and you will become less anxious when these thoughts and images arise. As you become less anxious, you will also become less preoccupied with the thoughts and images and will probably start having them less frequently.

Sarah: Are there are other people with the same problem as me? With thoughts about stabbing people or setting fires?

A common practice in the cognitive treatment of obsessive-compulsive disorder is to cite the research by Salkovskis and Harrison (1984), which demonstrated that over 90 percent of community and laboratory samples of people had intrusive thoughts. Furthermore, many of the intrusive thoughts contained content similar to that of individuals with obsessive-compulsive disorder. The difference between people with and without obsessive-compulsive disorder is not the thought itself but rather the interpretation that is given to that thought.

Between 50 percent and 70 percent of clients with obsessive-compulsive disorder significantly improve when treated with cognitive-behavioral therapy, and research has shown this rate to be similar to treatment involving only exposure with response prevention (Abramowitz, 2006; Whittal, Thordarson, & McLean, 2005).

Dr. Laslow: Yes, lots. In fact, the thoughts and images you describe are very typical of people with obsessive-compulsive disorder.

Sarah: That makes me feel better somehow. I guess I assumed I was the only person in the world with such bizarre and perverse thoughts.

Dr. Laslow: No, not at all. In fact as I said, most so-called normal people will have a bizarre or perverse thought on occasion. Your problem is that you become excessively preoccupied with these thoughts.

For the remainder of the session, the psychologist further explained the exposure and response prevention treatment, describing the principles behind it and indicating how it would be applied to Sarah. The client indicated that the treatment plan made sense to her and she was ready to proceed.

Dr. Laslow recommended an app that Sarah could download to keep track of her obsessions and compulsions for the coming week. Then, at the end of the week, Sarah could easily print out her data and take it to her appointment with Dr. Laslow.

Session 2   Sarah kept the requested records, and from these 3 separate categories of obsessive-compulsive anxieties were identified: (a) household anxieties, (b) driving anxieties, and (c) anxieties over destructive thoughts and imagery. They spent the session setting up exercises that would pertain to the household anxieties.

To begin, they made a complete list of all of Sarah's household checking compulsions. The items that Sarah felt compelled to keep unplugged included the hair dryer, the microwave, the toaster, the laptop, the television, and the air conditioner. Light switches and lamps merely had to be shut off, not unplugged, to Sarah's way of thinking. Other items that she felt compelled to check were the stove (to make sure the burners were off), the faucets (to make sure they were not dripping), and the door (to make sure it was locked).

For exposure and response prevention exercises, Dr. Laslow proposed focusing first on the items that Sarah felt had to be unplugged or turned off. The psychologist suggested not only that Sarah plug these items in before leaving for work but also that she turn a few of them on (specifically, the television, the air conditioner, and some lights) and leave them running for the whole day.

Sarah said she couldn't see any way she could bring herself to do what Dr. Laslow was proposing. Accordingly, a less extreme procedure was devised. Sarah would not be required to leave any items on; instead, she would simply plug them in. Beginning the next morning, she was to plug in each of the feared appliances and leave them that way for the rest of the day. Sarah felt that this exercise was within her capability and agreed to carry it out. In addition, she was to allow herself only one check of the lights, faucets, stove, and lock each morning.

Dr. Laslow cautioned Sarah about not surrendering to any urges to do unauthorized checks, no matter how strong. She compared obsessive-compulsive disorder to a machine that needed fuel, explaining that every time Sarah yielded to a compulsion to check, she was adding fuel to that machine, whereas every time she resisted the urge, she was taking fuel away. Therefore, whatever benefit might be provided by the exposure exercises would be undone if Sarah gave in to the urge to check.

Session 3   Sarah reported that she had carried out the instructions every day in the past week. By the end of the week, she found to her surprise that plugging in the appliances was producing no anxiety whatsoever. On the other hand, the urge to recheck the stove, lights, faucets, and lock was still present, although reduced. Nevertheless, as instructed, she had succeeded in limiting herself to one check for each item.

Sarah was pleased by her accomplishment and encouraged by the practical benefits of the new morning procedure. Instead of spending an hour or more with her checking routine, the current procedure could be accomplished in a few minutes, essentially just the time it took to briefly unplug and then replug the various appliances. This was already having a significant impact on her quality of life. Dr. Laslow suggested that now was the time to start limiting the checking even further. After some discussion, it was decided that Sarah would stop checking all light switches, while still allowing herself one check of the stove, faucets, and lock.

The psychologist also spent some time reviewing with Sarah her ultimate fears about household items. Sarah reiterated what she had stated in the first interview: Her greatest fear seemed to be a fire or a flood due to her negligence. She could envision the havoc and destruction and being blamed; the very thought of it made her visibly upset.

Dr. Laslow suggested that in order for Sarah to overcome her preoccupation with this thought, some of the emotionality associated with it would have to be reduced. She proposed that the treatment of Sarah's household anxieties include prolonged and repeated exposure to images of her building being destroyed.

Sarah: You are saying it would be beneficial to eliminate or reduce the anxiety I feel when thinking of my building being destroyed. But isn't this anxiety appropriate? I mean, isn't it normal not to want the building destroyed?

Dr. Laslow: Yes, that is normal. But there is a difference between not wanting the building destroyed and getting anxious at the very thought of it. The first is appropriate, but the second is causing you difficulties. Of course you don't want the building to be destroyed, but you also don't want to be getting anxious at the very thought of it.

Dr. Laslow then explained the mechanics of exposure to anxiety-provoking thoughts or images. Sarah would have to develop a detailed description of the

Certain antidepressant drugs (for example, clomipramine, fluoxetine, and fluvoxamine) also bring improvement to 50 percent to 80 percent of those with obsessive-compulsive disorder (Taylor, 1995). Selective serotonin reuptake inhibitors (SSRIs) are recommended as the first-line medication treatment for obsessive-compulsive disorder (Bandelow et al., 2012).

building being destroyed, perhaps by fire and flood simultaneously. The description would include the hideous aftermath, the people whose lives would be lost or ruined, their awareness that Sarah was to blame, and their everlasting loathing of her. Together the psychologist and Sarah worked on a written scenario. Next week, the session would be devoted to recording a 50-minute description of the event. Sarah would then listen to it on her phone a number of times throughout the week.

Sarah's instruction for the coming week was simply to keep all appliances plugged in and not do any checking except once for the stove, faucets, and door lock. She was to follow the same procedure before going to bed.

Session 4 Sarah reported that she had been able to keep to the new morning and evening checking procedure 95 percent of the time during the past week. She continued to keep appliances plugged in all the time, saying it now felt totally normal to her. She mentioned, however, that she did make one or 2 unauthorized checks of the stove. These extra checks seemed to have been provoked by her use of the stove that morning or evening.

On hearing this, Dr. Laslow instructed Sarah on a new exposure and response prevention exercise. Specifically, Sarah was to use the stove at least once in the morning and once in the evening every day, even if only to turn it on and off. Then she was to walk away without checking it further.

The remainder of the session was devoted to recording her script of her building being destroyed. According to this procedure, Sarah sat back with her eyes closed and imagined the scene as vividly as possible. She then began her verbal description: "I accidentally leave the water running as I leave the apartment. The overflowing water reaches an electric outlet, causing a short circuit. The walls ignite. Flames start shooting up to the apartment above me. The people are trapped . . . " Sarah continued for about 10 minutes, ending with the destruction of the building and her being blamed by the survivors. The psychologist then provided a second description, Sarah a third, and so on until a 50-minute recording was produced.

In addition to the stove exercises discussed earlier in the session, Sarah was given an assignment to listen to her script daily, rating her anxiety prior to each visualization, at its peak during each visualization, and at the end of each visualization.

Session 5 Sarah reported she had been able to listen to the recording 5 times during the week, and she was indeed becoming less reactive to it. She also reported that her general feelings about causing a disaster seemed to be undergoing a shift of sorts as a consequence of listening to the script. She noted that in thinking about being blamed for a disaster, her reaction was becoming one of "healthy defiance." Specifically, she was thinking, "I suppose I could cause a disaster, but so could anybody; if I did do it, it wouldn't be on purpose, and to hate me for it would be ridiculous."

Sarah was enthusiastic about the positive effects the recording appeared to be having on her: and she even seemed to look forward to listening to it again this week, feeling it led to more positive attitudes with each listening.

Regarding her other exercises, Sarah continued to keep all appliances plugged in. She also limited herself to one check of the stove, faucets, and lock in the morning and evening. As a new exercise, Dr. Laslow asked Sarah to leave several lights on every day while she was away at work and to stop checking faucets.

Next the psychologist raised the idea of Sarah's starting to limit some of her compulsions during the drive to work: the excessive inspection of the rearview mirror, driving too slowly, mentally reviewing events on the road to reassure herself, and keeping lane changes to a minimum. Dr. Laslow suggested that instead the client now start normalizing her driving habits, driving at least 50 miles per hour on the highway and making at least 5 unnecessary lane changes while driving both to and from work. She also instructed Sarah to check the rearview mirror only as required for monitoring traffic.

> Most people with compulsions recognize that their repeated acts are unreasonable, but they believe that something terrible will happen if they do not perform them (Foa & Kozak, 1995).

Sessions 6 and 7   At the sixth session, Sarah reported that she had been able to follow through with the new instructions about changing her driving habits. To all outward appearances, her driving habits probably now seemed normal to onlookers. More important, these changes seemed to have reduced Sarah's obsessions about causing accidents.

It was decided that the next 2 weeks would be devoted to consolidating all of the changes that Sarah had made thus far. In addition, during the 1st of the 2 weeks, the client was to leave her laptop on all day while she was away at work, and during the second week, the television. In driving she was to continue with the current procedures.

Regarding the recording, by Session 7 Sarah reported that she could listen to the disaster scenario with hardly any reaction at all; if anything, she was getting bored with it. Accordingly, Dr. Laslow said she could stop listening to the script.

In summary, by Session 7, Sarah's household obsessions and compulsions had virtually been eliminated. When driving, she was checking the rearview mirror much less frequently and even felt free enough to listen to morning radio broadcasts rather than obsessing over the possibility of an accident. The next step was to work on her anxiety about committing deliberate destructive acts: stabbing people and setting fires. For the coming week, Sarah's task in this area was simply to use her app to keep track of the thoughts and her behavioral responses.

Session 8   Sarah reported that over the past week she had continued to maintain her gains in the household and driving areas. In fact, she sometimes amazed herself with how different she had become in household matters.

As instructed, she had kept records of any anxieties associated with destructive thoughts. She reported several typical incidents. Twice, while out to lunch at a restaurant, she was disturbed by the thought of stabbing her lunch companion. More frightening to Sarah, the same thought occurred when James, her fiancé, came over for dinner at her apartment. Similarly, thoughts and images about setting fires arose whenever Sarah came in contact with matches.

She also tried to observe her behavioral responses to these images or to her obsessions about knives and matches in general. She noted that she took pains to keep all knives hidden in drawers while at home, particularly if she had company. She also made a point of never having any matches in the house.

Dr. Laslow proposed that they begin working on this problem with some in vivo exposures. First, as a response prevention measure, Sarah was to stop avoiding knives and matches. Indeed, she was to make special efforts to start exposing herself to these items. Specifically, at home she was to take all of the knives out of the drawers and leave them on the kitchen counters for the entire week. In addition, she was to buy a box of matches and place several books of matches in plain view in each room of her apartment.

| Repeated cleaning and repeated checking are the most common kinds of compulsions. |

Session 9 Sarah reported that she had carried out the instructions concerning knives and matchbooks throughout the week. At first it had made her quite anxious to have these items out in plain view, but after a couple of days her anxiety subsided and she became accustomed to it. Still, she wondered how she would fare if anybody came to her house while the knives were accessible. She was concerned that the thoughts of stabbing someone might be overwhelming.

At this point, Dr. Laslow proposed some new exposure exercises for the coming week. Sarah was now to carry a Swiss Army knife in her purse at all times, to give her prolonged experience with having a knife accessible. In addition, the psychologist suggested that Sarah have James over to dinner with all of the knives laid out on the kitchen counter. If practical, Sarah was actually to use a sharp knife in his presence; for example, she could have him come into the kitchen to chat while she cut vegetables.

In addition, Sarah was to increase the intensity of her exposure to matches. Specifically, she had to strike several matches every day, blow them out, and then discard them.

Finally, Dr. Laslow suggested that the next session be devoted to recording another imaginal exposure exercise, one involving the violent imagery associated with knives and matches. Sarah herself suggested that the scenario focus on her fiancé, since he was often the subject of her violent imagery, a factor that made the images particularly disturbing.

Sessions 10 to 13 At Session 10, Sarah and Dr. Laslow recorded the new visualization exercise: a 50-minute description of Sarah stabbing James and then setting fire to his building. As with the first exercise, the client reported high anxiety while visualizing the scene, but the anxiety tapered off slightly by the end. For the next 2 weeks, Sarah listened to the recording daily, and as with the first visualization exercise, her anxiety lessened with each listening. At Session 13, she informed Dr. Laslow that she was barely feeling any emotional reaction at all when listening to the recorded scenario.

During this 2-week period, Sarah also kept a Swiss Army knife with her constantly. At first, the knife made her anxious, fueling her image of herself as "some kind of secret killer." However, as time passed, the knife seemed no more remarkable than her keys or wallet. It was just another item in her purse. She even used it on several occasions to slice tomatoes for lunch at her desk.

Sarah also scheduled the fateful evening with her fiancé. James came for dinner and she deliberately handled knives in his presence in the kitchen. In so doing, she experienced the usual violent image—she had an image of stabbing him—but she followed the instruction not to try to force the image out, as she had in the past. Instead, she just let the image occur and carried on normally with her conversation and dinner preparations; as she did so, her anxiety eventually subsided. Sarah also invited James over a second and third time during this period. On each occasion, she still saw the image, but she became less and less anxious and preoccupied with it.

In the other areas—household and driving—Sarah had been faithfully following the specified procedures, which were beginning to feel like second nature. Now, in the morning, she was free of any extraordinary urges to check and often did not bother with her one allotted check of the stove and lock. In driving to work, she felt like any other bored commuter. Occasionally, she said, she had a flashback to one of her former obsessions (about causing a car accident), but now it felt like just a vague memory of former times.

At Session 13, it was decided that Sarah would stop carrying out any active therapeutic procedures, which by now consisted mainly of turning on items before leaving for work and listening to the recorded slash-and-burn scenario (as Sarah called it).

Session 14 Sarah reported on her first week of "normal life." She was not feeling anything more than an occasional urge to check, which she resisted. A plan was made to meet at 2-week intervals for the next 2 sessions and at 3-week intervals for the 2 sessions after that. The goal was simply to keep an eye on Sarah's status and advise her on adjustments to any new situations. As it happened, in 3 weeks' time, Sarah and her fiancé would be married and beginning their life together in a new apartment.

Obsessions may take such forms as obsessive wishes (for example, repeated wishes that one's spouse would die), impulses (repeated urges to yell out obscenities at church), images (fleeting visions of forbidden sexual scenes), ideas (notions that germs are lurking everywhere), or doubts (concerns that one may make the wrong decision).

Therapists will explain to clients how "forcing the image out of their mind" is counterproductive. By trying to get rid of the image, the client focuses more attention on the thought itself, which increases anxiety. Also, holding the belief that one must force the image out reinforces the belief that the thoughts were bad and dangerous in the first place.

Sessions 15 to 18   These follow-up sessions were held over a period of 2½ months. Throughout this period, Sarah was free of obsessions and compulsions in the household and driving areas. Living with James, now her husband, turned out to present few unexpected challenges. As expected, however—and Dr. Laslow had advised the client about this—Sarah had initially experienced more frequent violent images. However, in keeping with all she had learned, she did not try to force the images out and did not treat them as a threat. After the first couple of weeks with her husband, the images lessened markedly.

Because everything continued to go well during this period, they decided not to schedule any more therapy sessions. The psychologist asked only that Sarah return for one more visit in 6 months' time to report on her progress.

Even though effective treatments for obsessive-compulsive disorder exist, only a small percentage (approximately 5 percent) of individuals actually receive this treatment. Newer treatment options, such as Internet-based cognitive behavior therapy have been shown to have efficacy rates similar to those of face-to-face treatment (Andersson et al., 2012)

Epilogue

At her 6-month follow-up visit, Sarah reported that all was continuing to go well. Her only lingering symptom was an occasional violent image. On the other hand, she said such images were causing hardly any anxiety. Generally, she was extremely pleased, and she expected that these images would continue to lessen with time. Overall, she reported feeling like a different person, certainly different from the woman who had entered therapy a year ago and also different from the person who had had less severe obsessions and compulsions for several years prior to that. Now able to focus on events and activities without the constant intrusion of frightening thoughts and images, and without the burden of complex compulsions, she found life much easier and more enjoyable than she had ever thought it could be.

Assessment Questions

1. When do obsessive-compulsive behaviors begin for most individuals?

2. What were Sarah's primary obsessions and compulsions?

3. Why did Sarah finally decide to seek treatment?

4. What type of therapy did Dr. Laslow decide to try to help Sarah overcome her obsessive-compulsive disorder?

5. Dr. Laslow asked Sarah to keep track of her obsessions and compulsions. What did Sarah learn from entering this information, and how did

Dr. Laslow use this information to assist in her treatment program?

6. What was the purpose of recording Sarah's visually imagined disaster scenes?

7. How many sessions did it take for Sarah to overcome her household obsessions and compulsions?

8. Obsessions may take different forms. List 3 forms cited in the text.

9. How many sessions were necessary for Sarah to overcome her obsessive-compulsive disorder on household and driving issues?

CASE 3

Hoarding Disorder

Contributed by Danae L. Hudson, Ph.D.
Missouri State University

Table **3-1**	
Dx Checklist	
Hoarding Disorder	
1.	Persons are repeatedly unable to give up or throw out their possessions, even worthless ones, because they feel a need to save them and want to avoid the discomfort of disposal.
2.	Persons accumulate an extraordinary number of possessions that severely clutter and crowd their homes.
3.	Significant distress or impairment.

(Based on APA, 2013.)

Jenny, now 35, had a privileged but lonely childhood. The only child of Paul and Grace Irvine, she grew up attending various social and charity functions with her parents. For the first few years of her life, Jenny was Daddy's girl, but as she got older, she often felt sad and lonely because her dad was frequently away on business. Paul was a well-known photographer who started his business by taking engagement and wedding pictures in the Charlotte area. By the time Jenny was 4 years old, Paul was being asked to photograph weddings and other momentous events throughout North Carolina and neighboring states. Her mother, Grace, worked full time as an assistant bank manager and was rarely home before 6:00 P.M. Before Paul became a renowned photographer, he stayed home during the day to take care of Jenny while Grace went to work. This arrangement continued until Paul's work required more travel, at which time Ms. Teresa was hired as a full-time nanny for Jenny. Jenny liked Ms. Teresa very much but found that she was busy much of the day keeping the house and doing the laundry. Jenny spent a lot of time in her room playing with the numerous toys she received from her parents and other family members.

> Hoarding affects more males than females, but women are much more likely to seek treatment for the disorder (APA, 2013).

> Although hoarding is conceptualized as a variant of obsessive-compulsive disorder, research has found that symptoms of inattention (not obsessive-compulsive disorder) predict severity of clutter, difficulty discarding, and the acquiring characteristics of hoarding disorder (Tolin & Villavicencio, 2011).

Jenny Early Difficulties in School

Jenny started kindergarten when she was 5 years old. Grace would drop her off every morning and Ms. Teresa would pick her up at the end of each day. Jenny enjoyed being at school; she was a sociable child and made friends easily. While she performed adequately in her academic subjects, Jenny's teacher would often send notes home stating that she kept a messy desk and appeared to be thinking about other things when she should have been paying attention to the teacher. Her parents tended to brush these comments off, as they knew their daughter had a very active imagination. They did, however, talk with

Ms. Teresa about beginning to give Jenny responsibility for picking up her own toys at the end of the day.

By the second grade, Jenny was starting to fall behind in a variety of school subjects. Her teacher requested a number of parent-teacher conferences and attempted to explain to Paul and Grace how Jenny's apparent attentional problems were affecting her academic performance. The evenings after a parent-teacher conference tended to go the same way each time: Her parents would lecture Jenny about needing to pay more attention in school and then Paul would go up to her room, find one her favorite toys, and take it away to "donate to another little girl who appreciated the importance of a good education." Jenny developed the habit of hiding her most precious toys from her father. She remembered one afternoon in particular when she realized that she had forgotten to put her dollhouse back in her closet before she left for school. She hurried up to her room and found that it was gone. With her heart pounding she ran downstairs and asked her mother if she knew what had happened to her dollhouse. Grace responded in a soft voice that they received a call from the principal, who expressed concern about Jenny advancing to the third grade. The principal suggested they have Jenny tested for attention deficit/hyperactivity disorder (ADHD). For the first time ever, Grace wondered if there really was some kind of problem, but Paul had responded with his typical anger. He marched upstairs to Jenny's room and left the house with her cherished dollhouse. Jenny remembered crying herself to sleep that night and many nights thereafter. To outsiders, it seemed as though she had everything she could ever want, but on the inside she felt that she could lose anything at any time no matter how hard she tried to hold on to it.

Two months later, Grace took Jenny to see Dr. Davis, a neuropsychologist, who after hours of testing, diagnosed her with ADHD, predominantly inattentive presentation. Dr. Davis explained that Jenny had a neurodevelopmental disorder that made it difficult for her to sustain attention for any length of time. Her ADHD was likely also contributing to her constant state of disorganization and mess. Given the impact of her symptoms on her academic functioning, Dr. Davis recommended they consult a child psychiatrist to discuss whether a trial of stimulant medication would work for Jenny's condition.

The waitlist for an appointment with a child psychiatrist was 6 months, so Grace took Jenny to her pediatrician, who was comfortable prescribing a trial of methylphenidate (Concerta). They agreed to give the medication a try for the remainder of the school year, with a plan to take a drug holiday over the summer.

Jenny The Beginning of Acquiring

The medication Jenny took for her ADHD was very helpful over the next several years. By the fourth grade, her grades had improved significantly, primarily as a result of being able to better focus in the classroom. She still struggled with keeping

---

Despite what was once thought of as an important etiological factor, material deprivation has not been found as a risk factor for hoarding. However, trauma and other stressful life events have been shown to be important correlates of hoarding behaviors (Landau et al., 2011).

While hoarding disorder is often comorbid with obsessive-compulsive disorder, studies have found that among individuals with hoarding disorder who have no history of obsessive-compulsive disorder, 28 percent were diagnosed with attention deficit disorder, inattentive type (Frost, Steketee, & Tolin, 2011).

Methylphenidate is a stimulant drug that often restricts the growth of children when taken for ADHD. These children tend to gain less weight and height than peers who don't take stimulant medication. Growth retardation is thought to result from decreased appetite, a side effect of methylphenidate. Some people believe taking a drug holiday, during which the medicine is discontinued over the summer, can help a child catch up to peers in terms of height and weight.

Indecisiveness has been identified as one of the prominent features in individuals with hoarding disorder (APA, 2013).

Individuals with hoarding disorder struggle with discarding possessions, typically because of the perceived utility or aesthetic value of the items. They also tend to have a strong sentimental attachment to their possessions (APA, 2013).

all of her books, notes, and personal belongings organized, both at school and home. By the eighth grade, it became evident just how much Jenny struggled with making the most basic decisions. What should she wear to school that day? What would she like for dinner? Which toys or electronics does she no longer play with, so they can be donated? As she was a child, many of her decisions were made for her, but now Jenny struggled with anxiety about making the right decision and the consequences of making the wrong one. One thing she struggled with in particular was throwing away boxes, mostly the small boxes that held jewelry but also the original boxes for her toys. She started out by saving the little jewelry boxes, along with empty toilet paper and paper towel rolls, thinking they would be great for various art projects, such as papier maché animals. She rarely had the time to use these materials for projects at home, but she knew they would come in handy for something one day, so she held on to them—for years.

She also felt that it was important to keep all of the original packaging for her toys, because she made an arrangement with her parents that if she sold the toys she no longer used on Craigslist, she could keep the money. She knew that an item would typically sell at a higher price if it were in the original packaging. While this idea was good in theory, Jenny had only been able to sell one game on Craigslist. It wasn't that her things weren't worth selling; she was having a hard time deciding what to sell and then following through with listing it online. She felt so attached to her things. Even though she knew objectively that she didn't play with a particular toy anymore, she couldn't help anticipating the loss she would feel when it was gone. She also questioned her own judgment, thinking, "Well, I don't play with this right now, but who is to say that I'm not going to want to play with it next week?"

Her "collections" didn't present a problem until one day her mother went into Jenny's room when she wasn't at home. Grace had bought Jenny some designer clothes that she found on sale at a local department store. Wanting to surprise her daughter, Grace went into Jenny's room to hang the clothes in her closet. Jenny's closet was full of clothes, toys, and cardboard boxes, so Grace decided she would move some of last season's clothes into her dresser to make room for the new clothes. She was shocked when every single dresser drawer she opened was full of small boxes and empty toilet paper and paper towel rolls. She had absolutely no idea why Jenny was saving all of these things. She was irritated that doing something nice for her daughter was now taking up so much of her time. She got a garbage bag and filled it with four drawers' worth of empty boxes and cardboard rolls. When Jenny came home from school, Grace told her she had a surprise for her and took her up to her room. She proudly showed Jenny how she had arranged her closet and filled it with new designer outfits. She explained that to make room that she threw out all of the junk that Jenny had been saving in her drawers. When she heard this, rather than running to see the clothes, Jenny ran to her dresser and frantically opened drawer after drawer. "You threw out my things? How could you do that?" she screamed at her mother. "Those were mine. I was saving them for something, and now they are gone." Jenny sat on the floor sobbing, without even noticing her new clothes. Grace just walked out of the room, astonished at how irrational her daughter could be and annoyed that Jenny didn't appreciate the time and effort Grace had put into buying her new clothes.

When Jenny was 14 years old, her 17-year-old cousin, Andrew, was killed in a motorcycle accident. Andrew was the only child of Olivia, Grace's sister. Grace and Olivia had an extremely close relationship and saw each other often, as they only lived about 20 miles from one another. Olivia and her husband, Brian, were completely devastated by the loss of their only child, and Grace grieved alongside her sister. For at least a month after Andrew's death, Grace left work early to come home and cook dinner and then drive it out to Olivia's house. Many nights Grace would just sleep at Olivia's house and go straight to work from there in the morning. Jenny and Andrew were actually quite close, and she felt the pain of his death and a sadness for her aunt that she had never experienced before. After about 3 months, Jenny felt as though she never saw her mother. Grace was still spending a lot of time at Olivia's house. Jenny decided that she would ask if she could come with her mom to help, which would give her the opportunity to spend some time with her mother. It was the first time she'd been back to her aunt and uncle's house since the funeral, and she was surprised by how empty it felt. Jenny carried some laundry upstairs, and while she was up there, she decided she would peek into Andrew's room. The door was shut, but she quietly opened it. She was shocked when she opened the door and saw that the room was almost completely full of boxes, which were all overflowing with what looked like Andrew's things and anything loosely related to him. Jenny asked her mother about this on the way home and Grace replied that Aunt Olivia seemed to be grieving by collecting and buying anything that reminded her of Andrew. Grace told Jenny that if she was disturbed by that bedroom, she should definitely not go into their basement.

Hoarding behavior has a genetic component, with about 50 percent of individuals who hoard reporting that they have a relative who also hoards (APA, 2013).

Jenny in Adulthood A Struggling Marriage

After graduating from college with a degree in English and Communications, Jenny was offered a job working in the graduate college at a local university. Her job entailed working with the doctoral students to ensure that their dissertations met the graduate school's detailed formatting requirements. She enjoyed the work, as she tended to be a detail-oriented person, but she did find it a little monotonous at times. Steven, a doctoral student in biomedical sciences and chemistry, wasn't the typical student she saw in her office. He actually made an appointment to ask for guidance before he started writing his dissertation. Most students she met with had already written the entire document, incorrectly of course, and were in a panic because the dissertation had to be submitted within a couple of days. Steven seemed to appreciate Jenny's help, and Jenny enjoyed listening to Steven talk about his grand ideas of changing the world through his inventions. In fact, Steven was working with one of his professors to develop a material that they hoped one day would be used in the 3D printing of human organs. Eventually, Jenny and Steven started dating, and he proposed to her the day after he received his doctorate.

Jenny and her mother were extremely excited to begin planning the wedding she had always dreamed of. Jenny started buying bridal magazines, following various wedding planning blogs, and printing pictures and ideas from Pinterest to show Steven and her mother. She became so consumed with wedding planning that she was having a hard time concentrating on her job. Furthermore, her office was beginning to look smaller and smaller as the magazines and papers piled up. She knew she needed to clean it up because she met with students in her office, but she kept telling herself that once she "got organized," there would be much less clutter. She tried to keep the door to her office shut as much as possible, but her boss did make a comment one day about her office not giving the right message to students. Jenny agreed with his observation and was happy when she was able to secure a small conference room that she could use for student meetings.

Jenny and Steven were married by the time she turned 26, and they were thrilled to be able to buy a house. Jenny was grateful to her parents for the financial help with the down payment, as she did not make a lot of money at the university. Steven's invention was about to be patented, but it cost much more money than it brought in at that point. The weekend Jenny and Steven moved into their new home was much more stressful than either had expected. Steven was shocked to see box after box after box coming out of Jenny's parents' home. He thought to himself, "How could any 26-year-old possibly have that much stuff?" He knew Jenny's family came from a different socioeconomic background than he did, so he assumed she would have more to move than he would. But this was even more than he could have imagined. He wondered where they were going to store everything and how long it would take Jenny to unpack. As they moved boxes into their small basement storage area, Steven couldn't help but open a few just to take a look inside. He was shocked to see what looked like boxes of garbage and old papers. There seemed to be no rhyme or reason to the way things were packed, and one huge box was full of empty toilet paper and paper towel rolls! When Steven confronted Jenny with his discovery, she became defensive and angry. She told him that it was none of his business and that he shouldn't be going through her things. He responded by telling her that now that they were married, it was his business, especially if all of those things were taking up more than half of their house.

Jenny and Steven's first year of marriage was stressful on many levels. They were learning how to live together and how to divide household duties, and Steven was acclimating to Jenny's packrat nature. She did make significant progress in terms of unpacking boxes, but as a result, almost all of their open space was occupied with her possessions. Steven wondered what was going to happen when they had children.

Two years later, they had their first child, a daughter named Claire. Jenny struggled with balancing the demands of motherhood and a full-time job. Steven's invention was now receiving a lot of good press, and he was starting to travel more to make presentations to hospitals and biomedical research centers. Jenny had days when she felt pretty down and alone. She wondered if she had postpartum depression. She recalled some of these same feelings from when she was a child and her father spent a lot of time away from home. She took care of herself and Claire but didn't have much motivation to keep up the house. The clutter began to pile up, and despite Steven's comments when he returned from a business trip, she justified the mess by claiming that she was still a new mother and was having to take care of everything at home because he was off gallivanting around with his friends and colleagues.

While Jenny's mood improved over the coming months, Steven noticed that anytime there was a significant change in the household, Jenny started collecting things that she believed were important. Furthermore, she refused to throw any of these things away, and the house became more and more cluttered. She repeated this same pattern two years later, after their son, Jeremy, was born. By this time, Steven's invention was being sold to a number of large medical research institutes and they could afford for Jenny to quit her job. Jenny had developed a hobby of scouring the Internet, particularly eBay and Craigslist, for baby and toddler gear. She prided herself on always being able to find fantastic deals on items that would sell for double on Amazon. Steven told her that she didn't need to worry about money so much anymore, but she explained to him that the thrill was related to getting a great deal, not about whether they could afford it. As a result of this newfound hobby, Jenny and Steven began acquiring a number of items that they didn't need or use. These items ultimately ended up being stored in the garage. Jenny assured Steven that she was going to sell many of these items for a profit on eBay or Craigslist. Steven had heard this before many times, but never once had he seen Jenny actually sell anything.

> General life stress, particularly interpersonal stress, has been found to be associated with hoarding. Studies have suggested that emotional intolerance, the belief that emotional stress is intolerable and must be avoided, is partially responsible for the relationship between stress and hoarding (Timpano, Keough, Traeger, & Schmidt, 2011).

Steven Through a Husband's Eyes

I felt myself becoming more and more emotionally distant from Jenny. I'm sure she could feel it too, but she didn't seem to care. The only thing she really seemed to care about was her stuff. She is a good person and has been a good mother to our children, but I believe they too are starting to suffer the consequences of her issues. Our daughter, Claire, is now in first grade, and she would come home talking about how all of her friends were having playdates at their houses. When I told her that she was welcome to invite friends over to our house, she put her head down and mumbled that she was embarrassed to invite her friends over because of how messy our house was. Hearing that broke my heart, and when I looked around

Spouses and family members often don't see the severity of the hoarding behaviors because the accumulation of items happens slowly over a long time, often years.

our house that night I felt like I was really seeing it for the first time. It was appalling, really; every counter and every table was completely covered with junk. The kitchen garbage was starting to smell; it had been there for weeks because it was hidden behind so much stuff. How did Jenny even cook in there? I had to admit to myself how blind I had been over the past year. I had been traveling a lot, which I guess I used as an escape. Then when I was home, I just forced myself not to look around. But now that I had seen it, I mean really seen it, there was no going back. I went through every room of the house, opened every closet door, and looked down in the basement. I realized I hadn't been in the basement since we moved into the house after we got married. I will never be able to get that scene out of my head. There was stuff, brand new stuff that I'd never seen, literally stacked from floor to ceiling. I felt as though I couldn't breathe. How could I have been so blind to this? How much money has she spent on all of this stuff? But the most difficult thought I had was: "How could I have let my children live in this condition?" That was enough to cause me to fall to my knees and start sobbing. I knew at that moment that as much as I loved Jenny, I couldn't allow our kids to grow up like this. By the time Jenny and the kids got home that evening, I had packed up a few things I could actually find in the piles around the house. I told her that I was taking the kids to my parents for a while so she and I could work out a plan about what we were going to do. I remember she just looked at me like I was crazy. She said she didn't understand what I was talking about and that it was fine if I wanted to leave but there was no way I was taking the children. She really didn't get it and was starting to get angry. I threatened to call the Department of Family Services and report her if she didn't let me leave with the kids.

The kids and I lived with my parents for the next few weeks while Jenny and I tried to work out a plan. I told her that I had done some research on psychological disorders and that I thought she had hoarding disorder. She responded in her typical way, which was angry and defensive. I suggested that we go see a marriage counselor to help us work through this rough patch in our marriage. I was shocked that she reluctantly agreed, and this gave me a glimmer of hope.

Unfortunately, that glimmer of hope faded. In the middle of our second session, Jenny stormed out after the therapist asked her if she thought her hoarding tendencies played a role in our marital problems. She later claimed that the therapist didn't know what he was talking about and that he was obviously on my side because he was a man. I tried to explain to her that I thought her hoarding problem was one of the major reasons our marriage was failing, but she just refused to acknowledge that fact. I felt like I had no choice; I had to do what was best for my children. I had been offered a job in Raleigh, and I made the decision to accept the job, file for separation, and move with the kids to Raleigh. It was by far the hardest thing I've ever done in my life. I don't think it was until the kids and I drove away pulling a trailer of our things that Jenny finally realized what she had lost.

Jenny Treatment as a Last Resort

In the weeks after Steven left with the kids, Jenny was devastated and had difficulty getting through the day. She rarely left her house and had trouble sleeping. She ignored her mother's phone calls and only answered the phone if she saw that it was Steven calling. He was good about having the kids call her every day or two. Her mother frequently called ahead and then brought food over and left it at the front door. But one day, she showed up at Jenny's house unannounced. It had probably been over a year since she had been inside the house, because Jenny never invited anyone over. Grace was worried about her daughter and kept banging on the door telling Jenny she wasn't leaving until she let her inside. Eventually, Jenny conceded and let Grace in. Steven had tried to prepare Grace for what she would see, but no one could have been adequately prepared. Her jaw dropped as she looked around and saw only a small pathway from the front door leading into the living room and kitchen. Her daughter's house looked like it could have been on one of those reality TV shows. Grace looked at her daughter, a ghost of who she once was, and begged her to get some help. She told Jenny that there was no way a judge was going to grant her any custody rights to her children as long as she was living in those conditions. Jenny broke down sobbing, and with tears streaming down her face, she agreed to go get treatment.

Sessions 1 and 2   Jenny agreed to go see Dr. Michael Strader, who specialized in the cognitive-behavioral treatment of hoarding disorder. According to his Web site, he worked with a whole team of people, including professional organizers and a psychiatrist. Grace attended the initial assessment with Jenny, primarily because she was afraid Jenny would cancel if left to herself. When Dr. Strader asked Jenny what brought her to treatment, she responded, "I've lost my husband and my children because my house is a mess." Dr. Strader had a difficult time pulling the entire story out of Jenny, but he knew this type of defensiveness and lack of insight were common in individuals who had hoarding disorder. Grace was willing to fill in some of the important information that Jenny was leaving out of the conversation. At the end of the 50-minute session, Dr. Strader told Jenny and Grace that he believed Jenny had hoarding disorder but that he was confident that his team could help her. He was careful not to guarantee that she would be completely symptom free after therapy, because he knew that while cognitive-behavioral therapy was an empirically supported treatment for hoarding, complete remission was rare. However, Dr. Strader believed that with a multidimensional cognitive-behavioral approach Jenny could have significant emotional relief, clean up her living environment, and function at a higher level. Jenny agreed to give it a try to get her family back and scheduled an appointment with Dr. Strader for the following week.

Insight refers to the ability of the patient to recognize the irrationality of the behavior. Treating hoarding is a challenge because many of these individuals exhibit poor insight, which makes them unlikely to seek treatment on their own; and if they are in therapy, relatively noncompliant with treatment recommendations (Frost, Tolin, & Maltby, 2010).

In the second session, Dr. Strader described the cognitive-behavioral model of hoarding to both Jenny and her mother. He explained that hoarding consists of excessive acquisition and difficulty discarding items, which result in extreme clutter in the living environment. He went on to say that there is a lot of evidence to suggest that hoarding stems from a combination of information-processing deficits, problematic beliefs and behaviors, and emotional distress and avoidance. Jenny appeared confused and slightly agitated.

Cognitive-behavioral therapy has been found to produce clinically significant improvement in clients who complete the treatment. Cognitive-behavioral therapy can be provided in individual or group settings (Gilliam et al., 2011; Steketee, Frost, Tolin, Rasmussen, & Brown, 2010). There is also some evidence that hoarding can be successfully treated in non–professionally facilitated, biblio-based support groups (Frost, Pekareva-Kochergina, & Maxner, 2011). These action-oriented groups use a self-help book for hoarding disorder that has been shown to be effective in reducing and/or eliminating hoarding symptoms.

Jenny:	I have no idea what any of that means.
Dr. Strader:	Okay, well let me put it another way. People who develop hoarding behaviors tend to have a history of difficulty sustaining attention, making decisions, and organizing their belongings.
Jenny:	Well, that definitely describes my life.
Dr. Strader:	Furthermore, the cognitive-behavioral model suggests that individuals who hoard have very strong emotions about their possessions. On the one hand, they have powerful negative emotional reactions, such as anxiety, grief, or guilt, that lead to avoidance of discarding or organizing things. On the other hand, they have very positive emotions, such as pleasure and joy, from acquiring and saving possessions. The relief that results from the avoidance of discarding and the pleasure from bringing new items into the home are a powerful combination that makes this a difficult problem to change on your own.
Jenny:	Now I understand what you are talking about, and that has pretty much been my experience for the past few years.
Grace:	I would have to say that your description pretty accurately describes how Jenny has been for most of her life.
Dr. Strader:	It is common for many of these behaviors and beliefs to begin in adolescence or even childhood. You can probably trace these behaviors back a long time; it is just that now they have reached a point where they are having very negative consequences for your life.
Jenny:	(Sniffing as she nods) I just don't know anything different at this point.
Dr. Strader:	That makes perfect sense, and that's why this treatment is educational as well as therapeutic. Lifelong problems take a long time to change. So we can move at a pace that is comfortable for you. Does that sound okay?
Jenny:	Yes, that sounds good to me.

The standard individual cognitive-behavioral treatment for hoarding disorder lasts 26 sessions over approximately a year.

Sessions 3 to 6   Jenny attended the next few sessions by herself. She was pleasantly surprised that Dr. Strader didn't want to come to her house and make her throw out all of her stuff like they did on those reality shows. Instead, he asked her a lot of questions regarding her understanding of how her hoarding began and the kinds of things in her life that maintained the behavior. Dr. Strader attempted to understand Jenny's core values, or what was most important to her in life, and asked her about her personal goals. Where did she want to be in 5 years? What were some of her dreams that she never imagined were attainable because of her disorder? Dr. Strader knew that most patients with hoarding disorder struggled with being ready to make changes, so he wanted to move slowly. But he also wanted Jenny to recognize both the pros and cons of changing and that it was okay if a part of her didn't want to change. He asked her to brainstorm a list of all of the possible pros of changing and then all of the possible cons. The most striking part of the exercise was when Jenny came to the realization that there were many pros *and* many cons. This recognition allowed Dr. Strader to empathize with Jenny about her ambivalence about changing. It also gave him the opportunity to work with her to shift the balance toward the good things about changing in an effort to increase her motivation for the work to come.

> Ambivalence refers to the mixed feelings of patients with respect to giving up their disorder. On the one hand, they know the disorder is ruining their life in many ways, but on the other hand, their disorder provides them with a sense of comfort. In Jenny's case, her hoarding gives her the opportunity to avoid anxiety and other negative emotions.

Sessions 7 to 10   The next four sessions were devoted to teaching Jenny some specific skills that would help her through decluttering and maintaining the decluttered environment. Dr. Strader had Jenny meet with Susan, a professional organizer, to talk about developing organizational skills. Susan would assign Jenny a very small task to practice at home between sessions, such as finding one box to put by the front door in which she would keep all of the mail that was brought into the house.

Dr. Strader also worked with Jenny on decision-making and problem-solving skills. These were issues that Jenny had struggled with since childhood. She felt some relief finally to have a system to use to make a decision or solve a problem. They also started to work on cognitive restructuring of some of the beliefs Jenny held about the importance of acquiring and keeping possessions. Dr. Strader helped Jenny figure out what some of those beliefs were.

Dr. Strader:	Can you give me an example of something in your home that you are holding onto that other people would think you should throw out?
Jenny:	Well, that probably describes most of the things in my house. But I guess if I had to pick something I would say the broken bicycle in my living room.
Dr. Strader:	Okay. How long has your bicycle been broken?
Jenny:	It's actually not my bicycle; it's my cousin Andrew's. He's the one I told you about who was killed when I was 14 years old.
Dr. Strader:	Yes, I remember you telling me about him and how difficult that time was for you and your family. So why do you think you're holding on to his broken bicycle?
Jenny:	I don't know, I guess I just feel like throwing it out would be like throwing him out, and I don't have many things of his because

	my aunt had a hard time letting anyone take anything out of his room.
Dr. Strader:	So in some way, you feel like throwing away a broken possession of his would be disrespectful to him?
Jenny:	A little bit, I guess.
Dr. Strader:	It also sounds like you have some fear that if you were to throw the bicycle away, you would be choosing to lose some of your memories of Andrew, or even worse, forget about him all together?
Jenny:	(Choking back tears) Yes, that could be it.
Dr. Strader:	Where do you think the memories of Andrew are held? Are they stored in the broken bicycle? Or, are they stored within you?
Jenny:	Well, they are within me of course. But the bicycle helps me remember him.
Dr. Strader:	So the bicycle serves as a reminder for you to not forget Andrew.
Jenny:	Yes, I guess it does.
Dr. Strader:	Are there any times during the day or week that you think about Andrew when the bicycle isn't around?
Jenny:	Sure, sometimes something outside will remind me of him, or I'll just have a random memory about something from our childhood.
Dr. Strader:	So I wonder if you aren't giving yourself enough credit to trust that your memories of Andrew will be with you forever and that you don't need a reminder every time you walk in your house to remember him. My guess is you don't look at the broken bicycle every time you walk in your house and then take a moment to think about Andrew.
Jenny:	No, not at all. I can hardly even see the bicycle now because it is behind so much other stuff.
Dr. Strader:	So you really don't need it for any of the reasons you originally thought?
Jenny:	No, I suppose I don't. In my heart I know that I'll never forget Andrew.
Dr. Strader:	That's right. So how about we try this? When you get home today, can you move the bicycle to a place where it is completely out of your sight? Then we can really test whether or not it is the bicycle that helps you to remember Andrew. Then, any time during the next few weeks that you think about or have a memory of Andrew, make a note of it in your phone. If at the end of that time you have had thoughts or memories of him that weren't triggered by the bicycle, you'll bring the bicycle in to our next session and we'll discard it together.
Jenny:	Just hearing you say that makes me nervous, but I'm willing to give it a try.

Sessions 11 to 14 After collecting her own data, Jenny was able to let go of her belief that it was necessary to hold on to a broken bicycle to remember her cousin. She took the bicycle to her twelfth session with Dr. Strader, and together they threw it away in the dumpster behind his building. Jenny felt significant anxiety during this process, but Dr. Strader helped her to use the coping strategies that she had learned in treatment so far.

The next sessions took place in Jenny's home. Dr. Strader attended the first of these sessions with Susan, who was going to work with Jenny to develop an organizational system. Dr. Strader and Susan helped Jenny to learn the difference between things that she needs and things that she wants. They also reminded her that her identity did not come from her possessions. With Dr. Stader's help, Jenny began to realize that she could get rid of some of these things, still be who she is, and have a much happier life because her children would be able to come back.

Over the next couple of months, Susan helped Jenny to sort the things in her house, room by room. Susan brought in large bins that were labeled Trash, Recycle, Donate, Sell, and Undecided. The Sell and Undecided bins were significantly smaller than the others, and once they were full, Susan didn't allow Jenny to put anything else in there. Over the course of the next month, Jenny was surprised by the progress she had made. She could actually see the floor in some places, and some small countertop space was visible. At times, she struggled with feeling overwhelmed at the sheer amount of work to be accomplished, but if she stayed focused on the task at hand, by using some of the strategies Dr. Strader taught her, she managed quite well.

Sessions 15 to 26 Jenny had found her rhythm. With Susan's help she developed an organizational system, and she worked on it for at least 30 minutes each day. Jenny agreed to spend a minimum of 30 minutes a day organizing as homework, but many days she found herself organizing for hours. Dr. Strader had asked Jenny to take before and after pictures. He asked her to text him the before picture prior to beginning the cleanup of that area and then text him the after picture once she felt that she had made enough progress to move on to another area of the house. This strategy was helpful for Jenny because it gave her some accountability and she really wanted Dr. Strader to be pleased with her progress. This strategy enabled Dr. Strader to maintain regular contact and monitor what was going on in Jenny's home without having to make numerous trips.

In addition to decluttering her home, Jenny worked with Dr. Strader to develop skills to stop herself from acquiring new possessions. Jenny found it very difficult to throw things away, but she was surprised that it was almost as difficult at times to resist bringing new things into her home. Jenny identified her high-risk situations for acquiring new items, such as eBay, Craigslist, the local freecycle site, flea markets, and garage sales. She agreed to deactivate her accounts on eBay,

Craigslist, and the freecycle site for a while to help reduce her urge to acquire stuff, and she avoided flea markets and garage sales. Dr. Strader helped her develop a hierarchy of stores she could visit with the goal of not buying anything. The hierarchy started with stores that were only minor triggers and ended with those where Jenny would always buy something. Jenny began these exposures a few times each week, and as she felt confident that she could visit a store without the urge to take something home, she was able to move up to the next store on the hierarchy. With each passing week, Jenny began to feel more confident and truly started to believe that she could change her life for good.

Epilogue

Jenny attended regular therapy appointments for over a year. Even after she met all of her goals, which included decluttering her home, having it professionally cleaned, and maintaining the organization and cleanliness, she continued to meet with Dr. Strader once every few months just to check in. She found that the little bit of accountability helped her keep on track if she started to slip back into old habits. Not falling back into her old ways was a daily battle for Jenny, but as each month passed, she felt that this battle got easier to fight.

Follow-up research studies have indicated that treatment gains can be maintained over a long period; however, individuals with high levels of preexisting perfectionism are more likely to relapse (Muroff, Steketee, Frost, & Tolin, 2013).

As Jenny looked back at the last few years of her life, she could hardly believe how chaotic her life had been. She struggled with the guilt of what she'd put Steven and her children through but tried to stay focused on the changes she could make in the present. Jenny didn't know what the future would hold for her and Steven; she desperately hoped that he would come back to her, but she knew that he had to make that decision in his own time. She was incredibly grateful, however, that he was open to having the children visit her often and spend some weekends and holidays with her. When Jenny saw the smiles on her children's faces the first time they came back to their house, she knew that all of her hard work in treatment over the past year and a half was worth it.

Assessment Questions

1. What characteristics did Jenny have as a child that are common in individuals who develop hoarding disorder?

2. Who in Jenny's family appeared to have hoarding tendencies? What situation appeared to trigger an episode?

3. How is it that Jenny didn't think she had a problem until after she had been in treatment for some time?

4. Describe the cognitive-behavioral model of hoarding.

5. List some of the beliefs Jenny had about why it was important to hold onto things.

6. Why would it not have been effective just to call a junkman to clear everything out of Jenny's house and make a clean start?

7. How did Jenny's hoarding interfere with her life?

CASE **4**

Posttraumatic Stress Disorder

Table 4-1

Dx Checklist

Posttraumatic Stress Disorder

1. Person is exposed to a traumatic event—death or threatened death, severe injury, or sexual violation.

2. Person experiences at least 1 of the following intrusive symptoms: • Repeated, uncontrolled, and distressing memories • Repeated and upsetting trauma-linked dreams • Dissociative experiences such as flashbacks • Significant upset when exposed to trauma-linked cues • Pronounced physical reactions when reminded of the event(s).

3. Person continually avoids trauma-linked stimuli.

4. Person experiences negative changes in trauma-linked cognitions and moods, such as being unable to remember key features of the event(s) or experiencing repeated negative emotions.

5. Person displays conspicuous changes in arousal and reactivity, such as excessive alertness, extreme startle responses, or sleep disturbances.

6. Person experiences significant distress or impairment, with symptoms lasting more than a month.

(Based on APA, 2013.)

At age 65, Elaine, a retired professor of social work, was living a full and active life. Although retired, she had never been one to sit back and let life pass her by. She had always been an energetic and outgoing woman, something of a social butterfly who enjoyed good friends and good food. She was a regular subway rider, traveling all over the city to go to her favorite shops, restaurants, museums, and lectures and to visit her numerous friends from the university community.

Elaine A Woman of Energy and Optimism

In fact, Elaine's energetic and optimistic life in retirement was consistent with the robust and challenging state of mind with which she had always approached life. Indeed, she had never had any psychological difficulties to speak of, or even a significant physical illness. On the other hand, she certainly had her share of trauma

Interest in stress disorders intensified during the Vietnam War, when clinicians observed that increasing numbers of returning veterans were having flashbacks (intense recollections of combat traumas) and were generally alienated from everyday life.

earlier in her life. She spent her childhood living in Alabama during the civil rights movement. Her father, an African-American man who became an outspoken local leader for civil rights, was a frequent target of hate mail and community protests. Throughout her early childhood into her teenage years, Elaine witnessed marches and nonviolent protests that were often met with threats and violence. At age 14, she was one of the first African-American students to attend a desegregated high school in her hometown. At best, her white classmates ignored her; at worst, they mocked and bullied her. Elaine got used to eating lunch alone and staring stone-faced into the distance as the white high school students taunted and mocked her. Even in her own community, some people expressed hatred for her and her family. Every night as she and her parents watched the nightly news, she saw the stories of the many people who had been hurt or killed during the civil rights movement. She became skilled at walking through the hallways of her school and the streets of her town with her head held high, ignoring the frequent taunts and occasional shoves. She became skilled at avoiding situations that seemed ready to erupt, and her ability to overcome taunting and isolation, as well as cope with danger, had instilled in her a fierce pride in her self-sufficiency, mental acuity, and physical resilience. She likened herself in those times to a cat: someone who quickly sized up a situation and made the right move almost instinctively, always landing on her feet.

Following high school, Elaine went to a Northeastern university to study for a bachelor's degree in social work. She eventually earned a doctorate and obtained a faculty appointment at a major university in the Northeast, where she remained for 30 years.

At the university, she threw herself wholeheartedly into her career, devoting her life to teaching, research, and writing. Her intense involvement in her work was legendary, and anecdotes circulated in her department of how she had occasionally been found asleep at her desk when colleagues arrived in the morning; apparently, she had become so absorbed in her work that she had ended up staying the night.

With her devotion to her career, there was no doubt in Elaine's mind that her personal life had suffered. As she remained unmarried, her colleagues and students became her family. (Both of her parents had since passed away, and her siblings remained in the South.) Sensing her devotion, students flocked to receive the benefits of her wisdom and experience, which she generously bestowed. She, in turn, took great personal interest in her students' progress, maintaining contact with them and following their careers, sometimes for decades, after they had graduated.

And so it was, both prior to and during retirement. Elaine was a picture of emotional and physical strength—a woman of incredible poise, self-confidence, and direction. Then, in one brief moment, everything seemed to change. She was struck by a catastrophe that took her life and state of mind in a direction that she could never have anticipated or imagined.

Elaine Disaster Strikes

Elaine was taking the subway home from a shopping trip when it struck a stationary train on the track ahead. Although her train was not traveling at high speed—perhaps 20 miles an hour at most—the impact was forceful enough to hurl the passengers from their seats and partially crush the metal cars. Elaine herself had been standing at the moment of impact. As she was thrown forward, her left leg struck a seat jutting out in front of her, wrenching her knee, and her head struck a metal pole, knocking her out. When Elaine regained consciousness, she was lying in a pile of other passengers who had been thrown together in the same corner of the car. As far as she could make out in the dim light, most were unconscious and bleeding. Elaine put her hand to her own forehead and it came back wet with blood. She was horrified. What if she was bleeding to death and no one could reach her to stop the flow? She tried to get up but could not overcome the weight of the other passengers. She spent the next half hour lying there, paralyzed with fear, wondering if she would be able to survive until help arrived.

When the rescue squad finally did arrive on the scene, the injured passengers were taken out of the train on stretchers. Only 4 were judged to require hospitalization—Elaine among them—and they were taken to separate emergency rooms in the vicinity of the train wreck.

The initial examination in the emergency room determined that Elaine did not have a critical loss of blood. Now, as she lay on a gurney awaiting further tests, the terrified woman stared wide-eyed at the gruesome scenes paraded before her: people being brought in as a result of stabbings, shootings, drug overdoses, and the like. A tough-looking stabbing victim with only superficial wounds seated himself next to Elaine and winked at her; Elaine was aghast. She turned her head away from the derelict, hoping to escape his further notice, but she felt she might be set upon at any moment.

Elaine spent 3 hours in this highly anxious state, restrained by the straps on the gurney, until she was finally taken to the radiology department for tests. At first she was relieved to be removed from the throng, but then, as she was wheeled down a dark corridor, she began to wonder if her relief was premature. Overcome by her fears, she even wondered whether she was being taken away to be raped or killed by the hospital orderly, of all people.

Once her X rays and a computed tomography (CT) scan were done, Elaine was returned to the waiting area, where her fears further intensified. Now she

> Stress disorders can occur at any age, including childhood.

> Generally, the more severe the trauma and the more direct one's exposure to it, the greater the likelihood of developing a stress disorder.

began to focus on the risk of contagion. Numerous patients were coughing persistently, and Elaine became afraid that she was being exposed to tuberculosis, which had been making a well-publicized comeback in city hospitals. She glanced at the disreputable-looking man hacking away next to her. He seemed extremely haggard and sickly, practically spitting on the floor, and she became convinced she was about to contract a drug-resistant strain of tuberculosis.

After another 2 hours, the doctor finally arrived and informed Elaine that the X rays and CT scan had revealed no fracture or brain hemorrhage. He then helped her up from the gurney and tested her gait, physical mobility, and neurological signs. Everything seemed normal. The doctor told Elaine she was free to go home as soon as the nurse dressed her head wound. To play things safe, however, he also advised Elaine to see a doctor for follow-up.

Elaine was relieved to be released finally. However, she glanced at the clock and saw that it was now 1:00 A.M., 6 hours from when she had originally been brought to the hospital. The idea of venturing out into the night at this hour, in this condition, in this neighborhood, was, like everything else, terrifying. She was in a tremendous conflict. This horrifying emergency room was the last place on earth that she wanted to be in. But the alternative, leaving the emergency room to be discharged into the unknown, seemed even worse right now. She soon positioned herself in the same waiting area that moments before she had so fervently been hoping to flee. The frightened woman sat there amid the other patients' coughing, shaking, vomiting, and bleeding. In fact, she waited there until the first glimmer of dawn, and then hobbled out to a taxi waiting at curbside.

The taxi carried her through the awakening city. It was a strangely quiet, dreamy ride, completing the journey Elaine had begun on the subway some 12 hours before. She arrived at her apartment house in 20 minutes and dragged herself out of the cab and into her building, where she took the elevator up to her floor. Once inside her apartment, she collapsed on her bed, happy to be home at long last. What had begun as a simple trip home from a downtown shopping expedition had turned into a nightmare. Elaine slept for almost a full 24 hours.

Elaine Aftermath of the Trauma

The next day, Elaine called some close friends to tell them what had happened. In the light of day, she now realized that one of the most disturbing elements of the whole experience had been coming face-to-face with the prospect of physical disability. As someone who lived alone and had no close living relatives, she realized that even a temporary inability to care for herself could be disastrous. Fortunately, she had a close-knit network of friends and colleagues from the university where she had taught until a few years ago. With her calls this

Women are at least twice as likely as men are to develop a stress disorder. About 20 percent of women who are exposed to a severe trauma develop such a disorder, compared to 8 percent of men.

morning, she hoped to reassure herself that her friends would indeed step in if the need arose.

Her friends were sympathetic and asked her if she needed anything. But oddly, Elaine felt disoriented and found it difficult to answer their questions. The previous day's experience was now jumbled in her mind, and explaining it required considerable effort. It was tiring just to talk for a few minutes. By the time she had made the third call, her voice was so weak that her friend felt great concern and suggested she see a doctor sooner rather than later.

Elaine set up an appointment with a neurologist for 3 days later. In leaving her apartment—for the first time since the accident—she was alarmed at how noisy and confusing it was just to be outside. The city traffic seemed unbearably loud, and Elaine wondered if she would even be able to cross the street. Her body still ached from the accident, but more important, she became concerned that history might repeat itself. She had never been in an accident before and had never been concerned about crossing the street. Now, however, she found herself jumping back and running from cars as they zoomed past, even though she was still on the sidewalk.

Eventually, Elaine reached the doctor's office exhausted and out of breath. She was panting noticeably, as much from running as from her anxiety about the traffic. She didn't even speak to the receptionist when she first arrived. Instead, she collapsed on the nearest seat, closed her eyes and gulped for air, as though having just escaped some grave danger. After a few minutes, the receptionist noticed her sitting there and walked up to greet her. At the sound of the receptionist's voice, Elaine practically jumped out of her seat, she was so startled to find someone suddenly upon her.

The neurologist gave her a thorough examination and reviewed the X rays and CT scan taken in the hospital emergency room. He said that all results seemed normal, but that judging from the cuts and bruises on her head and her complaints about fatigue, noise sensitivity, and disorientation, she might well have sustained a concussion. He told her it was mild, but the symptoms could take several days or even weeks to go away. In the meantime, she should take it easy and get all the rest she needed.

Noticing that Elaine's knee seemed quite swollen, the neurologist also referred her to an orthopedist. Two days later, the latter physician determined that Elaine must have torn the cartilage in her knee as a result of the accident, and now it was becoming inflamed. He said that for the time being, he would treat the knee with an anti-inflammatory drug; but if the inflammation did not improve or if it worsened, arthroscopic surgery to remove the inflamed tissue would be necessary.

Elaine returned home from her appointment with the orthopedist with a vague sense of unease that gradually built to a feeling of impending doom. She had not expected to hear surgery mentioned, and the idea was unusually threatening

Studies indicate that survivors of severe stress, especially those who develop stress disorders, experience abnormal activity of the neurotransmitter norepinephrine and the hormone cortisol.

to her. She shuddered at the thought of going back to a hospital. She recalled her emergency room experience and practically shook with fear as she considered the terrifying scene.

As time passed. Elaine's postconcussion symptoms—her fatigue, noise sensitivity, and disorientation—subsided. Physically, she started to feel more her old self, but she couldn't seem to shake her fearfulness. Each trip outdoors was extraordinarily stressful. Crossing the street was consistently anxiety provoking, as she couldn't get over her preoccupation with being in another accident, this time as a pedestrian. Taking the bus or subway was simply out of the question. The very thought of getting on a train made her shudder. Accordingly, her travels were confined to small local trips in her neighborhood, just to do the necessities: buy food and go to doctor appointments.

It seemed that Elaine's accident and emergency room experience had transformed her entire outlook on life. Somehow, having spent several hours in a highly charged emotional state, focusing almost exclusively on the prospect of dying or being raped or murdered, her mind had started to see everything through this lens. And there was no escaping the memories. When home, in what she considered a safe environment, her memories of the subway car or the emergency room would constantly intrude. As she watched television, her eyes would glaze over as some particularly harrowing element of her experience forced itself into her consciousness: the pile of bodies in the subway car, the grim ride down the hall to the X ray room, or one of the bleeding or coughing "thugs" sitting just a few seats away. Then she would try to shake the memory loose, forcing it out of her mind and trying to focus on something more pleasant, only to find it returning in bits and pieces throughout the evening.

> People who generally view life's negative events as beyond their control seem more prone to develop a stress disorder when confronted with a traumatic event (Regehr et al., 1999). Nevertheless, even people like Elaine, who have hardy attitudes and personalities, may develop a stress disorder.

Previously a sound sleeper; she now found herself waking frequently from dreams that contained images of her subway or emergency room experience. They were not exactly nightmares; rather, they were mostly accurate renditions of her all-too-real experience. She couldn't escape the images, even in sleep.

Elaine Drifts Away A Friend's Perspective

During the weeks immediately following the accident, Elaine talked on the phone to friends regularly, endlessly sharing her experience. At first, her friends were deeply interested and supportive. It pained them to consider what this grand elderly lady had gone through. But after a while, as Elaine turned every conversation back to her "horrible experience," her friends began to lose patience.

Even Fiona, perhaps Elaine's closest friend, came to dread her daily phone calls from Elaine. In a later conversation with her sister, Fiona tried to explain such a reaction and to describe the course that her relationship with Elaine had traveled in the months following the accident.

At first I hung on every word, trying to grasp the horror that had befallen her. I worried about her terribly, wanted to help her through this, wanted to be there for her. But after a few weeks a sameness began to set in in our conversations. No matter what we talked about, Elaine found a way of turning the discussion back to her accident or her fears. If I told her about a film I'd seen, she would ask, "Did you take the subway?" and then she'd tell me for the fiftieth time how dangerous the subway is, how many crimes are committed in movie theaters, or some other tale of peril. Eventually I felt unimportant to her, just an excuse to describe the danger she now saw everywhere. Sometimes, it didn't even seem as if she was even talking to me—just reciting her terrible litany out loud. It didn't matter that I was her best friend—anyone would have done fine. Once I realized what was happening, I would try to divert her attention from these topics. I would offer gossip about someone at the university, bring up items from the news, or recall a funny or interesting event from past times. Nothing. Elaine showed no interest in anything except her newfound fears.

I would try to make plans to see her in person, rather than just talk on the phone. Elaine would not consider going out to a restaurant or movie; however, she would "let" me come over to visit her. Of course, during these visits we would just wind up talking about her fears again. Over time, the visits became shorter and shorter. Finally, I began to feel like a delivery person. Elaine would "allow" me to take groceries to her or to pick up some laundry from the cleaners. Our whole relationship became empty and superficial. I tried letting her talk about her fears; I tried not letting her talk about her fears. But nothing seemed to help. In time, it became a moot point, because Elaine pushed me out of her life.

By 3 months after the accident, she had stopped calling me and would only occasionally answer my calls. Our communications were brief and very superficial, as if Elaine couldn't wait for them to end. She seemed very fearful over what had happened to her and, worse, over what might happen to her in the future. Loving her, I truly felt for her. But, she also seemed to become increasingly angry, nasty, and cynical, not at all the friendly and warm woman I have known for so many years. She acted as if she blamed me—I'm not sure for what—perhaps for not having gone through the same ordeal or maybe for not seeming to care enough or to do enough now. All I know is that after a while conversations or interactions with me seemed to further agitate Elaine. If I suggested that she see her doctor again or gave her advice regarding her bad knee, she would act like I was bothering her and sticking my nose where it didn't belong. So I pretty much stopped. I stopped making suggestions or trying to coax her back into the world. It seemed easier for Elaine that way; it was certainly easier for me.

You know, in an odd way, I feel like I was a victim of that train accident. For the most part, I have lost my dearest friend. I have been forced to stand by and watch her drift away. This warm, energetic, and worldly woman who added so much

> One-third of victims of serious traffic accidents may develop a stress disorder within a year of the accident (Stallard et al., 1998).

richness and love to my life has been replaced by a stranger—an obsessive, self-centered, angry woman—who seems to resent me and wants little to do with me. I am just so frustrated and sad and a little angry as well, I guess. For now, Elaine and I have an implicit understanding to keep some distance between us.

Elaine in Treatment The Journey Back to Normalcy

Over the next few months, Elaine's life became more isolated. Her fearfulness did not improve, and her outdoor activities remained restricted to what she considered safe situations, although nothing felt completely safe. At the same time, her injured knee became more and more painful. When the orthopedist, during a subsequent visit, talked more certainly about the need for surgery, she burst into tears and cried out, "I cannot face going back into that horrible place. My life has already been ruined by this accident. If I go back into the hospital once more, I know I will never survive." Soon realizing that his patient was in need of more than physical help, the physician suggested that Elaine make an appointment with Dr. Martin Fehrman, a psychologist, just to discuss her situation and see if the psychologist had any helpful suggestions about her lingering fears and upsets. The next morning, after yet another fitful night's sleep, she decided to call Dr. Fehrman.

At the psychologist's office, Elaine recounted her "nightmare" and how her life had unraveled overnight. As a former professor of social work, she was rather sophisticated about psychological matters and had spent some time pondering her predicament. She told Dr. Fehrman that on the one hand, she felt that her current state was an understandable result for anyone undergoing such a horrifying experience. But on the other hand, given her previous level of functioning, she would not have expected to be so completely undone by what she knew objectively to be just an accident. Her whole identity had been consumed by this accident and its aftermath. She felt like a different person.

After listening to Elaine's story, Dr. Fehrman concluded that her condition met the DSM-5 criteria for posttraumatic stress disorder. First, she had been exposed to a traumatic event that posed a threat of death or serious injury; moreover, her response to the event entailed intense fear. Second, the traumatic event was followed by months of intrusive symptoms—in Elaine's case, in the form of intrusive recollections and intense psychological distress in response to cues that resembled the original trauma (subways, buses, traffic, and strangers on the street). Third, Elaine persistently avoided stimuli associated with the trauma and experienced numbing (in the form of diminished interest or participation in activities and the sense of a foreshortened future). Fourth, she exhibited persistent negative emotions and a significant change in her own thoughts about herself and the dangers of the world. Finally, Elaine also exhibited increased arousal, including sleep difficulties, hypervigilance, and exaggerated startle response. This had been going on for 5 months now, and her functioning had been greatly impaired as a result. Dr. Fehrman believed that Elaine had developed an acute stress disorder in the immediate aftermath of the train crash but that as her early symptoms continued and even intensified after the first month, she now had posttraumatic stress disorder.

A specialist in stress disorders, Dr. Fehrman knew that both behavioral and cognitive approaches have often proved helpful in cases of posttraumatic stress disorder. The behavioral approach involves exposing the person—with either in vivo or imaginal exposure—to anxiety-provoking stimuli. The cognitive approach, called cognitive restructuring, guides the individual to think differently about the trauma itself and about possible current dangers. Dr. Fehrman typically used a combination of the approaches when treating clients.

In vivo exposure is used to help clients react less fearfully to stimuli and events around them. The in vivo exposure procedure for the posttraumatic stress disorder client is similar to that used with other anxiety disorders, such as phobias. A hierarchy of anxiety-provoking situations, ranging from the least to most threatening, is constructed by the client and therapist. The individual is then given assignments to enter these situations and to remain there for a time, usually until he or she has a significant drop in anxiety. The therapist generally has the individual repeat the exposures on several occasions until only minimal anxiety manifests during the exposure. Such exposure assignments proceed up the hierarchy until the most threatening item is mastered.

Imaginal exposure is used to help clients with posttraumatic stress disorder react less fearfully when recalling the original trauma. The individual repeatedly visualizes the entire sequence of events involved in the trauma for a long period, on a repeated basis. In visualization exercises, the client usually listens to a lengthy recorded description that he or she has provided. The purpose of the exposure is to desensitize the client to the memory of the trauma in the same manner that someone would be desensitized to any phobic object through repeated exposure. In essence, the meaning of the traumatic memory as a danger signal is changed by the exposure, and it eventually stops producing a sense of threat. Ultimately, the traumatic memory can be readily put aside like any other long-term memory.

Cognitive therapy, which more directly challenges the accuracy of the individual's negative cognitions, can further bring about changes in the fearful reactions of persons with posttraumatic stress disorder. In one cognitive strategy, a client might be guided to write down or practice less catastrophic, less self-damaging interpretations of the trauma, often in connection with exposure exercises. Thus, Dr. Fehrman, like a number of professionals, included this approach in his treatment program. Under his care, Elaine embarked on a treatment program that extended over 19 sessions.

> If the stress symptoms begin within 4 weeks of the traumatic event and last for less than a month, the person has acute stress disorder. If the symptoms continue longer than a month, a diagnosis of posttraumatic stress disorder is appropriate.

> Many cases of acute stress disorder develop into posttraumatic stress disorder.

Session 1 In the first session, Elaine described the anxiety she had been feeling for the past 5 months. She also described the accident and its aftermath in the emergency room. She explained that the feelings resulting from that experience—mainly the fear of injury or attack—seemed to have colored her entire approach to life. "I just can't seem to get past this horrible experience. This is not me. It's like I've become somebody else. I've got to get my old self back."

Dr. Fehrman said he was optimistic that Elaine would be able to get back to her former self. He explained that she had posttraumatic stress disorder, the anxiety syndrome that arises following an intensely frightening experience. He also explained that after such an event most people go through a stressful period in which they feel especially vulnerable.

The psychologist then outlined the basic treatment strategy. He said one component of the treatment would be to survey all of the different ways in which Elaine's life had been changed by her current fears and anxieties, paying particular attention to curtailed activities. Then the two of them would arrange the activities along a scale ranging from the least to the most threatening. Together, they would construct weekly exercises in which Elaine would enter—expose herself to—the situations she was avoiding, according to carefully specified procedures. Dr. Fehrman explained that Elaine's anxiety should ultimately improve after she repeatedly entered situations for specified durations and frequencies each week.

The second component of treatment, the psychologist explained, also involved exposure, but in this case, exposure to the traumatic memory itself. He noted that the memory of the trauma was provoking a strong emotional reaction in Elaine, and as long as this was the case, it would intrude on both her waking and her sleeping life. He indicated that the emotional reaction provoked by the traumatic memory could be reduced by prolonged exposure to the memory itself.

Elaine was puzzled by the logic of this approach. She remarked that she already was repeatedly exposed to the traumatic memory; indeed, it seemed to intrude numerous times each day, but her emotional reaction remained as strong as ever. Dr. Fehrman noted that with these naturally occurring intrusions, the exposure often lasts only a few minutes; in addition, people are inclined to block out some of the more disturbing elements of the intrusion. The psychologist explained that in general, improvement occurred only with prolonged exposure, perhaps 45 to 60 minutes at a time, and only when all the elements, including the most disturbing ones, were faced.

For the coming week, he asked Elaine to start monitoring her feelings and behavior. She was to note particularly any instances of fear and anxiety, including the circumstances that provoked the anxious reaction and any associated thoughts. In addition, the psychologist asked Elaine to start taking note of the various activities

About 3.5 percent of people in the United States have acute or posttraumatic stress disorder in any given year; 7 percent to 9 percent have one of these disorders within their lifetime (Peterlin et al., 2011; Taylor, 2010; Kessler et al., 2009, 2005).

In many cases of stress disorder, antianxiety drugs are also used to help control the client's tension and exaggerated startle responses; antidepressants may help reduce the occurrence of nightmares, panic attacks, flashbacks, unwanted recollections, and feelings of depression (Friedman, 1999).

she was avoiding, so that he and she could begin constructing a series of in vivo behavioral exposure exercises.

Session 2   Elaine began the next session by reporting that she had not kept any of the requested records. She explained that at her most recent visit to the orthopedist, he had once again voiced his skepticism that her knee would improve without surgery, although he could not rule it out. Elaine said that since this consultation, she had been completely consumed with deciding whether or not to have the surgery. The decision laid before her by the orthopedist had sent her into a state of anxiety and conflict that was overshadowing everything else.

Dr. Fehrman suggested that inasmuch as the orthopedist had told Elaine that there was no immediate need to make a decision, the client might consider removing that pressure entirely for a defined period. Specifically, the psychologist suggested that Elaine shelve the whole question of surgery for a month. Elaine expressed tremendous relief at this idea. Suddenly the future seemed brighter to her. She said she now felt prepared to throw herself wholeheartedly into the treatment.

At the same time, Elaine expressed concern that her physical limitations might prevent her from proceeding at a reasonable pace with in vivo exercises (that is, doing things she had been avoiding). It was decided, therefore, that for the time being, greater emphasis should be given to the imaginal exposure and that the next session would be devoted to discussing the subway and emergency room experiences in more detail. Still, Elaine would try a couple of brief shopping trips in the coming week if she felt physically capable.

Session 3   Dr. Fehrman asked Elaine to relate the details of her traumatic episode, including the accident and its aftermath in the emergency room. Dr. Fehrman recorded Elaine as she began describing the episode matter-of-factly. She soon closed her eyes in a trancelike fashion, as if trying to focus her efforts on an intensely painful task. She then described the whole episode in a detailed monologue lasting approximately 45 minutes. She included the bodies in the darkened subway car, the blood on her forehead, her helpless posture on the gurney, the threatening characters in the emergency room, and so on.

When she had finished, Elaine appeared drained. Dr. Fehrman praised her for her tremendous effort in recounting those experiences. He then asked her to estimate her level of anxiety at its peak during the monologue and at the end of it, using a 0-to-10 scale. Elaine assigned ratings of 8 and 5, respectively, indicating that some reduction of anxiety had occurred by the end of the monologue.

Session 4   Elaine and the psychologist listened to the recording together. While listening, Elaine closed her eyes and, as instructed, tried to imagine the events

In one form of exposure therapy, eye movement desensitization and reprocessing, clients move their eyes in a saccadic or rhythmic manner from side to side while recalling or imaging traumatic and phobic objects and situations. Some people with stress disorders have been helped by this approach (Cahill et al., 1999).

as vividly as possible. This time, she said she seemed to have had some new insights. First she said she now realized that one of the most troubling elements of the whole experience was the sense of loss of control—in this case, being at the mercy of various ambulance and hospital workers and not being able to fend for herself. She drew a direct connection to her childhood experience during the civil rights movement, when physical and mental quickness were her most prized possessions, which she equated with life itself. She now realized that her accident and emergency room experience had dealt a severe blow to this most precious aspect of her self-image.

Dr. Fehrman tried to offer Elaine a means of viewing the experience in a less negative fashion, suggesting that occasional episodes of loss of control are a normal part of life and that people are not necessarily diminished or demeaned by their occurrence. On hearing this, Elaine seemed tentatively prepared to accept the idea. She herself noted that yes, even during her adolescence, when she felt so independent and vital, she had once been in the hands of the police while jailed for a day for civil disobedience along with both of her parents. Nevertheless, she had later been able to view that episode as a transient interlude in an otherwise independent existence. When freed, she had felt prepared to pursue her independence even more vigorously than before. She said she could now see how it might be possible to view the recent accident in a similar light.

Sessions 5 to 8   During the next 4 weeks, Elaine was instructed to listen to the recording almost every day. She recorded her peak anxiety level for about half of these imaginal exposures. Elaine's anxiety level declined progressively, and by the end of the fourth week, her anxiety reaction to the recording was virtually extinguished. Decided shifts in Elaine's thinking accompanied these reductions in anxiety. After about 2 weeks, when her peak anxiety had lessened considerably, Elaine told Dr. Fehrman that listening to the recording was making her feel that many of her fears had been overblown. By the third week, when Elaine's anxiety had decreased still further, she said that the reduction in anxiety seemed to be carrying over to other parts of her life. She had resumed taking short bus and subway trips, at first with friends and then alone; moreover, she said she felt much closer with her friends, who had remarked on and rejoiced over the improvement in her spirits. Elaine also observed that repeated listening to the recording had made her feel that the episode was "now part of my experience." The memory was no longer constantly "in the back of my mind"; nor did she feel compelled any longer to shut it out when she did think of it. In other words, its intrusive properties had been eliminated. By the eighth therapy session, Elaine reported that she had actually fallen asleep during a couple of listenings, so relaxing had the recording become.

> Some people with a stress disorder also benefit from group therapy, where they can discuss with other trauma victims their lingering fears and other symptoms, their feelings of guilt or anger, and the impact that the trauma has had on their personal and social life.

> According to one survey, posttraumatic stress symptoms last an average of 3 years with treatment but 5.5 years without treatment (Lessler & Zhao, 1999).

During these same 4 weeks, Elaine also spontaneously began to take trips downtown, both by subway and bus, to places that she hadn't visited since the accident (again, first with friends and later on her own). At about the same time, her fear of youths on the street also declined.

The psychologist felt Elaine no longer needed to listen to the recording at this point, suggesting that the most benefit would come from Elaine's increasing the range of her behavioral activities through in vivo exposure. The therapist and client designed a plan for Elaine to take at least one local shopping or subway trip per day, plus a couple of downtown shopping trips per week.

Sessions 9 to 13   During these sessions, held over a 4-week period, the emphasis remained on the in vivo behavioral exercises. Elaine continued to become more comfortable using public transportation and now did so without hesitation. At the same time, however, her physical condition was starting to deteriorate. Her knee had grown so tender that she was finding it difficult to walk at all. The orthopedist was again pushing for surgery.

Intellectually, Elaine felt that the surgery was the rational solution to her problem, but she didn't know whether emotionally she could face going into a hospital. Thus, Dr. Fehrman suggested that perhaps this anxiety could be reduced through some exposure to preliminary aspects of the medical process. He suggested that Elaine begin taking some of the steps that would be involved if the surgery took place, as a type of hypothetical exercise. The first step would be to make an appointment with the orthopedic surgeon to inquire about the surgical procedure, including such matters as the preoperative testing, the duration of the surgery, the length of the hospital stay, and the recovery.

Sessions 14 and 15   Elaine carried out the assignment and reported on the information she received from the orthopedic surgeon. It turned out that surgery would be arthroscopic, a couple of small incisions, through which the inflamed and torn cartilage would be removed. There would be a recovery period of several weeks, but after the first week she shouldn't be any more debilitated than she was now, and she should steadily improve after that point. Acquiring this information seemed to allow Elaine to consider the idea with some objectivity for the first time.

To further promote Elaine's psychological preparedness, Dr. Fehrman suggested that she now look into the arrangements that would have to be made for a home recovery—again, hypothetically. At Session 15, Elaine reported that the home recovery arrangements could apparently be made without much difficulty. The psychologist then asked her to call the orthopedist's office manager and ask how one would go about actually scheduling the surgery, should she decide to do so.

Sessions 16 to 19 Returning for Session 16, Elaine discussed her phone call to the orthopedic surgeon's office. In fact, she had gone ahead and scheduled the surgery, reminding herself that she could always cancel or reschedule it. By Session 19, the surgery date was only a week away, and she felt only limited hesitation about proceeding.

Epilogue

Elaine had the surgery and reported to Dr. Fehrman that it had gone "marvelously." From beginning to end, she was impressed with the professionalism and caring of the medical staff. Her only remaining task was to recover physically, which she expected would take several weeks. From a psychological standpoint, she felt she had now come full circle. It had been just about a year since her accident, and here she was, once again emerging from a hospital, but this time in good spirits and filled with optimism, this time embracing her friends and their offers of help rather than pushing them away

Dr. Fehrman contacted Elaine by phone 3 months later and learned she had made a full recovery from the surgery. She said she now felt fully restored, both physically and mentally. Her traumatic accident had finally come to an end.

> One study conducted 2 to 3 years following the 9/11 terrorist attacks found that 12.6 percent of people living in lower Manhattan had posttraumatic stress disorder (DiGrande et al., 2008).

Assessment Questions

1. What event precipitated Elaine's posttraumatic stress disorder?

2. Which neurotransmitter and which hormone often have abnormal activity in survivors of severe stress?

3. Why do friends and relatives eventually distance themselves from a person who has had a traumatic incident?

4. Why did Elaine finally decide to seek treatment?

5. Why did the doctor diagnose Elaine with posttraumatic stress disorder rather than acute stress disorder?

6. What modes of therapy did Dr. Fehrman select to assist Elaine with her disorder? Give an example of each type of therapy.

7. During the first session, Dr. Fehrman gave Elaine 3 components of her therapy. Describe those 3 components.

8. What was the purpose of recording the traumatizing incident?

9. Why did Elaine fail to take notes of her feared activities as part of her treatment plan? How did Dr. Fehrman handle this problem in his session with Elaine?

10. What other incident in Elaine's early life may have contributed to her posttraumatic stress disorder?

11. According to the text, how long does it typically take for people to recover from posttraumatic stress disorder? What percent of people continue to experience symptoms even after receiving treatment for many years?

CASE **5**

Major Depressive Disorder

Table 5-1

Dx Checklist

Major Depressive Episode

1. For a 2-week period, person displays an increase in depressed mood for the majority of each day and/or a decrease in enjoyment or interest across most activities for the majority of each day.

2. For the same 2 weeks, person also experiences at least 3 or 4 of the following symptoms: • Considerable weight change or appetite change • Daily insomnia or hypersomnia • Daily agitation or decrease in motor activity • Daily fatigue or lethargy • Daily feelings of worthlessness or excessive guilt • Daily reduction in concentration or decisiveness • Repeated focus on death or suicide, a suicide plan, or a suicide attempt.

3. Significant distress or impairment.

Major Depressive Disorder

1. Presence of a major depressive episode.

2. No pattern of mania or hypomania.

(Based on APA, 2013.)

Carlos was born in 1975 in Philadelphia, Pennsylvania. His parents were both born in Puerto Rico but moved to the mainland before their 4 children were born. Trained in Puerto Rico as a plumber, Carlos's father readily found profitable work in the continental United States. Eventually he moved into selling wholesale plumbing parts and supplies. He worked hard to make his business work and involved all 4 children in the fledgling company at early ages.

Carlos A Comfortable Climb

By the time Carlos graduated from high school and began working in the family business full time, it was a solid company that sold supplies to plumbers, builders, and contractors in several states. Carlos's family assumed that he would make a career for himself in the plumbing supply business. Only an average student in school, he couldn't imagine what would have become of him if he had had to make it on his own. He was proud to carry his load in the family business, and indeed, he felt he had a certain business expertise that his father and brothers respected.

Most people with a mood disorder have unipolar depression; that is, they have no history of mania and return to normal or nearly normal mood when their depression lifts. Bipolar disorder, in which people alternate between depression and mania, is the subject of Case 6.

On the other hand, as the baby in a family business, he had a lower status than his brothers during the early years of the business. His brothers did not dominate him deliberately; there were just occasional moments when they would pull rank, so to speak. At the same time, Carlos felt a certain safety and security in what was basically a loving family atmosphere.

At age 22, Carlos married Sonia, whose family was also from Puerto Rico. They dated in high school and got engaged 2 years after graduation. Two years later they were married in a large church wedding. They set up a relatively traditional household, with Carlos working in the family business and Sonia working part-time while taking college courses online. She gave birth to a daughter within a year of their marriage; another daughter followed 4 years later, then a son, and then another son.

Carlos A Sudden Decline

At age 39, Carlos, by now the successful part-owner of his family's plumbing supplies business and the proud father of 4 children, became increasingly preoccupied with his health. His cousin, who was about 15 years older than Carlos, had recently died of a heart attack. Carlos was saddened by the loss but didn't think much more of it at the time. However, within a few months he started to worry about himself and ultimately was convinced that he might also have a heart condition. He began taking his pulse constantly and putting his hand to his chest to decide whether his heartbeat was palpable, believing that a pounding heart could be the sign of a heart attack.

Eventually, Carlos went to see his doctor, even though he had just had a checkup a few months before. The doctor performed an electrocardiogram (EKG) in his office; the results were completely normal. Carlos left the doctor's office reassured in a factual sense, but somehow it didn't help his mood. "A heart attack is still possible," he thought.

In the succeeding weeks, he could not get over the idea of disaster striking. He envisioned the effect his death would have on his wife, children, and brothers and found it devastating. On several nights he awoke with an overwhelming sense of despair and sobbed quietly to himself while Sonia lay asleep next to him.

At work, Carlos lost all interest in his usual activities and could barely focus his thoughts at times. What did anything matter, he thought, when such tragedy could strike? At home he just sat and moped. He looked at his children as if they were already orphans, and tears would come to his eyes.

Carlos decided to see his doctor again. This time, the physician told Carlos that his preoccupation with the idea of a heart attack was getting out of hand. "You're fine, my friend, so stop your worrying." As the doctor spoke, Carlos's eyes welled up with tears, and the doctor realized that this patient was more troubled than he

According to the DSM-5, it is now possible to diagnose an individual with major depressive disorder even in the context of bereavement. Ultimately, clinical judgment is used to determine whether the reaction is considered appropriate to the loss or a major depressive episode is present in conjunction with the expected symptoms of loss (APA, 2013).

Of persons with depression, 41 percent initially go to a physician with complaints of feeling generally ill, 37 percent complain of pain, and 12 percent report fatigue (Katon & Walker, 1998).

had at first suspected. The physician recommended that Carlos see a psychologist, Dr. Alex Willard, who was also a member of their church, and he told Carlos that a few months with the psychologist would probably be enough to set him on the right track.

Upon hearing Carlos's recital of his symptoms—feelings of despair, poor concentration, difficulty sleeping, loss of interest in usual activities, and tearfulness—the psychologist told Carlos that he believed he had depression and would benefit from psychological treatment. Dr. Willard also recommended that Carlos consult a psychiatrist, who could advise him on the benefits of antidepressant medication.

Carlos left the psychologist's office shaken. He had not expected to hear an actual diagnosis, and the idea of medication gave him the feeling that the real threat to his well-being was not a heart attack but rather mental illness. In fact, Carlos's older sister had been diagnosed with schizophrenia years ago and had spent the past 2 decades in and out of institutions. Despite the psychologist's assurances that Carlos did not have any symptoms of schizophrenia, the troubled man now focused on the possibility that a similar fate could befall him.

Eventually, he went to see the psychiatrist, Dr. Charles Hsu, who had been recommended by Dr. Willard. After interviewing Carlos, Dr. Hsu concurred with the diagnosis of depression. He also reiterated that Carlos's symptoms had nothing to do with schizophrenia. Dr. Hsu then recommended that Carlos begin taking antidepressant medications.

The psychiatrist explained that antidepressant drugs are ordinarily very effective. Carlos would simply have to follow the medication regimen, taking one or 2 capsules of fluoxetine (Prozac) per day, and this might well be enough to relieve his depression and tide him over this difficult period. When Carlos asked whether he would have to undergo psychotherapy as well, Dr. Hsu replied that many people found taking the medication and undergoing psychotherapy at the same time very helpful, while others improved with medication alone. Carlos decided to try sticking with the medication alone for the time being.

He began taking Prozac but after a few days concluded that he didn't like the side effects. He called Dr. Hsu and told him that he felt like he was about to "jump out of his skin." The psychiatrist explained that the jitters were sometimes an initial side effect of Prozac but that they often dissipated with time. He urged Carlos to continue with the medication a bit longer. However, Carlos simply couldn't stand this feeling and pushed for a change.

Dr. Hsu switched Carlos to a similar antidepressant, sertraline (Zoloft). Although the patient had fewer jittery side effects, he didn't seem to derive much benefit from the new medication. Furthermore, the sexual side effects were more than he could handle. His feeling of despair persisted, apparently fueled by his sense of defeat at not getting better with Prozac in the first place. The longer Carlos remained depressed, the more he became convinced that he was indeed

Approximately 8 percent of adults in the United States have a severe unipolar pattern of depression in any given year, while another 5 percent have mild forms (Gonzalez et al., 2010; Kessler et al., 2010, 2005). About 19 percent of adults have an episode of severe unipolar depression at some point in their lives.

About 60 percent of people with severe unipolar depression respond well to antidepressant medications (Hirschfeld, 1999). However, a recent meta-analysis suggests that the combination of pharmacotherapy and psychotherapy is more effective than either treatment on its own (Cuijpers et al., 2013).

headed toward a nervous breakdown, like his sister before him. Eventually, he was refusing outright to go to work, and Dr. Hsu felt it would be best to hospitalize him so a concentrated effort could be launched to find an effective medication regimen. Unfortunately, this also meant that Carlos's worst fears were now (in his eyes) about to be realized.

Carlos spent 3 weeks in the hospital, where various combinations of antidepressant and antianxiety drugs were tried. Ultimately, one combination provided some relief. Carlos was discharged from the hospital, with the plan of continuing to see Dr. Hsu once a week.

Although no longer hospitalized, Carlos was nevertheless struggling mightily. He hoped that if he just continued to take the medication and kept the demands on himself to a minimum, he would gradually recover. Accordingly, he cut his work hours by half, stopped seeing customers, and restricted his activities at the office to paperwork and occasional meetings with his brothers. In his spare time, he thought it best to lead a minimalist existence. At home, he told his wife he could no longer help take care of the children or do any other household chores. Accordingly, he spent his spare time napping, jogging in the park, and trying to watch an occasional television show.

The summer went fairly well by Carlos's current standards. As in the past, the family made their weekend trips to the beach, and Carlos resumed playing softball in his summer league. He was starting to feel a little bit better. Maybe, he thought, this whole horrible business would soon be behind him. As the summer drew to a close, however, Carlos started to get an uneasy feeling, which gradually built into a sense of impending doom. Somehow, he had gotten it into his mind that the end of summer would signal a turning point for him. He became convinced that with the approaching fall, he would either recover or descend into an abyss.

Unfortunately, it was the latter. When fall arrived and Carlos still did not feel completely better, he lost hope of ever recovering, and his condition started to deteriorate again. He became preoccupied with the possibility of becoming sick again, and in due time this preoccupation grew into the previous symptom picture: depressed mood, poor concentration, and loss of interest in usual activities.

> Studies have demonstrated that exercise compares favorably to antidepressant medications for mild to moderate cases of depression (Carek, Laibstain, & Carek, 2011).

> Approximately 40 percent of people with unipolar depression begin to recover within 3 months, with 80 percent recovering somewhat within a year (APA, 2013).

Sonia's View Sinking Along with Carlos

Carlos was not the only person affected by his depression. His wife, Sonia, and their children—the people who lived with him and cared about him—were hurt by it as well. And like Carlos, they were confused by the dramatic changes that they had seen in him. As Sonia explained to her sister:

> For years I lived with this strong man who was a good father and caring husband and who worked hard every day to provide a good life for all of us. Then over the

course of weeks, I watched him change into a sad, frightened, weak person who could think of nothing but himself—his pain, his health, his unhappiness.

It seemed innocent enough when it first started. When Frank [the cousin] died, we were all upset, and it was natural to think about how young he was and how something like that could happen to any of us. But while the rest of us—his brothers, his cousins, and I myself—got over it and got back to our lives, it seemed to trigger something in Carlos that wouldn't let go of him.

First it was his fear of having a heart attack. Then his concern about dying. Then worrying about every little thing, overprotecting himself, seeing doom everywhere. I would walk into the family room and find him sobbing. Over what? He was healthy, he was successful, he had a beautiful family, yet he was sobbing.

Time and again, I tried to point out the brighter side of things, to snap him back to his old self, but nothing helped. I talked my guts out, but it was always, "Yes, but this" or "Yes, but that." He felt doomed and hopeless about everything; nothing made a difference.

It was horrible to see him so upset, but worse was the way he stopped doing anything. At home he stopped being a father and husband. The kids would need help with their homework or have to be driven somewhere. The sink or car would need fixing. Or I would need to talk about finances with him. He could do none of it. He would just sit there, usually staring into space, sighing, or crying. He became like a fifth child. Actually, it was worse than that. At least I could reason with the children, get them to do things, have fun with them.

At work it was the same. His brother Enrique called one day, worried to death about Carlos. He was no longer doing anything there; he hardly was coming into work at all. The brothers had to pick up his work and they were worried. They were angry, too. They couldn't really understand what was going on, and sometimes they resented the way they had to cover for him, the way he pitied himself, the way he turned them away. What could I tell Ricky? I too was confused and worried and angry. I too was watching him sink.

I was relieved when he went to the hospital. The medicine was not helping and he was only getting worse, and his behavior was really upsetting the children. In addition, I felt that I was in over my head. He was sinking and nothing I did made a difference. What if he decided to do something to himself? He certainly was dropping enough hints in that direction. Finally, I thought, we'll get this fixed. Actually, it was much easier at home while he was hospitalized. We didn't have to tiptoe around Carlos or worry about upsetting him or disturbing him. We missed him and were worried about him, but at the same time, the cloud of darkness was temporarily lifted from the house; our spirits improved as well.

Overall, the hospitalization seemed to help him, and his new medications brought some relief. After his return home, he was very shaky at first. In fact, he did even less than before. But then he seemed to gradually be getting better. By

About half of people with severe unipolar depression also have an anxiety disorder (Fava et al., 2000). In most such cases, the anxiety symptoms precede the depressive symptoms, often by years (Regier et al., 1998).

Between 6 percent and 15 percent of people with severe unipolar depression commit suicide (Mulholland, 2010; Taube-Schiff & Lau, 2008).

the middle of the summer, I was sure that he had turned the corner. He was more active again, seeing friends and even playing ball again. And he started to do more with the children. I really felt hopeful that I was getting my husband back.

That was a big mistake. For some reason, Carlos crashed down once again in the autumn, just like the leaves falling from the trees. It was like the summer had been a vacation from his depression, and now the vacation was over. I love him, but I don't think I can take another bout of this. Neither can the children. I doubt that Carlos can take it anymore, either. You know, I used to dismiss it when he said that he wasn't going to recover, wasn't ever going to feel happy again. Now I wonder whether he might be right. One thing is for sure. Something has to be done. I told Carlos and his psychiatrist that more must be done. The hospitalization did not work. The medications are not working. More must be done. Last night, I found a video that we made at the beach a year ago. It shocked me. Carlos was a totally different person. I had almost forgotten how confident and happy he used to be. I almost couldn't recognize him. For his sake, and for ours, we must find that man again. In the meantime, I've lost my husband and my children have lost their father.

Carlos in Treatment Focusing on Cognitions

Given Carlos's latest decline, Dr. Hsu suggested that now was the time to consider psychotherapy, which Carlos had initially hoped to avoid by taking the medication. The psychiatrist explained that he would continue trying to find a medication combination that provided some benefit, but that they should now cover the bases that had been missed up to this point. In particular, Dr. Hsu explained, there was a cognitive form of psychotherapy, suited specifically for depression, that might provide the missing ingredient in the treatment Carlos had received up to this point. He wanted very much for Carlos to see a specialist in this kind of psychotherapy.

Carlos, now more willing to pursue psychotherapy, began treatment with Dr. Robert Walden. Dr. Walden was a psychologist who had trained with Judith Beck, daughter of Aaron Beck, a pioneer in the development of cognitive therapy, at Beck's Center for Cognitive Therapy in Philadelphia. Dr. Walden agreed with Dr. Hsu and Carlos's previous practitioners that their client met the DSM-5 criteria for a diagnosis of major depressive disorder. He exhibited a depressed mood most of the time, had markedly reduced pleasure or interest in his usual activities, had difficulty sleeping, and had lost both his energy and his ability to concentrate.

About 60 percent of people with severe unipolar depression respond successfully to cognitive therapy (DeRubeis et al., 2000).

Like other cognitive therapists and researchers, Dr. Walden explained and treated depression largely by focusing on a person's style of thinking. Although a disturbance in mood is the most obvious symptom of this disorder, research suggests that disturbances in cognition have an important—perhaps primary—role in the disorder. Cognitive therapists believe that depressed individuals have a severe negative bias in their perceptions and interpretations of events, a bias that leads them to experience themselves, events in their lives, and their futures in very negative—depressing—terms. The goal of cognitive therapy is to change this negative bias and negative style of interpretation, and in so doing, remove the source of depression.

Although straightforward in principle, the application of cognitive therapy is no small matter. Concentrated methods have to be brought to bear to rid depressed persons of their cognitive bias. The process includes psychoeducation, self-monitoring by clients, self-examination, sustained questioning by therapists, personal research by clients, and retraining in how to think about things. In addition, behavioral methods are typically used to enhance the cognitive techniques.

Session 1　Most of the first session of psychotherapy was devoted to a discussion of Carlos's current condition and the events leading up to it. In spite of his obvious distress, Carlos related the events of the past year in a coherent and organized fashion. At the same time, the desperation on his face was almost painful to observe, and his voice trembled with distress. He said he just wanted to know one thing: whether Dr. Walden believed that he could ever be cured. He stated that he had been through a lot and felt that he was down to his last hope. He said he just wanted the straight truth: Was he ever going to get back to normal or not?

Like most mental health professionals who encounter a seriously disturbed patient, Dr. Walden found himself wondering for a moment whether Carlos could indeed be restored to his former self. At the same time, the psychologist knew that his own fleeting misgivings were the last thing that Carlos needed to hear right now. The psychologist told him that nothing was guaranteed but that he had agreed to treat Carlos because he had every expectation of bringing about a full recovery. Carlos pressed the matter further, wanting to know specifically when he could expect to be restored to normal. "How many months?" he asked. "Why can't you tell me?"

Dr. Walden felt no antagonism in Carlos's close questioning about the timetable. Rather, he knew the questioning reflected Carlos's sense of desperation, his utter fear that he might be a hopeless case. He was obviously hanging on the psychologist's every word, looking for some glint of reassurance.

The psychologist felt he had to walk a fine line. On the one hand, he wanted Carlos to have confidence in getting better. On the other hand, given Carlos's history of becoming unduly focused on his rate of progress and then alarmed at not improving according to a self-determined timetable, Dr. Walden wanted to avoid setting up expectations for improvement by specific dates, foreseeing that if expectations were not met, it would fuel Carlos's negative view of the future.

> As many as 20 percent of the relatives of severely depressed people are themselves depressed (Kamali & McInnis, 2011; Berrettini, 2006).

Dr. Walden: I know you're anxious to get better, and I don't blame you. It's natural to wonder when this is all going to end. As I said before, I'm seeing you because, as I told Dr. Hsu, I expect you will recover from this depression and I can hasten the process. At the same time, I am reluctant to place an exact timetable on it, simply because it has been my experience that the rate of improvement varies from person to person. I could, of course, hazard a guess as to when you'll be better, but I'm concerned that if you don't have a complete recovery by that date, you might think it means more than it really does.

Carlos: I know. I would be upset.

Dr. Walden: So I think it best that we leave the timetable open for now. If the time ever comes when I truly think we're not getting anywhere, I'll let you know honestly and we'll consider our options.

Carlos: OK. I guess I can live with that.

Dr. Walden spent the remaining 15 minutes of the session giving Carlos a brief overview of the cognitive theory of depression and the implied treatment. He used Carlos's sensitivity to the timetable of recovery as an example of how certain negative perceptions or interpretations can have powerful effects on the way one feels. In particular, the psychologist noted that a different point of view, one that placed less importance on the exact timetable of recovery, would result in a less catastrophic response to the absence of a full recovery by a certain date.

The psychologist went on to explain that a major part of therapy would be discovering those aspects of Carlos's thinking and behavior that were undermining his capacity to feel well and then helping him develop alternative ways of thinking and behaving that would ultimately reduce his depression. To begin, the psychologist explained that Carlos would be asked to monitor his emotional reactions throughout the next week, recording all thoughts or events that produced distress (sadness, anger, anxiety, or whatever) and rating their intensity. In the next session, Dr. Walden explained, they would discuss these matters so as to bring out Carlos's thinking about them. In addition, the psychologist asked him to keep a record of his activities.

Atypical antipsychotic medications (traditionally used to treat schizophrenia and other psychotic disorders) are often added to an antidepressant to augment its effectiveness in people with treatment resistant depression (Schlaepfer et al., 2012).

Later that evening, the psychologist called Dr. Hsu, as the 2 had agreed (with Carlos's permission) to keep in close contact to coordinate their treatments. Dr. Hsu indicated that unless the psychologist had any particular objections, he would like to add a low starting dose of aripiprazole (Abilify) to his medication regimen. The psychologist agreed, so the plan was for Carlos to start the new medication the next day.

Session 2 Dr. Walden reviewed Carlos's records of both his moods and his activities, and these provided the focus of discussion. A distressing thought that Carlos had written down several times each day pertained to the seriousness of his current condition, expressed in several forms: "I'm a basket case." "How did I get so sick?" "I can barely function." These thoughts seemed to arise spontaneously, particularly when Carlos was inactive.

Dr. Walden engaged Carlos in the type of Socratic dialogue that is typical of cognitive therapy.

Dr. Walden:	You say you are a "basket case" and can barely function. What leads you to those conclusions?
Carlos:	Well, I've been hospitalized. That's how bad it's been. I just can't believe it.
Dr. Walden:	I know we discussed it last time, but tell me again what led to that hospitalization.
Carlos:	I sort of got panicked when the medicine didn't help, and I stopped going to work or doing anything else. Dr. Hsu figured that as long as I wasn't working, I might as well go into the hospital, where I could try different drugs without having to manage all the side effects on my own. I also was pretty miserable at the time. I told Dr. Hsu my family might be better off without me.
Dr. Walden:	Do you think they would be better off?
Carlos:	I don't know. I'm not doing them much good.
Dr. Walden:	What would life be like for them without you?
Carlos:	It would be terrible for them. I suppose saying they'd be better off without me is going too far. As bad off as I am, I'm still able to do a few things.
Dr. Walden:	What are you able to do?
Carlos:	Well, I'm not in the hospital anymore. And I don't think I will be back either. When I went into the hospital, I didn't really feel any worse than I do now. I mainly went in because I thought I could get better treatment or whatever. But it didn't pan out, so what would be the point of going back in?
Dr. Walden:	So the fact that you were in the hospital isn't really a sign that you are now or ever were a "basket case," which I take to mean someone who is completely helpless and can't function.
Carlos:	No. If I knew then what I know now, I probably wouldn't have been hospitalized at all. In looking back on it now, it was all basically voluntary. But that doesn't erase the fact that I'm still a mess.
Dr. Walden:	How much of a mess are you?
Carlos:	I can't work, I can't help out at home, I can't even watch a television show. What else do you want to know?
Dr. Walden:	A couple of minutes ago you said you were still able to do a few things. What are those?

Carlos: I can drive to work and . . . I guess it's an exaggeration to say that I can't work at all. There are a few things that I do at the office.

Dr. Walden: Like what?

With continued discussion, the psychologist helped Carlos to recognize the various capabilities that he did have, and how, in practical terms, he wasn't as compromised as the terms "basket case" and "barely able to function" implied. Dr. Walden also pointed out that Carlos really didn't know the limits of his capabilities because he had deliberately reduced the demands on himself under the questionable assumption that "stress" would worsen his condition. The psychologist suggested that they start testing this assumption by having Carlos make a few simple additions to his activities. After some discussion, it was decided that each day Carlos would make a concerted effort to get up and leave for work at 8:00 A.M., the same time he used to leave before his depression set in. Second, it was decided that Carlos would read a bedtime story to his 2 younger children each night; moreover, it was specified that he try hard to attend to the content of the story, rather than allow his thoughts to drift off into his own concerns. He was to note on his activity record his daily success in carrying out these 2 assignments.

Finally, Dr. Walden asked that Carlos continue to keep a record of his unpleasant emotions and the thoughts associated with them. This time, however, the client was also to try to produce alternative, more realistic thoughts by considering whether his initial thoughts truly reflected all the evidence. Furthermore, the more realistic thoughts were to be written down.

Session 3 Carlos appeared upset when he came in for the third session. He said that he had begun taking the Abilify 5 days ago—he had put off starting it, even though Dr. Hsu had written the prescription almost 2 weeks ago—and he had pronounced light-headedness. He stated that the medication only made him feel worse, and he was inclined to stop.

The psychologist's private feeling was that Carlos, although having actual side effects, was becoming unduly alarmed over the sensations and as a result was experiencing the effects more intensely than he might otherwise. He needed some help in tolerating the sensations psychologically until his body adjusted. Dr. Walden was particularly concerned that Carlos not repeat the scenario of 6 months ago with Prozac, when he became panicked over the initial side effects, insisted on going off the medicine, and lapsed into despair over his prospects of recovery.

Dr. Walden: Tell me exactly what you've been feeling since you started the medicine.

Carlos: I feel light-headed, dizzy, especially when I get up suddenly.

Dr. Walden: Have you spoken to Dr. Hsu about it?

Studies have found that depressed subjects have a variety of biases in attention, interpretation, and memory for negative events. They recall unpleasant experiences more readily than positive ones, denigrate their performance on various tasks, and expect to fail in various situations (Gotlib & Joormann, 2010; Wenze, Gunthert, & German, 2012).

When nondepressed subjects are manipulated into reading negative statements about themselves, they become increasingly depressed (Bates et al., 1999).

Sales of antidepressant drugs total $11 billion annually. Antidepressants are also the third most prescribed class of drugs, just behind analgesics and antihyperlipidemics (CDC, 2010).

Carlos:	Yeah. He says that this sometimes happens when people start this medicine, but it will probably get better.
Dr. Walden:	Why does it bother you so much?
Carlos:	I don't know. It makes me feel like I might topple over or something.
Dr. Walden:	Have you toppled over?
Carlos:	No. It just feels like I might.
Dr. Walden:	Has the light-headedness prevented you from doing anything? Were you able to drive here, for example?
Carlos:	I drove. In fact, while I'm driving I don't seem to notice it that much.
Dr. Walden:	Is there anything that you feel you can't do because of the symptoms?
Carlos:	Well, I didn't leave for work at 8:00, like we had agreed. I figured, given the way I'm feeling, why push myself?
Dr. Walden:	What about reading to the kids?
Carlos:	I did that! It worked out fine. I made a point of focusing just on the story for the 15 minutes or so that it lasted, and I was amazed I could actually do it. I've read them a story every night this week.
Dr. Walden:	Great! I'm glad that you made that effort, and it sounds like you got some satisfaction from it.
Carlos:	Yeah. But this light-headedness, it really bothers me.
Dr. Walden:	Remember last week when I pointed out the principle of considering all the evidence both for and against a particularly upsetting thought that you have and then trying to produce a more balanced thought? How about trying your skill at this situation with the light-headedness? What is your immediate thought about the light-headedness? Why does it bother you so much?
Carlos:	Well, I guess my immediate thought is, "This light-headedness is terrible, I'm not going to be able to function at all."
Dr. Walden:	What is the evidence?
Carlos:	I guess the evidence shows that I'm still doing at least as much this week as I did last week, in spite of the light-headedness. Also, considering what Dr. Hsu said, it probably won't last, or it should get better.
Dr. Walden:	So what is the more balanced thought?
Carlos:	I guess it is that this is a damn nuisance, but it's a known side effect of the medicine and does not mean that something is going wrong or that I'm going downhill.

Based on his more balanced conclusion for his behavior, Carlos decided it was worth putting up with the light-headedness temporarily to see if the medicine would benefit him. Second, he decided he should not eliminate any of his activities on account of the light-headedness unless there was clear evidence that carrying out the activity presented a physical hazard. This meant that if he noticed a surge of light-headedness, he would persevere with his ongoing activity. In addition, it was decided he would once again attempt last week's assignment of leaving for work every morning by 8:00 A.M. and continue reading to the kids for 15 minutes every night.

Session 4   Dr. Walden asked Carlos first about the behavioral assignments. The client reported that he had continued to read to the children each evening throughout the week and was doing so with a "clear head." On the other hand, he complained that for the rest of the evening, he would just sit around and mope, sometimes sitting in the living room chair for an hour or more worrying about his condition and his inability—or lack of desire—to do anything else while the rest of the family went about their normal activities. Dr. Walden asked him about his negative thoughts during this period, and the client replied that it was the same old thing, meaning thoughts about being a basket case and unable to function. The psychologist asked Carlos if he was able to refute such thoughts when they arose. The client replied that he was carrying out the exercise of weighing the evidence and forming alternative thoughts, but that within a few minutes the negative thoughts would return. Then he would carry out the thought exercise all over again. It was getting to be repetitive.

On hearing this, Dr. Walden reviewed with Carlos their earlier discussions about the objective extent of Carlos's disability. The client acknowledged that his characterization of his condition as being a basket case was exaggerated, but he seemed to have trouble holding on to this more accurate assessment and had to remind himself constantly that he was in fact functioning reasonably well, all things considered.

Dr. Walden felt that the next step was for Carlos to bring the force of behavior behind his reformulated thoughts. That is, it was time for Carlos to participate more fully in the family's evening routine. Such participation would help to refute his exaggerated perceptions of being dysfunctional and promote greater belief in the alternative: that he was temporarily depressed but still capable of doing more than he allowed. Second, more activity would provide a wider range of stimulation, thus diverting Carlos's thinking from its strictly depressive content. Finally, from the standpoint of family dynamics, becoming more active would help to bring Carlos's existence more in tune with the family's, leading to a more normal family environment and at the same time reducing some of the tension with Sonia, who was becoming increasingly angry at being the only responsible adult in the household.

A large portion of this session was therefore devoted to working out in detail the appropriate routine for Carlos to follow in the evening at home. It was decided that he would follow a set routine upon returning home from work: (a) talk to his wife about her day, (b) eat dinner with the family, setting aside his own concerns and attending as closely as possible to the conversation, including asking the children some questions about their day, (c) assist the children with their homework, (d) read the newspaper or watch television, (e) read to the children before bed, (f) do household or work-related paperwork, (g) go to bed.

At the end of the session, the psychologist asked Carlos about his success in leaving for work by 8:00 A.M. Carlos reported that he had found he could do it but had learned that it was important not to get caught up in what he termed a "stall mode" in the morning—by which he meant becoming so wrapped up in his thoughts that he paused and brooded for several minutes at a time before proceeding to the next task. The best strategy, he observed, was to maintain his momentum by going directly from one task to another. As for the light-headedness, Carlos noted that it was greatly reduced this week, as Dr. Hsu had predicted, so he was less concerned about it.

The main assignments for the coming week were outlined on paper: (a) Continue to leave for work at 8:00 A.M. consistently, avoiding the "stall mode," (b) follow the new evening routine, and (c) continue to record negative thoughts and to produce more balanced alternatives.

Session 5   Carlos reported that he had been able to follow the prescribed routine at home. He found that keeping his attention focused on the concrete tasks before him—reading the kids a story, asking them questions about school, doing some paperwork—had a way of reducing his pattern of depressive thinking. He told Dr. Walden he was pleased with his ability to do these things, and he was even starting to enjoy some activities. In fact, he spontaneously decided to go to the playground a couple of times to play catch with his older son and had a pleasant time. His wife, on the other hand, was not so pleased with the changes, Carlos remarked.

Carlos: Well, she obviously prefers me this way as compared to the old way, but now she's asking me why I couldn't do these things before. Her idea, basically, is that it is too little too late. She said she's had a year of misery.

Dr. Walden: What are your thoughts on why you couldn't do those things before?

Carlos: I don't know. It's still sometimes a struggle to do them now, but I feel better doing them. I never realized the connection between how I was thinking and acting and how I felt. Also, I wonder if the new medicine has anything to do with it. I'm feeling better, but I tried at least a dozen different medicines in the past and none really seemed to do that much. Do you think this one is helping? I don't want to be taking something that isn't necessary.

| Dr. Walden: | There is no way of knowing for sure how much the medicine is helping. The 2 treatments—the psychotherapy and the drug therapy—were started more or less at the same time, so your improvement could be due to the medicine, the psychotherapy, or the combination. Regardless, the good news is that you are improving, so I don't think we should even consider your going off the medicine for the time being. |

Further discussion returned to the question of Sonia and her resentment of the past. Carlos's initial thinking was, "She's self-centered; she has no appreciation for what I've been through; she's just going to make my condition worse and undo my progress. Pretty soon I'll just be back in the same boat." Dr. Walden had him weigh the evidence both for and against such notions. The client recognized that most of Sonia's actions in the past year had indeed been supportive, even if she did have occasional lapses into frustration. He also recognized that he would get worse only if he himself strayed from his current regimen, and he had no intention of doing so. His more rational conclusion was, "She's been a good wife throughout all of this, especially considering the hard time she's been through. If I just show some understanding, it will probably help her frustration. In the meantime, she's not doing anything that would prevent me from getting better."

The next discussion turned to Carlos's routine at work. He reported that he was spending about 6 hours a day at work (9:00 A.M. to 3:00 P.M.), but he found himself frequently feeling depressed there. Apparently he had severely cut down his activities at work under the assumption that stress could exacerbate his condition. As a result, he had a lot of dead time on his hands, which he would spend sitting at his desk, staring at his computer and brooding over the extent of his disability and his rate of progress. Carlos was doing his best to refute his negative thinking—reminding himself of his improvements—but it seemed like a never-ending process.

Dr. Walden pointed out the inconsistency between Carlos's attempts to refute his negative thoughts and his actual behavior in the situation:

Dr. Walden:	It's good that you're challenging the incorrect idea that you're a basket case and can't function. But if you really know that such thinking is wrong, why are you still limiting your activities at work?
Carlos:	I guess I'm afraid that any increased stress might ruin my progress.
Dr. Walden:	What happened when you started taking on more responsibilities at home?
Carlos:	I got less wrapped up in my worries.
Dr. Walden:	What lesson does that seem to teach for the work situation?
Carlos:	That I should start doing more things. I'm not even doing the minimum. And I can't say that I ever had that much stress from work. I

As many as half of depressed clients may have marital problems. In such cases, couple therapy may be as helpful as cognitive therapy (Teichman et al., 1995).

People who consistently ruminate—that is, repeatedly dwell on their moods without acting to change them—are more likely to become clinically depressed than people who do not generally ruminate (McLaughlin & Nolen-Hoeksema, 2011; Zetsche et al., 2012).

mean, I'm one of the owners. I set my own pace. I always put in a
good day's work—at least I used to—but I never saw any point in
going overboard.

Dr. Walden: So getting back to my original question about how to conduct yourself at work . . .

Carlos: I know, I know. It makes no sense at this point to be slacking off
like I am.

Carlos agreed to gradually start building up his activities at work. Specifically,
he would (a) leave the office at 5:00 P.M. rather than 3:00 P.M., (b) resume handling telephone sales calls, and (c) resume attending the daily sales meetings with
his brothers and the sales associates. For now, he would omit seeing customers
face-to-face, going on sales visits, or taking overnight business trips.

All other aspects of the treatment program (record keeping, thought exercises,
the home routine) remained in place.

Later, the psychologist once again contacted Dr. Hsu to exchange observations. Dr. Hsu said he had met with Carlos the previous day and was impressed with the gains he was making. He said he normally would be inclined
to increase the Abilify dose at this point but decided to hold off, since Carlos
was doing so well at the low dose. In Dr. Hsu's experience, every increase in
medication caused a level of disturbance in Carlos that it was probably better
to avoid. Dr. Hsu indicated that he planned to maintain Carlos's current medications indefinitely.

> If people who respond to antidepressant medications stop taking the drugs immediately after obtaining relief, they run as much as a 50 percent risk of relapsing within a year. The risk of relapse decreases considerably if they continue taking the drugs for 5 months or so after being free of depressive symptoms (Kim et al., 2011; Ballas, Benton, & Evans, 2010).

Session 6   This session focused on Carlos's adjustment to the fuller day at
work. The client's overall impression was that it was going well. He noted particularly that when he was actively engaged in practical activities—talking on
the phone to customers, attending meetings, speaking to co-workers about
business concerns—he tended not to brood. In contrast, when he retreated to
his office and sat idly at his desk, he became caught up in depressive thoughts
and images.

Dr. Walden suggested that Carlos use this observation to his advantage and
do what he could to minimize the brooding. The psychologist recommended
that he follow a 4-step mental procedure to cope with periods of brooding.
Step one was simply to recognize that he was getting caught up in depressive
thinking. Step 2 was to identify the specific negative thoughts he was having. Step
3 was to consider the evidence and then produce more rational or balanced
thoughts. Step 4 was to put the issue aside and turn his attention to practical
matters.

Carlos liked the idea of having a concrete procedure to follow and remarked
that he had already applied a similar strategy on his own in a few situations. But
why couldn't he just sit and do nothing without getting depressed? Dr. Walden

explained that there was no such thing as doing nothing. The mind is always active; if it is not engaged in one thing, it is engaged in something else. The point was for Carlos to keep his mind engaged in rational and constructive activities rather than irrational and destructive ones.

Sessions 7 to 9   Over the course of the next 3 weeks, Carlos applied the 4-step procedure as consistently as possible and was reaping the benefits. He was becoming more and more engaged in the practical aspects of daily life and less consumed with negative thinking. As a result he was feeling normal most of the time. He was participating fully in the family routine, and at work he was meeting the responsibilities he had set for himself. As he functioned better, it strengthened his conviction that he was not headed for a permanent mental collapse.

During this period Carlos had an episode of anger after his eldest brother questioned a decision that he had made at work. An extended therapy discussion revealed Carlos's negative thinking: "Ricky thinks I'm incompetent; he has no respect for the good work I do around here; he thinks he's smarter than anybody." With Dr. Walden asking Carlos to weigh the evidence, he came to realize that this characterization was not accurate. Far from thinking he was smarter than anybody, Ricky was a nervous person who fretted constantly about the smallest business details, worrying about mistakes he might have made, and generally making a pest of himself with everybody. Carlos now recognized that when Ricky questioned one of Carlos's decisions, it reflected his brother's own insecurity more than anything else. With this understanding, Carlos felt he could take his brother's comments more in stride.

Studies reveal that depressed people who lack social support remain depressed longer than those who have a supportive spouse or warm friendships (Moos & Cronkite, 1999).

Sessions 10 to 14   In the 4 weeks comprising Sessions 10 to 14, Carlos had returned to full functioning and was in good spirits most of the time. He had even resumed going on overnight business trips. Accordingly, the therapy sessions themselves were now devoted to relapse prevention. The goal was to help Carlos understand the basic beliefs underlying much of his depressive thinking.

It was, for example, apparent that the client's most fundamental depressive belief was a so-called vulnerability to harm and illness schema—a belief that disaster is about to strike at any time and that the client is helpless to protect himself. This particular belief seemed to be the basis of Carlos's original preoccupation with heart disease and his preoccupation later on with the prospect of a total mental breakdown.

Session time was spent reviewing the various negative thoughts that had arisen from this belief. The goal was to improve Carlos's ability to recognize when the belief was active and to take it as a cue to confront the resulting negative thoughts.

As one exercise, the therapist had Carlos practice verbally refuting those negative thoughts.

In a related vein, Carlos's current behavior patterns were scrutinized for any remaining practices that might inappropriately be producing a sense of vulnerability in him. In this regard, he noted that he was still cutting short his exercise regimen, a remnant from the time when he was preoccupied with heart attacks. He decided he would now reinstate an exercise level more in tune with his athletic interests and his true physical capacity.

Epilogue

Because Carlos had had such a severe depression prior to cognitive therapy, both Dr. Walden and Dr. Hsu decided to follow up with him monthly and have him continue to take a low dose of his medicines for at least 18 months. Carlos continued to feel well during this period, and his symptoms did not return after the medicines were withdrawn. With each day, he became more convinced that a dark cloud had been lifted from his life—more accurately, that he had lifted the cloud. It was not that he felt happy every minute of every day, but rather that he felt armed to cope with and even conquer life. Problems were now perceived as challenges—challenges that could be overcome, challenges from which he could grow. The dark cloud had indeed been lifted.

> As many as 30 percent of depressed patients who respond to cognitive therapy may relapse within a few years after completing treatment (Cameron et al., 1999; Shea et al., 1992). More recent research has identified specific symptoms, such as increased anxiety, increased loss of appetite, and increased loss of libido, to be among risk factors for relapse after 2 years (Taylor, Walters, Vittengl, Krebaum, & Jarrett 2010).

Assessment Questions

1. What are the first signs that a person might be depressed?

2. Why did Carlos initially see his family physician?

3. What symptoms did Carlos present that prompted his family physician to suggest a psychologist?

4. Why did his psychologist, Dr. Willard, recommend a psychiatrist?

5. What was the initial antidepressant prescribed, and why did Carlos decide not to continue taking this medication?

6. Why did the psychiatrist decide to hospitalize Carlos?

7. What concerns did Sonia, Carlos's wife, have about her husband's depression?

8. What type of psychotherapy did Dr. Walden use with Carlos?

9. What were the criteria for Carlos's diagnosis of major depressive disorder?

10. What are some of the concentrated methods that must be used to rid depressed persons of their cognitive bias?

11. Carlos wanted to know how long it would be before he felt normal again. Why did Dr. Walton not want to give Carlos a definite timetable?

12. What was the first assignment Carlos was given for the first week of therapy?

13. Why did Dr. Walton want Carlos on medication as well as the cognitive therapy approach?

14. What was the homework assignment given in Session 2? What was the purpose of this assignment?

15. Why was it important to get Carlos to set up an evening routine of activity?

16. This case study mentions that about half of depressed clients may have marital problems. What factors led Sonia to become frustrated with Carlos's behavior?

17. Why is it suggested that clients continue to take their medication for several months rather than quitting once they begin to feel better?

18. At approximately what point in treatment did Carlos return to full function?

CASE 6

Bipolar Disorder

Table **6-1**

Dx Checklist

Manic Episode

1. For 1 week or more, person displays a continually abnormal, inflated, unrestrained, or irritable mood as well as continually heightened energy or activity, for most of every day.

2. Person also experiences at least 3 of the following symptoms: • Grandiosity or overblown self-esteem • Reduced sleep need • Increased talkativeness, or drive to continue talking • Rapidly shifting ideas or the sense that one's thoughts are moving very fast • Attention pulled in many directions • Heightened activity or agitated movements • Excessive pursuit of risky and potentially problematic activities.

3. Significant distress or impairment.

Bipolar I Disorder

1. Occurrence of a manic episode.

2. Hypomanic or major depressive episodes may precede or follow the manic episode.

(Based on APA, 2013.)

Gina, an only child, was raised in a prosperous family. Her mother was the chief executive officer of a major charitable organization, and much of her work entailed the hosting of fundraising events to support charitable projects. Through these events, Gina's family acquired a wide array of prominent people as family friends and acquaintances.

Gina attended an exclusive private school for girls, where she was an above-average student. She did not seem to have any unusual psychological problems during childhood and early adolescence. A popular girl who got along well with others, she had many friends. At about age 17, however, there was an incident that as it turned out foreshadowed the problems to follow.

The mean age of onset for bipolar I disorder is approximately 18 years (APA, 2013).

Gina The First Incident

In her senior year of high school, Gina became deeply involved in a school play production in which she had a minor acting role. As the production progressed, she became more and more absorbed in the work. Her presentation on stage during rehearsals became increasingly theatrical, and she became more involved in her costuming and makeup. The other students initially were in awe of the teenager's increased level of creativity and comfort on stage. However, with time, her behavior became bizarre. Once, for example, in the coffee shop where students would gather after rehearsals, Gina became so giddy and talkative that she approached strangers for rambling conversations, telling some that she was a famous actress. Once, she actually burst out in song, reveling in the attention she got, which was actually not admiring.

Soon the other cast members were distancing themselves from Gina. As matters progressed, Gina's joy shifted to paranoia. She became convinced that the other students were plotting against her, trying to undermine her road to fame and glory. She became increasingly guarded and ultimately withdrawn. Over a period of weeks she became depressed, crying all the time and refusing to go to school; she believed that everyone hated her and she wished she were dead. Unable to cope with this dramatic downslide, her parents sought professional help, and Gina was soon admitted to a private psychiatric hospital.

While hospitalized, she improved with low doses of an antipsychotic (olanzapine, or Zyprexa) and antidepressant (fluoxetine, or Prozac) medication and was released after 6 weeks, feeling more or less like her old self. She received her high school diploma after making up missed work over the summer, and she began college as planned in the fall. Things progressed well during her first year in college, but in her sophomore year she had another depressive episode, which led to her doctor increasing her antidepressant medication. The increased dose of antidepressant was likely responsible for triggering her second manic episode, which ultimately brought about another hospitalization.

Gina The Roller Coaster Continues

During her sophomore year in college, Gina became increasingly absorbed in her course work in astronomy, to the point of neglecting her other studies. She would spend large amounts of time at the library, reading astronomy materials and becoming extremely excited about the idea of interplanetary travel. Eventually she spent 3 days in her room almost without sleeping, plotting voyages across the heavens and developing grandiose plans for colonizing the solar system.

The resident advisor (RA) of her dormitory eventually became aware that Gina had stopped attending classes and was up at all hours of the night. When the RA asked her about her activities, Gina offered an excited discourse on the benefits of space travel. Realizing something was amiss, the RA urged Gina to visit the student health center, telling her that she looked exhausted. In response, Gina got annoyed and stormed off. The RA finally decided that Gina's behavior might

Bipolar disorders are about equally common in women and men. The lifetime male-to-female prevalence ratio is approximately 1.1:1 (APA, 2013).

Antidepressant drugs can trigger a manic episode for some people who have bipolar disorder (Barak et al., 2000). Thus, clinicians must carefully monitor the impact of these drugs when prescribing them for people with such a disorder.

be a health emergency and contacted the dean of students' office for guidance. The dean called Gina's parents, who drove to the campus and realized that their daughter was in a state similar to the one that had preceded her depression in high school. It was not long before Gina found herself in a psychiatric hospital for a second time.

While she was hospitalized, Gina's mania received psychopharmacological attention. She was given the antipsychotic drug paliperidone (Invega), which produced dramatic relief within a few days, restoring her to a normal condition. She was discharged from the hospital with a prescription for extended-release Invega, with the hope of stabilizing her mood for a longer time.

This medicine appeared to work well for her, and it became the mainstay of her treatment for the next several years. Later, she began having some extrapyramidal side effects from the antipsychotic medication, so her doctor decided to change her to lithium carbonate (Lithium) in combination with eszopiclone (Lunesta) for sleep. The problem was that Gina felt incapable of taking medications consistently. Although recognizing the benefits, she often felt "straitjacketed" by the drugs she was taking. When medicated, she was free of manic episodes, but at the same time she felt she had lost her spark; her emotions felt dulled, and she sometimes longed for a few mild highs in her emotional life, a feeling of excitement or of "just being alive," as she put it. When the longing became intense, Gina would stop taking the medications, often without immediate negative consequences and with a return of her desired emotional highs. Unfortunately, she also became more vulnerable to manic episodes and the depression that often followed.

The result, over the years, was a life greatly hampered by periodic bipolar episodes. Because of several further hospitalizations during the next few years and other disruptions caused by more hypomanic, or depressive, episodes, Gina was unable to complete her bachelor's degree on time. She moved back into her parents' apartment and lived there for several years while taking a reduced course load at a community college. Ultimately she earned a bachelor's degree and found work, ironically as a sales representative for a pharmaceutical company.

Unfortunately, Gina continued to ride an emotional roller coaster after obtaining employment. Her manic episodes were more frequent than her depressive episodes and in her opinion more of an obstacle to her professional and social goals.

At the outset of any manic episode, there was no obvious indication that something was wrong. Rather, the first sign was usually a feeling of happiness that gradually grew to a glorious outlook on life. At this early stage, Gina felt immensely pleased, considering herself the smartest, sexiest, most talented woman alive. These feelings were in sharp (and initially welcome) contrast to the feelings

> Lithium is a silvery white metallic element that occurs in nature as a mineral salt.

> Unlike Gina, most people with bipolar disorder tend to have depressive episodes more often than manic episodes (Julien et al., 2011). Depressive episodes may even occur three times as often as manic episodes.

she would have when depressed, when she would consider herself the most miserable failure who ever existed. Even when not depressed, Gina often would hold herself in somewhat low regard, unhappy with her work, her love life, and her appearance, which actually was attractive.

The feelings that preceded a manic episode were therefore hard to resist. Gina went shopping for new clothes, often spending large amounts of money, which forced her parents to provide her with financial assistance. Gina also became almost unbearably outgoing and friendly, chatting with strangers on the bus or subway and calling up friends in search of stimulating conversation late at night.

As the euphoric feelings progressed, her behavior crossed acceptable boundaries. Of particular concern were her sexual impulses. Because of her family's social connections, Gina often attended charity balls and other gala social events. When she was manic, these parties were the focus of her sexual interests as she became intent on picking up men and having sex with them the same evening. There was one extremely short red dress that she favored for such events. Her typical strategy was to put on that dress and then apply lavish makeup. When finished, she felt as though she could have been a Hollywood actress.

At the party itself, she made a grand entrance and soon became the focus of attention of several men with whom she flirted. Gina loved the attention, and her sense of euphoria and self-satisfaction increased with each passing hour. As the evening progressed, one of the men inevitably would suggest to Gina that they leave the party together, and Gina would almost automatically go. She had sex with 50 men under such circumstances over the course of several years.

Her work activities also offered opportunities for picking up men when she was in a manic state. One of her functions as sales representative at the pharmaceutical company was to coordinate conferences and meetings among doctors to promote sales. When manic, Gina would arrive at the meeting wearing the provocative red dress or a similar outfit. Her language would become flowery and fast-paced. Although she was often noticed at the meeting, it was after the conference, at the customary social hour, that she made her presence truly felt. As at parties, she found men to flirt with and inevitably wound up hooking up with one of them.

This behavior had its negative consequences. Aside from medical problems—she contracted a sexually transmitted disease—she acquired a reputation. Thus, even when no longer manic, she might be approached by men who assumed they could take liberties with her, given her behavior on prior encounters. On one occasion, word got back to her employer when the director of a medical department requested that Gina's company send someone "a little more low-key" to organize the conference for the following year.

Like depressive episodes, some manic episodes include psychotic symptoms. Some persons with mania, for example, may hold delusions of grandeur. They believe that they have special powers or that they are especially important beings, even a deity.

As her mania progressed, her contact with reality would increasingly slip away, and she was capable of developing many grandiose ideas. For example, she once became convinced that she had a natural talent for interior design and was going to surprise her parents, who were on vacation, by redecorating their entire 5,000-square-foot house for them. Completely taken with this idea, Gina got in her car and spent several days buying paint, wallpaper, curtains, and various furnishings.

Gina ultimately purchased several thousand dollars' worth of supplies and furniture and spent the next few days stripping wallpaper, mixing paint, and pulling up carpet, a process she carried out on only a couple of hours of sleep per night. One week later, Gina received a phone call from her mother on her way home from the airport. When she heard her daughter talking about a "huge surprise" she had for them at their house and that she had been working on it for a week straight, she knew that Gina was once again manic. Racing back to her house, her mother found her in their living room, looking like a creature from another planet—white as a ghost, covered from head to toe with various colors of paint and what looked like plaster. The living room and kitchen were painted with multicolored polka-dots; one wall had the wallpaper half removed; and there were many odd pieces of furniture and decorations that she didn't recognize.

Gina excitedly told her mother that she planned to open he own interior design business and that their home would be featured in her portfolio. Her mother, who found it difficult to concentrate because of her anger, tried explaining that her idea was unrealistic and that she didn't have any experience with interior design, but Gina became irritated with her mother's failure to support her. When her mother begged Gina to call her psychiatrist, she refused, saying she had finally discovered her own special talent and all her mother could think about was putting her away. Eventually Gina's mother called the psychiatrist herself and was advised to call an ambulance.

When the paramedics arrived, they tried persuading Gina to come with them to a hospital where she had been taken once before. Only when they promised that she would be released right away if an examination by her psychiatrist proved that everything was all right did she agree to go.

Many states have established procedures by which physicians can temporarily commit patients to a psychiatric hospital in an emergency. The procedure is usually called a *physician emergency certificate*. Today, certification by nonphysician mental health professionals is allowed in many states.

Gina was confined at the hospital on the basis of a physician emergency certificate, which allowed the hospital to hold her for 3 days without a court order or involving the coroner. She was again given medications, and she lost her desire to return to her redecorating project, which she eventually saw as absurd. Gina felt intensely guilty for what she had done to her parents' house. Her mother tried to pacify her by saying she had wanted to redecorate anyway, but Gina knew her mother was just trying to reduce any stress in her life.

When she was depressed, Gina's feelings were almost the mirror image of what she felt when manic. She lost all interest in normal activities, called in sick at work, and slept 16 hours each day. Even when awake she could barely leave her bed. Instead, she spent most of her conscious hours mindlessly surfing the Internet, sobbing, and thinking she was a miserable failure at every aspect of life. Occasionally she might put on some old clothes and go to the store to buy a few basic things, barely looking at anyone she might encounter. At such times, she had no concern for her appearance and ate only enough to keep going.

In between her mood episodes, Gina was intelligent, responsible, serious about her work, and considered a capable sales representative by her employer. However, even then she was not completely free of difficulties. She suffered from chronic low self-esteem. Although perfectly capable in her work, for example, she often doubted her abilities; and after organizing successful meetings she would spend considerable amounts of time and energy analyzing flaws or faults. Similarly, any hint of criticism had a way of overshadowing the praise that she generally received in her work. This sensitivity led to great anxiety and suffering. In her love life, Gina's lowered self-esteem would interfere with her ability to find a suitable partner. Actually, her relations with men were mostly confined to sexual escapades while manic, as if she had nothing else to offer.

Between 1 percent and 2.6 percent of adults around the world have bipolar disorder at any given time (Khare et al., 2011; Merikangas et al., 2011).

A Friend's View Along for the Ride

It was a challenge, to say the least, to be friends with Gina. Actually, it was easy—even seductive—to become her friend, especially if a person met her during the early stages of a manic episode. Her wit, energy, and upbeat disposition would bowl people over. But it was very hard to stay friends with Gina. As she became increasingly manic, friends would find themselves confused, appalled, and ultimately frightened. If she crossed over into depression, they might feel pulled down by her misery and pain. After witnessing one of her manic or depressive episodes, some friends would decide to end the relationship. Others might understand that she had a severe disorder and would try to pick up the relationship where it had left off. But in many cases, such efforts were unsatisfactory. A line had been crossed; the friend's trust or confidence in Gina and in her stability had been broken, and so things were not quite the same. A line had also been crossed for Gina. Embarrassed and humiliated by how she might have acted, especially during a manic episode, she later found it hard to feel comfortable, or even respectable, in the presence of those who had witnessed her bizarre behaviors.

Cyndi, another sales representative at work, was one such individual. Her relationship with Gina started as a source of great joy, but it progressed, along with Gina's manic behaviors, into a troubling, painful, and desperate experience that Cyndi had trouble putting behind her. She later described the relationship to Andrea, one of the newer representatives in the pharmaceutical company:

I didn't think too much about Gina at first, because she generally kept to herself. The first year that I worked with her, we never talked too much, even when we were at a sales conference together. In fact, she kind of had a reputation for not talking to anyone. She didn't have a lot of friends. She was a damn good salesperson, but that was about all I knew about her. Everyone seemed to have their own theory about her, and I heard some talk about a psychiatric hospital, but I figured it was just a rumor.

So I was really surprised at one sales conference when Gina suddenly approached me and started talking to me with great gusto and interest. She told me that she'd always wanted to ask me if I spelled my name the way I do after Cyndi Lauper, and I told her that the singer had nothing to do with it. I said I took complete and utter credit for the name Cyndi, and we had a good laugh. It turned out that we enjoyed the same kind of music and we both enjoyed going out to clubs dancing. We also talked about movies and favorite TV shows. Looking back, it wasn't really what we talked about, I guess, but the way the talk happened. She seemed really excited to be getting to know me, and I was happy that I was making friends with someone at work. Soon we arranged to sit next to each other at marketing meetings, and we would start to have little private jokes that we'd share.

I was really enjoying my friendship and having a lot of fun with Gina. I guess the first time I noticed that something might be a bit off was half a year or so after we started really being friends. One night she called me up at 4:00 A.M., which was very unusual, and I immediately assumed there'd been some sort of emergency. She seemed extremely excited and when I could get her to calm down and tell me what was going on, she said, "You know that guy Dave who reps for us in Seattle. Well, you'll never guess. I totally hooked up with him! I went home with him and we had an amazing time!" I tried to find a way to get off the phone, but she just kept talking a mile a minute, telling me every detail I didn't want to know.

I was pretty shocked that she was having sex with someone from work who she hardly knew. Then she told me that she'd hooked up with a whole lot of the guys who worked in the field offices. A few months later, as luck would have it, Dave was transferred to our office. By the end of his first week there, Gina was telling me that she was deeply in love. After a couple of weeks of hearing about her perfect relationship, I must admit I was getting pretty tired of it, but I had to be polite. Then, by the end of just a month, she was talking to me about marriage. I would say, "Listen Gina, don't you think this is a little fast? I mean, you guys aren't ready to be talking about marriage."

She wasn't even fazed. "Oh, Dave and I are going to do this; it's gonna be like that." She even asked me my opinions on flower arrangements for the wedding.

Finally, I said to her, "Listen, I think this is too soon. As your friend, I have to say I just don't think you're ready to get married, and it doesn't sound like Dave is either.

I mean, you guys haven't even told anyone at work besides me that you're seeing each other, and you won't even let me tell him that I know."

She screamed at me, "But I love him so much! We're going to be together forever! You're the best friend I've ever had and you're going to be my maid of honor. How dare you say we're not ready to get married!" This really scared me, not least because I hardly thought that we were each other's best friend ever.

I decided I had to act. She was starting to make me nervous; she was so jumpy all the time. There seemed to be a real desperation to the way she felt about this relationship, and so I decided to talk to Dave about it.

First thing he said was, "How did you find out about that?"

I just said, "Look, Dave, I know, okay? She told me. And because she's my friend, I want you to know I don't think she's ready for marriage." And he just stared at me like I was from Mars. He told me he'd seen her a couple of times but it was no big deal.

Now I was really scared, so I told her what happened. She got so mad at me, screeching over the phone, "You ruined everything. We were taking it slow, but I know he wanted to marry me, and you ruined it! I hate you, I hate you!" She hung up on me and wouldn't talk to me for months. At work, her behavior kept getting stranger and stranger, more and more outrageous. Needless to say, Dave wanted nothing more to do with her, and quite truthfully, after a while, I began to feel the same way. I mean she was so bizarre and frightening. By then, of course, I realized that she was terribly troubled. Yet for a long while I couldn't shake the thought that I had done something terribly wrong. Now that I know about her problem it makes more sense. We're still friends, kind of, but not nearly like before. I went on one of those rides with her for several months, and I'll never forget it. On the other hand, what must it be like for her to live through them again and again?

Gina in Treatment One More Time

As Gina approached age 32, she decided to seek treatment with a new psychiatrist. Her emotions were stable at the time, due largely to a combination of the medications lithium and eszopiclone. Nevertheless, she knew from experience that this stability would eventually change unpredictably, because of either changes in her reactions to the medications or a change of heart about taking them. She had grown ever so weary of the roller-coaster ride, weary of making and losing friends, weary of all the unpredictability and pain, and she hoped that perhaps a new psychiatrist could help her gain better control over her symptoms.

She contacted Dr. Shara Rabb. She had heard of Dr. Rabb from a friend, a man whom Gina had first met 2 years before at a group for people with mood disorders. The friend himself had been seeing Dr. Rabb for 4 years. He said that the psychiatrist had been able to help him settle down where others had failed.

Bipolar disorders occur in people of all socioeconomic classes and ethnic groups. However, bipolar disorder appears to be more prevalent in lower socioeconomic groups (Schoeyen et al., 2011). Specifically, a negative association has been found between the number of days spent in a manic or hypomanic state and income level (Bauer et al., 2011).

Various genetic studies have linked bipolar disorders to possible gene abnormalities on chromosomes 1, 4, 6, 10, 11, 12, 13, 15, 18, 21, and 22 (Wendland et al., 2011; Baron, 2002).

He couldn't have been more positive, and so Gina, feeling that she was running out of time to live a normal life, decided to see Dr. Rabb. It was certainly worth a try. Thus began a doctor-patient relationship that was to continue for 17 years.

A Psychiatrist Prepares for Treatment A Delicate Balance

Experience taught Dr. Rabb that medicating mood disorders, especially bipolar disorder, is complex and can involve a certain amount of trial and error. The stereotype of the bipolar patient who simply takes lithium, a mood stabilizer, to be free of symptoms was, unfortunately, more the exception than the rule. Most such patients require other medications at different phases of their disorder. Many need a combination of antidepressants and atypical antipsychotic drugs for both their major tranquilizing and their antipsychotic effects.

Dr. Rabb knew that for prescribing lithium it was necessary to achieve a balance between the drug's therapeutic efficacy and its unpleasant side effects—side effects that often would lead patients to just stop using it. In addition, a special problem in the case of bipolar disorder was the pleasure that patients often would get from their manic symptoms. Even with minimal side effects from lithium, the patients might be tempted to discontinue the drug to get the high.

Added to this was the issue of helping patients with bipolar disorder to accept the reality that they have a lifelong disorder and that they probably will have to be on medications for most of their life. Dr. Rabb had come to appreciate that the psychological management of patients was an important adjunct to medication management. A psychiatrist had to be very sensitive both to the patient's concerns about medication side effects and to the changes in emotional life brought about by the medication. Additionally, treatment often had to include behavioral strategies to help patients recognize and seek help for their manic episodes before the episodes fully blossomed, as well as psychotherapy for unresolved conflicts about having a chronic illness.

> Possible side effects of lithium include gastrointestinal irritation, tremor, metallic taste, cognitive dulling, weight gain, excessive thirst, and muscular weakness (Bowden, 1995). Effects on the renal system ultimately leading to kidney failure are a primary concern among patients who take lithium for a significant portion of their lives (Müller-Oerlinghausen, Bauer, & Grof, 2012).

The First Session After gathering a description of Gina's symptoms and history, Dr. Rabb was certain that the patient's condition met the DSM-5 diagnostic criteria for bipolar I disorder. Gina had had both manic and depressive episodes. Her manic episodes were characterized by inflated self-esteem (sometimes called grandiosity), decreased need for sleep, increased talkativeness, increase in goal-directed activity, and excessive involvement in activities with a high potential for painful consequences (especially sexual indiscretions and buying sprees). Conversely, her depressive episodes were marked by severely depressed mood, loss of interest in nearly all activities, excessive sleep, fatigue, feelings of worthlessness, and loss of appetite. Moreover, the episodes brought significant distress and impairment.

> Gina typically had full manic episodes. In contrast, a hypomanic episode is an abnormally elevated mood state that is not as severe as a manic episode. It produces little impairment.

The psychiatrist explained to Gina her basic plan for treating bipolar disorder. She noted first of all that Gina was encountering a common problem for people with bipolar disorder, namely difficulty in adhering to the medication regimen. In discussing this problem, Dr. Rabb felt it was important not to convey this observation in a critical fashion. Given Gina's somewhat girlish self-presentation and her involvement with her parents even at this stage of her life, the psychiatrist concluded that there might have been an adolescent-type rebellion in Gina's problems with medication compliance in addition to the usual reasons patients fail to take their medications.

Since Dr. Rabb would now be assuming the role of an authority figure, she worried that Gina might decide to resist her recommendations as another way of demonstrating rebellion. Thus, Dr. Rabb's first tactic was to empathize with Gina's spotty record of medication compliance. She remarked that the medications used to control manic episodes often had the effect of reducing even a normal sense of high spirits, and as a result, many patients were tempted to omit their medications occasionally.

Gina readily agreed, and she began to open up about the dilemma posed by medications. The feelings that resulted from omitting the medication were indeed pleasurable; moreover, once her feelings progressed to a manic phase, she was no longer capable of rationally considering the advisability of taking medication or of getting medical help. Gina wondered out loud how she could ever be helped out of this dilemma; it seemed she had to choose between a chemical straitjacket and destructive bipolar episodes.

The psychiatrist explained that the first step was to see what could be done to maximize the antimanic benefit of medication while permitting a greater range of emotional feeling. She remarked that there had been some inconsistency in Gina's care to date, as her hospitalizations had led to involvement with a variety of mental health professionals, none of whom had been able to follow her for any length of time. The psychiatrist said she would like to set matters on a different course and asked for Gina's commitment to remain in treatment with her for the next year. Gina agreed, and the first stage of treatment was devoted to finding a medication regimen with which Gina could comply.

The First Year of Treatment

Dr. Rabb's goal during the first months of treatment was to determine the lowest therapeutic dose of lithium for Gina—specifically, a dose that would keep the patient's moods stabilized but that was not so powerful as to flatten Gina's mood completely or produce intolerable side effects.

When Gina first consulted the psychiatrist, she was taking 900 mg of lithium daily and 2 mg of eszopiclone for sleep. Blood tests ordered by the psychiatrist at

In bipolar I disorder, full manic episodes alternate or intermix with major depressive episodes. In bipolar II disorder, hypomanic episodes alternate or intermix with major depressive episodes.

first seemed to indicate that this dose of lithium was operating at a therapeutic level. However, after listening carefully to Gina, the psychiatrist suspected that the patient's medication compliance problems in the past year might have been due not so much to her search for emotional highs as to impaired judgment brought on by her repeated manic episodes. That is, as Gina declared again and again that she had really been trying in the past year to take the medication properly, the psychiatrist came to believe that the main problem might be that her dose of lithium was too low.

Dr. Rabb discussed this impression with Gina and suggested that as long as she was taking medication, she might as well be taking enough to get some of the intended benefits. The psychiatrist proposed increasing Gina's dose gradually, with the goal of raising the patient's blood level to the higher end of the therapeutic range. Gina agreed to this proposal, and over the course of the next couple of weeks, the daily dose was gradually raised.

Months 2 and 3   Unfortunately, even this higher dose did not bring about the desired results over the next few months. The first sign was Gina's arrival at a treatment session dressed more strikingly than Dr. Rabb had yet seen her. There was nothing outlandish in her appearance; she was simply wearing more jewelry and makeup than usual. Gina said she had decided to start dressing up a little to present a more professional image. She added that colleagues seemed to treat her more professionally when she attended more to her appearance. In fact, she thought she might be considered for a promotion soon and wanted to look the part in case there was any chance of her influencing things favorably.

Dr. Rabb asked Gina if she was continuing to take the lithium at the prescribed dose, and she replied that she was. In fact, she said she was very satisfied with the medicine. She took it regularly and felt that it was controlling her moods and helping her get back on the road to recovery. To be on the safe side, the psychiatrist had Gina visit the lab for another test of her lithium blood level.

A few days later the lab report came back indicating that Gina's blood level was the same as before—the lithium blood level had not increased despite the increase in medication. In the meantime, it soon became clear that something was indeed amiss behaviorally, as Gina failed to appear for the next scheduled session with the psychiatrist. It turned out that she was in the midst of a 10-day manic episode, marked by increasing euphoria and flirtatiousness, which culminated in a one-night stand with a participant in one of her medical conferences. When Gina's sexual partner informed her the next morning that he was headed home to his wife, Gina grew furious and began hurling hotel furnishings around the room, smashing lamps and ashtrays. Finally the hotel manager was called, and Gina was ejected, along with her companion, who was grateful to have someone intervene on his behalf.

Because lithium and other mood-stabilizing drugs help prevent bipolar mood episodes, clinicians usually continue to prescribe these drugs even after a mood episode subsides (Connolly & Thase, 2011).

Gina descended on her parents' house, where she encountered her mother. Recognizing a manic episode, Gina's mother asked her daughter when she had last seen her psychiatrist and insisted that Gina get in touch with Dr. Rabb right away. Gina said she didn't want to bother. Her mother made the call herself, which made Gina furious. As her mother spoke on the phone, Dr. Rabb could hear Gina shrieking in the background. Eventually, Gina came to the phone and agreed to come to the psychiatrist's office that evening.

Gina arrived in the company of both parents, who wanted to ensure that their daughter kept the appointment. During the session she was irritable and pouty. She berated her parents for treating her like a child but at the same time was very much acting the part of a child. On their side, Gina's parents—her father in particular—made snide references to Gina's "inability to keep her pants on" and her general failure to live up to their expectations. Throughout it all, Gina was extremely agitated; she spoke rapidly in a shrill voice and periodically rose from her seat and gestured wildly to emphasize a point.

After listening to everyone, Dr. Rabb asked to speak with Gina alone. After making sure that her patient was still taking her medication, the psychiatrist concluded that the dose was inadequate. Gina at first resented this pronouncement, complaining that "everything good that I do is called an illness." Dr. Rabb was wary of confronting Gina with the facts of the past 10 days. She elected instead to focus on Gina's current state, asking her how she felt and whether she was up to going to work. With this shift, Gina acknowledged that she needed help to return to work. The psychiatrist therefore advised her to increase her dose of lithium yet more; and at the same time, she gave her chlorpromazine to calm her right away.

The next evening, Gina called the psychiatrist, obviously in a much calmer state because of the chlorpromazine. She had gone back to her own apartment and had made arrangements to resume her work appointments on the Monday of the following week.

Early that week, Dr. Rabb met with Gina once again and determined that her mood had indeed stabilized. The psychiatrist ordered blood tests, and this time her lithium blood level came back at the high end of the therapeutic range. The plan was to taper off the chlorpromazine with the hope that the higher dose of lithium, if taken properly, would prevent further bipolar episodes.

Months 4 to 8 The new medication regimen appeared to control Gina's mood swings. In fact, she led a calm existence for the next 4 months, meeting all of her work demands and leading a quiet personal life. During this period she practically went out of her way to avoid men.

After about 4 months of this existence, Gina began to grow increasingly more cynical about her "boring" life. Finally, she decided to stop taking her lithium. She called Dr. Rabb and told her that she just couldn't see herself living this way

Identical twins of persons with a bipolar disorder have a 40 percent likelihood of developing a similar disorder, whereas fraternal twins and other siblings have a 5 percent to 10 percent likelihood (Craddock & Jones, 1999).

If people with bipolar disorder have four or more mood episodes within a year, their disorder is further classified as rapid cycling.

indefinitely. She had grown up with enough "domination" from her parents, and now she was being dominated chemically; she felt she was being deprived of her freedom. Furthermore, the new level of lithium seemed to produce enormous thirst, which led her to gulp water constantly, leading in turn to constant trips to the bathroom. She stated she just couldn't take it anymore. The psychiatrist strongly advised Gina to keep to the medication, reminding her of her last manic episode. But all that Dr. Rabb could really do at this point was urge the patient to keep her informed about how she was doing and to call her at the earliest sign of either a manic or depressive episode.

Months 9 to 12   For the next couple of months Gina felt fine. She was happy to be off the lithium and feeling more like her "normal" self. As the weeks progressed, however, her feelings of contentment progressed to euphoria and then mania, which led to one of the most traumatic experiences of her life.

It began at a society fundraising function where Gina, in her manic state, began flirting with a philanthropist from Mexico. As the evening progressed, the man suggested that Gina fly back with him to his country that night. Gina, in high spirits and needing little encouragement to do almost anything, readily agreed, and the two headed for the airport directly from the party. On the plane, Gina was in a boisterous mood, feeling she was the life of the party and adored by everyone. Her companion was so taken with her vivacity that, upon arriving at their destination, he hired a limousine to take them to a hotel in grand style.

At the hotel, Gina and her companion settled in for a high time of fine dining, alcohol, and later, sex. After 3 full days of an extravagant, reckless existence, Gina's companion raised the idea of Gina's "entertaining" a couple of his friends. Gina was shocked by the suggestion but ultimately agreed, and there followed what she later described as "the most degrading week of my life." It all came to an abrupt end when her companion, tiring of the arrangement, checked out of the hotel, leaving Gina on the curb with nothing but cab fare back to the airport. Alone in a strange country and with only a few dollars, Gina called her parents and explained her predicament. Her father immediately made plans to retrieve his daughter. Gina spent the next 24 hours awaiting her father's arrival, sitting on a lonely seat in the airport fuming to herself and kicking at any objects within reach.

Once home, Gina spent 2 weeks in her parents' house, now overcome with depression. She felt she was a complete misfit who would never succeed in life or love, and all she wanted to do was die. In view of her condition, her parents begged her to get back in touch with Dr. Rabb. Gina agreed to schedule a visit, and she tearfully related the Mexican episode to the psychiatrist.

Dr. Rabb prescribed the anticonvulsant drug *lamotrigine* (Lamictal) to treat Gina's acute depression and reinstated the previous high level of lithium. Gina's depression lifted 2 weeks later. After a couple of months, the psychiatrist gradually tapered the anticonvulsant in the hope that Gina's mood could be stabilized once again with just the lithium.

Gina had thus come full circle. She was once more taking the lithium that she so detested, and her mood swings were under control once again. As one might predict by now, before long she was expressing the same old complaints. She couldn't stand the side effects, she felt like she was wearing a straitjacket, and so on. She began omitting the lithium for a few days at a time, saying that she deserved a "couple of days of freedom" now and then.

Dr. Rabb felt that Gina was not facing up to the reality of her situation. Like a rebellious adolescent, she continued to see taking the medicine as something imposed on her rather than something that she was doing for herself to avoid alternatives that were even worse. Thus, the psychiatrist suggested that Gina might benefit from some psychotherapy to help sort out her feelings. Psychotherapy, she explained, might also be helpful with some of Gina's other concerns, her problems with relationships, for example. The patient agreed to see a psychologist, Dr. Michael Kohl, for a consultation.

Second Year of Treatment

Gina saw the psychologist, Dr. Kohl, for intensive insight-oriented therapy during the next 12 months. For the first 3 months of therapy, they focused on Gina's relationship with her parents. Gina complained that her parents devalued her and her problems. Specifically, she believed that they saw her mainly as a disruption to their otherwise tidy lives and fancy social concerns. Sometimes it seemed they resented her very existence and held Gina responsible for her manic and depressive episodes, as though somehow she was causing them deliberately.

The cause of bipolar disorders is not clear. However, some theorists point to improper transport of sodium and potassium ions between the inside and the outside of a person's neuron membranes.

Further discussions helped Gina recognize how extensive her resentment of her parents had grown. Time and again, she seemed bent on retaliation, keeping her parents constantly informed of her suffering by phone calls. Also, she often would try to rub their noses in her problems by causing crisis states—for example, by omitting medication—that forced them to come to her assistance. Dr. Kohl pointed out this pattern to Gina, suggesting that she was running her life much like an adolescent whose main goal was rebellion against her parents. The obvious conclusion was that she needed to stop making rebellion against her parents the primary guiding force of her life.

Armed with these insights, Gina spent the next 3 months of therapy trying to make some important changes. For example, she found a new apartment farther from her parents' home, which would cut down on the frequent impromptu visits from both sides. In addition, the patient decided to cut down on her calls to her parents, in which she would seek their advice on even minor matters. At times the telephone calls were hard to resist, but as Gina got more used to handling simple things on her own or talking them over with her friends or Dr. Kohl instead, her parents became less enmeshed in the details of her daily life, and they became less of a factor in her thoughts and actions.

The next step was for Gina to begin thinking about her own goals in life. Previously, she now realized, her parents' reactions had been such a powerful motivating factor for her behaviors that she had seldom considered her own needs and desires. Over the next 3 months of therapy, Gina decided that what she wanted most was a "normal" life—a life uninterrupted by the manic and depressive episodes that now checkered her past. As discussions on this theme progressed, the patient acknowledged that the medication she was now taking had been the one guarantee of control over these horrifying episodes. As therapy continued, Gina came to view the medication as the guarantor of her hopes to be a normal person rather than an instrument of parental control. Furthermore, she recognized that the medication helped her to live a truly independent life. The question was whether she could accept the trade-off that the medication required, including the loss of certain pleasures and excitement that manic periods initially produced.

Intellectually, Gina said she felt prepared to accept this trade-off, holding out for herself the hope that one day a better medication might be found or that at some point she might no longer need medication. In the meantime, she felt that the advantages of the lithium outweighed its disadvantages.

The remainder of the year in psychotherapy was spent helping Gina achieve a more gratifying existence without manic episodes. The focus was on her relations with the opposite sex, which up to now had been restricted to picking up men for casual sex while in a manic state. With Dr. Kohl's encouragement and coaching, Gina began to date men in a more conventional fashion, typically holding off sexual activity until the relationships progressed to the point where some true feeling developed.

Many bipolar treatment programs now include individual, group, or family therapy as an adjunct to medication. The adjunctive therapies focus on the need for proper management of medications, psychoeducation, improving social and relationship skills, and solving disorder-related problems (George et al., 2000).

The 3rd Through 7th Years

By the 3rd year of treatment, Gina's life truly began to stabilize. She developed independence from her parents and acquired a steady boyfriend for the first time. She remained in psychotherapy with Dr. Kohl for the next 5 years and continued to see the psychiatrist, Dr. Rabb, once a month. Throughout these years, there were occasions when Gina would omit her medication, but it usually involved skipping only a dose or two rather than stopping completely. Whenever she was tempted to discontinue, she would recall the painful episode in Mexico.

With greater emotional stability and a more mature self-concept, Gina was able to make greater progress in her professional life. She started applying herself more seriously to her work, took business courses, and was eventually promoted to regional manager. As she experienced the pride of professional success, the pleasures derived from manic episodes seemed less important to her. This helped her to take her medications even more reliably as time progressed.

After 7 years of treatment with Dr. Rabb, Gina reduced her visits to the psychiatrist to just a few times per year, while continuing to consult with Dr. Kohl, the psychologist, periodically.

Epilogue

A few years later, during one of her visits to Dr. Rabb, Gina raised the idea of taking some lithium holidays. She told the psychiatrist that she still missed some of the "normal" highs that she used to experience when not taking the drug and wanted to see if she could function without the lithium at least a few days of the week. She pointed out that as it was, she was sometimes skipping a day here and there—against medical advice—without any bad consequences. She thought it made sense to try to do this in a more regulated fashion, with the psychiatrist's supervision. Dr. Rabb was persuaded, and she worked out a plan for Gina to begin omitting her lithium one weekend day each week.

This plan proceeded without any problems for a full 6 months, and the decision was then made to omit the lithium for the entire weekend. Once again, Gina appeared to tolerate the omission without any difficulty. She continued to lead her stable, productive existence.

Over the next 10 years, Gina stopped seeing Dr. Kohl but continued to see Dr. Rabb for her medication needs. In a sense they were growing older and wiser together. As the clinical field came to learn more about bipolar disorders and to develop some alternative treatments, Dr. Rabb was able to cut back on lithium and introduce a newer medication, such as *aripiprazole* (Abilify), an atypical antipsychotic. The new combination of medications allowed some of the emotional richness that she longed for back into her life—yet without heightening the risk of new bipolar episodes.

These changes were all done through a slow process of trial and error. The key to their success was that Gina had become a wise and attentive watchdog. She always knew to call Dr. Rabb as soon as the short red dress in her closet—which she hadn't worn for years—started to look appealing again. Over the years, she obtained a business degree, advanced further in her profession, and developed a long-term romance. At last, her emotions—and her life—had indeed calmed down.

> More than 60 percent of patients with bipolar disorder improve while taking lithium or another mood stabilizer (Gao et al., 2010).

> Two anticonvulsant drugs, carbamazepine (Tegretol) and valproate (Depakote), are also used in the treatment of bipolar disorder. They are about as effective as lithium and often have fewer side effects.

Assessment Questions

1. What event prompted Gina's first symptoms of bipolar disorder?

2. What events may have turned her mania into depression?

3. What was the reason for her second hospitalization?

4. What medications were used in the beginning of her treatment and then several years later to assist in reducing Gina's symptoms?

5. Why did Gina decide to stop taking her medications, and what was the result?

6. Which of her manic behaviors became a concern to her parents?

7. Gina suffered from delusions of grandeur. What was her specific grandiose idea?

8. Explain the concept of the physician emergency certificate. Why was this necessary in Gina's case?

9. Why do friendships suffer when an individual is bipolar?

10. Genetic studies have linked bipolar disorder with gene abnormalities on which chromosomes?

11. Why did Gina decide to begin therapy with Dr. Rabb?

12. Why did Dr. Rabb choose the diagnosis of bipolar I?

13. Why did Dr. Rabb want to increase Gina's lithium level?

14. What is meant by the term *rapid cycling*?

15. Why did Dr. Rabb suggest that Gina see a psychotherapist, Dr. Kohl?

16. What type of therapy did Dr. Kohl use with Gina?

17. How many years did it take for Gina's moods to stabilize?

18. What new medication was used to replace the lithium? What are the advantages of these newer medications over lithium?

CASE **7**

Somatic Symptom Disorder

Contributed by Danae L. Hudson, Ph.D.
Missouri State University

Table **7-1**	
	Dx Checklist
	Somatic Symptom Disorder
	1. Person experiences at least 1 upsetting or repeatedly disruptive physical (somatic) symptom.
	2. Person experiences an unreasonable number of thoughts, feelings, and behaviors regarding the nature or implications of the physical symptoms, including 1 of the following:
	(a) Repeated, excessive thoughts about their seriousness.
	(b) Continual, high anxiety about their nature or health implications.
	(c) Disproportionate amounts of time and energy spent on the symptoms or their health implications.
	3. Physical symptoms usually continue to some degree for more than 6 months.
	(Based on APA, 2013.)

The next two cases—Case 7 (Somatic Symptom Disorder) and Case 8 (Illness Anxiety Disorder)—feature two disorders whose symptoms are similar in certain ways. And, in fact, the disorders are sometimes confused by experienced diagnosticians. To help you distinguish these disorders, we are including these two cases that reflect each disorder.

According to the DSM-5, people with somatic symptom disorder have somatic symptoms that cause them disproportionate distress or excessive life disruption. In contrast, people with illness anxiety disorder become preoccupied with the notion that they have or are developing a specific serious illness, despite the fact that they have no somatic symptoms at all or very mild somatic symptoms at most.

Somatic symptom disorder is significantly more common among women than men.

Sadie Millgram stormed out of her doctor's office convinced that it was "impossible to find any physician who knows what they are doing in this town." She was a 31-year-old woman, yet she felt as though she were being treated as a child. Sadie had spent so much time, energy, and money trying to get her health under control, but no one seemed to care. She and Luis had been married for 6 years, and while he was generally quite supportive and understanding, even he seemed to be pulling away from her. She just didn't understand it, because now more than ever, she needed to be healthy. Sadie was 3 months pregnant with their first child.

Sadie A History of Childhood Illnesses

Sadie was born to Jack and Janet Millgram as a healthy 7-lb, 11-oz baby. Her parents were beyond excited to finally have a family. Janet had severe endometriosis, which her doctors believed contributed to years of infertility. Finally, after much emotional pain and financial expense, Janet became pregnant. She tried to enjoy and cherish her pregnancy; she and Jack had already decided that this would be their only child because they couldn't go through trying to conceive again. Even with that knowledge, Janet was a nervous wreck for 9 months. She was so anxious about losing the baby that by the time Sadie was born, she felt relief more than anything else.

Sadie was a happy baby with an easy temperament, and being the first grandchild in the family, she never lacked attention. At 4 months old, she came down with her first cold, which led to a night when she refused to sleep for more than 30 minutes at a time. She screamed and cried in pain, and her mother completely panicked. Janet rushed her to urgent care first thing in the morning to discover that Sadie had infections in both ears. This scenario repeated itself four more times that year, until Sadie had a set of tubes in her ears at 11 months old.

As a child, Sadie was well-behaved and respectful. She struggled some with making friends because she tended to be a little reserved and anxious in new situations. On many occasions, Sadie would complain that her stomach hurt in the morning before school. Janet took her to numerous doctors and specialists to try to find out what was wrong with her stomach and eventually had to accept what the doctors had suggested all along, which was that Sadie was likely subject to separation anxiety. Despite the doctors' recommendations about sending Sadie to school, Janet would often allow Sadie to stay home. Sadie was quite happy with this arrangement; she enjoyed the time with her mother, and she looked forward to visiting the doctor because she knew she would always leave with a sucker and a sticker.

> Many people with somatic symptom disorder have a history of childhood illness (Kenny & Egan, 2011). Furthermore, children with functional abdominal pain are vulnerable to developing anxiety disorder as children (Shelby et al., 2013).

Sadie's pattern of stomachaches tended to ebb and flow over the years, and at age 10, after reading recommendations on the Internet, Janet decided to take Sadie to see an allergist specializing in food allergies. The allergist conducted extensive testing and concluded that Sadie was allergic to gluten, which was the likely cause of her frequent stomachaches. She recommended a gluten-free diet and asked Janet to bring Sadie back for a checkup in 8 weeks. Janet left that appointment feeling overwhelmed about how much she was going to have to change their family's eating patterns, but she also felt vindicated that there actually was something medically wrong with Sadie. She had just known it all along, but everyone assumed that Sadie was just an anxious kid.

> Behavioral theories of somatic symptom disorder suggest that the individuals are rewarded for illness behavior. Rewards can come in the form of gaining something positive or escaping from an undesirable activity or situation (Witthoft & Hiller, 2010).

Sadie A Scary Experience

When Sadie was 11 years old, her parents took her on a summer vacation to Disney World. She had been there before, but she was excited to return again. The family stayed in a hotel close to the park, where the parents slept in one bed and Sadie in the other. She enjoyed the closeness she felt with her parents during this trip. At the end of second day, Sadie was exhausted and quickly fell asleep. In the middle of the night she was awakened by terrible stomach pain. She reached for her mother's iPhone and turned on the flashlight so she could find her way to the restroom. She struggled to get up and when she did she was horrified to see that her sheets were covered in blood. Her first thought was "I've been stabbed!" Realizing that wasn't possible, she assumed that her stomach had finally exploded after all of those years of stomachaches. She was paralyzed with fear. She tried to scream for her parents, but she could not make a sound. Instead, she lay in her in bed crying for an hour until the sun started to come up. When Janet woke up, she heard her daughter whimpering and immediately jumped out of bed and turned on the light. When she saw the bloody sheets she started screaming uncontrollably but her screams quickly changed to tears as she held her daughter and sobbed that "her little girl was growing up." Janet explained to Sadie that her stomach had not exploded but that she had started her menstrual period. Sadie felt completely unprepared to deal with such grown-up things and even less prepared to deal with the terrible cramps and heavy bleeding she would have each month. Even worse, every month Sadie was reminded of that terrifying night in the hotel room where she lay paralyzed for an hour thinking she was dying.

> Many individuals with somatic symptom disorder report traumatic experiences in childhood; these may include emotional, physical, and/or sexual abuse (Brown, Schrag, & Trimble, 2005; Imbierowicz & Egle, 2003).

Sadie High School and Beyond

Sadie enjoyed the opportunities that high school provided. She had a few close friends, took her academics seriously, and played varsity volleyball. She loved the sport, and in her senior year, her team was considered a contender for the state championship. Early in the season, during a game against a local rival school, Sadie and one of her teammates collided when both girls were running to return the ball. The collision was a serious one, knocking the girls to the ground. Sadie and her teammate had to be taken by ambulance to the ER. Sadie was diagnosed with a mild concussion and had torn ligaments in her lower back. Her back pain was excruciating at first, but she was determined to do whatever was necessary to get back to playing volleyball. She was devastated when her orthopedic doctor told her that she would not be able to return to volleyball or any other sports for at least the rest of that year. She had worked so hard, and she was counting on a scholarship for college. In an instant, she felt it all being taken away from her. For the next month, she spent a lot of time at home vacillating between feeling depressed and doing nothing to avidly researching her back injury along with conventional and unconventional medical treatment. Sadie was excited by the prospect of many "alternative" treatments, but when she brought up the subject, her mother told Sadie that their insurance did not cover such treatments and they couldn't afford to pay for them out-of-pocket. Feeling hopeless, Sadie confided in

> Many individuals with chronic pain seek relief via complementary and alternative medicine, such as massage, acupuncture, qigong, or hydrotherapy (Hassett & Gervirtz, 2009).

her mother, telling her that she thought she was depressed, but her mother just tried to reassure her by telling her that it made perfect sense that she was feeling sad and that most people who are in chronic pain have those types of feelings. Sadie spent the rest of the school year attending classes and going to various doctor appointments and physical therapy. One of Sadie's doctors had recommended that she start attending a support group for adolescents with chronic pain. While she was hesitant at first, she quickly realized that the others in this group were the only people who truly understood how she was feeling. She was supposed to be moving away for college soon, and she started to doubt whether being a few hours away from home was such a good idea. Janet reminded Sadie that she had been accepted into a competitive journalism program in which she could specialize in video production and that this opportunity was too good to pass up. So with some hesitation Sadie agreed to give it a try for a year.

Janet A Mother's Perspective

I was really proud of her for having the strength to move away for college. Sadie's an only child, and she was used to having her father and me close by to help her with whatever she needed. While I was very sad to see her go, I knew in my heart that it was going to be good for her. Her last year of high school was awful; she was in so much pain and wasn't able to do much except watch Netflix on her phone. There were many times that I thought she was in her room sleeping, but when I checked on her, I found her reading up on her injury and other medical conditions. In fact, it was a little strange, but she sort of became obsessed with her medical issues. She was always researching new treatments and support groups and talking about the ways that having back pain was going to interfere with her life. I thought that going off to college would give her a fresh start and provide another avenue for her to direct her focus and energy.

Sadie appeared to adjust to college life quite well, and I could tell that she was becoming more comfortable when she no longer called me once or twice a day. She told me that she was attending a support group at the university health center and that she had made some friends through this group. Jack and I were just starting to enjoy the idea of being empty nesters when everything changed.

After a routine physical, Jack was informed by his doctor that he had prostate cancer and needed immediate surgery. When I heard the word *cancer*, I was just devastated. My own father died of cancer when I was in high school, so I have always been terrified that someone in our family was going to get cancer and die. Even though the doctor was optimistic that he would be able to remove the prostate, we didn't know if it had metastasized or not. We waited a few days before telling Sadie because we knew how scared she would be. When we did tell her, she wanted to come home immediately, but we were able to persuade her to stay at school for just a few more days and then come home for the surgery. Unfortunately, the surgery was anything but routine, and Jack had significant complications, including a minor stroke. He was in the hospital for a week and then needed almost constant care at home for at least a month. He had muscle weakness on the left side of his body, difficulty swallowing, which made it very likely that he would choke on his food, and difficulty speaking. The doctors told us that they felt confident these symptoms would get better as his brain healed, but I wasn't so sure. Honestly, that month for me was a complete blur. I was hardly sleeping or eating, and despite everyone telling me I had to take care of myself, I just couldn't seem to focus on anything but the fear that I might have lost the husband I've always known. I know Sadie was worried about both of us— and scared herself, I'm sure. She drove home every Thursday night and stayed through Sunday night until she had to get back for school on Monday morning. I could tell that she was physically exhausted and that her back was bothering her, probably from all of the driving. I tried telling Sadie that she didn't have to come each week to take care of me, but she wouldn't listen, and honestly, I was really glad to have her there.

The doctors were right, and over the course of the next couple of months Jack improved tremendously. He was not exactly the same as he was before the surgery; he walked with a slight limp and sometimes had difficulty finding the right word to express his thoughts. But other than those things, he really was the same old Jack. The best news was that the doctors were able to remove all of the cancer—it had not spread—and all of his subsequent scans have been clear.

> Observing a sick parent or sibling has been found to be an important factor in the development of somatic symptoms (Mai, 2004).

Sadie Focusing on Her Symptoms

Sadie was surprised that it didn't take her long at all to acclimate to college life. With her first semester under her belt, she became more active in the journalism club in the spring and was starting to get to know some of the other students and faculty from the school of journalism. She performed well on her midterms and was feeling confident about the rest of the semester until she received the call from her mother telling her that her dad had cancer. Sadie was shocked and worried because she remembered her mother talking to her about how awful it was when Janet's dad was diagnosed with cancer; and he didn't survive! After her father had a serious complication from surgery, Sadie spent the rest of the semester traveling back and forth to her parents' house to help take care of her parents. Sadie saw her mother as somewhat fragile and had the sense that Janet needed someone to take over. So for one month, every Thursday through Sunday, Sadie would cook, clean, and take care of her parents while trying to maintain good grades and honor her commitments to her classmates and friends in the journalism club. She knew it was taking a toll on her; and her back was having spasms

> Stressful life events can precipitate or exacerbate somatic symptoms.

on a regular basis. She noticed that she was starting to feel depressed again but figured that was normal given the circumstances.

Sadie was thankful that her father's health improved quite quickly and that he remained cancer free. Sadie struggled with her back pain and eventually began attending physical therapy again at the clinic on campus. She had not experienced this kind of back pain for at least the past nine months, and now she found herself wondering if something else was wrong. Maybe she had cancer? She did a little research and figured it was highly unlikely that she had bone cancer, but nonetheless she started to follow the American Cancer Association on Twitter. She told herself that since her dad did have cancer, it would be important for her to stay up-to-date with the most recent cancer news and discoveries.

As the college years went by, Sadie learned to manage her back pain and became well aware of the connection between her level of stress and how much her back hurt. Most of the time she was determined not to let it get in the way of her living her life. Sadie was particularly excited to be accepted for an internship during her senior year: She worked with a local not-for-profit agency committed to helping children who had lost parents as a result of disease or natural disasters. This opportunity was an eye-opening experience for her, and during that year Sadie realized that this was the type of work she wanted to do for her career.

Sadie was both excited and nervous when she was given the opportunity to travel to New Orleans after Hurricane Katrina. As part of her internship she spent 2 weeks in the city, working with displaced children and their families. At the end of each day she would write notes about her experience, which would be used to make a short video to be shown at a fundraiser later that year. On the days leading up to her departure for New Orleans Sadie struggled with nervousness and stomachaches reminiscent of her childhood. She knew she would be working in an office with other college students but didn't expect to know anyone. So she was pleasantly surprised to bump into Luis when she arrived at the office in New Orleans. She and Luis had been in a couple of classes together over the years, but they had had little contact. During the 2 weeks, she and Luis spent a lot of time together. Sadie felt very comfortable and safe with Luis. He was strong but also sensitive and caring. They talked about all aspects of their lives, and she felt that he was the first person who really understood all of the medical issues and difficulties in her life up until that point.

Sadie and Luis fell in love in New Orleans, and while a career was important to both of them, they also planned to get married after graduation and wanted to have a family. They were married after a 10-month engagement, and both felt grateful that they were able to find good jobs in the same city. Over the next 4 years, Sadie threw herself into her work. A gifted video producer, Sadie had a talent for providing a real picture of children's suffering without too much drama. Her bosses noticed her work, and over time they started assigning her higher-profile jobs. She was happy to have the opportunity to allocate her time to projects both in the United States and abroad. She spent time in Uganda working with local children's agencies, and 3 years later she made a number of trips to Joplin, Missouri, to produce a video that was shown at a large fundraiser to help victims of the tornado. Despite receiving national attention for her work and achieving many of the goals she had set for herself, Sadie had a difficult time feeling truly happy. Luis told her that he thought she was getting too wrapped up in her work, and she acknowledged that she was having a difficult time putting her work away. Then, in an instant, all of that changed when Sadie discovered that she was pregnant.

Sadie and Luis were thrilled, as they had always planned to have a family and this appeared to be perfect timing. Sadie began to focus on her pregnancy much more than her work, which Luis saw as a welcome change. However, it wasn't long before Sadie's elation turned to overwhelming anxiety about having a miscarriage. She also worried about how her back would handle the weight gain and whether the emotional toll of her job would cause too much stress for her and the baby. Sadie downloaded a number of pregnancy books, and while she tried to focus on the positive, she couldn't help thinking about all of the things that could go wrong.

Over the next couple of months Sadie struggled with the symptoms of early pregnancy. She felt nauseated most mornings and felt irritable and sometimes sad. Sadie worried about postpartum depression, since she knew she was already susceptible to depression. There were days when Sadie woke up after a full night's sleep but still felt tired. She would usually force herself to go to work but would spend most of the day feeling as though she was coming down with something. Luis told her that she had to remember that she was pregnant and that she was probably working too hard, but she didn't agree. She had a feeling that it was something more than that. One night, while lying in bed trying to fall asleep, Sadie was struck by the thought that maybe she had contracted a disease during her trip to Uganda. She tried to reassure herself that she had been careful to make sure that she received all of the necessary vaccinations prior to her trip, but she couldn't help thinking that it was impossible to vaccinate against everything. She grabbed her tablet and started searching for information about diseases and parasites in Uganda. Her heart started pounding when she saw numerous articles and postings about the outbreak of African sleeping sickness in Uganda in 2008, the year she was there. She read that human African trypanosomiasis was a parasitic disease spread by tsetse flies. She recalled seeing a lot of flies while she was in Uganda but hadn't thought anything of it. She wondered if it was possible for the disease to lie dormant for so long. But maybe she had been infected for years and had just brushed off the symptoms as stress from work? As she read through the symptoms, she became more and more convinced that she had this

Between 48 percent and 90 percent of patients with a pattern of somatization, or multiple long-lasting physical complaints, have also been diagnosed with depression (Hurwitz, 2004).

disease. In a matter of minutes, she saw her life flash before her eyes and started to panic at the thought that she might not be able to carry this baby if she was infected. Even worse, what if she did have the baby but died young, leaving her child to grow up with no mother? Sadie felt herself starting to panic, so she leaned over to wake Luis up. He awoke startled and concerned. With tears in her eyes, Sadie related the information she had discovered. Luis's concern quickly turned to irritation as he realized this was another one of Sadie's "crazy fears about being sick." Luis thought of himself as a patient man, but this behavior was really testing his limits. At least once a week Sadie was waking him up in the middle of the night to announce her latest medical issue or discuss a new treatment option she had found for an existing problem. He was getting tired of constantly having to reassure her, and while he didn't communicate this to Sadie, part of him was wondering about her ability to be a good mother when she appeared to be most concerned about herself.

Sadie The Search for a "Good" Doctor

Sadie and Luis didn't talk much of her "African sleeping sickness," but Sadie had a hard time letting go of the idea. She knew she needed to talk with a doctor, just so she could know for sure whether she was right about having this illness. She didn't want to see her primary care physician because he was a generalist, and she was worried that he might not be familiar with this parasitic disease or its possible effect on pregnancy. Furthermore, she had already been to see him three times in the past month for various other concerns, and after her last appointment, she got the impression that he didn't really take her concerns seriously and was just trying to push her out the door. She considered changing primary care physicians again, but she had already seen a number of doctors from her health insurance provider's list, and she was starting to lose hope that there was anyone decent who contracted with her insurance company.

After a little research on the Centers for Disease Control and Prevention Web site she decided to consult a travel medicine specialist. There were only 2 to choose from, so Sadie chose the doctor who had the most credentials. Dr. Don Benson specialized in travel-related illnesses, and he was also an endocrinologist. Sadie felt hopeful about Dr. Benson, because as an endocrinologist he should appreciate her concerns about the implications this disease could have for her unborn child.

Dr. Benson was kind and took time to listen to Sadie's entire medical history and list of current symptoms. He told her that it was extremely rare for travelers to return from Africa with human African trypanosomiasis but that he was happy to run some tests for that illness and various other possible explanations for her fatigue. Sadie had to wait 2 very long weeks before her follow-up appointment with

There are many similarities between somatic symptom disorder and illness anxiety disorder. Both disorders involve overconcern and worry about physical symptoms and/or medical illness. In somatic symptom disorder the symptoms or illness are present and experienced by the patient, even if an organic basis has not yet been found. With illness anxiety disorder, the anxiety surrounds the *possibility* of developing a serious illness. In this case, the symptoms are either absent or only very mild. It is suggested that there is a high comorbidity between somatic symptom disorder and illness anxiety disorder, although the actual prevalence rates are unknown because both disorders are new to the DSM-5 (APA, 2013).

Doctor shopping is a common feature of somatic symptom disorder. Individuals with this disorder have been found to have very high rates of health care utilization (Puri & Dimsdale, 2011; Tomenson et al., 2012).

Dr. Benson. She and Luis had a big argument that morning because she wanted him to take off from work to attend the appointment with her, but he told her that he had already taken too much time off to attend her various appointments. She was hurt that he couldn't see the potential seriousness of this situation and wondered what had happened to the man who had once been so gentle and caring.

Dr. Benson had seen Sadie's lab results and reported that she tested negative for trypanosomiasis but that she did have hypothyroidism, and it was likely that her low levels of thyroid-stimulating hormone (TSH), in addition to pregnancy hormones, were causing her symptoms. Upon hearing this news Sadie burst into tears. Dr. Benson sat with her and empathically reflected that she must feel so relieved to not have tested positive for trypanosomiasis. Sadie looked up at him, confused, and tearfully explained that these were not tears of relief but that she was devastated to have been diagnosed with a severe endocrine disease. Dr. Benson tried to reassure Sadie that hypothyroidism was very common and easily treated with medication, but Sadie didn't appreciate his patronizing tone and how he downplayed the seriousness of this condition. She abruptly left his office thinking that she needed to find a different endocrinologist, one who knew what he was doing.

> Patients with somatic symptom disorder often exhibit an attentional bias toward pain and illness. Most people would think that Sadie should be relieved that she didn't have a rare parasite, but instead she was focused on the development of a new "disease."

Sadie waited for Luis to come home from work, and when he did, she had an emotional breakdown. She tried to tell him about her diagnosis, her fears for their baby, and her complete frustration with the medical community. Luis listened to her for over an hour and then finally told her that she needed to see a different kind of doctor. This announcement got Sadie's attention, and she listened as Luis explained that he had been doing his own research and that he believed Sadie had been seeing the wrong type of doctor. He recommended that she make an appointment with Dr. Maureen Weston, a psychologist specializing in health concerns. Sadie felt enraged that Luis would suggest that her problems were all in her head and said she wouldn't make an appointment with that kind of doctor. She was shocked when Luis told her that it wasn't an option and that if she wanted their marriage to be happy again, she would keep the appointment that he had already scheduled for her.

> Cognitive-behavioral therapy is an empirically supported treatment for somatic symptom disorder (Gili et al., 2013; Magallón et al., 2008).

Session 1   At Dr. Weston's request, Luis accompanied Sadie to her first appointment. Sadie didn't speak to Luis for the entire drive to Dr. Weston's office. She didn't appreciate the fact that he was coming to her doctor' appointments now only because he thought she was crazy. Dr. Weston, who was younger than Sadie expected, explained that she was a clinical psychologist specializing in health psychology. She expressed interest in hearing about Sadie's entire medical history, including her current medications and concerns related to her health. She was also interested in Luis's perspective and how Sadie's illnesses had affected their relationship.

At first, Sadie attempted to avoid answering Dr. Weston's questions by providing her with a detailed medical history she had typed up in chronological order, beginning with her chronic ear infections as a baby and ending with her diagnosis of hypothyroidism. The 10-page document was thorough and well organized. Still, Dr. Weston was interested in other aspects of Sadie's life that she hadn't described in the document. Sadie respectfully answered her questions, and over the course of the hour she felt herself relaxing. Dr. Weston actually seemed interested in what Sadie had to say and appeared to understand how much she had suffered.

Session 2   At the follow-up appointment the next week, Dr. Weston explained to Sadie and Luis that she believed Sadie had somatic symptom disorder, recurrent major depressive disorder, and various medical issues including chronic back pain and hypothyroidism. Sadie felt her frustration increase as soon as she heard Dr. Weston start talking about psychological disorders. However, the way Dr. Weston explained it did make some sense. She referred to Sadie's illness as a neurobiological illness with both biological and psychological components. Dr. Weston made a special attempt to validate Sadie's medical issues. They were indeed real, she said, and if Sadie was to feel better, she and Sadie would have to work in conjunction with the primary care physician and endocrinologist. Dr. Weston obtained Sadie's permission to write a consultation letter to both physicians explaining the treatment plan and asking them to join the treatment team.

Dr. Weston went on to explain that her role in Sadie's treatment would involve providing individual cognitive-behavioral therapy to decrease her medical issues' interference in her life. She proceeded to explain that somatic symptom disorder tended to develop in individuals with a significant medical history and as a result of a complex interaction of (a) prolonged attention to bodily sensations; (b) misinterpretation of bodily sensations as a sign of a catastrophic illness or disease; (c) neurochemical changes; and (d) the influence of illness behaviors that inadvertently reinforce and maintain the focus on the physical symptoms. Dr. Weston assured Sadie that they would be returning to talk about each of these factors numerous times in their treatment, so she should not be concerned if the entire concept didn't make sense yet. For now, Dr. Weston wanted to consult with Sadie's primary care physician about her diagnosis and the proposed treatment plan. She also showed Sadie an app that she could download to her phone to keep track of her physical symptoms throughout the day. Dr. Weston wanted to gather some baseline data to determine how often Sadie was attending to her physical symptoms and the number of illness-related behaviors she was engaging in throughout the day. By the end of the session, Sadie was feeling hopeful that maybe she had finally found a doctor who understood her.

Including the patient's medical doctors as part of the treatment team is an important part of therapy. Sometimes even one consultation letter sent to the primary care physician leads to lessening of symptoms (Kashner, Rost, Smith, & Lewis, 1992; Looper & Kirmayer, 2002). It is assumed that labeling the symptoms by providing a diagnosis reduces the clinical uncertainty of the medical doctor. Furthermore, a consultation letter may prevent the patient from undergoing potentially harmful and invasive examinations as a result of diagnostic uncertainty (Hoedeman et al., 2010).

Approximately 6 percent of health-related mobile phone apps are categorized as relating to mental health. Mobile apps can be used for self-monitoring, including mood tracking, psychoeducation, and treatment delivery. Text messaging is often used to enhance therapist and client communication between sessions (Morris & Aguilera, 2012).

Sessions 3 to 5   Prior to each session Sadie downloaded the data from her self-monitoring app and emailed the spreadsheet to Dr. Weston for review before their session. Dr. Weston began Session 3 by congratulating Sadie on her meticulous recording of her various symptoms, thoughts, and behaviors in the past week. She was interested in Sadie's experience of self-monitoring:

Dr. Weston: I'm wondering what this was like for you, having to record every physical symptom and your thoughts about it.

Sadie: It was kind of interesting, actually. On the one hand, I liked it because I felt like by writing it down it was making it real. I've spent a lot of time in my life thinking that people don't believe me. On the other hand, though, I noticed that I was feeling pretty nervous throughout the week.

Dr. Weston: What were you nervous about?

Sadie: I think just looking at everything recorded made me have to face all of the medical issues I have.

Dr. Weston: Did you have any new medical problems this week?

Sadie: No.

Dr. Weston: So having to pay attention to every physical symptom caused you to think about the symptoms more, and thinking about the symptoms more made you anxious.

Sadie: Yes, I guess that's true.

Dr. Weston: I wonder if in some way this is what you've been doing all along; you just haven't been recording it.

Sadie: What do you mean?

Dr. Weston: Well, one of the things we know about people who have somatic symptom disorder is that they tend to be overly perceptive and overly sensitive to physical symptoms. So that means that you are extremely good at detecting even very minor changes in your body. This is not necessarily a bad thing, but you also tend to misinterpret those physical symptoms in a catastrophic way. This means that you tend to jump to the worst-case scenario in your mind. Having those scary thoughts leads you to feel very anxious, which ultimately leads you to engage in what we would call illness behavior to reduce your anxiety so that you'll feel better.

Sadie: Wow, I've never thought about it like that before. But that really does sound like me!

The remainder of the session and the next 2 sessions were devoted to introducing the concept of cognitive distortions (errors in thinking) and helping Sadie see that the illnesses or physical symptoms themselves were not actually the problem. The problem was the way Sadie was interpreting those symptoms as a medical catastrophe. Dr. Weston was very careful never to suggest that the pain, symptoms, or illnesses were not real, but that just the way Sadie experienced and interpreted her pain, symptoms, or illnesses was interfering with her life. They also discussed Sadie's beliefs about coping. Sadie discovered that she held very strong beliefs that she was susceptible to illness, injury, and disease; that she had little power to control the situation; and that she was weak and needed someone to take care of her. Dr. Weston pointed out how these beliefs reinforced Sadie's focus on her symptoms and helped to keep her in the patient role. They began to brainstorm and practice new coping statements and strategies that empowered Sadie to have more control over the outcomes in her life.

Sessions 6 and 7 Sadie continued to monitor her symptoms, but now she was also recording her distorted thoughts and identifying which cognitive distortion the thought represented and how she could challenge that thought. Ultimately, she would record a new, more balanced thought. Sadie was surprised that once she got the hang of the procedure, she really did feel less anxious.

In session 6, Dr. Weston asked Sadie to make a list of all the things she did in response to feeling nervous or concerned about her medical symptoms. They brainstormed a long list of behaviors, including going to the doctor, frequently looking for any changes in the symptoms, talking with Luis or her mother about her concerns, and looking up symptoms and/or treatment on the Internet. Dr. Weston helped Sadie to see how these behaviors inadvertently reinforced her excessive focus on her symptoms and catastrophic misinterpretation of them.

Dr. Weston	When you feel nervous or anxious about your health and you engage in one of these behaviors, how do you feel afterward?
Sadie:	Usually, much better.
Dr. Weston:	So when you engage in some kind of checking behavior or reassurance-seeking behavior, you feel better after you do that? Why do you think that is?
Sadie:	Well, because I was worried about something but then was able to get some kind of information that I was really okay.
Dr. Weston:	Right! But there are two major problems with that way of responding. First, engaging in that kind of illness-related behavior relieves your anxiety, which means you are much more likely to engage in that type of behavior again in the future when you feel anxious. Second, allowing yourself to practice those illness behaviors reinforces your beliefs that the symptoms are bad and scary and that you are unable to manage them on your own.
Sadie:	Okay, I can see that. But what are you saying? That I can never go see a doctor again? That's not realistic. I already have appointments to see my obstetrician every month.

Dr. Weston: You're right, that's not realistic, and it's important to keep all of your scheduled appointments regarding your pregnancy. But it would be good for us to put some parameters around some of the illness-related behaviors you engage in when you are feeling anxious. For example, we have already been working with your primary care physician, and she has agreed to see you for very brief checkups every month for as long as you feel that you need that. These checkups are in addition to your obstetrician appointments and are not in response to specific symptoms that arise; they are already scheduled. So you will just attend the appointment even if you don't have anything to talk about. What that also means, though, is that you will agree not to make any doctor appointments outside of those times. Obviously, if something serious happens or you are concerned for the welfare of your baby, then Luis should take you to the doctor or urgent care. Otherwise, any minor concerns or questions will have to wait until your next appointment with your primary care doctor. Furthermore, we are going to have to set some boundaries around your researching of medical symptoms and treatments on the Internet. All that these behaviors do is keep your mind focused on your physical symptoms. We want you to start focusing on other things and learn to manage the symptoms in unobtrusive ways.

Sadie: I don't know if I can do this.

Dr. Weston: It won't be easy. It will actually be very difficult at first. But I think you'll be surprised at how quickly it becomes easy. So if you can just persevere for the first few times by resisting the urge to engage in any of these behaviors, you'll realize just how much they were keeping you stuck in your symptoms.

> Providing brief, frequent, and regular visits to the primary care physician has been found to be an effective part of the overall treatment for somatic symptoms. Requiring the patient to follow the appointment schedule begins to break the pattern of seeking immediate relief of health anxiety by seeking reassurance from a doctor.

Dr. Weston had Sadie monitor her urges to check and seek reassurance and the anxiety that accompanied resisting. As predicted, her anxiety ratings were very high at first, but within a few days they started to decrease. Sadie felt proud of herself when she realized that she didn't have to look up every little symptom on the Internet or rush to her doctor to make sure she wasn't sick. She was amazed that not only could she manage to take care of herself on her own, but she actually felt relieved. As the days progressed, Sadie realized that long periods would pass when she did not feel anxious about any physical symptoms.

Sessions 8 and 9   By Session 8, Sadie was starting to feel like a different person. She was still monitoring her illness thoughts and behaviors but she had very little to record compared to when she started therapy. She could hardly believe that she still had the same medical problems and her back still hurt, probably more as she was progressing in her pregnancy, but she wasn't bothered by them as she had been before. She was starting to trust that she really could manage her symptoms on her own and that worrying about what might happen was just not a good use of her time.

Dr. Weston helped Sadie reflect on how far she had come in just 2 months and warned her that she would likely have a setback at some point. They discussed how having a baby could trigger many anxieties, and Dr. Weston reminded Sadie that her tendency was to focus on her own physical symptoms in those situations. Together they developed a relapse prevention plan that identified high-risk situations and coping strategies to use when confronted with them. Their plan also included step-by-step instructions in case she felt herself slipping back into old habits. Dr. Weston assured Sadie that she would be happy to see her if she needed any booster sessions, but they agreed that Sadie would try to get back on track on her own for 2 weeks before calling to make an appointment.

Epilogue

Four months after her last session with Dr. Weston, Sadie and Luis welcomed Samuel into their family. Sadie's delivery was long and had some minor complications, but she was able to manage her anxiety by following the plan she had developed with Dr. Weston. Sadie continued to have periodic scheduled appointments with her primary care physician, and they discussed the possibility of her beginning a trial of fluoxetine (Prozac) if she had any postpartum depression or an exacerbation of her somatic symptoms. Sadie never developed postpartum depression, and she found that she rarely even thought about it or any other illnesses or diseases. She and Luis had a number of months together to strengthen their marriage before Samuel was born. Luis frequently told Sadie how proud he was of the changes she had made and that he could really see how much happier she was and how much he enjoyed spending time with her again. While it wasn't easy, Sadie thanked Luis for stepping in and scheduling her first appointment with Dr. Weston. She had had no idea that that would be the day her life changed forever.

> Antidepressants have been found to be effective for some patients with somatization disorder, even in some patients with no evidence of a depressive disorder (Mai, 2004).

Assessment Questions

1. What experiences did Sadie have in her childhood that likely contributed to her development of somatic symptom disorder?

2. What role did Sadie's mother and father play in the development of Sadie's disorder?

3. Even though Sadie appears to overreact to her various medical problems and injuries, the conditions she experiences are real. Which diagnosed conditions is Sadie having to deal with as an adult?

4. Finding out that she is pregnant appears to be a trigger for some of Sadie's anxiety and somatic symptoms. Why might this be?

5. Sadie spends a lot of time researching symptoms, possible illnesses, and treatments. What function does this behavior serve for her, and how is it contributing to her disorder?

6. Dr. Weston described Sadie's somatic symptom disorder as a complex interaction of four factors. What are these factors?

7. Dr. Weston recommended that Sadie download a mobile phone app to keep track of her symptoms. What role could technology play in Sadie's treatment?

8. The cognitive theory of somatic symptom disorder involves attentional bias and catastrophic interpretations of illness or medical situations. What evidence from Sadie's life supports this view?

CASE 8

Illness Anxiety Disorder

Table **8-1**	
	Dx Checklist
	Illness Anxiety Disorder
	1. Person is preoccupied with thoughts about having or getting a significant illness.
	2. In reality, person has no or, at most, mild somatic symptoms.
	3. Person has easily triggered, high anxiety about health.
	4. Person displays unduly high number of health-related behaviors (e.g., keeps focusing on body) or dysfunctional health-avoidance behaviors (e.g., avoids doctors).
	5. Person's concerns continue to some degree for at least 6 months.
	(Based on APA, 2013.)

In the previous case, Sadie Millgram displayed somatic symptom disorder. In this case, Andrea Hilgard displays a similar but distinct, disorder—illness anxiety disorder. In contrast to Sadie, Andrea's somatic symptoms are extremely mild, but she continues to experience significant anxiety and is particularly concerned that she is developing a specific serious illness.

Looking back, 37-year-old Andrea Hilgard thought she first began to worry about her health at about age 10, when she was playing with some friends after school. At that time, she was seized with "a sudden awareness of my own mortality." She was in the midst of a kickball game, and the emotional pall that came over her at that moment grabbed her attention for the rest of the game. While her friends were enjoying themselves and were completely caught up in the fun, Andrea could not shake her feeling. Afterward, she went home, where she found her mother doing her usual household activities, and the feeling gradually subsided.

Since that "awakening," Andrea felt that her emotional life was never quite the same. Although a basically happy, well-adjusted child, she was now sensitive to life's negative possibilities in a way that others did not seem to be. Occasionally she would be at school or playing at a friend's house, and she would be seized by the thought that her parents or sisters could have been in a car accident without her knowing. The thought would keep her distracted and worried for the remainder of the day, at least until she could go home and make sure that the worry was unfounded.

Despite their upsetting impact, such episodes did not dominate Andrea's childhood. In fact, her childhood was generally positive and the family environment

Many people with illness anxiety disorder had a serious illness during childhood or experience with disease of a family member (APA, 2013).

loving. Her father was a salesman who made a comfortable middle-class living, and her mother was a full-time homemaker. Andrea excelled in school; after graduation from high school, she attended an exclusive Ivy League college and then law school. After graduation, she moved to a major metropolitan area where she worked for a few years as an associate in a law firm. At age 30, she took a job as house counsel in a brokerage house.

Andrea had dated a number of men during her 20s. At age 32, however, she "panicked" at the thought of not finding a husband and ended up marrying a man whom her better judgment was telling her to avoid. He was a self-described musician who obtained occasional gigs with his rock band at underground clubs. His lifestyle seemed exciting to her, but a more reasoned analysis of his situation would have told her that he was immature and self-absorbed, with no real means of support. In addition, he had a cocaine habit that Andrea was at first willing to overlook.

Soon after marrying this man over her family's objections, Andrea was struck by the stark reality of their life together: she had assumed the responsibility of supporting a self-indulgent parasite who showed no prospect of ever becoming a full partner. She would leave for work in the morning with her husband still in bed; when she returned after a long day's labor, the apartment would be awash with dirty dishes and beer bottles. In addition, as time passed, it was clear that he was using large portions of her salary to support his cocaine habit.

Although Andrea was a successful lawyer, she felt paralyzed by her marital distress, both personally and legally. Eventually, she swallowed her pride and asked her family to help her escape from this situation. They swiftly came to her assistance and helped her obtain an annulment and get this man out of her life.

Following the annulment Andrea went through a period of despondency and entered counseling for about a year. Among the important insights she gained in therapy was the realization that in her dating she had been favoring men who were "interesting, offbeat, or unpredictable." However, these attributes were not usually consistent with her long-term goals: children, financial security, and a stable home life. Over the course of counseling, she began dating men whom she previously would have overlooked as too boring, and she discovered that in many instances the boredom had been of her own creation. Eventually, at 33 years of age, she met Paul, a high school science teacher, and they were married 6 months later. Her son, Jimmy, was born a year after that.

Andrea Bodily Concerns Take a Serious Turn

For the first 34 years of Andrea's life, her tendency to worry had remained in check. True, she was always capable of suddenly becoming concerned about the safety or health of her parents, sisters, or husband, but such worries were usually mild and infrequent. It was not until she became pregnant that her occasional anxieties became more frequent and focused specifically on the medical area. During

Although illness anxiety disorder can begin at any age, it starts most often in early adulthood. It affects 1 percent to 5 percent of the population (Abramowitz & Braddock, 2011).

her pregnancy she made the usual visits to the obstetrician and loaded up on various books about pregnancy. She also underwent the usual blood tests, sonograms, and other procedures that a modern-day pregnancy entails. As she moved deeper and deeper into the process, however, she became aware of the many possible threats to her health and to the baby's. With each passing month, the various tests and changes in her body produced increasing levels of anxiety that could be reduced only with the doctor's strenuous reassurance or a favorable test result.

When her son, Jimmy, was born, Andrea actually went through a period of calm, as she could see that he was healthy and strong. Before long, however, she returned the focus to her own health. Her bodily concerns increased in intensity and frequency over the next 2½ years. Although she did not find them a constant problem, she had more and more episodes in which she would become consumed with the belief that she had a serious, possibly fatal, illness.

Andrea Bodily Concerns Take Over

Illness anxiety disorder is one of the somatic symptom and related disorders, that is, physical illnesses or ailments that are explained largely by psychosocial causes. Other somatic symptom and related disorders are somatic symptom disorder, conversion disorder, and pain disorder.

Most of the time, Andrea felt fine. However, once one of her health fears struck, she could not rest until she got medical reassurance. Sometimes a single visit to the doctor was enough to put her mind at ease; but other times she required several visits to several doctors. Due to her persistence—with telephone calls, follow-up visits, and more telephone calls—doctors soon became exasperated with Andrea, and some even refused to see her. These medical visits were not enjoyable for Andrea, either. Indeed, they were among the least pleasant activities she could imagine. She sought the visits only because she had no other method of coping with her terrible fears.

A typical crisis unfolded one weekday morning in November, when Andrea awoke with a curious sensation of numbness in her right arm. Concerned, she tried prodding her skin at various locations to determine how much sensation she had lost. While there was no doubt she had some feeling, it was obviously blunted.

Andrea thought of rousing Paul, her husband, to get his opinion. However, she hesitated, as just the day before she had asked him to feel the back of her skull, to get his opinion on whether a bony projection there had always been present. At that time, she had even insisted on feeling his skull to see if he had a similar projection—he did not—and she was only reassured upon feeling her son's skull and discovering that it resembled hers. And the day before that, she had asked Paul to comment on the appearance of a pimple on her neck. He had responded that it seemed like a typical pimple, and he begged her to wait just one day to see if it would disappear before concluding that it was cancer or smallpox, or some other dread disease. Andrea took his advice; happily, the pimple was almost gone the next day.

The numbness in the arm, however, really worried her. She recalled having read an article in the newspaper a few weeks prior, "Multiple Sclerosis: The

Stalker of Young Adults." The article noted that multiple sclerosis typically strikes between age 20 and 40. Andrea was horrified to learn that she was in the prime risk period. Still, when reading the article, she was at least thankful that she didn't have any of the symptoms listed: weakness, vision problems, numbness. Now, however, she undeniably had a sensation of numbness.

Andrea could not resist eventually rousing her husband and describing her fear. As she spoke, she could tell that Paul viewed her problem with a skepticism born of many false alarms in the past. He tried to get her to see reason, asking her to consider logically how seriously ill she could be if she could still move her arm normally and still had feeling in it. As in the past, he suggested that Andrea let the problem ride for a day before calling the doctor.

Paul's opinion did not hold her for long, however. The article had explicitly stated, Andrea recalled, that the initial symptoms of multiple sclerosis could indeed be minor, but the illness to follow could be devastating. If the disease progressed rapidly, she could be reduced to a wheelchair within a few years.

Andrea decided to see her doctor that day. She raced to get herself and her son dressed and on their way. The first stop was the nursery school, where she exchanged the usual morning pleasantries with the teachers and other parents. However, while there, all she could think about was how lucky they were to be in good health, whereas she might now be gravely ill. Andrea then gave Jimmy a kiss good-bye and raced to her office.

Andrea called the doctor and was relieved to learn that she could get an appointment at 11:00 A.M. She left immediately, and when she arrived at the doctor's office, she settled down in the waiting room, nervously flipping through a magazine. While she waited, anxiously anticipating the verdict on her symptoms, Andrea thought about her predicament. Why was it, she wondered, that she was subject to these alarming symptoms? How ironic, she thought, that she should be plagued in this fashion. Other people took their good health for granted—foolishly so, in her estimation. She recalled once reading a story about people who had survived various disasters, such as airplane hijackings. These people reported that prior to their harrowing ordeal, they had had all the wrong notions about what mattered in life: careers, income, a nice house or car. Afterward they emerged with a new appreciation of life's true gifts: the health and well-being of their family and friends.

In recalling the article, she thought, "I already know this without the benefit of a disaster striking. The only thing I've ever cared about is my family and their health. So why should I, of all people, be singled out for this kind of treatment? Why can't an illness strike somebody who needs a little shaking up—someone who smokes or who thinks her career is such a big deal, or who doesn't pay any attention to her kids?"

The doctor came into the waiting room and took Andrea into the office. Andrea explained about the numbness, and the physician performed a standard neurological exam. All findings were normal. When Andrea raised the question of multiple sclerosis, the doctor replied that it couldn't be discounted completely—a statement that visibly alarmed her. Seeing Andrea's distress, the physician hastened to remind her that the results of the neurological exam were normal; therefore, it was unlikely that her numbness was serious. The physician suggested that they wait a few days to see whether the numbness subsided before conducting any further investigations.

Andrea left the office feeling not at all reassured. She wanted a definitive answer. Almost immediately, she made another appointment, this time with a neurologist, who might be better able to assess her condition. By the time she got to see the neurologist a week later, the numbness had disappeared. Still, she kept the appointment just to hear what the neurologist would say. After an exam and several tests, the specialist, too, concluded that the numbness was not a serious problem; perhaps a muscle ache had caused the feeling of numbness.

The numbness did not reappear, and about a week later, Andrea's concern with multiple sclerosis had more or less subsided. She got back into her regular routine of work and family and felt happy and content that she had no symptoms to worry her. Indeed, under these conditions, she was at complete peace with the world. The way she saw it, she had a wonderful husband and son, 2 loving parents, and a job that provided a reasonable living and a sense of doing something worthwhile. If only things could just stay this way, with no more symptoms or illnesses to worry about.

Things did stay that way for about 2 weeks, during which time Andrea maintained her sunny outlook. Then one morning she awoke with blurry vision and became frantic that it might be another sign of multiple sclerosis. She asked her husband to take Jimmy to school and then called in sick, determined to find an ophthalmologist who would see her that day.

She was finally able to obtain an appointment for that afternoon. Over the course of the morning, the blurriness disappeared. Still, she was deeply concerned because she had learned, during a morning of searching online, that the symptoms of multiple sclerosis can come and go.

The ophthalmologist examined Andrea's eyes, paying particular attention to the state of the optic nerve, since she had raised the multiple sclerosis question. He soon informed Andrea that everything appeared normal, and inasmuch as the blurring had vanished, he assumed it had just been a transient disturbance due to some eye irritation or a minor infection. He gave her eye drops to counter the possible infection. Andrea thanked him and left the office feeling more reassured.

When she arrived home, she had time to consider her experiences of the past three years. She was very unhappy with the contrast between the secure adult image that she wanted to project to her young son and the utterly helpless

> Illness anxiety disorder affects 1.3 percent to 10 percent of the population (APA, 2013).

creature she seemed to be whenever she was preoccupied with a medical concern. Also, she could tell that Paul was getting more and more exasperated with her. Not too long ago, after a particularly frenzied period of medical fears, he had even told her that he was at a loss as to what to do for her. Perhaps, he suggested, she should get "some professional help" for the problem. That evening, Andrea told Paul that she was indeed ready to seek therapy. With his encouragement, she soon made an appointment with a psychologist, Dr. Frances Lloyd, through the referral service of her managed care network.

A Spouse's View Living with Imagined Illness

When Andrea informed Paul that she was ready to seek therapy, he felt as if he were being given a "new life." He had just about given up hope of his wife ever improving—or of her taking the steps needed to improve. For the most part, he had kept his exasperation to himself. He loved Andrea and thought it would be cruel to belittle her or threaten her. Besides, when he did express upset or anger, things always seemed to get worse. She seemed to become even more convinced that a terrible illness was overtaking her. No, it was usually better to just calmly reassure her and make gentle suggestions that she might be overreacting.

On the outside, Paul tried to be calm and understanding. But on the inside he was boiling. He was able to hide his feelings—at least some of them—from Andrea, but he would periodically open up to a close friend or family member. Indeed, he felt he had to open up or else he would explode. Just a week ago, in the middle of his wife's multiple sclerosis scare, he had confided to his brother that he was, for the first time, considering seeking a separation.

Her behavior is truly unbearable. I mean, I'm not sure I can continue in the marriage. You know, she never gave any indication that she had problems this serious when we first met. We fell in love, and everything seemed wonderful. I guess that's what comes from marrying someone you only know for 6 months. I knew we were rushing things, but I was so sure. I never thought there could be any reason I wouldn't want to spend the rest of my life with her.

Everything was great for about a year. Then she started in with her ridiculous "medical problems." It started with "The baby's going to be deformed. . . . He's going to be stillborn. . . . He's going to die within 6 months." At first I worried right along with her because she seemed so sure that something was going to be wrong. I thought it just might happen. But then the doctors told us everything was going to be fine, and her attitude was, "What if they're wrong? What if he dies?"

Then I thought, well, she's just nervous about becoming a mother. But the sheer strength of her worries finally convinced me that her thinking was really disturbed. Then again, I told myself that the pregnancy must be wreaking havoc on her entire system and that she'd soon be back to normal. But after Jimmy was born and he was fine, I realized that she wasn't going to get any better.

It was cancer one week and tuberculosis the next. She might have a brain tumor during the day and a curvature of the spine by nighttime. Do you know how hard it is to repeatedly explain that the world isn't going to collapse, to repeatedly remind your wife that she's not gravely ill? It's been like living with Chicken Little, constantly screaming that the sky is falling. When she panics, even though I realize that she's not right and that there's no real problem, I can't help but get caught up in her emotion at first. Sometimes she's even able to convince me that this time it's for real—it's a problem that will change everything. But then it soon becomes obvious that it's the same old story—another false alarm—and I'm back to my usual job of trying to convince her that everything's going to be fine.

Men and women are equally likely to have illness anxiety disorder (APA, 2013).

I guess what upsets me the most is that the woman I married no longer seems to be an adult. Here we are trying to raise a child, and she's behaving like a child herself. It's both surreal and depressing when you have to hold your wife while she cries in your arms because she has a headache or a cold that won't go away. I also get really nervous when I think about what this may do to Jimmy if it continues. When she tucks him in at night or drops him off at school, she sometimes gets teary, and even says things like, "Remember that Mommy always loves you, even if I go away!" I mean, for heaven's sake. When I think about what she's starting to put him through and how he may feel when he really starts to understand what she's saying—well, that frankly makes me mad. It's got to harm him, maybe seriously. How anxious, nervous, or all-around screwed up is he going to be?

After three years of this nonsense, I think I've had enough. I don't need this nightmare, and I certainly don't want my son exposed to it. But then again, I love her, and I don't want to hurt her. And really, I don't want to leave her. I just want her to change and for our lives to become normal. But then I come back to the fact that I'm running out of steam. I don't know how much longer I can be the patient, understanding husband, especially when I don't understand anything about this.

Fortunately, Paul didn't have to act on his thoughts of separation. It was as if he and Andrea had reached bottom at the same time. When she came to him, saying that she was ready for therapy, he knew that this was the right direction—not separation or arguments or accusations. Of course, even as Andrea made her appointment with the psychologist, Paul realized that there were no guarantees that everything would turn out all right. But at least she—and he—now had a chance.

Andrea in Treatment Achieving a "Healthy" Perspective

Upon listening to Andrea's tale of suspected illnesses and repeated anxieties, Dr. Lloyd concluded that the young woman's condition met the DSM-5 criteria for a diagnosis of illness anxiety disorder. She had been preoccupied with fears of serious illness (based on misinterpretations of symptoms) for the past three years; her somatic symptoms were mild (e.g., transient numbness or blurry vision); she had high levels of anxiety about her health; and this preoccupation had led her to engage in excessive health-related behaviors such as checking her body for signs of illness and making frequent medical appointments.

Dr. Lloyd's reading of clinical studies had convinced her of the parallels between illness anxiety disorder and obsessive-compulsive disorder. In illness anxiety disorder, a patient's anxious and intrusive focus on bodily sensations and physical symptoms is often equivalent to the obsessions with germs or disaster displayed by patients with obsessive-compulsive disorder. Similarly, the efforts of patients with illness anxiety disorder to cope with fears of illness—repeatedly seeking reassurance, seeing doctors, reviewing medical texts, and monitoring their physical state—are reminiscent of compulsions.

To many clinicians, such parallels suggest that the treatment for illness anxiety disorder should take its lead from that for obsessive-compulsive disorder. Thus, psychiatrists who specialize in drug therapy often give patients with illness anxiety disorder medications that benefit obsessive-compulsive patients, particularly fluoxetine (Prozac). Similarly, psychotherapists often offer patients with illness anxiety disorder a treatment program of exposure and response prevention similar to the behavioral treatment used in cases of obsessive-compulsive disorder. Many such psychotherapists also include cognitive interventions similar to the cognitive approaches used for anxiety or depression.

> People with illness anxiety disorder receive an additional (that is, comorbid) diagnosis of obsessive-compulsive disorder only when their obsessions or compulsions are not restricted to concerns about illness (APA, 2013).

In Andrea's case, Dr. Lloyd decided to use the psychological approach first and to refer the client for drug therapy only if psychotherapy failed. Exposure in the treatment of illness anxiety disorder involves bringing the person into contact with the stimuli—sensations, thoughts, or images—that provoke illness anxieties, with the goal of extinguishing those anxieties. In the response prevention component of treatment, clients with illness anxiety disorder are prevented from performing the behaviors—for example, reading medical information online or seeking reassurances—that they usually turn to when they fear illness.

Session 1   At the first session with Dr. Lloyd, Andrea related her history. Not now in one of her "crises," she was in good humor as she discussed her difficulties. She told the psychologist that in between the crises she had no real complaints. She enjoyed her work, loved her family, and was generally an upbeat and enthusiastic person. Still, she always felt mildly apprehensive, as she knew the slightest thing could set her off and plunge her into an acute and terribly painful anxiety episode.

As the first step in the treatment, Dr. Lloyd explained to Andrea the theoretical treatment model. To start, she cited the role that Andrea's self-scrutiny, reassurance seeking, reading of medical material, and doctor visits were playing in maintaining her problem. The psychologist explained that it was completely understandable that Andrea should engage in these behaviors as a means of coping with her fears; indeed, most people with illness anxiety disorder responded in the same way. The problem was that while these behaviors often provided a certain measure of relief, in the long run they maintained the fear. Thus, the first step in the treatment, Dr. Lloyd explained, was to begin limiting some of these "coping behaviors" (the prevention component of the treatment).

Andrea: Don't I need to go to the doctor to make sure I'm okay? I mean, what if there was something seriously wrong with me and I neglected it? What harm is there in going?

Dr. Lloyd: From a medical standpoint there is no harm in going. From a psychological standpoint, however, the visits fuel the feeling that something is wrong and rob you of any opportunity to learn to cope with the illness fears in another way. For our purposes, you need to limit the doctor visits that are psychologically harmful.

Andrea: How do I tell one from the other?

Dr. Lloyd: I admit it's not always easy, but we will devise some guidelines. What is your impression concerning the necessity of the doctor visits you now make?

Andrea: At the time I make them they seem absolutely necessary. I mean, I get a symptom and I just have to know what it indicates or that it's not serious. But I know that what I'm doing is not normal, because the doctors usually get fed up. Often they start out being nice and understanding, but then things go to pot when I start calling too much.

Dr. Lloyd: So it would appear that some of these visits are unnecessary.

Andrea: Yes, but how do I tell which ones?

Dr. Lloyd said she would like to put the question of specific guidelines for medical visits on hold for now and concentrate first on Andrea's other problematic coping behaviors. To begin, she wanted Andrea to start recording her illness concerns, using a written log containing the following elements: (a) the eliciting symptom or sensation, (b) her immediate concern about the symptom, (c) how she coped with her concern, and (d) the result of her coping efforts.

Next, Dr. Lloyd explained the exposure component of the treatment. She said that generally it would be a good idea for Andrea to limit her coping behaviors (for example, asking Paul for constant reassurance) whenever she was in the midst of a crisis; this resistance would help lessen her anxiety over time. In addition, rather than just wait around for crises to occur, therapy could speed along the process by causing conditions that produced illness anxiety and regularly exposing Andrea to such conditions. At the same time, the psychologist noted that causing such conditions presents logistical problems—one cannot readily

Illness anxiety disorder can present a clinical picture very similar to that of somatic symptom disorder, the somatic symptom and related disorder marked by one or more somatic symptoms that are distressing or result in significant disruption in daily life.

manufacture unexplained physical symptoms—so the 2 of them would have to develop some type of substitute, such as a visualization exercise, in which Andrea would imagine in detail having such symptoms.

Andrea said she could see the value in exposure exercises, even remarking, "I guess it's the same as what you do if you're afraid of snakes—have more and more contact with snakes until the fear diminishes." At the same time, she expressed doubt that just visualizing herself ill would have any emotional impact. She assumed that there would be no therapeutic benefit in an exposure exercise unless there was some real anxiety to extinguish.

Dr. Lloyd and Andrea agreed to give this question some thought for the coming week. In the meantime, Andrea would keep the log of her symptoms and responses to them.

Session 2   Andrea returned with blank record forms, saying she simply had not been troubled by any symptoms during the week. She noted that this was not unusual for her. She could go for a couple of weeks without a crisis occurring.

Dr. Lloyd said she would like to devote the session to 2 main matters. First, she wanted to devise some specific guidelines for limiting Andrea's coping behaviors, should any be provoked in her real life. Second, she would like to work out an exposure procedure, especially since Andrea was not having any spontaneous fears that might be used for therapeutic purposes. Regarding the guidelines for limiting coping behaviors, the psychologist suggested the following:

1. Stop doing online medical searches, whether provoked by symptoms or not.
2. Stop taking blood pressure at home.
3. Refrain from seeking reassurance from family or friends if a symptom arises.
4. Refrain from calling the doctor for at least 2 days when faced with symptoms that cause only minor discomfort.

Andrea agreed to try to observe these guidelines if any symptoms arose.

Next, she and Dr. Lloyd discussed an exposure procedure. The client remained firm in her belief that visualizing herself having an illness would not be compelling enough to produce anxiety. She said that her fears just didn't seem to have a visual component. She even tried closing her eyes in the session and imagining herself on a sickbed, but she had trouble conjuring up any image. She said it just seemed artificial.

Accordingly, to help develop an appropriate exposure procedure, Dr. Lloyd asked Andrea to explain the exact sequence of events when a spontaneous fear of illness arose. Andrea replied that the process usually began with her noting a particular abnormality in her appearance or an abnormal sensation; next, she thought of a dreaded illness that might be implied by the abnormality; and then

---

There are many similarities between somatic symptom disorder and illness anxiety disorder. Both disorders involve overconcern and worry about physical symptoms and/or medical illness. In somatic symptom disorder the symptoms or illness is present, even if an organic basis has not yet been found. With illness anxiety disorder, the anxiety surrounds the *possibility* of developing a serious illness. In this case, the symptoms are either absent or only very mild (APA, 2013)

she frantically sought reassurance, usually first by approaching her husband, doing online searches, and then by calling or visiting the doctor.

Dr. Lloyd devised an exposure procedure modeled on this natural sequence. She suggested a written exercise, as follows: Three times a day for the next week, Andrea was to take time out from her normal activities and briefly survey her body's appearance and sensations. Then, based on a particular attribute that she identified, she was to manufacture a particular illness fear (a different one each time) and write it down in a notebook. By doing this three times a day, she would produce 21 illness fears by the end of the week. Should the fear be great enough to provoke a desire to engage in any coping behaviors, Andrea was to follow the guidelines described earlier in the session for limiting the behaviors. To test the exercise, Dr. Lloyd asked Andrea to carry it out right then. Andrea focused on her body for a few seconds and then remarked that she had a slight tingling sensation in her right foot, due, most likely, to the way she had been crossing her legs for the past half hour. Dr. Lloyd then asked Andrea to proceed to the next step, namely to think of a dire illness that the symptom might signify. Andrea was very hesitant, saying it would cause her great anxiety actually to verbalize an illness. The psychologist persevered, however, encouraging Andrea to proceed. Finally, in a soft voice, Andrea speculated that the tingling could be a sign of multiple sclerosis.

Dr. Lloyd praised Andrea for this effort and suggested that the client next carry out the exercise on paper, following the procedure outlined for the coming week's assignment. Accordingly, Andrea wrote down: "(a) My foot is tingling." Next, the client should have written: "(b) I have multiple sclerosis." But once again, Andrea hesitated. She said that she was seized with the fear that writing down the words might become a self-fulfilling prophecy. Dr. Lloyd empathized with Andrea's concern but then led the client in a rational discussion of whether writing down an illness could actually have any role in producing it. Andrea replied that intellectually she knew it was nonsense, but somehow writing it down filled her with fright. Yet, at the same time, she felt intuitively that writing down the sentence—"I have multiple sclerosis"—would be therapeutic for her. All of a sudden, Andrea said that she wanted to go ahead and do the written exercise. She thought that if somehow she could accomplish it, she would feel like she was defying her fears. She took the pen in her hand and wrote the sentence down.

Dr. Lloyd and the client agreed that Andrea would continue to carry out the exercise three times a day in the coming week, each time trying to think of a new illness or at the very least not using the same illness more than once in a day.

Session 3 Andrea reported that she had carried out the exercise faithfully each day. For the first few days it was quite stressful. Each time she wrote down an illness, she almost felt as if she had doomed herself to the disease. However, as the week progressed, she noticed a shift in her feelings. She felt less and less

Illness anxiety disorder and other somatic symptom and related disorders are among the least-researched mental disorders. One online search found around 300 literature selections for illness anxiety disorder over the past decade, compared to 3,000 for specific phobias, 7,700 for alcohol abuse, and 16,000 for depression.

threatened by the writing, and she seemed to become bolder and bolder in her thoughts. Furthermore, the more she wrote, the less threatened she felt.

Dr. Lloyd reviewed the entries that Andrea had made, one by one, and noted the increasing detail and daring as the week progressed. A typical entry for the first couple of days read: "(a) I had poor posture in sitting at a meeting at work," and "(b) I am getting osteoporosis." By the end of the week she had written: "(a) I have a slight headache," and "(b) It is a brain tumor, which will invade my brain, rob me of my senses, and leave me a vegetable in a hospital bed."

Andrea said she was amazed at what she was eventually able to write. The illnesses were still unpleasant to write about, but the fear was drastically weakened.

As to the general effect of the exercise on her illness anxiety disorder, the client said this was difficult to assess. She had not been subject to any spontaneous illness fears this week, but this was not necessarily a sign of improvement because even in the past she could go for weeks without an incident. Still, this was her 3rd consecutive week without a problem, and it was getting close to the longest time in the past years that she had ever gone without a medical concern. She wondered if the deliberate focus on symptoms had replaced her usual fears. Dr. Lloyd said she would also like to discuss the cognitive component of Andrea's fears. To begin, she asked Andrea to consider her worst-case scenario should she become ill:

Andrea:	It's funny you should ask. When all this started about three years ago—when I got pregnant—I was focused mainly on my own fear of dying. I was just thinking, I don't want to die. But since Jimmy was born, dying itself doesn't seem like such a big deal. I mean, I still don't want to die, but it seems that my main reason now for not wanting to die is the impact it would have on my husband and son.
Dr. Lloyd:	My next question may seem a little strange, but to overcome a preoccupation with illness and death, it is usually helpful to think things through completely. So my question is, Why would your dying be so bad for them?
Andrea:	It seems obvious. Their lives would be ruined. Isn't it terrible to lose your wife or mother?
Dr. Lloyd:	Yes, it is terrible. Did you ever know anyone who lost a parent at a young age?
Andrea:	I had a childhood friend whose father died.
Dr. Lloyd:	What happened?
Andrea:	Well, he died suddenly. I think it was a heart attack. Afterward, my friend Sheila had to leave school for a month. She was really upset. And of course she really missed her dad.
Dr. Lloyd:	What happened to her eventually?

In addition to their illness concerns, people with illness anxiety disorder often have fears of aging and death (APA, 2013).

Andrea:	Her mom got remarried after a few years to a really great guy. But it wasn't like having her own dad back. She had a very hard time.
Dr. Lloyd:	Was her life ruined?
Andrea:	She's married now and has 2 kids. I guess you couldn't say her life was ruined. Still, I wouldn't want anything like that to happen to Jimmy.
Dr. Lloyd:	If something did happen to you, if you did die, what do you think the effect would be?
Andrea:	Oh, boy. This is hard. I can't believe we're talking about this. But I think I know what you're driving at. If I can learn to see it just a little less hysterically, I might be a little less hysterical about the whole illness thing.
Dr. Lloyd:	Possibly.
Andrea:	(Sighing) Well, if I died, everyone in my family would be sad, and I know I would be missed. I think Jimmy would take it very hard. But on the other hand, I think Paul is the type to remarry, and I think that would help. I just hope he would choose a woman who would be a good mother to Jimmy. I think he would. I also hope Jimmy would remember me, but mainly I would just want him to be happy. (Long pause) I hope my family never has to face my early death, but I guess they would eventually handle it.
Dr. Lloyd:	I know that was hard to think through. What you just did was something known in psychotherapy as decatastrophizing, taking an event that you assumed you couldn't bear even in your thoughts and figuring out a way that it could be faced and accepted. Having done this with an event as extreme as your own death, you may find it easier to do the same with lesser events, such as serious illnesses.

Dr. Lloyd then went on to explain the other aspect of thinking that produces anxiety, namely, overestimating the likelihood that a particular symptom signifies something serious. The psychologist reviewed with Andrea several of her most recent illness fears, noting how none of them came to pass. For example, her numb arm turned out just to be a muscle ache, not multiple sclerosis; her eye problem turned out to be a minor infection, not multiple sclerosis; and the bump on her skull was just a normal bony projection, not a tumor. The psychologist suggested that Andrea would benefit from learning to identify and correct her overestimation sooner rather than later.

Thus, the psychologist suggested an expanded exercise for the coming week. First, as before, Andrea would survey her body three times a day, identify a symptom, and think up a disease on the basis of the symptom. Now, however, in addition, she was to describe the catastrophic aftermath of the disease—as she imagined it—so as to increase the intensity of the exposure.

In a bizarre coincidence, on February 17, 1673, the French actor-playwright Molière collapsed on stage and died while performing in *Le malade imaginaire [The Hypochondriac]* (Ash, 1999).

The new exercise included a cognitive component as well. Having formed her disease thought, Andrea was to produce a more reasonable interpretation of the symptom. In so doing, she could draw on her experience. Thus, for example, if she were to note numbness in a finger, in addition to forming the thought that it could represent multiple sclerosis, she was to produce a more rational alternative, such as that it probably represented a mere muscle ache or some other less dire condition.

Session 4   Andrea reported that she had carried out the exercise more or less as prescribed. She did find, however, that on some days she had difficulty coming up with three symptoms and three disease thoughts. She said she didn't know whether this was a sign of progress or just an indication that she was running out of ideas. She thought it could be a sign of progress, for she could never imagine herself at a loss for illness ideas in the past. She also noted that her attempts at decatastrophizing the aftermath felt very artificial at the beginning of the exercise but that toward the end of the week her renditions seemed more believable.

Andrea also reported that she had had her first spontaneous disease fear since treatment began. One night, when entertaining guests, she noticed an abnormal swelling in her armpit. It was quite a noticeable lump, and the thought of a tumor arose. In a departure from her previous habits, she did not excuse herself to conduct a Google search, although she was tempted. Instead, she tried to apply her new cognitive skills by forming a more likely disease thought: "It's just a boil." This held her until the guests left, but then she felt compelled to ask her husband for his opinion. She didn't think that this represented a violation of the prohibition on requests for reassurance, as she didn't feel she was seeking reassurance, just "an unbiased opinion." Paul, for his part, didn't know what to think.

> Many people with illness anxiety disorder also have an anxiety disorder, depression, or another somatic symptom and related disorder (APA, 2013).

The next day, Andrea was in a quandary as to whether to call the doctor or not, in view of Dr. Lloyd's guideline concerning waiting 2 days for symptoms that caused only minor discomfort. The symptom did seem quite unusual—even her husband eventually recommended calling the doctor—so Andrea decided to call, although without actively seeking an appointment (another departure from her usual habit).

She followed her usual routine that morning, taking Jimmy to school and going directly to work. She then placed a call to the doctor without conveying any sense of urgency, just requesting that the doctor return her call when he was free. The doctor called back about an hour later, and Andrea described the swelling. After a few questions, the doctor concluded that the swelling was probably an infected hair follicle that would clear up in a few days. Andrea felt immediately reassured, which was a distinct departure from the past. Previously, she would have insisted on an appointment.

Andrea felt this experience represented a sign of improvement. Not only had she conducted herself differently, to honor the guidelines, but she also felt different in the process, as she did not experience the usual sense of fear or hysteria. She was pleased with her reaction.

Dr. Lloyd agreed that the client was showing signs of improvement. She advised her to continue her exercises and adherence to the coping rules for the coming week.

Session 5   Andrea said she thought she had reached the limits of her imagination, as the entries in her writing exercises seemed to be getting more and more far-fetched. For example, by the end of this week, one of her selected symptoms was: "The hair on my arm looks slightly blonder than usual." The corresponding disease fear was: "My hair is turning white because I'm getting one of those accelerated aging diseases—advanced senescence!" The psychologist agreed that the exercise had probably outlived its usefulness.

In the realm of natural disease fears during the week, Andrea revealed that she had had only some brief concern with a cough that she developed. Consistent with the guidelines, Andrea did not ask Paul for reassurance, and she refrained from calling the doctor for 48 hours; her impulse to call was not strong in any event. By the end of the 48 hours, the cough had subsided somewhat and the impulse to call had gone. Andrea expressed delight, not only at her rather minimal fear, but also at being spared the burden of leaving work, arranging a doctor's visit, traveling to the doctor's office, and enduring the humiliation of the doctor's annoyance.

Reviewing her experiences of the past several weeks, Andrea felt that there had indeed been some basic change in her feelings. She believed that if she just continued to observe the behavioral guidelines, she might eventually be able to return to her normal self of three years ago.

The plan for the next week was for Andrea to stop the written exercises. If she had a spontaneous disease fear, she was to cope with it using the behavioral guidelines and cognitive reinterpretations. Dr. Lloyd also suggested that if the week proved uneventful and Andrea was able to continue observing the guidelines, future sessions would be scheduled less often.

Sessions 6 to 8   Andrea returned for the sixth session, once again reporting an uneventful week. She said she was starting to grow more confident that she might have overcome the problem. A review of the week's events indicated that the client had had some appropriate concern over a high fever that her son had developed, but otherwise she had been anxiety free and not preoccupied with her own health.

At Session 7, held 2 weeks later, Andrea offered basically the same report, and at Session 8, held a month after that, she still had not had any new illness fears. She and Dr. Lloyd agreed to stop therapy at that point, with the understanding that the client would call if any difficulties arose.

Epilogue

Dr. Lloyd called Andrea 6 months after the last session, and the client reported she had more or less maintained her progress. There had been a couple of isolated instances when she was unreasonably anxious, but by using cognitive reinterpretations and following the behavioral guidelines, she had managed them pretty well. Generally, she continued to be aware—too aware—that life always carried a potential for tragedy, but her day-to-day feelings and behavior were not adversely affected by this awareness. Moreover, she found that she was also able to hold onto the flip side of this awareness, that is, an appreciation of the blessings of life and good health. The positive view more than counterbalanced the negative view. In a way, she felt that she had returned to 2 kinds of health—physical and psychological. She considered treatment a roaring success.

> Most cases of illness anxiety disorder are chronic, but complete recovery does occur in some cases (APA, 2013)

Assessment Questions

1. What event(s) usually precede individuals' preoccupation with their health, that is, illness anxiety disorder?

2. What event precipitated Andrea's preoccupation with her health?

3. Why is illness anxiety disorder labeled a somatic symptom and related disorder?

4. What was the first serious disease that Andrea diagnosed for herself?

5. Why did Andrea decide to consult a psychologist?

6. Why did Paul, Andrea's husband, become frustrated with Andrea to the point of thinking about a separation?

7. What other psychological disorder parallels illness anxiety disorder?

8. What therapy did Dr. Lloyd decide to use with Andrea?

9. What 4 steps did Dr. Lloyd outline for Andrea to begin her written log for treatment?

10. What is the difference between the diagnosis of illness anxiety disorder and somatic symptom disorder, according to Gorenstein and Comer?

11. What were the 4 guidelines for limiting coping behaviors outlined by Dr. Lloyd?

12. How did the exposure treatment eventually help Andrea?

13. Describe the concept of decatastrophizing as a treatment procedure.

14. How many sessions before Andrea was able to control her illness anxiety disorder?

15. Do individuals with illness anxiety disorder often completely recover, as Andrea did?

Bulimia Nervosa

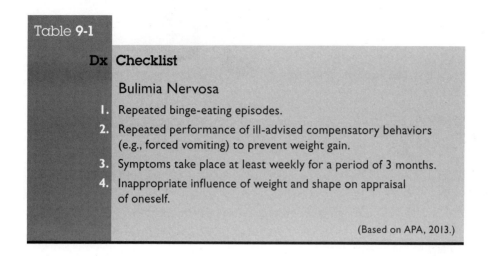

Table **9-1**

Dx Checklist

Bulimia Nervosa

1. Repeated binge-eating episodes.
2. Repeated performance of ill-advised compensatory behaviors (e.g., forced vomiting) to prevent weight gain.
3. Symptoms take place at least weekly for a period of 3 months.
4. Inappropriate influence of weight and shape on appraisal of oneself.

(Based on APA, 2013.)

Rita was a 26-year-old manager of a local Italian restaurant and lived in the same city as her parents. Her childhood was not a happy one. Her parents divorced when she was about 5 years of age. She and her three older brothers remained with their mother, who often seemed overwhelmed with her situation and unable to run the household effectively. Rita would often refer to her childhood as utterly chaotic, as if no one were in charge.

She nevertheless muddled through. When her brothers were finally all off to college or beyond, Rita entered high school, and the household seemed more manageable. Ultimately, she developed a close relationship with her mother, indeed too close, Rita suspected. Her mother seemed like her closest friend, at times the entire focus of her social life. They were both women alone, so to speak, and relied heavily on one another for comfort and support, preventing Rita from developing serious friendships. The two often went shopping together. Rita would give her mother an update on the most recent fashion trends, and her mother would talk to Rita about "how important it is to look good and be put together in this day and age." Rita didn't mind the advice, but sometimes she did wonder if her mother kept saying that as a way of telling her that she didn't think she looked good.

Rita later attended a local public college, majoring in business. However, she quit after 3 years to take a job at the restaurant. She had begun working in the restaurant part-time while a sophomore and after 2 years was offered the position of daytime manager. It was a well-paying job, and since her interest was business anyway, Rita figured it made sense to seize an attractive business opportunity. Her mother was not very supportive of her decision to leave college, but Rita reassured her that she intended to go back and finish up after she had worked for a while and saved some money.

Within a 12-month period, 1 percent to 1.5 percent of individuals will meet the diagnostic criteria for bulimia nervosa; at least 90 percent of cases occur in females (APA, 2013).

Just before leaving college, Rita began a serious relationship with a man whom she met at school. Their interest in each other grew, and they eventually got engaged. Everything seemed to be going well when out of the blue, her fiancé's mental state began to deteriorate. Ultimately he manifested a pattern of schizophrenia and had to be hospitalized. As his impairment extended from days to months and then to more than a year, Rita finally had to end the engagement; she had to pick up the pieces and go on without him. She felt as if he had died.

A period of psychotherapy helped ease her grief and her adjustment following this tragedy, and eventually she was able to move on with her life and to resume dating again. However, serious relationships eluded her. Rita knew that she was a moody person—she judged people harshly and displayed irritation easily—and she believed this discouraged potential suitors. She suspected that her employees didn't like her for more reasons than the fact that she was the boss, and she found it hard to make close friends.

Rita Fundamental Concerns About Weight and Appearance

Body dissatisfaction, depression, and self-reported dieting are important risk factors in the development of eating disorders (Stice, Marti, & Durant, 2011).

Throughout her adolescence and young adulthood, Rita had always been sensitive to people's opinions about her appearance and weight, particularly the opinions of other women. She recognized that this sensitivity likely came from the not-so-subtle messages from her mother about her appearance. She can still remember the day they went to a local pool with friends when she was 12 years old. She overheard her mother talking to the other mothers, telling them that she wondered if Rita was going to have "hormonal problems" because she seemed to be chubbier than all of the other girls. Rita didn't initially think of herself as chubby, but socially she always seemed to fall in with a group of women who were equally preoccupied with dieting and weight control. To Rita, their preoccupation seemed to be based not on vanity but on anxiety. They lived under a cloud of concern that their weight and eating might somehow grow out of control. Typically, her acquaintances did not have significant weight problems, nor were they unusually vain or intent on being popular. In fact, most of them had serious academic interests and career goals. Thus she found it almost ironic that they in particular were so focused on their physical image. But focused they were, and Rita became no exception.

From age 14 to 25 she always tried to keep her weight between 121 pounds and 123 pounds, a standard that began in the ninth grade, after she had a slightly overweight period. She would rigidly follow what she called her weight watcher plan, although she had never actually gone to the program of the same name. The eating plan consisted, when she was being "good," of a breakfast of dry toast and juice, a lunch of turkey or dry tuna on diet bread, and a low-fat frozen meal at dinnertime. On some days, when she was being "bad," it also included a couple of candy bars or two large gourmet chocolate chip cookies. She tried to keep "bad" days to a minimum, but there were probably three or four of them each week. Rita felt she could tolerate such days, however, as she was a regular exerciser, attending spinning classes at the gym or doing Pilates at home at least 3 nights per week. During a particularly bad week, however, she might go to the gym a couple of extra times to exercise on her own.

In addition, she developed the habit of weighing herself several times a day to reassure herself that the reading did not exceed 123 pounds. When the scale showed that her weight was at or below 121, the young woman felt enormous satisfaction, similar to what other people might feel if their bank statement showed a comfortable balance. Rita saw her 121 pounds as the well-earned reward for sustained and concentrated effort. And like a miser who counts her money over and over, she would get on the scale frequently to recapture that feeling of satisfaction, especially when other aspects of her life felt less than satisfying. One evening at home, when she saw that her weight was 119, she returned to the scale a dozen times to experience the pleasure at seeing that number.

At the same time, the frequent weighing had its downside. Sometimes she would weigh 124 or 125 pounds and have a very negative reaction: She would feel fat and bloated and would resolve to limit her eating to a much stricter version of her weight watcher plan. In addition, she might throw in extra exercise sessions for good measure. In the meantime, to avoid anyone seeing her "fat" body, she would hide it under bulky sweaters and other concealing clothing. This way, at least other people would not gossip about her.

> Repeatedly engaging in body-checking behaviors (e.g., weighing self, checking in the mirror, comparing body to others, measuring body size with clothes or other instruments) has been found to be a maintaining factor of eating disorders (Shafran, Fairburn, Robinson, & Lask, 2004).

The more she felt upset about her body, the more she tended to check her body shape and size. She would try on different-sized clothes from her closet to see how they fit. She had one pair of "skinny jeans" that she fit into a few years prior, but only for a short time. She saved them, swearing that she would fit back into those again one day. She would stand in front of the mirror and suck her stomach in as far as she could and see if that made her feel any better. It tended to make her feel worse, but it did give her more motivation to have a really "good" day the next day.

Rita: Caught in a Binge-Purge Cycle

Shortly after her 26th birthday, Rita's eating habits became much more troubled. First she began to have eating binges, perhaps two to three times per week. Typically she would become aware of the urge to binge sometime in the afternoon while at work. Because she restricted her food intake during the day as much as she could, she was hungry, and the food smelled so good. As the afternoon progressed, the urge would build into a sense of inevitability, and by the end of

A *binge* is defined as consuming an objectively large amount of food during a relatively short time (less than 2 hours) and is accompanied by a feeling of loss of control (APA, 2013).

the workday, she knew she would be spending her evening on a food binge. She would then start to fantasize about the foods she would be buying on the way home.

The foods that figured in Rita's binges were items that she had labeled as "bad"—foods that in her mind should never be eaten if she had any hopes of maintaining proper weight. On one binge day, for example, the young woman made three stops on the way home from work. The first was a fast food drive-through, where she ordered an extra-large combo cheeseburger meal. The next stop was a gourmet cookie shop, where she bought three large super chunk chocolate chip cookies. The final stop was the grocery store, where she bought half a gallon of ice cream, which, as usual, was heavily laden with chocolate chips and nuts.

Once home, Rita locked the door behind her and put her phone on silent. Something about the secrecy, the single-mindedness, and what Rita called the depraved indifference of her binges made her feel as if she were committing a crime. Yet once the eating began, she felt powerless to stop it. After the first mouthful, the binge was destined to run its course.

On this particular evening, Rita tore into the cheeseburger first while she sat in her kitchen checking Facebook, Instagram, and Twitter on her iPad. She ate rapidly, without pause, taking little notice of the stories or photos. After the cheeseburger came the cookies; these were gone in a matter of minutes. After about a 20-minute break, during which Rita changed out of her work clothes, she proceeded to the ice cream. This she ate in her living room at a slower, more leisurely pace while she watched the food network on TV. Within about an hour and a half she was scraping the bottom of the carton. Spoonful by spoonful, she had devoured all of it. In fact, within a 3-hour period, Rita had consumed more than 4,000 calories.

The young woman often felt as though she were in a changed state of consciousness during such binges. Nothing else in the world seemed to matter when she was eating like this. She would avoid answering the phone or doorbell.

Although Rita viewed the binge overall with disgust, she couldn't deny there was some pleasure in it. It was the only situation in which she could eat foods that appealed to her. Under normal conditions, eating was not a source of pleasure, because she would restrict herself to unappetizing foods. For her, normal eating meant dieting—avoiding all foods that she enjoyed. She was convinced that if she regularly ate foods that she did like, she would set in motion a process that she couldn't stop. And now, indeed, her binges seemed to be bearing this theory out.

Once the binge was over, the next step, in Rita's mind, was to repair the damage. By the time she was through, she was left with feelings of both physical and psychological revulsion. Physically she would feel bloated. The blow to her self-esteem was even more pronounced. Binge eating was so inconsistent with her

Typically, binges are followed by feelings of extreme self-blame, guilt, and depression, as well as fears of gaining weight and being discovered (APA, 2013).

usual style of behavior that she wondered if she was developing some sort of split personality: the competent, striving Rita versus the irresponsible, out-of-control Rita. She was becoming concerned for her mental health.

Most important, the binge posed a severe threat to the one area of life by which she measured most of her success and worth as a human being: her weight. After a binge, she felt that if she didn't do something about it, she might see a 5-pound weight gain on the scale the next morning. During her first 2 or 3 months of binge eating, she would attempt to avoid weight gains by trying to fast for a day or two. Then she came across a documentary on YouTube featuring women with bulimia that examined purging behavior at length. The message of the documentary was to avoid this fate at all costs. However, with her binges becoming more extreme and her weight reaching an all-time high of 127 pounds, Rita saw purging as the solution to her problem: a way of eating what she wanted while avoiding undesirable consequences.

She started to purge at home several times a week. She would stand over the toilet, touch her finger to the back of her throat, and throw up as much of the binge food as she could. The first time Rita tried this, it was not so easy. Indeed, she was surprised at how hard it was to stimulate a gag reflex strong enough to bring up the food. Eventually, however, she often didn't have to use her finger at all; the food would seem to come up almost automatically as she bent over the toilet.

In the early stages of her disorder, Rita's purging felt gratifying. It typically brought an immediate sense of release, as though some terrible wrong had been set right. The bloated feeling would go away, and Rita would avoid seeing a weight gain the next day. But over the next few months, the need to purge grew and grew. Even after eating normal meals, Rita would feel fat, and she couldn't get the thought of purging out of her mind.

Beyond purging, the young woman would try additional practices to undo the effects of binge eating. For example, she tried hitting the gym to exercise each day. Before going, however, she had to follow a particular ritual in front of the mirror. She had to convince herself that she looked thin enough to appear in a gym environment. She put on her workout clothes and inspected herself in the mirror from every angle. Rita's weight was within the normal range: she was 5 feet 5 inches tall and weighed 125 pounds. Her body mass index (BMI) was 20.8, which was at the lower end of the normal range of 18.5 to 24.9. Anyone would have described her as slim. However, there were aspects of her body that caused her repeated concern. She felt that her center of gravity was too low, meaning she was heavy in her hips and thighs. If, after surveying herself in the mirror, she believed that she looked dumpy, she would abandon her plan to go to the gym. She just couldn't face going there "looking fat."

Usually, however, if Rita spent enough time in front of the mirror, she was able to convince herself that her appearance was not entirely repulsive. Sometimes to

People with bulimia nervosa often have numerous inaccurate and disturbed attitudes toward their body size and shape. Compared to individuals without an eating disorder, people with bulimia have a tendency to overestimate their body size in a laboratory setting (Delinsky, 2011; Farrell, Lee, & Shafran, 2005).

do this she had to change outfits, moving to more concealing clothing. She would spend at least 2 hours at the gym, alternating between jogging on the treadmill and baking in the sauna. Going to the gym achieved two things in her mind. It burned calories and it kept her away from food. When she returned home, usually at about 9:30 P.M., she drank a couple of cans of diet soda and tried going to bed. Unfortunately, the long workout often left her ravenous, and frequently she found herself getting up again to binge and purge.

When she was not bingeing or skipping meals, Rita would try to follow her diet plan: a breakfast of dry toast and juice, a lunch of half a sandwich of dry turkey or tuna on diet bread, and a dinner of a low-calorie frozen meal. Sometimes she would allow herself a snack of fat-free cookies or vanilla frozen yogurt. When eating in this way, she felt she was in an odd harmony with the universe. The restrictive eating gave her a sense of control, competence, and success. She felt more worthy as a human being, and more at peace.

Unfortunately, the controlled feeling could not be sustained. Eventually, she would give in to periodic binges. And after bingeing she felt compelled to begin the cycle all over again.

A Coworker's Perspective: Piecing Things Together

Even as Rita's pattern of bingeing and purging at home was increasing month after month, she was able to keep it under control at her job. She sensed that allowing the pattern to enter her work life would mark the beginning of the end of her promising career. To be sure, there had been some slips. One afternoon, for example, she ate a whole order of lasagna in the break room. The full feeling that resulted was so intolerable that Rita went to the employees' bathroom and purged. However, afterward, she felt horrified at the idea of someone observing or finding out about her purging, and she promised herself that she would try with all her might to limit the practice to home. It was not easy to do, but for the most part, she was able to keep her bingeing and purging out of the workplace.

That is not to say that Rita's problems totally escaped the notice of people at work. Coworkers were increasingly able to tell that something was amiss, and some began to piece things together. Kate, a 22-year-old server and friend, was one such individual.

Working under Rita in the restaurant for the past year, Kate had developed a cordial relationship with her manager. Although the two of them were not close friends outside of work, they had gone to an occasional movie or out to a bar together. In recent months, however, Kate noticed that Rita had become more distant and withdrawn at work, and she became concerned for her coworker's well-being. "I always knew that she wasn't the happiest person in the world and

People with bulimia nervosa are more likely than other people to be diagnosed with comorbid depressive disorders and/or anxiety disorders. Approximately 30 percent of people with bulimia struggle with a problem with substance use (particularly alcohol or stimulant use) (APA, 2013).

that she was certainly unhappy about not having any boyfriends," Kate later told another manager at the restaurant.

Of course, that was true of a lot of people, so at first I didn't give it much thought. However, after a while I started to notice a troubling pattern in Rita. She would be very cheerful and friendly—for her—when I'd first arrive for my shift around 11:30 A.M., but as the day wore on her mood would turn distant and sour. From about 3:00 onward, she would hardly talk to me or anyone else, and she often seemed to be staring into space as though she was thinking about something far away.

Not long after this started Rita stopped making plans to see me outside of work. Since we didn't get together all that often, at first it didn't seem that unusual. She was always "busy," too busy to spend time with me outside of the restaurant. A couple of times, I asked her what she was so busy with. Not that I was prying, but I was curious about what she was up to, since I really didn't think she had anything going on besides work. But when I would ask her, she would suddenly seem nervous and say something like, "Oh, just a few things I'm working on. Stuff for friends, you know."

I didn't know, but her tone made it clear to me that I shouldn't pry further. After about 2 months of this, it was apparent that she didn't want to spend any time with me outside of work. She never had any time to get together. And if I said, "Well, we really should find time to get together soon," she would brush the whole issue aside. Her moodiness at work was getting worse, too, and I wasn't the only one who noticed it. Of course, we all knew that she's not the most jovial of managers, but now she seemed totally distant and nervous at work. And she always was in a tremendous hurry to get out of the restaurant at the end of the day. I kept wondering what was going on in her personal life—what was she so desperate to get to after work—and why she wanted to shut me out of her life altogether.

Her appearance was also suffering. She seemed to be gaining some weight, nothing too alarming. But the way she carried the extra weight was a bit disturbing. Her face, especially around the eyes, seemed kind of puffy, like she wasn't getting enough sleep. Her eyes were also red. It looked as if some extreme upset or unhappiness was showing in her face. She also seemed very tired at work. I knew something was wrong, but I was afraid of asking her what was going on.

Finally, I decided that I was worried enough about her to go ahead and ask what was going wrong, regardless of what her reaction was. It seemed more important than maintaining our friendship. So I just asked one day, "Rita, I can tell that you're very upset about something. You seem like you're very unhappy and secretive all the time, and frankly you don't look very healthy. Is there something that I should know about? Or something you'd like to get off your chest? You know, I do consider you a friend, whatever you think of me, and I do care about you."

Americans spend more than $60 billion each year on weight-reduction products and services (Marketdata Enterprises Inc., 2011).

She just looked at me very coldly and said, "I don't know what you're talking about. You have some tables to bus." But her coldness led me to believe that she knew very well what I was talking about. Then I noticed that her weight, while generally on the increase, seemed to be going up and down every few days. I started to suspect that there was some kind of eating disorder going on. Of course, I'm no expert, but I had a feeling that maybe she was so depressed about something that she'd taken to binge eating or something. I knew that this was dangerous, but what could I do? She was uninterested in pursuing our friendship or in responding appreciatively to any offers of support. Eventually, her responses to me became downright nasty. So finally I decided that I had no choice but to wash my hands of the whole situation and stop trying to lend my hand. I had done what I could.

Rita in Treatment: Gaining Real Control

After 6 months of bingeing, Rita found that she was falling further and further behind. As the binges and snacking had become more regular, she gradually gained 10 pounds, ballooning, as she called it, from 123 pounds to 133 pounds. She had never been this heavy before, and she felt desperate to lose the weight. All the purging, dieting, and exercise were adding up to nothing.

Rita was also becoming increasingly worried that she might resort to more extreme measures, such as purging at work, to lose weight. Ironically, her only temporary relief from these anxieties was achieved through bingeing. But after the binge and purge were over, Rita would often find herself sobbing. Overwhelmed, she contacted a behavior therapy program for weight management at a nearby medical center. There she was directed to Dr. Francine Heston, a psychologist with expertise in the treatment of eating disorders.

During her first interview with Rita, Dr. Heston concluded that the 26-year-old woman's eating behavior and related attitudes about food and weight fit the DSM-5 criteria for a diagnosis of bulimia nervosa. First, the client had recurrent episodes of binge eating, over which she felt little or no control. Second, she engaged in inappropriate compensatory behavior in response to the binges—mainly purging and occasional fasting, but some inappropriate exercising as well. Finally, Rita's self-concept was largely influenced by her body shape and weight.

Most therapists tend to use a combination of approaches—primarily cognitive and behavioral—to treat persons with this disorder, and Dr. Heston was no exception. Her treatment program had two main components: (a) changing the patient's bingeing and compensatory behaviors; and (b) changing the patient's distorted attitudes about weight and shape and any other thinking patterns that might cause distress and hence lead to bingeing. Her techniques included educating patients about their eating disorder; helping them perform more appropriate weighing and eating behaviors; teaching them how to control binges and eliminate purges; and leading them, through cognitive therapy, to identify dysfunctional ways of thinking and to develop more accurate cognitions.

Session 1   Rita framed her problem mainly in terms of the bingeing. She stated that the binges were increasing in frequency and were causing her to gain weight. What was most upsetting, she didn't seem to have any control over the binges at this point. Her weight was inching up and she felt helpless to stop it.

Dr. Heston listened sympathetically and expressed optimism that Rita's problem could be solved. She then showed the client a diagram that depicted a model of bulimia nervosa (Figure 9-1), explaining to Rita that although bingeing was her main complaint, it was really just one element in a system of interconnected parts. That is, the bingeing was the result of such elements as unpleasant emotions, concerns about shape and weight, and strict dieting. Furthermore, in a vicious cycle, the bingeing was also helping to intensify these other parts of the system. Similarly, it was both causing and being caused by purging, another element in the system. To stop a bingeing pattern, treatment had to bring about changes in all of the system's elements. It could not focus on bingeing alone.

Dr. Heston then outlined the treatment approach. First, she explained that certain steps usually help to reduce the urge to binge. Chief among these is structuring eating in a manner that keeps physical and behavioral deprivation to a minimum. In addition, the therapist noted, it is usually helpful to develop certain measures for heading off binges should the urge arise. Finally—and this is where Dr. Heston felt

Dr. Heston's combination of cognitive and behavioral therapies for bulimia nervosa is similar to the successful approach developed by Fairburn (2008).

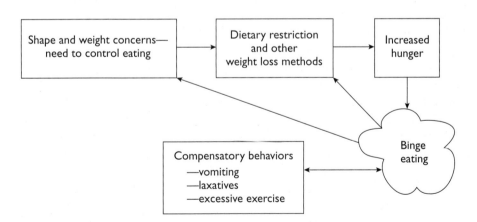

Figure **9-1**

Cognitive-behavioral theory of the maintenance of bulimia nervosa

it advisable to tread lightly initially—it is usually helpful with this kind of problem to become less preoccupied with eating and weight matters. She explained that when people have a problem with binges, it is sometimes because such matters have assumed a greater role in the person's thinking than is desirable.

The psychologist also told Rita that she would like her to start keeping track of her eating and related stresses. Dr. Heston allowed Rita to choose whichever method felt most comfortable to her: using one of the apps that she recommended, keeping detailed notes in her phone, or writing everything down on a record form which she could then scan and email to her. Rita expressed some reluctance about such record keeping. She explained that she had tried keeping records of her eating in the past and had not found it helpful. If anything, it had increased her focus on her eating. Dr. Heston acknowledged that Rita's past record keeping might not have been helpful, but suggested that it would be used more constructively now. Now the record keeping would be part of an overall strategy, and clinical experience showed that it was quite important. It would allow the therapist to understand Rita's eating better and help the young woman make appropriate changes.

Dr. Heston did acknowledge that, as Rita suspected, the record keeping might initially increase her preoccupation with her eating and weight but said that such increases would be temporary. Over time the client would become less focused on the whole problem. Rita agreed to download the recommended app and give it a try for the coming week.

Session 2 Rita's food records indicated that during the week, she had binged on 3 evenings after work. Each consisted of a cheeseburger meal followed by some cookies or cake; then, later in the evening, a pint or two of ice cream. Rita always purged afterward. During the day, her eating was severely restricted; on one of the days she was virtually fasting, consuming only no-calorie beverages (coffee, tea, diet soda) before surrendering to several large cookies in the late afternoon. On the 3 postbinge days, Rita reported skipping lunch and later having an apple and a couple of rice cakes before once again surrendering to high-calorie snacks. On days when she followed her "normal" weight-watching diet, her total calorie intake was around 800, about half the requirement for someone of Rita's weight and activity level. In contrast, on binge days, Rita was consuming 4,000 to 5,000 calories.

Dr. Heston did not discuss the specific calorie values with Rita, knowing that it can be counterproductive for patients with bulimia to monitor calories too closely. It creates a dieting mentality that the treatment is trying to discourage. Instead, the psychologist simply noted that soon they would begin the process of trying to fashion a more regular eating pattern for Rita, one that might lower some of her urges to binge.

They spent most of the session reviewing basic facts about weight and eating. Dr. Heston explained that it would be important for Rita to recognize first that her current weight of 133 was not considered excessive according to standard criteria and second that the deprivation needed to maintain the very low weight of 121, her "ideal" weight, could in fact lead to physically overpowering food cravings.

Rita said she understood that 121 was on the low side but voiced strong reservations about accepting anything higher, particularly 133, as a weight for her. Dr. Heston suggested that there was no need to decide on an appropriate body weight for Rita now, only to recognize that her assumptions about proper body weight might call for some reexamination sooner or later.

The psychologist then recommended that the client stop weighing herself more than once per week, explaining that frequent weighing was fueling Rita's preoccupation with her weight. Moreover, frequent weighing gives false feedback, as day-to-day scale fluctuations often reflect water retention or a particular state of the excretion cycle, rather than true weight gain or loss based on body fat. Rita replied that this would be a big change for her, but on the other hand, she liked the idea of not being a slave to the scale.

Dr. Heston made one additional recommendation, that Rita stop skipping lunch at work, a habit that she had developed. The therapist said she understood Rita's motivation—concern about weight gain—but explained that skipping meals ultimately produces overeating.

The weight of people with bulimia nervosa is typically within a normal to overweight range (i.e., body mass index [BMI] between 18.5 and 29.9) (APA, 2013).

Rita: I just don't see how I can do what you're proposing. If I don't skip some meals, I'll turn into a blimp. As it is, I've gained 10 pounds in the past 6 months. The only thing that is keeping me from gaining another 10 is skipping lunch now and then. Wouldn't it make more sense for you to tell me to stop bingeing?

Dr. Heston: Yes, I could tell you to stop bingeing. But bingeing is probably the thing that you have the least control over right now. Instead, it's better to focus on something that you have more control over, such as whether you eat lunch or not. I know you feel that skipping lunch is helping you to maintain your weight, but skipping meals actually produces the urge to snack or binge. Not skipping meals will eventually help you to stop overeating.

Rita: It makes me nervous to think of eating lunch every day.

Dr. Heston: I know this will take some getting used to. But let's try it out this week, and we'll review how you feel about it next time.

Rita: OK, I'll try it.

Dr. Heston closed by giving Rita three main instructions for the week: (a) continue to keep the food records, (b) weigh herself only once, and (c) eat lunch every day.

Research has found that normal subjects on very restrictive diets develop a tendency to binge. For example, after participating in a very low calorie weight loss program, 62 percent of the subjects, who had not previously been binge eaters, reported binge-eating episodes (Teich & Agras, 1993). Similar results have been found in animal studies; they appear to be related to increased stress as a result of caloric restriction (Pankevich, Teegarden, Hedin, Jensen, & Bale, 2010).

Session 3   Rita's records indicated that she had had two binge nights during the preceding week. As instructed, she had made an effort to eat a lunch every day, which for her, was still the "diet" meal: for example, half a sandwich of dry tuna on diet bread. In addition, the client had limited weighing herself to only once during the week. Dr. Heston asked how Rita felt making these changes.

Rita: To tell you the truth, it's making me very nervous. I feel I must be gaining weight. Not only am I still snacking and bingeing, but I've added regular lunches.

Dr. Heston: What does the scale say?

Rita: 132 pounds.

Dr. Heston: So your weight is basically the same. Even if it were higher, it wouldn't mean that you were necessarily gaining weight. As we've discussed, one week's weight reading doesn't tell much about the overall trend.

Rita: Well, it just feels wrong not to skip lunch occasionally.

Dr. Heston: I know how difficult this must have been, and I appreciate the effort you've made. However, you will eventually benefit from this change. I'm afraid, though, that what I'm going to ask you to do next will not be any easier. However, I think you're ready for it, and it's important that we keep moving forward.

Rita: Don't tell me you want me to start eating even more!

Dr. Heston: Yes. That's exactly it. As we discussed in the beginning, your calorie intake on your so-called normal days is too restricted and is therefore producing binges. You need to start consuming more calories in the course of your regular meals.

Rita: But how do I do it? I have no idea what else to eat. I've been eating this way for so long.

Dr. Heston: One way is to match your eating to what others eat, perhaps even take your cue from friends, coworkers, or even recipe books. Right now you seem to be having half a sandwich for lunch. As you probably know, most people eat the whole sandwich; therefore, I'd encourage you to do the same. For breakfast, most people have some cereal, fruit, or eggs in addition to toast and juice, so you could add that as well.

Rita: I guess I could try it.

Most cases of bulimia nervosa begin after a period of dieting.

Session 4   Rita reported having made the suggested meal changes, adding cereal to her breakfast and eating a whole sandwich for lunch, although complaining that eating the whole sandwich made her feel fat for the rest of the afternoon. Dr. Heston praised the client for these changes and reminded her that there was a difference between feeling fat and actually gaining body fat. The psychologist suggested that Rita relabel the feeling that she got after a regular meal as feeling full, which has nothing to do with a true weight gain.

Rita's food records during the week indicated two episodes that the client labeled as binges, each consisting of two slices of pizza and a pint of ice cream. This amount of food was less than in her past binges, yet she still described them this way because of the frame of mind she had been in at the time: She was focused only on the eating and afterward felt the usual guilt and shame. And she purged afterward. Dr. Heston observed that nevertheless, eating somewhat more during the day had seemed to promote less ravenous eating in the evening.

The psychologist now suggested a two-pronged approach, in which Rita would further normalize her meals and would also develop some strategies for eliminating binges at night. With respect to meals, Dr. Heston observed that Rita was still limiting herself to a diet frozen dinner in the evening. She suggested that instead she start to have a regular dinner: meat with rice or potatoes, plus a vegetable. It had been a while since Rita had prepared a regular dinner, and so the client was concerned that the sheer effort might force her back to the frozen meals. Thus the therapist suggested that she at least eat conventional frozen dinners, rather than the dietetic ones.

Next, Rita and Dr. Heston discussed some measures for avoiding binges, should the urge arise. First, the psychologist advised that she plan an evening activity at least 3 nights a week: a movie, a dinner out, or a moderate exercise class. Second, Rita should buy all of the food for the week in one or two shopping trips, preferably on the weekend; she should shop from a list and go to the store on a full stomach. Third, Rita should change her route home from work so as to bypass the stores in which her binge foods were usually purchased.

Finally, Dr. Heston said she thought the time was right for Rita to start refraining from purging. The client's better eating habits had already reduced the severity of her binges, and so she was better off just accepting the full caloric consequences of those binges, as opposed to purging. The psychologist emphasized that purging was actually helping to produce bingeing by making Rita feel that she could protect herself from the consequences of a binge. In other words, knowing she could purge, she was feeling freer to binge. Rejecting purging, on the other hand, would help Rita to try to control her bingeing. Dr. Heston also pointed out that if Rita retained the calories from the binge, she would be less likely to feel deprived afterward, thus reducing the need to binge later.

Rita expressed agreement with the goal of not purging, saying it made her feel disgusting. But once again she was concerned about gaining weight. Dr. Heston reminded the client that the proposed measures did not, according to experience, cause people to gain weight. That is, the increased calories that might result

Individuals with bulimia nervosa are more likely than other people to have symptoms of depression, including sadness, low self-esteem, shame, pessimism, and errors in logic (Burney & Irwin, 2000; Paxton & Diggens, 1997).

Vomiting fails to prevent the absorption of at least half the calories consumed during a binge (Garner et al., 1985; Wooley & Wooley, 1985).

occasionally from not purging would be offset over time by a reduction in over-eating. This could be verified by keeping track of Rita's weight. Rita said she would do her best not to purge.

Session 5   Rita reported that she had followed the new meal plan, eating a regular breakfast, a whole sandwich for lunch, and on most nights, a complete dinner—sometimes frozen, sometimes a meal she prepared. Snacks consisted of fruit and rice cakes. Also, as advised, the client had scheduled activities for herself on several nights.

   Still, there were two episodes that Rita described as binges: a pint of ice cream on one night and a couple of large chocolate doughnuts on another night. The quantities of these "binges" were not really extraordinary—it now appeared that her more regular meals were holding down her cravings—but Rita considered them intolerable, and she purged on both occasions.

   She said that she had decided to purge because she just felt so fat after eating those foods. Still, she asserted, "I really want to stop purging," and she asked for another chance to try during the coming week. Dr. Heston encouraged the client to try again but asked that she bring some so-called bad foods to the next session. The psychologist explained that they could do a practice exercise in which Rita would eat the foods with Dr. Heston and then practice tolerating the feeling of fullness.

Session 6   Rita reported having purged after two episodes of "overeating" at home in the evening. In one case, she purged two large chocolate chip cookies that she had bought in a gourmet shop; in another, she purged two pieces of chocolate cake. She had intended not to do any purging this week, but once she ate those foods and felt as if she had gained weight, she couldn't stand it.

   Dr. Heston asked the client whether she had brought any "bad" foods, as advised. Rita at first stated that she had forgotten, but then admitted that she had deliberately not brought the foods in the hope of avoiding the eating exercise. The psychologist, having anticipated this complication, informed Rita that she had brought some chocolate doughnuts to the session herself. The client reluctantly agreed to do the eating-without-purging exercise during the session. She said she might as well get it over with, as it appeared she could not do the exercise on her own right now.

   Dr. Heston brought out two large chocolate doughnuts and suggested that they each eat one. Rita balked, saying she hadn't expected the doughnuts to be so large, and she asked whether she could just eat half. The psychologist explained that the exercise would be of no value if Rita restricted her eating to an amount that felt safe. "I know," Rita replied, "but I'm afraid of gaining weight."

Dr. Heston then asked Rita to estimate how much weight she would gain by eating the doughnut. "I don't know; 2 pounds?" she guessed. In response, the psychologist gave Rita some facts on eating and weight gain. First, the doughnuts themselves did not weigh more than 3 ounces each; so ingesting one of them could not increase her weight by more than 3 ounces. Moreover, like all foods, some of the doughnuts' weight reflected their water content, which would be excreted eventually; most of the rest would be burned off in the natural course of events. Dr. Heston suggested they conduct an experiment in which the client would weigh herself on the office scale just prior to eating the doughnut and then immediately afterward.

Rita agreed to eat the doughnut, first weighing herself on the office scale; her weight was 132. She then ate her doughnut slowly, as if taking a bitter herb, but at the same time she admitted that she liked it. After finishing, the young woman remarked that she felt really fat and had a strong desire to purge. The psychologist suggested that she return to the scale. Rita discovered that her weight did not show any increase. Dr. Heston used the finding to make the point that feeling fat after eating and actually being fat or gaining weight are not the same. The therapist also noted that sometimes eating a large quantity of food will indeed produce a considerable weight gain immediately afterward, but most of this gain is water and will be excreted eventually. In order to get used to this, however, Rita would have to stop purging.

The behavioral technique that requires clients to confront their fears by eating taboo foods to show that eating can be harmless and even constructive is similar to the exposure and response prevention therapy used in cases of obsessive-compulsive disorder (Steinglass et al., 2012).

For the remainder of the session, Rita and Dr. Heston focused on other matters, reviewing Rita's meal plan, binge control strategies, and evening activities. All three areas seemed to be going smoothly. At the end of the session, the psychologist asked Rita how she felt about having eaten the doughnut. The client replied that she still felt fat, but not as much as before. She said it had been a long time since she had let such a feeling stand without purging afterward. Dr. Heston repeated the importance of Rita's not purging after she left the office or undertaking any other compensatory measures. The young woman indicated she thought she could comply.

Finally, the psychologist asked Rita what the prospects were of her refraining from all purging during the coming week, should she get the "fat" feeling after eating. Rita replied that she thought the prospects were better now. If she could keep this doughnut down for the rest of the night, she thought the experience would help her resist purging on future occasions.

Session 7   Rita reported that she had gone the full week without purging. There were a couple of occasions when she had been sorely tempted—once after she ate a whole pint of ice cream at night and another after eating a couple of large chocolate chip cookies. When she first selected those foods, she had in fact planned to purge afterward. However, she later willed herself not to do it, recalling her success in the therapist's office.

Dr. Heston praised Rita for this accomplishment and said she wanted to help the client lock in these gains by once again eating some "bad" foods together. Today, the psychologist explained, she had brought some large chocolate chip cookies. "I was afraid of that," Rita replied, but she was clearly more willing to conduct the exercise this week.

Once again, they ate together and Rita agreed not to purge either these cookies or any other foods in the coming week. As usual, she was to continue eating regular meals, observing the binge control strategies, and scheduling activities at night.

Sessions 8 to 11 During the next four sessions, Dr. Heston and Rita continued to eat foods that the young woman would normally have avoided—potato chips, pizza, and cake—and again Rita refrained from purging. In fact, she succeeded in not purging throughout the 3-week period, despite several occasions when she ate "bad" foods at home.

During this period, the combination of regular meals plus the lack of purging seemed to be naturally reducing the client's desire to binge. By the 11th session, she reported bingeing only occasionally, and the quantities were actually rather modest.

Also during this period, Dr. Heston had Rita add some taboo foods to her diet. By the 11th session, the client was deliberately eating such items as pizza or a sausage-and-peppers hero for lunch, chips or candy bars for afternoon snacks, and barbecued chicken for dinner.

Throughout this whole period, Rita worried about gaining weight, but the scale indicated that her weight was remaining the same—131 to 134 pounds. Still, she complained that this eating pattern made her feel fat.

> Many individuals with bulimia nervosa have severe oral and dental problems, including dental erosions, dental cavities, periodontal disease, and gum disease. Esophageal complications, some of which can be life-threatening, are fairly common (Mehler, 2011).

Rita:	I know the scale says my weight is the same. But when I eat such large meals during the day, I feel fat and bloated. My clothes are tight, I feel that people can tell I'm fat. Before, I didn't have this feeling. I miss that feeling of being in control.
Dr. Heston:	How were you in control before?
Rita:	By dieting, by following my weight watcher plan.
Dr. Heston:	But what about the binges?
Rita:	Well, except for the binges I was in control.
Dr. Heston:	I don't think you can separate one from the other. Your dieting was causing binges. Besides, the term *control* doesn't really describe what you were doing when you dieted. You weren't controlling your food, you were being controlled by a vicious cycle of dieting, bingeing, and purging.

Rita: Well, I had a feeling of control when I dieted. It made me feel good—like I was accomplishing something.

Dr. Heston: You seem to be equating control over food—or what you thought was control—with accomplishment. Does that stand up?

Rita: Well, maybe it's not the control part. I mean, I can see that the idea of controlling food is sort of dumb by itself. It doesn't make you accomplished or anything. It's more my weight that matters. Maybe I wasn't going about it in the best way, but 133 pounds is fat as far as I'm concerned, and nothing in the world is going to convince me not to lose that weight.

Dr. Heston: What's wrong with 133 pounds?

Rita: It's more than I should be weighing.

Dr. Heston: But we've seen that 133 is normal for your height.

Rita: I don't care. I *am* fat at 133.

Dr. Heston: I'd like you to consider the possibility that your thinking on this matter is really groundless. For example, what evidence do you have to support the idea that you're fat?

Rita: I feel fat.

Dr. Heston: That's just a feeling. We're trying to see if the feeling is justified. What evidence do you have?

Rita: Well, I used to weigh less—that's evidence—but I suppose you would say I used to be too thin. How about the fact that my love life is non-existent? I haven't had a date in months.

Dr. Heston: What was your love life like when you weighed 121 pounds?

Rita: Not that great either, I suppose. People don't want to go out with me because I'm so miserable more than because I'm fat.

Dr. Heston: But you still believe you're fat.

Rita: Well, I guess I'm not actually obese. I just look heavy at this weight.

As many as half of elementary school girls have tried to lose weight, and 61 percent of middle school girls are currently dieting (Hill, 2006).

This discussion seemed to shift Rita's view of her weight slightly: She moved from declaring she was fat to thinking that maybe she just looked heavy. Still, Dr. Heston felt that her client's thoughts had not yet shifted far enough. It was critical that she arrive at a more neutral view of her weight.

Thus, the psychologist asked Rita to consider all the ways in which her current behavior differed from the way she had behaved at 121 pounds. Rita noted that at her current weight she tended to: (a) wear a bulky sweater or jacket at the office, (b) check her body shape for extended periods in a full-length mirror before leaving the apartment, (c) wear concealing clothing at her gym, (d) avoid swimming, (e) spend most of her time alone in her office at work, and (f) rarely accept dates.

Dr. Heston explained that these actions were actually all serving to strengthen Rita's belief that her weight was terrible. The therapist thus suggested behavioral exercises to help Rita change such behaviors, and they agreed to devise the first set of exercises at the next session.

Sessions 12 to 15 Rita and Dr. Heston devoted the next four sessions to planning and carrying out behavioral exposure exercises and cognitive reinterpretation exercises to help eliminate Rita's fear and avoidance of various activities. In these exercises, Dr. Heston systematically guided her client to perform and reinterpret those activities that, according to the previous week's list, Rita had been avoiding or eliminating from her life.

> Research indicates that individuals with bulimia nervosa are extremely focused on weight matters and virtually define their self-worth in these terms (Fairburn et al., 2003; Fairburn, 2008).

The first exercise was for the young woman to remove her sweater at work and venture around the restaurant for a minimum of 1 hour—later 2 hours—each day. When she carried out the plan initially, Rita felt enormous anxiety. As instructed, the client recorded her negative thoughts and then tried to refute them in writing. In one instance, for example, Terry, a "slim" coworker, had seen Rita and had given her a critical look. Rita's first impression was that Terry must be thinking that she had grown fat. As part of her written exercise, Rita also considered contrary evidence—for example, that Terry had not actually said anything about her appearance. Rita then produced an alternative interpretation of her interaction with the coworker—namely, that Terry's so-called critical look could just as easily have been a meaningless glance or a reflection of some other concern.

At first, such counterarguments didn't feel very convincing to Rita. But after continued written thought exercises, coupled with the behavioral exposure, her thinking and feelings started to shift. In fact, after 2 weeks of not concealing her shape, Rita was no longer feeling self-conscious in this activity.

The client's anxiety was also reduced following repeated exposure to other activities, coupled with the thought exercise. By the 15th session, she no longer felt the need to wear concealing clothing at work or at the gym, and she was leaving her apartment with just a quick glance at the mirror. Rita had even gone swimming several times at her gym and felt pretty comfortable doing so by the fourth venture.

Rita: By doing these things over and over I'm getting used to them. I'm back to doing normal things in spite of my weight. People don't really seem to view me any differently. More likely, they simply don't care one way or the other. I guess I need to consider why I care so much.

Dr. Heston: What thoughts do you have?

Rita: I guess I've been equating my weight with some sense of worthiness, like I don't deserve anything unless I'm thin. Where do you think I got that?

Dr. Heston: I don't know, but obviously our culture promotes that concept to some extent. In any case, the important thing is to recognize that you've fallen prey to that idea and need to counteract it.

Rita: I think these exercises have helped to some extent. But I can't help feeling that being successful or worthwhile is tied to being thinner.

Dr. Heston had Rita consider arguments both for and against the belief that thinness is a sign of success. Rita concluded that being thinner might be desirable from an appearance standpoint but that it did not represent any form of merit. To further this, the psychologist had Rita carry out a new exercise. The client agreed to survey the appearance of women whom she considered attractive or successful, particularly at the gym and the swimming pool. Rita was to attend specifically to the flaws in body shape they might each possess. Such observations would help her recognize that she might have given her own flaws in body shape unfair emphasis.

Sessions 16 and 17 By the 16th session, Rita had been almost binge-free and purge-free for 8 weeks. She was continuing to eat regular meals, including formerly forbidden foods. And she had eliminated most of the behaviors that had been inspired by anxiety over her weight and shape.

By the 17th session, the client had spent 2 weeks carrying out the exercise of noticing other women's body shapes. She noted that the exercise was very different from the way she normally directed her attention to other women. Usually, she would focus on their most flattering attributes. If one had a small waist, she would focus on that; if another had toned legs, she would look at them, all the while making unfavorable comparisons with herself. With this new exercise, she was forcing herself to do the opposite, and it was quite an eye-opener. She learned, for example, that Terry, the coworker Rita had always considered the epitome of thinness, was actually quite thick in the calves and had large feet. Similarly, she noted that a woman at the pool, one Rita had consistently admired, had dimpled thighs. These observations, in combination with the ongoing behavioral exposure exercises, were helping her to see her own situation in a different light. She was starting to consider that maybe her dissatisfaction with 132 pounds was overblown. Although she still would prefer to weigh 120 to 125, she was now thinking of postponing any further weight loss; the effort might not justify the result.

Dr. Heston was very supportive, suggesting that it would be best to put the whole weight loss question on hold for at least several months. This would give Rita time to lock in her more realistic views on weight and body shape. Then the client could consider the question of weight reduction objectively.

Cognitive-behavioral treatments for bulimia nervosa produce significant improvement in 40 percent to 60 percent of clients. Differences in outcome statistics depend on when the treatment outcome is assessed and how it is defined (reduction in symptoms versus complete remission) (Mitchell et al., 2011; Poulson et al., 2014).

One follow-up study indicated that patients who received either cognitive-behavioral therapy or exposure with response prevention treatment for bulimia continued to improve over a 5-year period. By 5 years after treatment, 83 percent of individuals no longer met the criteria for bulimia nervosa, but only 36 percent had been abstinent from bulimic behaviors for the past year (McIntosh, Carter, Bulik, Frampton, & Joyce, 2011).

Sessions 18 to 22   The next five sessions were devoted to the consolidation of Rita's behavior and attitude changes and to relapse prevention. During this period, she had been instructed to stop her daily food records and behavioral exercises. In addition, the sessions were spread more and more apart, to give the client practice in functioning for longer periods without supervision. All continued to go very well, and treatment ended after the 22nd session. In the final session, Dr. Heston advised Rita to keep on the lookout for any signs of slipping into old habits: for example, skipping meals, avoiding many foods, excessive weighing, and of course purging. If she were to detect any such signs, she was to counteract them right away; if this proved too hard to do on her own, she was to contact Dr. Heston for booster sessions.

Epilogue

Six months after the final session, Rita contacted Dr. Heston. She said that she had successfully maintained her progress, although there had been one occasion, about a month after the treatment ended, when she purged. Rita said she regretted the purging immediately afterward and had been purge-free for the past 5 months. She continued to follow a regular meal plan, although she had to admit that her old dieting habits were often tempting. Her weight remained about the same throughout this period.

Her main reason for getting in touch, she told Dr. Heston, was that she was not doing well in her dating relationships: on more than a few occasions, she had driven off guys by being too critical and moody. She asked Dr. Heston for the name of a therapist who was experienced in interpersonal problems. The psychologist suggested a colleague and asked Rita to continue to keep in touch. The therapist was of course not pleased that her former client was still struggling with relationships, but she was very pleased indeed with her continued success in the realm of eating and appearance. With those problems under control, Rita's chances of addressing her interpersonal problems, or any other problems for that matter, were greatly improved.

Assessment Questions

1. What was the concern that Rita had, along with many others who have bulimia nervosa?

2. Describe Rita's eating plan, including her "good" and "bad" eating habits. Do you think her diet plan was reasonable?

3. When did Rita's eating behaviors begin to become pathological?

4. What prompted Rita to decide to purge after her binges?

5. What was Rita's nonpurging activity to lose weight?

6. According to the information provided in the text, how do individuals with bulimia generally perceive their body size compared to control subjects?

7. How did Rita's eating disorder affect her relationships with her coworkers?

8. Why did Rita finally decide to seek treatment?

9. Describe the cognitive-behavioral model of the maintenance of bulimia nervosa.

10. Dr. Heston asked Rita to keep a record of her eating behaviors. What did Dr. Heston see as advantages to this exercise, and why was Rita reluctant to participate in this assignment?

11. At what age do most cases of bulimia begin?

12. Describe at least two medical problems that may occur with continued bingeing and purging.

13. From reading about Rita, list all of the reasons you think were factored in to why she developed bulimia nervosa.

14. For clients seeking treatment for bulimia, what are the statistics regarding improvement in behaviors?

CASE 10

Alcohol Use Disorder and Marital Distress

Table 10-1

Dx Checklist

Alcohol Use Disorder

1. Individuals display a maladaptive pattern of alcohol use leading to significant impairment or distress.

2. Presence of at least 2 of the following within a 1-year period:

   (a) Alcohol is often consumed in larger amounts or for longer than intended.

   (b) Unsuccessful efforts or persistent desire or to reduce or control alcohol use.

   (c) Much time spent trying to obtain, use, or recover from the effects of alcohol.

   (d) Failure to fulfill major role obligations at work, school, or home as a result of repeated alcohol use.

   (e) Continued use of alcohol despite persistent social or interpersonal problems caused by it.

   (f) Cessation or reduction of important social, occupational, or recreational activities because of alcohol use.

   (g) Continuing to use alcohol in situations where use poses physical risks.

   (h) Continuing to use alcohol despite awareness that it is causing or worsening a physical or psychological problem.

   (i) Craving for alcohol.

   (j) Tolerance effects.

   (k) Withdrawal reactions.

(Based on APA, 2013.)

Kirk was never a moderate drinker. He began drinking in high school and right from the start consumed large amounts of alcohol. Throughout high school, he limited his drinking to weekends. He and his friends would get a case of beer and a couple of bottles of scotch or rum and then drive to a wooded parking area in the suburbs. There they would turn on the radio, open the car doors, sit out in the open, and get what Kirk described as blissfully buzzed.

Kirk generally returned home from these parties after his parents fell asleep, so they never fully appreciated the extent of his drinking. They themselves were just social drinkers, and it never occurred to them that their son's drinking might warrant attention. Moreover, Kirk and his friends never got into any trouble as a result of their drinking.

One study showed that 44.9 percent of high school students reported drinking alcohol in a given month, and 28.8 percent of high school students reported engaging in binge drinking (Miller, Naimi, Brewer, & Everett Jones, 2007).

Kirk Drinking on the Rise

In college, Kirk joined an off-campus fraternity, and he continued his high school drinking pattern, only it became more regular. Almost every Friday and Saturday night, the fraternity brothers would get together for free-flowing beer and liquor. At least a couple of other fraternity brothers equaled or exceeded Kirk's sizable capacity for alcohol, so the young man felt more and more at home with his own drinking.

Upon graduation, Kirk married Michelle, whom he had been dating since high school. Michelle herself enjoyed an occasional drink but always stopped at one, since she did not like feeling light-headed. She was aware that Kirk drank heavily, but she assumed that all college men drank as he did and she expected his pattern would change when he later took on the responsibilities of a family and a career. The pattern did later change. But rather than drinking less, Kirk began drinking more.

Soon after graduation, he obtained a good job in a prestigious telecommunications corporation. His new job afforded him an opportunity to drink almost every day, both at lunches and at parties with colleagues and clients. In addition, the young man would "reward" himself after each workday by pouring himself expensive scotch and rum at home. Within a few months of joining the work world, he was averaging 12 drinks daily. This pattern continued for the next 17 years.

In spite of his high level of drinking, Kirk received positive work evaluations and promotions throughout the 17 years. Nor did he have any legal problems due to drinking. Although he regularly drove with a blood alcohol level over the legal limit, he had not had any accidents or arrests.

Each year, American college students spend $5.5 billion on alcohol, mostly beer (Eigan, 1991).

Michelle Awareness on the Rise

What Kirk could not ultimately avoid was the toll his drinking took on his marriage. For the first several years, Michelle tolerated her husband's drinking, not recognizing it as a problem. A man with a drinking problem, to her way of thinking, was someone who couldn't hold a job, got into fights, stayed out all night in bars, or beat his wife while drunk. Kirk, however, came home every night and enjoyed a quiet dinner with her either at home or at a restaurant.

This was the pattern for the first 8 years of their marriage. During this time, Michelle worked as an office assistant. However, when she gave birth to their daughter, she quit her job to become a full-time stay-at-home mother. Four years after that, their son was born.

When their daughter entered school full-time and their son was a toddler, Michelle began to do child care at home, 5 days a week, for several preschoolers. Although it was demanding, she enjoyed the work, and the extra money helped. However, after a while, she began to feel a need for more adult contact. In addition, she began to feel the effects of Kirk's drinking, as he was unable to provide much companionship or assistance in the evenings. To compensate, Michelle began joining volunteer organizations in her community. Before long, she was going out every weeknight to attend one volunteer function or another. Kirk responded by withdrawing into his drinking even more.

Alcoholism and Marriage Don't Mix

At age 40, Kirk seemed to be the picture of success—on the surface. The father of a 9-year-old daughter and a 5-year-old son, he was vice president in charge of sales for his company, earning a high salary and regular bonuses. He supervised 20 individuals and was respected for his business acumen. He arrived at work consistently at 9:00 A.M., rarely missed an important meeting, and usually met his deadlines and sales quotas. Moreover, he was providing comfortably for his family.

At the same time, Kirk was continuing his long-term pattern of having 12 drinks a day, mostly scotch or rum, along with a few beers. He usually took his first drink of the day at lunch, when he went out to eat with colleagues or clients. To start off, the businessman would have a couple of scotches while waiting for his meal. When his food arrived, he would order a couple of beers to go with the meal. Kirk was under the impression that he was drinking no more than his lunch companions. However, he was actually doubling their consumption—not that they took special notice of his drinking. Although outgoing and gregarious at these lunches, Kirk's general behavior didn't differ much from that of the others. His heavy drinking over the years had caused him to develop a tolerance to alcohol, so his four drinks affected him no more than one or two drinks might affect someone else.

At least 2 days a week, Kirk had another work-related drinking opportunity. This was at a private club where his company entertained important clients. The club had an open bar, with waiters who took drink orders and automatically brought refills as soon as an empty glass was detected. It would be hard not to drink in such a place, Kirk once reflected. And of course he had no intention of making any such effort.

The purpose of the parties was to entertain visiting clients. The idea was to build relations with them on a personal as well as business basis. Kirk's company was looking for every edge possible, and if this meant spending several hundred dollars on a party that would help to secure accounts worth millions, it was considered well worth the investment.

Kirk was acutely aware of the pressure to be friendly, jovial, and well-liked at these parties. In fact, the parties were a trial for him. There were high expectations for him to be entertaining, and each time, he was doubtful of his ability to carry it off. The alcohol took an edge off his anxiety, loosening him up and allowing him to mix freely. It took at least three drinks for him to reach this point and at least another two to keep the feeling going for the rest of the party.

> Among individuals with alcohol use disorder, men outnumber women by at least 2 to 1 (Johnston, O'Malley, Bachman, & Schulenberg, 2011).

When the concentration of alcohol reaches 0.09 percent of the blood volume, the drinker usually crosses the line into intoxication.

Once home from work, whether on a party night or not, Kirk felt the need to unwind. One Tuesday evening was typical. He came home and had a couple of scotches before having dinner with his wife and their two children. He had planned to drink nothing more, aside from two beers with dinner, for the rest of the evening. But as usual, things went well beyond that. After dinner, Michelle had to go to a PTA meeting, and when she left, Kirk felt neglected and bored. He knew that his wife would like him to do the dishes or entertain the kids while she was gone, but looking at the pile of pots and pans in the kitchen did not inspire him. Anyway, the kids seemed perfectly satisfied watching television in the living room. He made a half-hearted effort to ask them if they wanted to play a game or listen to a story, but they barely looked up from their show.

Feeling he had done his duty, Kirk poured himself a drink and retired to the den to watch television. He sat there watching sports for the next hour and a half, pouring himself another couple of scotches along the way.

When Michelle returned, she found a quiet house with two television sets glowing—one with cartoons, the other with a basketball game—and felt her usual resentment. The dishes in the kitchen were untouched and the kids were still dressed and nowhere near ready for bed. And as usual, Kirk was drinking. Some nights, Michelle would just ignore the situation, get the kids ready for bed herself, and do the dishes. But that night she tore into her husband, telling him he was lazy, irresponsible, and self-centered. Kirk seized on the "self-centered" part and told his wife she should try applying the label to herself. She was the one who was out every night pursuing personal interests, not he. Michelle asked what point there was in staying home to watch television with a drunk. For his part, Kirk denied he was drunk, saying he had every right to have a couple of drinks to unwind. What did she care anyway, since she wasn't even home?

Then the phone rang and Michelle went to answer it. It was one of Kirk's colleagues. Michelle didn't even consider turning the phone over to her husband; she carried out her usual policy of shielding him whenever he got calls this late in the evening and this deep into his drinking. She simply told the caller that he was out visiting a friend. After hanging up, she decided just to drop the whole matter and get on with things. Why waste any more time banging her head against a wall?

Spouses and other family members often shield problem drinkers from some of the negative consequences of their drinking. The spouses may, for example, make excuses for the drinker or fulfill the drinker's social or business obligations. This is sometimes called *enabling*.

Arguments such as these left Michelle feeling increasingly unhappy with their life together. Indeed, she and Kirk now barely had any life together. In the evenings, they went their separate ways. On weekends, they—mainly Michelle—did household errands. For recreation, she would attend activities tied to her volunteer work; he would watch sports on television while drinking himself into isolation. The children would either tag along on Michelle's errands or hang around the house, receiving only limited supervision from Kirk. Over time, Michelle began to consider leaving him.

The Incident

Kirk and Michelle sat down one evening to do some paperwork for their taxes. As usual, Kirk had been drinking throughout the evening, but he was still quite alert and had no problem in sorting receipts, organizing records, and carrying out calculations. It was a 2-hour project, and the couple actually worked effectively together, chatting and even joking throughout the task. It was one of their rare periods of togetherness; how ironic, Michelle thought, that it should come over an activity like taxes. They got the whole job done that night and both went to bed in good humor.

The next morning, however, Kirk said something that floored his wife. He asked her when she wanted to get together to do the taxes. She stared at her husband in disbelief, but soon realized he was absolutely serious; he had no recollection of having completed the paperwork the night before. Michelle told Kirk that they had already done the taxes, and he didn't believe her. "How could I forget doing taxes?" he asked. At this, Michelle ran to get the evidence, the paperwork from the night before. Kirk was shaken. Michelle was right. He had done the taxes, but for the life of him he could not remember it. It was as if somebody else had done the whole thing for him.

Truly upset, Kirk decided that from then on he would have no more than a couple of beers in the evening. However, after a few days, his determination broke down and he returned to his usual pattern of drinking.

After the incident with the taxes, Michelle took to quizzing Kirk routinely about events from the day before, and it soon became clear that the tax affair was not an isolated event. There were many mornings when he could not recall details from the night before. Michelle finally persuaded her husband to seek professional help with his drinking problem. She had seen an advertisement describing a community clinic that specialized in treating alcohol use disorder and related marital problems through the use of marital therapy. Michelle called for information and then, with Kirk's agreement, arranged an appointment for them.

> Over a year, 8.5 percent of all adults in the United States exhibit a pattern of alcohol use disorder (APA, 2013).

Kirk and Michelle in Treatment A Marital Approach

While interviewing Kirk and Michelle, it became clear to Dr. Daniel Aronson, a psychologist who had been in practice for over 20 years, that Kirk had alcohol use disorder. The client had developed a tolerance to alcohol. He often drank larger amounts than he intended; he had a persistent desire for alcohol; he drank to intoxication on a daily basis and had done so for many years; he neglected household obligations because of his drinking; and he continued his drinking despite realizing that it was possibly causing memory difficulties.

Dr. Aronson used a behavioral model, the so-called SORC model, in his work with drinking problems. The acronym SORC stands for the chain of events—stimulus, organism, response, consequences—that lead to a given pattern of

> When people develop tolerance to a substance, they need increasing amounts of it to keep getting the desired effect.

behavior. In the SORC model of alcoholism, *stimulus* refers to external situations that prompt drinking, such as being at a bar, being with certain friends, or having an argument with one's spouse. *Organism* denotes events that take place within the individual, such as thoughts, emotions, or withdrawal symptoms. *Response* refers to the specific drinking behaviors prompted by stimulus events and organismic states. And *consequence* refers to the results of drinking behavior, such as the reduction of anxiety or reduction of productivity.

According to the SORC model, each instance of drinking is a response to stimulus events or organismic states, and drinking is maintained because the consequences are in some way reinforcing. Correspondingly, to eliminate excessive drinking and to help people develop more adaptive behaviors, therapists must try to change each element in the SORC chain.

Whenever a client's drinking was destroying his or her marriage, Dr. Aronson would conduct treatment within a couples therapy format, in which he would use a combination of cognitive and behavioral techniques, applying them in three stages. In the first stage, he would teach the drinker skills for reducing and eliminating excessive drinking. In the second stage, he would help the spouse to see his or her role in the partner's drinking, both as a trigger and as a consequence. In the third stage, he would offer communication and problem-solving training to help improve marital functioning. Throughout treatment, he would use the language and principles of the SORC model.

> Research suggests that including the spouse in the treatment of people who abuse alcohol increases the probability of a successful outcome (McCrady, 1990).

Session 1 After gathering a complete picture of Kirk's problems and of Kirk and Michelle's marital difficulties, Dr. Aronson explained to them the logic behind his treatment approach. Specifically, he presented the SORC model, noting that drinking can be viewed as a behavior that an individual carries out in response to certain situations or feelings, which the psychologist labeled *triggers*. Sometimes the drinking may occur out of habit; other times it may be a means of coping with the triggers themselves. For example, the drinking may be a way of coping with feelings of anxiety, loneliness, or the need to be sociable. The psychologist explained that the goal of treatment was for Kirk to develop alternative ways of responding to these triggers.

Dr. Aronson also noted that sometimes the triggers themselves should be changed. That is, certain situations, be they marital or work situations, may have some undesirable features, in addition to promoting drinking. The psychologist pointed out that although it would be important for Kirk to learn to respond to such circumstances without drinking, it might be equally important to eliminate or reduce some of the undesirable features themselves. For example, if Kirk was drinking because he was lonely, it might be helpful to see what could be done to decrease his loneliness.

At this, Michelle voiced concern that she was being blamed for Kirk's drinking. She stated that if her husband were lonely, he had only himself to blame. It was hard enough dealing with Kirk's drinking—and for her to be considered responsible was the last straw.

Dr. Aronson clarified his point, explaining that from a treatment vantage point the person with the drinking problem should be viewed as entirely responsible for his or her drinking. At the same time, the psychologist noted, it would be important for both Kirk and Michelle to examine the changes that each was willing to make to help him avoid alcohol. Under no circumstances, however, would Michelle be asked to make changes that she felt were unfair.

Next, the psychologist explained the behavioral monitoring that would be used throughout treatment. Both Michelle and Kirk would complete a monitoring record each day. Both Michelle and Kirk had smartphones, and they agreed that the easiest method to do the monitoring would be to use a self-monitoring app that would provide a daily alarm prompt to complete the form. On his app, Kirk was to record any urges to drink, the intensity of the urges (on a 1-to-7 scale), the type and amount of drinks consumed, and his marital satisfaction that day (also on a 1-to-7 scale). On her app, Michelle would record her perception of Kirk's urges to drink, the level of drinking she perceived that day, and her level of marital satisfaction.

Also, Dr. Aronson instructed Kirk to complete a trigger sheet (Figure 10-1) during this first week, both to assess his drinking in SORC terms and to help him see the triggers and consequences of his drinking. Because Kirk was so shaken by his memory lapses and concerned about his health in general, Aronson felt that

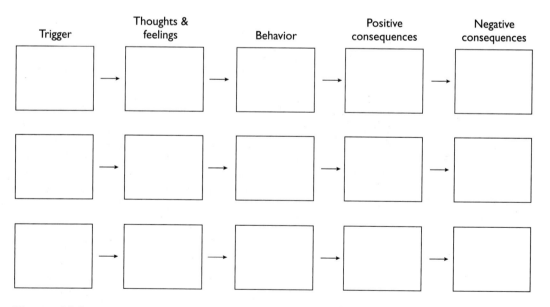

Figure **10-1**

"Triggers" sheet used by Kirk (from McCrady, 2014)

his motivation to stop drinking was strong. Nevertheless, he gave the client an additional homework assignment that involved listing both the advantages and disadvantages, as Kirk saw them, of continued drinking versus abstinence.

Session 2 Dr. Aronson, Kirk, and Michelle examined Kirk's drinking in detail, based on the records of the past week. The client's trigger sheet indicated that there were three main circumstances in which his drinking occurred: business lunches, business parties, and watching television in the evening. During the business situations, the following thoughts often occurred:

"They expect me to drink."

"I need to drink to be part of the crowd."

"I can't be upbeat enough with the clients if I don't drink."

According to the trigger sheets, his drinking in these situations had two positive consequences: the feeling that he was doing what was expected of him and the ability to be more outgoing with the clients. Although Kirk was unable to cite any negative consequences, Dr. Aronson noted one that he could see: By drinking consistently in business situations, Kirk kept himself from ever learning whether his assumptions about the need to drink were valid. Perhaps Kirk was overestimating the external pressure to drink at business functions. Dr. Aronson suggested that he test this possibility by observing the drinking of others—not just the heavy drinkers—to see if everyone was drinking as much as he.

According to the trigger sheets, two thoughts often occurred in the other major drinking situation, watching television at home when Michelle was out: "There's nothing else to do" and "I need a drink to unwind." Kirk also noted that a positive consequence of drinking at home was a feeling of comfort and relaxation, while negative consequences included his failure to do anything constructive with his time, distancing himself from his children, and upsetting Michelle.

Dr. Aronson suggested that for the coming week Kirk begin reducing his drinking in either the business or home circumstances. Kirk volunteered to reduce it at home. He agreed to try to limit his home drinking to one scotch before dinner. In fact, he stated that he felt bad about neglecting his household responsibilities, and he hoped that cutting back his drinking at home would bring him and Michelle closer together. Michelle was clearly touched by her husband's wish to improve their relationship. She volunteered to stay home every evening if this would help him in his effort. It was decided that she would still go to one monthly PTA meeting.

Dr. Aronson noted that with these changes in the home, some consideration should be given to the evening's structure. If Kirk were simply to follow his usual pattern of watching television by himself, Michelle would feel neglected and become resentful, leading him back to alcohol in short order. Thus, it was decided that Kirk would not watch any television on his own during the coming week. Instead, after dinner, the couple would do the dishes together. Then Kirk would help their daughter with her homework. After that Michelle would give the kids their baths and Kirk would read them bedtime stories. With the kids in bed, the couple would do any remaining household tasks or read or watch television together until bedtime.

Session 3   The couple reported that Kirk had successfully limited his drinking at home to the one scotch before dinner. In addition, the two of them had followed the new evening schedule. Michelle was very pleased with her husband's progress, especially with the renewed sense of togetherness that the new evening routine was producing.

At the same time, Kirk expressed some areas of concern. Although his drinking had decreased, his urges to drink remained frequent and intense, perhaps more intense than ever. Indeed, his records showed that on most days he was rating the intensity of his urges as 5 to 7 on a 7-point scale. He was worried that he would not be able to keep up the new pattern.

Dr. Aronson explained to Kirk that these intense urges were a common and predictable result of his reductions in drinking. The psychologist pointed out that when people habitually use a drug under certain circumstances, they can develop a craving for the drug whenever those circumstances arise. If the craving is not satisfied with drug intake—in this case, having a drink—then the craving will rise and may become intense. This is what Kirk was now experiencing in the evenings. On the other hand, Dr. Aronson emphasized that if Kirk continued to resist drinking, the urges would gradually weaken.

Toward the end of the session, Kirk also mentioned that he had decreased on his own the amount of drinking during business lunches. As directed, he had observed the drinking behavior of his colleagues at lunch and was surprised to see that he was drinking much more than the others. He was above all surprised to learn that one of his most respected colleagues abstained from alcohol entirely during lunch. In turn, he decided to start having only one scotch before lunch and only one beer with the meal.

Between home and the business lunches, Kirk had lowered his daily average from 12 drinks to 4. Since the change was so large, Dr. Aronson did not press for any further reductions for the coming week.

Session 4   The couple reported that things were continuing to go well with the evening routine. Kirk continued to limit himself to the one drink before dinner, and the couple was dividing up the household and child care tasks. With Michelle continuing to stay home each evening, Kirk was starting to feel that he had his wife

The DSM-5 does not have separate diagnoses of substance abuse and substance dependence. Rather, the separate criteria for abuse and dependence in the DSM-IV have been collapsed into one set of criteria for the DSM-5 (APA, 2013).

back; with Kirk remaining sober and sharing household responsibilities, Michelle was starting to feel that she had her husband back. The rewards produced by the new routine seemed to be locking in the couple's commitment.

Kirk also reported that he had reduced his drinking even more. He was now going without beer at lunch. With this reduction, he was now averaging only about two to three drinks per day.

The client expressed concern, however, about his ability to reduce the drinking further. So far, he had made no attempt to change his drinking at business-related dinners and cocktail parties, which would occur 2 to 3 days a week. He continued to have four or five drinks at each event. Reducing his drinking in these circumstances seemed like an impossible task, he said. Kirk noted that his colleagues and clients drank heavily at these functions and expected him to join them. If he didn't drink, they might perceive him as less friendly—and he might truly be less friendly without alcohol.

Dr. Aronson encouraged Kirk and Michelle to work together to develop a solution to this dilemma. He suggested that they draw on their experience in treatment so far, as well as on ways in which each had coped with other difficult situations in the past. Kirk noted that he usually favored a logical approach, breaking a problem down into specific goals and then proposing individual steps to help achieve those goals. Michelle noted the importance of emotional support from friends and family.

Thus, Kirk first identified the goal at hand: to attend his business functions without drinking, but remaining friendly. He considered that perhaps he could hold a glass of club soda in his hand throughout the evening, but he seriously doubted whether he could socialize effectively without alcohol. He just knew it wouldn't be the same.

> Alcohol plays a role in more than one-third of suicides, homicides, assaults, rapes, and accidental deaths, including 30 percent of fatal automobile accidents in the United States (Gifford, Friedman, & Majerus, 2010).

Dr. Aronson:	How do you know it wouldn't be the same?
Kirk:	I just know. I need the alcohol to get loose. There's a lot of pressure on me to be a regular guy; you know, to entertain the clients and keep them amused.
Dr. Aronson:	Did you ever go to one of these functions without drinking?
Kirk:	No.
Dr. Aronson:	Then there's no way of knowing for sure whether your sociability would suffer if you didn't drink.
Kirk:	I suppose that's true.
Dr. Aronson:	Also, you seem to be assuming that the mood you achieve through drinking is the only acceptable mood at these parties. Is it possible that you don't have to be as outgoing as you think?
Kirk:	It's very important to be outgoing.
Dr. Aronson:	Is everyone as outgoing as you?

Kirk:	No, not everyone. My boss is kind of a quiet guy. He's the relaxed, confident type.
Dr. Aronson:	Do you think that clients are put off or offended by his behavior?
Kirk:	No. In fact, I think he puts the clients at ease. I could never be that way, though. I'm just too hyper by nature.
Dr. Aronson:	Perhaps there is some middle ground between your boss's quiet style and the high-pressure style you usually display.

Kirk agreed to conduct an experiment of sorts. He would try keeping a glass of club soda in his hand and observe whether abstaining from alcohol hurt his behavior at business functions. If he did experience strong urges to drink, he would deal with them by reminding himself of the experiment.

Michelle added that in the past, she had rarely attended these business functions, as she had long since decided not to link her social life with Kirk's. However, in listening to Kirk's plans, she felt that carrying them out successfully would be a tall order for him without some support. Accordingly, she thought she should start accompanying him to these functions. Her husband welcomed this offer.

Dr. Aronson complimented them on having arrived at a strategy on their own. He made one additional recommendation: that before each party Kirk and Michelle decide the specific length of time that they would spend there. This would help keep their task more limited and manageable.

Session 5   Kirk reported that he had remained abstinent for the two business parties he and Michelle had attended this week. He said that the urge to drink had been intense at both parties, but with Michelle distracting him and reminding him of his goals, he had been able to keep on track.

Kirk noted that carrying the club soda around had relieved him of any awkwardness. Also, contrary to his expectation, he found that he was as outgoing without the alcohol as he had been with it. All this time, he had been assuming that his social skill at these parties was due to the alcohol. Now he realized that he was a good mixer whether drinking or not.

With all the reductions Kirk had made—at home, at lunch, and at these two business parties—his total intake for the week was only 10 drinks, an average of about 1.5 drinks per day. Also, his urges to drink were less frequent, although the intensity of those urges remained high. Finally, he and Michelle felt that things were continuing to go well at home, as they had developed a regular routine for sharing household responsibilities.

Based on this success, Dr. Aronson asked whether Kirk was ready to consider total abstinence. The client responded, "I don't know. It seems like too big a step." Michelle, however, pointed out that in numerical terms her husband wasn't that far from abstinence, especially considering how far he had come. Kirk said he

The self-help program Alcoholics Anonymous has more than 2 million members in 116,000 groups across the United States and 180 other countries (AA World Services, 2011).

realized it was just a matter of eliminating the remaining drink or two each day, but somehow taking that added measure seemed too extreme; he said he'd feel like he was losing his safety valve.

Michelle replied that she felt Kirk was still not facing up to the full seriousness of his drinking problem. She appreciated all the effort he had made thus far, but she thought he was kidding himself if he thought he could maintain a safety valve. What he was describing was not a safety valve but an open pit.

After some thought, Kirk said that what really bothered him was the personal statement he would be making by becoming totally abstinent, practically "branding [himself] an alcoholic." Michelle responded that he was getting too hung up on terminology. If it made things any easier, she suggested, why not view himself as having an allergy to alcohol: Alcohol simply didn't agree with him, in the same way that some people can't tolerate dairy products. In the style of Dr. Aronson, she even suggested that Kirk view abstinence as an experiment. Why didn't he just try it out? He could then find out through experience whether complete abstinence was as difficult or stigmatizing as he feared.

Her suggestion seemed to strike a chord with Kirk. Once again, viewing a new step as an experiment seemed to enable him to move forward; it no longer seemed like such a leap. Thus, he devised a plan. He was scheduled for a knee operation in the next week, which would force him to spend a week at home recuperating. This, he felt, would be an ideal time to see what it was like to stop drinking entirely.

Under Dr. Aronson's guidance, the couple worked out the details. First, they would remove all the alcohol from the house the day before the operation. In addition, Kirk would buy some spy novels to keep him entertained during his recuperation. And Michelle volunteered to cut down on her child care work that week so she could spend more time with her husband.

Dr. Aronson further recommended that Kirk treat himself to a special reward during this period, since complete abstinence would represent a major loss of gratification. The client decided to buy some new furniture that he and his wife had been wanting.

Session 6 Kirk reported that he had remained abstinent during the entire period. He found that total abstinence was less difficult than he would ever have imagined 6 weeks ago, when he started treatment. Of course, the skills that he had been learning for managing his urges and cutting down on his drinking had set the stage for this accomplishment. At the same time, he recognized that the triggers encountered during this 1-week abstinent period had been limited and that the challenges would increase when he returned to his regular routine at home and at work.

Dr. Aronson agreed. However, he repeated the principle that Kirk's urges to drink would continue to weaken—extinguish—as long as the client continued

> One of the most debated areas in the clinical field is whether persons with alcoholism must become abstinent to overcome their disorder or whether they can simply learn to keep their alcohol use under better control. Research has not settled the debate, but it suggests that controlled drinking may be a better approach for some individuals, while the abstinence model may be more effective for others.

to resist drinking in various situations. The psychologist explained that treatment from now on would follow a relapse prevention mode, meaning that Kirk must always be looking for ways to maintain abstinence. Whenever urges to drink occurred, he was to view them as signals to devise alternative ways of coping with a situation, not as signs of weakness. In addition, Dr. Aronson cautioned both Kirk and Michelle not to react with alarm if a slip occurred. They should simply view such slips as indications of a need to be more watchful under certain circumstances and to develop better coping skills.

Sessions 7 to 9   At Session 7, Kirk reported on his 1st week of normal activities as a nondrinker. As expected, his urges to drink had increased but not as much as he had anticipated. One bit of welcome relief had occurred during lunchtime, when he had his first business lunch without drinking. He had been concerned that ordering a club soda would be ridiculed by his colleagues. Instead, no one seemed to notice. The others just ordered their drinks as usual, without paying attention to Kirk. The second time that he ordered a club soda, one colleague did ask him if he had given up drinking. Kirk replied, "I've decided alcohol really doesn't agree with me." The colleague accepted this as perfectly reasonable, although to Kirk it felt like a momentous revelation.

In Sessions 8 and 9, he reported that both the frequency and intensity of his urges to drink had declined quite a bit. He was now feeling only about two distinct urges to drink per day, and these were only moderately strong. In addition, he was continuing to devise new methods of coping with urges. He found, for example, that urges to drink often arose at parties when there was a lull in the social action. Previously, he would go refill his drink under such circumstances; now, however, he was using the urge as a signal to go talk to Michelle or someone else, and he was finding that this allowed the urge to disappear. Another strategy he found helpful was avoiding excessive hunger; if he ate more evenly during the day, he was less likely to feel strong urges to drink.

Sessions 7 to 9 were also devoted to a more direct focus on Kirk and Michelle's relationship. Over the course of treatment, Dr. Aronson had concluded that the relationship was basically loving and supportive, but because of Kirk's drinking, they had little positive interaction. To help reestablish more positive feelings, the psychologist recommended that they set aside a couple of periods each week to do fun activities together, such as play a game, go for a walk, or go out to dinner. The couple agreed to do this. At first, the activities seemed forced to them, but after doing them a few times, they started to look forward to them and sought out additional opportunities to do things together.

The next exercise that Dr. Aronson proposed seemed even more artificial to the couple at first. He had them designate a specific day each week on which they would go out of their way to please each other. For example, if Kirk thought that

> About half of treated couples say they are happily married at the end of couple therapy.

Michelle would be particularly pleased by his making the bed, he was to make the bed; if Michelle thought that Kirk would be pleased by her making him a cup of coffee, she was to make the coffee. The goal of this exercise was to lead each spouse to focus more on the needs or perspective of the partner, as well as to increase the number of positive interactions between them.

Sessions 10 to 15   The final 6 weeks of treatment took three main directions: (a) cognitive therapy to help Kirk manage his negative emotions more effectively, (b) communication training to help Kirk and Michelle get better at resolving marital difficulties on their own, and (c) relapse prevention.

The rate of alcohol use disorder is three to four times greater in close relatives of individuals with alcohol use disorder (APA, 2013).

Cognitive Strategies   Periodically, Kirk would brood about failings or mistakes he believed he had made at work. For example, he might become excessively worried about a client's long delay in returning a phone call. Typically he would think that he had somehow bungled the original phone call and offended the client, and he would consider the dire consequences of losing the client. Before long he would also be worrying about losing additional clients, as well as his job and his income.

When Kirk brought up one such incident, Dr. Aronson guided him to recognizing the errors in his thinking. First, the psychologist encouraged the client to consider the evidence both for and against his negative conclusions. He also encouraged Kirk to consider alternative interpretations of the troubling event. Upon carrying out this exercise, Kirk recognized that he had done nothing deliberate that could have offended this client. He also allowed that the client might have been delayed in returning his phone call because he (the client) had been busy, sick, moody, or just plain slow. Finally, Kirk recognized that it wouldn't make much difference in the overall scheme of things even if the client were to take his business elsewhere. Cognitive reviews of similar incidents brought similar results.

Dr. Aronson also had Kirk regularly write down the irrational thoughts that he had when alone and produce alternative, more balanced interpretations of the events in question. Kirk found that this exercise suited his logical way of thinking and improved his moods.

Communication Training for Marital Difficulties   Although making good progress, Kirk and Michelle still had a few basic issues to settle. One of these was the question of the day care work Michelle was doing in their home. She had started doing this when her younger child, Danny, entered nursery school. Currently, she was taking in three or four toddlers every morning, and the work was starting to wear on her. She was constantly busy from morning to night. Even with Kirk's help, she barely had time to read the newspaper, let alone do something relaxing or enjoyable, such as visit a friend or attend an exercise class.

Kirk had become much more aware of the burden his wife was under since he had taken over more responsibilities in the evening, so the couple was able to come to a quick agreement that 2 days a week of child care should be the limit for Michelle. Certainly their budget did not require any more. However, Michelle's desire to go back to some of her volunteer activities was not so easily worked out. She said that in spite of being much happier with Kirk's companionship, she needed a periodic change of scenery and wanted to explore some more meaningful interests.

According to the Department of Labor, 47.5 percent of American married couples are now dual-earner couples.

Kirk: What do you mean, more meaningful interests? What could be more meaningful than your family?

Michelle: Well, I just need to get out. You spend 10 hours a day away from the house at your job. I need an outside interest, too.

Kirk: My job is not an "outside interest." I work that job to support us. Somebody's got to be the breadwinner around here. How far do you think we'd get on the child care you do?

Michelle: I suppose you'd have me go back to work as an office assistant.

Kirk: The money you'd make as an office assistant would be almost nothing after taxes and babysitting costs are taken out.

Michelle: Well, we're not exactly living in the lap of luxury with your job.

Kirk: So what are you saying, that I should get another job?

Dr. Aronson pointed out how far the two of them had strayed from the issue. They had begun with the question of Michelle's doing more volunteer work and had ended up questioning the suitability of Kirk's job.

The psychologist pointed out that each of them had a tendency to view any statement of dissatisfaction from the other as an attack that required a counterattack. When, for example, Michelle seemed to compare Kirk's work to having outside interests, he quickly defended his role as breadwinner and pointed out Michelle's limited earning capacity. She then viewed the debate as a contest over the amount of money each earned. This led her to propose something—going back to work as an office assistant—that neither of them really wanted.

Dr. Aronson proceeded to teach them a communication strategy that might help avoid such misunderstandings and conflicts. Before expressing their own feelings, Kirk and Michelle were to try summarizing the meaning of the other person's previous statement, allowing the partner to verify or deny the accuracy of the summary. So, the psychologist explained, when Michelle said, "You've got your job; I need an outside interest too," Kirk could first try to summarize Michelle's meaning before responding.

Kirk said, "I guess your main message is that you find it harder to be tied down to the house than I realize. You feel that my job involves certain social opportunities that I take for granted. I guess that could be true. When I was at home all week recovering from the knee operation, I was practically climbing the walls after a while."

The psychologist then asked Michelle to summarize the meaning of Kirk's statement, "I work that job to support us. Somebody's got to be the breadwinner." She replied:

Michelle: I guess you seem to feel that I'm not recognizing the importance of your job to our survival. I didn't mean to imply it's not important. I know you work hard and it's not for your entertainment. But your work also gives you meaning apart from the breadwinning aspects. I want the same meaning.

Kirk: You feel that your family is not meaningful enough?

Michelle: My family *is* the most meaningful thing. I think it is for you, too. But that doesn't mean we can't have additional interests. You like to watch sports, for example. I wouldn't ask you to stop doing that just because it's not family-related.

Kirk: I guess you're saying that nobody can have a single purpose in life. I suppose I do get satisfaction from my job, and I suppose you're looking for similar satisfaction.

The couple eventually agreed that Michelle would spend one night out a week doing volunteer work. They continued to practice summarizing each other's meaning whenever they found they were starting to argue. They also learned additional strategies, such as avoiding complaints or criticisms that the other person could do nothing about (for example, "Your mother is so annoying").

Relapse Prevention   In preparation for the end of treatment, Dr. Aronson placed special emphasis on relapse prevention. The most important task was for both Kirk and Michelle to be alert to warning signs of relapse, particularly indications that Kirk might be at risk for taking a drink. The psychologist divided the warning signs into behaviors, cognitions, and moods. An example of a behavioral sign was Kirk's taking a long business lunch; a cognitive sign was Kirk's thinking that his drinking had not been a serious problem in the past; a mood sign was Kirk's becoming increasingly anxious or depressed. For each of these warning signs, the psychologist had the couple discuss strategies for managing the situation. They also agreed to call and arrange for a therapy session if Kirk ended up actually taking a drink. In addition, Dr. Aronson scheduled four follow-up sessions: for 1 month, 3 months, 6 months, and 1 year after the final treatment session.

Finally, toward the end of treatment, the psychologist had Kirk and Michelle enroll in a group for couples who had completed the same type of therapy. This was not a treatment group but a group for couples with a history of drinking problems to meet and discuss ongoing concerns and support one another.

According to surveys, almost two-thirds of adults believe that it should be harder than it is now for married couples with young children to get a divorce (Kirn, 1997).

It was led by a couple who themselves had once had drinking problems but who had been abstinent for over 10 years and had undergone training as lay counselors.

Epilogue

By the end of 15 sessions, Kirk had not had a drink for more than 2 months, and he remained committed to abstinence. In addition, he and Michelle reported they were communicating better and working out their problems more effectively.

Dr. Aronson saw them four times over the next year. Kirk continued to be abstinent throughout the year and reported having only a few urges to drink each week. Moreover, the couple's marital satisfaction remained high. They continued to attend the couples group once a week as part of Kirk's relapse prevention strategy. Overall, life without alcohol was good. As Kirk would often say, he had put the monster back in the bottle and along the way had rediscovered his wife, his children, and the many pleasures that life could bring.

Assessment Questions

1. What are the statistics for American high school students and their consumption of alcohol?

2. When did Kirk's drinking problem develop into pattern drinking?

3. Do you think Kirk developed a tolerance for alcohol? Give a reason for your answer.

4. Why did Kirk's wife, Michelle, not think of Kirk's drinking as a problem?

5. When did Michelle begin to realize that alcoholism and marriage don't mix?

6. What prompted Michelle to realize that Kirk needed professional help with his drinking problem?

7. Describe the SORC model that Dr. Aronson decided to use with Kirk and Michelle.

8. Why did Dr. Aronson feel it was important for Michelle to participate in the therapy with Kirk?

9. Describe the five components of the triggers sheet that Kirk used.

10. What are some of the alarming statistics that result from alcohol use and abuse?

11. What are two areas under debate regarding the use of alcohol once a person has developed alcohol use disorder?

12. What are some of the activities necessary to keep a couple together during therapy, with one family member suffering from alcohol dependence?

13. For children of alcoholics, what are the statistics for developing their own alcohol dependence problems?

14. What are some of the key features for relapse prevention?

15. What was the final outcome for Kirk?

CASE 11

Sexual Dysfunction:
Erectile Disorder

Table 11-1	
	Dx Checklist
	Erectile Disorder
	1. For at least 6 months, individual finds it very difficult to obtain an erection, maintain an erection, and/or achieve past levels of erectile rigidity during sex.
	2. Individual experiences significant distress.
	(Based on APA, 2013.)

Walter, a 59-year-old married man, the financial editor of a large city newspaper, was reared on the West Coast. Throughout his childhood he always found his father, a local politician known for strong-arm tactics, distant and unapproachable. His mother, who didn't work outside of the home, in contrast was warm although a bit smothering.

Walter did not have much sexual interest during adolescence, although he did masturbate some. He was raised in a conservative small-town community where teenagers' sexual behaviors were tame by today's standards. After high school he was drafted into the army. His first sexual experience was with a prostitute at a brothel visited by soldiers on the base. He found this encounter pleasurable, if awkward, and he continued to go to the brothel a couple of times each month.

> Sexual dysfunctions are a heterogeneous group of disorders in which persons are persistently unable to respond sexually or to experience sexual pleasure (APA, 2013).

Walter and Cynthia

After serving in the army, Walter went to college and majored in economics. There he met his first wife, Lisa, whom he would later describe as a hottie and a flirt. Their relationship was based largely on sex, and after about 4 years it became all too apparent that neither of them wanted to spend the rest of their lives together. Eventually they divorced. After this marriage, Walter decided to pursue an interest in journalism, securing positions of greater and greater responsibility in the newspaper business. Because of his knowledge of economics he eventually covered financial news.

During this time, he dated around for several years and had a few short-term relationships. Then he met Cynthia; he was 35, she 28. Cynthia was different from the other women Walter had been dating, who tended to be, in his words, "more the wild and crazy type." She was demure and serious, with a career as a registered nurse in a suburban hospital. They met when she was caring for Walter's mother during a hospital stay for gallbladder surgery. After they dated for a few months, Walter proposed marriage and Cynthia accepted. Their first child, a boy, was born about 3 years later; a girl followed a couple of years after that, and 2 years later another girl.

As Walter later remembered it, he and Cynthia did not have significant sexual problems during the first 24 years of their marriage. True, when they first began having sex, he did go through a temporary period of premature (early) ejaculation, but this was typical for him in adjusting to a new partner. As with prior partners, after a few weeks this difficulty passed. Granted, Walter found Cynthia less adventuresome sexually than his earlier partners—she rarely initiated sex or attempted something new on her own—but he accepted this as part of her personality.

For her part, Cynthia had been raised in a religious Roman Catholic household consisting of her parents and five siblings. Her relations with both parents were warm and loving, though it was often hard not to get lost in the large family. Cynthia was one of the younger children, and her older siblings did a lot of the caring for her. Both parents worked in a grocery store that they owned.

Cynthia attended parochial school through high school. After graduation, she went to college and earned a bachelor's degree in nursing. Her first sexual encounter was with a medical resident she began dating in nursing school and to whom she became engaged at age 24. The engagement did not last, however, as Cynthia became increasingly dissatisfied with her fiancé's total focus on his work and his unwillingness to make any compromises for the relationship. Ultimately he chose to make a cross-country move to accept a prestigious fellowship, and Cynthia stayed behind. After that she dated a few men, without any sexual involvement until she met Walter. Cynthia did not consider sex to be a key element of their marriage or of her life for that matter. Although she enjoyed sex with Walter, she had to admit that most of the time it was not something she cared to initiate on her own.

> Approximately 20 percent to 30 percent of men aged 18 to 70 years report concern about premature ejaculation. However, the DSM-5 has a new definition of premature ejaculation based on time (i.e., ejaculation occurring within a minute of vaginal penetration). With this new definition, only 1 percent to 3 percent of men would be diagnosed with this disorder (APA, 2013).

The Unfolding of a Sexual Dysfunction

During his 59th year, Walter was under extra pressure at the newspaper where he worked because of the downsizing of the editorial staff in his department. Although he was not affected directly, some of his junior colleagues had been laid off, and Walter now had to work hours that he had not put in since he was a night reporter on the city beat. He was feeling more tired than he had in years, and he also felt some degree of job apprehension. Although told that his own job was safe, he had been in the newspaper business long enough to know the score.

On top of all that, his financial responsibilities had increased, with two children in college and a third to be entering in 2 years.

Partly because of Walter's concern about his job, Walter and Cynthia began to have sex less frequently—perhaps once a month. However, one night in February, Cynthia was decidedly in the mood, and she was uncharacteristically unwilling to take no for an answer. As she made sexual overtures, Walter tried to dissuade her, telling her he was really too preoccupied with work. However, she became extremely insistent. To help him relax, she poured him a large glass of wine, which he accepted. He still did not want to pursue things, but then he accepted a second glass, as the first did seem to ease his concerns somewhat. After drinking the second glass of wine, Walter was prepared to put his preoccupations aside and attend to Cynthia. She had completely disrobed in front of him and was now stroking him in a provocative manner. Walter was starting to get aroused.

Usually, sex with Cynthia followed a formula. They would watch the evening news in bed on Saturday night, and Walter, if feeling amorous, would turn toward Cynthia and start kissing and fondling her. If Cynthia was similarly inclined, she would respond by relaxing her limbs and returning Walter's kisses. After a few minutes of foreplay, Walter would assume the superior position and complete intercourse.

That night, however, Cynthia was acting much more aggressively. As Walter sat on the edge of their bed, she pulled down his pants and undid his shirt. She continued stimulating him both manually and orally for a few minutes. Then she lay back on the bed and urged Walter to initiate intercourse. Now he was very interested.

As Walter positioned himself to enter his wife, he found, unbelievably, that his erection was starting to go soft. Completely bewildered, he tried and tried, but could not get firm enough to proceed. All the while, Cynthia continued to urge Walter on in a manner that he found indescribably enticing. However, the more he tried, the more he became aware of the flaccid state of his penis, and the less he succeeded. Finally, Cynthia asked Walter what was wrong, and he explained the difficulty he was having. He stimulated Cynthia to orgasm manually, and they both fell asleep.

At work the next day, Walter was in a state of confusion. True, his interest in sex had not been high in recent times; but now he was consumed with why he had failed to achieve an erection with Cynthia the night before, especially as she had been so enthusiastic and sexy. He wondered whether he would be able to perform the next time and finally decided to end his suspense by initiating sex with Cynthia at the next available opportunity.

That night, their evening followed the usual routine and they headed upstairs to watch the late news. As they watched television, Cynthia gave no evidence of the desire she had displayed the night before. Just as well, Walter thought, as he

Epidemiological surveys in the past 20 years suggest that approximately 30 percent to 40 percent of men over 40 have erectile dysfunction to one degree or another (Rosen & Kupelian, 2011).

didn't need any additional pressure in what he was about to attempt. As the news concluded, he leaned over toward his wife and began stroking her in the usual fashion. She relaxed her limbs, and Walter continued fondling her. He was pleased that this encounter seemed to be following their familiar pattern, but there was nothing familiar in his thoughts. The whole time, he was keeping track of the condition of his penis and whether he seemed to be showing enough responsiveness. About 5 minutes into the encounter, he realized he was only semierect, and for the life of him he couldn't remember whether or not this was normal for him during foreplay. He decided to end his suspense by proceeding to the main event. However, as he did so, his erection only got softer, and within a minute he concluded that all efforts at penetration were hopeless. Once again, he salvaged the situation by stimulating Cynthia to orgasm manually, all the while turning over in his mind the question of why he had failed once again.

Cynthia, sensing his upset afterward, tried her best to be understanding and to take the pressure off Walter. She told him to let the issue rest for a while. Maybe he was too stressed during this period to be interested in sex, and she had been wrong to force the issue the other night. By the same token, he should avoid forcing the issue now.

But Walter could not let the issue rest. Each night in the coming week he tried initiating sex with Cynthia, always with more or less the same results. He would become semi-erect during foreplay, but at the moment of penetration he would be acutely aware of any sign of difficulty, and this very awareness seemed to deflate him further.

Finally, he took Cynthia's advice and did try to let the matter rest for a while. Curiously, he found he could get normal erections when masturbating alone. He wondered whether this meant that he and Cynthia were sexually incompatible but then dismissed the idea as absurd, noting that they had had a good marriage and sex life for over 20 years.

In the next couple of months, things became only slightly better. Walter attempted intercourse with Cynthia on the average of about once a week. On a couple of occasions he succeeded in getting hard enough to enter her, but his frantic efforts to achieve an orgasm before getting soft seemed almost to guarantee that he could not maintain the erection. Moreover, each new attempt at intercourse had become an unbearable trial. After each disappointment, Walter brooded over the experience and its implications.

Throughout this period, Cynthia tried to soothe Walter, telling him that it wasn't important and that things would get better. However, Walter could tell that she herself was beginning to wonder what was happening. Once she hinted that maybe he needed to take a vacation—or see a doctor.

What Cynthia didn't know was how much this sexual problem was beginning to carry over into the rest of her husband's life. At work Walter had become painfully

> Most cases of erectile disorder result from an interaction of biological and psychosocial factors (Wincze & Carey, 2012).

> Erectile problems account for more than 400,000 visits to physicians in the United States each year (Ackerman & Carey, 1995).

self-conscious about his predicament. He felt like a weakling, less than a normal man, and also felt certain that others, if they knew about his difficulties, would mock him or think of him as a pitiful specimen. In meetings with male colleagues, he now felt a sense of distance and inferiority that he hadn't known since his days as a college intern, when he was awed to be in the presence of the gruff, competitive newspaper types. He felt like a fraud who didn't belong with the grownups.

After 6 months of disappointing results, Walter decided to seek medical assistance. As it happened, the television and Internet were being flooded at the time with a persuasive advertising campaign promoting "new, effective treatments for erectile dysfunction." He soon found his way to a physician who specialized in this sexual dysfunction.

The physician interviewed Walter about his difficulty and inquired about his medical and sexual history. He also gave Walter a standard physical exam and conducted some tests to assess the possible roles of neurological, endocrine, and vascular dysfunction, all of which are known physical factors in erectile difficulties.

The physician could find nothing physical to account for Walter's difficulty, although he noted that an undetectable physical component could never be ruled out completely. He outlined for Walter three main medical treatment options. One, a *penile implant* was considered by the physician to be a far too radical solution in Walter's case. The second was a *vacuum pump,* a device that draws blood mechanically into the penis, producing an erection; the erection is then maintained by the use of constricting rubber bands placed at the base of the penis. The third option was medication, specifically sildenafil (Viagra). Walter had certainly heard of this drug. Who in this society hadn't? The physician explained that a pill of Viagra increases blood flow to the penis within 1 hour of taking it, enabling a man to attain an erection during sexual activity. Given that Walter had no signs of coronary heart disease, the physician recommended this approach as a simple and safe way to solve his difficulties.

> Physicians wrote 120,000 prescriptions for Viagra during its first month on the market in 1998, making it the fastest-selling new prescription drug in history (Adler, 1998).

At the same time, the doctor suggested that Walter might want to consider psychological therapy. After all, the patient was able to achieve satisfactory erections with masturbation, which would suggest there was a situational component to his problem. Psychological treatment might assist him in expanding this existing capability to sexual situations with his wife.

Walter said he would have to think about it. He was very tempted by the Viagra option. It seemed so simple and was likely to bring immediate improvement. On the other hand, he was hoping to avoid an artificial solution. He didn't want to take pills for the rest of his life to have sex. He later explained the various options to Cynthia. After a few days, they both decided that it was preferable to start with the psychological therapy. The next day, Walter called Dr. Sandra Rostow, a psychologist who had been recommended by the physician, and made an appointment for himself and his wife.

A Spouse's Perspective "Concerned Yet Kind of Relieved"

When Walter first told Cynthia that he had consulted a physician for his problem, she felt a strange combination of concern and relief. Concern because the doctor visit confirmed that her husband's problem was real and in need of solution rather than a difficulty that would pass on its own. Relief because in one sweep the news of the visit had put to rest a whole slew of suspicions and worries that had been building within her for months. Later that week, Cynthia called her older sister and unburdened herself:

At first I thought he was having an affair: It was the lowest I've ever felt in my entire life. "You're such an idiot," I would say to myself, "you should have seen it coming." He was always such a sex fiend. Well, maybe not a fiend but he was certainly always interested in sex. I loved him, but I could never keep up with him. And he always seemed to want more. So I thought that he'd eventually gotten tired of me.

I thought, "What am I doing wrong?" I tried to be sexier for him, but more often than not it seemed to backfire. I kept picturing him with some 20-year-old fact checker or intern or secretary. I imagined the things they might do together, all the things he's tried to get me to do—things I would never do. I came to hate this perfect blond girl he was sleeping with—this girl who didn't exist.

I dressed up for him. I tried to say the things I thought he wanted me to say. But he just couldn't be excited about me. I would figure that he must be thinking about her. But then he would seem so genuinely upset when he couldn't have sex with me. He would get so upset about it, I couldn't be mad at him. I wanted to believe that he really had a problem, that he loved and wanted me but just had a problem. Much of the time, I did believe that. And of course I was concerned about him. So I told him to not worry about it.

Meanwhile, I myself had trouble thinking about anything else. I started going back to the gym, which I hadn't done in a few years. I bought a few new outfits, not that he noticed. But he just kept on being unable to perform. Other woman or no other woman, I kept thinking that I was just a failure, that my own husband would never desire me sexually again, that I was ugly and boring. I started to dread lying in bed at night, because he would so bravely start to be physical with me, and then he would try so hard, but he would lose his arousal and I would know that my husband wasn't being satisfied.

It was so hard to face the idea that I was disappointing him or that he had found someone else who was more exciting, but I didn't let him know how upset I was. I also missed the feeling of being close to him, of having him make love to me. I really—and I know this will sound crazy—I really thought I was going to lose Walter. I tried to be as reassuring and understanding as I could, and all the while I was a wreck inside. I told him everything was fine and that it was normal, when I knew in my heart that everything wasn't fine, that something was dreadfully

Despite 80 percent of men and women anonymously reporting that they would like sex to last more than 30 minutes, a survey of sex therapists and researchers indicates that intercourse that lasts between 3 and 13 minutes is considered normal (Corty & Guardiani, 2008).

wrong. I told him that maybe all he needed was a little rest, maybe a vacation, maybe a doctor even.

And then Monday Walter told me that he *had* gone to see a doctor. And I saw how scared he looked and I knew in an instant that there had never been another woman, that it had been ridiculous to even think such a thing. I felt relieved, but more than that I felt stupid. Stupid for being so jealous. Stupid for not knowing my husband. And stupid for not fully recognizing the fear and pain he must have been going through. Hopefully, this therapist—her name is Dr. Rostow—will make a difference. To be sure, it's better than doing nothing or, worse, imagining things that aren't true.

Walter and Cynthia in Sex Therapy Giving and Receiving Pleasure

Dr. Rostow spent two sessions obtaining background information from Walter and Cynthia. In the first session, she interviewed them together. In the second session, a week later, she met with Walter and Cynthia separately for about half an hour each.

By the close of these sessions, Dr. Rostow had determined that Walter's sexual difficulty fit the DSM-5 criteria for erectile disorder, a type of sexual dysfunction. That is, his difficulty had two key features: (a) a recurrent inability to attain or maintain an adequate erection until completion of sexual activity or decreased erectile rigidity that interfered with sexual activity and (b) significant distress or impairment over that inability.

Studies on erectile disorder had convinced Dr. Rostow that in many cases psychological factors help produce the problem. Initially the man may have an instance of erectile failure due to stress, fatigue, mild physical impairment, alcohol intake, discomfort with his partner, or another such reason. Once such a failure occurs, he places extra demands on himself to perform in a productive manner. Given the recent failure, however, such demands tend to provoke negative expectancies for the man. He may, for example, anticipate failure, disappointment, or ridicule. With such negative expectancies going through his mind, he focuses intensely on his performance during the sex act, searching for indications that he is not functioning adequately. This extra focus in turn produces an actual or perceived decrement in erection. The continued concern and focus on performance eventually lead to an actual decrement in erection, and the man becomes even more acutely focused on his performance. The cycle continues until the erection is lost entirely.

As a result of this episode of failure, the individual is primed for a similar result in the next encounter. Each encounter sets the stage for the next, causing negative expectancies, performance scrutiny, and erectile failure to become further

A revolution in the treatment of sexual dysfunctions occurred in 1970 with the publication of William Masters and Virginia Johnson's book *Human Sexual Inadequacy.* The combination of cognitive, behavioral, couple, and family interventions that they used to treat sexual dysfunctions is the foundation for today's sex therapy programs.

People with performance anxiety during a sexual encounter worry that they will fail to perform adequately. In turn, they take a spectator role during the encounter; that is, they keep observing how they are performing, rather than relaxing and enjoying the sensations of sexual pleasure.

and further entrenched. Dr. Rostow believed that this psychological process must be reversed if an erectile problem was to be overcome. Sex therapy as she conducted it included a combination of cognitive and behavioral techniques, all of which were intended to accomplish a fundamental goal: shift the man's focus from his performance to the sex act itself. As part of therapy, the psychologist also sought to reeducate clients about sexual matters and debunk any maladaptive attitudes about sex that they might have.

Sessions 1 and 2　The first two sessions were spent gathering both current and background information from Walter and Cynthia. Toward the end of the second session, Dr. Rostow explained the treatment plan to the couple. In practical terms, Walter and Cynthia would undertake certain exercises that would minimize performance anxiety in sexual situations. At first the exercises would involve various types of massage and sexual touching, but later they would progress to more explicit sexual activities.

In the meantime, it was important, the sex therapist explained, that Walter and Cynthia refrain from any "unauthorized" sexual activity. In fact, for the present, sexual contact should be limited to the specific exercises designed to further the treatment process. Both Walter and Cynthia expressed a sense of relief. As matters now stood, all attempts at sexual relations had become a trial for them; indeed, the sense of obligation to keep trying to have sex, combined with the disappointing results, was turning into an unbearable burden. With Dr. Rostow's recommendation that they stop making these attempts, that responsibility was off their shoulders. Walter particularly seemed to welcome the idea of simply following instructions, especially as, from the sound of it, the types of things the psychologist would require of him were far less demanding than what he was requiring of himself.

Dr. Rostow then explained what would be required of Walter and Cynthia during the coming week. They would perform an exercise called sensate focus, in which the goal was to engage in pleasurable touching and caressing while undressed but to avoid any genital touching. The point of the exercise, the therapist explained, was for them to recapture a state of physical intimacy without any sense of demand. When conducting the exercise, they were just to immerse themselves in the sensations each received during the caresses and also to note the pleasure they were giving while administering caresses. Dr. Rostow emailed Walter and Cynthia each a copy of written guidelines, including a suggested sequence of body areas to caress, as well as some pictorial supplements. The therapist recommended that the couple perform the exercise at least three times in the coming week.

> Sensate focus exercises are sometimes called nondemand pleasuring, or petting exercises.

Session 3　Walter and Cynthia reported that as instructed, they had refrained from sexual activity. In addition, they had carried out the sensate focus exercise three times. Cynthia volunteered that she found the exercises enjoyable. Walter echoed this but also observed that he had been tense during the first exercise, as it reminded him of his deficiencies. By the later two exercises, he had set aside his concerns and was giving himself up to the process; then he also found the exercises enjoyable.

Dr. Rostow explained the next exercise, which involved a procedure similar to the sensate focus but with the inclusion of genital touching. Cynthia and Walter were to take turns caressing one another as before but now were to include caressing each other's genitals as part of the sequence. The therapist noted that the inclusion of genital touching should not distract Cynthia and Walter from the goal of the exercise, which was the same as before: just to enjoy the sensations.

The psychologist, as before, sent Walter and Cynthia written guidelines for suggested approaches. For example, for Cynthia, part of the guidelines was as follows:

> Do as much of the general body caressing as you like initially. Then play with his penis. Play with the tip and the shaft and the testicles for a while. Then go to another part of his body. One that he likes. Caress his belly or his ears or his thighs, for example. Then go back to his penis. Use your fingers or lips as you and he please. (adapted from Kaplan, 1987, p. 46)

For Walter, the written guidelines included the following:

> Play with her whole body first. Then when you feel she is ready, or when she tells you, play with her breasts. Gently kiss and massage the nipples. Play with the pubic hair around her clitoris. Play around the vagina. Do not put your finger all the way into the vagina. Touch the clitoris lightly. Go somewhere else. Go back to the clitoris. Be as gentle and sensitive as you can. (adapted from Kaplan, 1987, p. 49)

Dr. Rostow emphasized once again that just as with the sensate focus exercise, the idea was simply to enjoy the sensations, no more and no less. Walter and Cynthia said smilingly that they would "do their duty."

Session 4   Walter and Cynthia seemed upset when they returned. Walter told Dr. Rostow that they had tried the new exercises, but they weren't working. The therapist asked Walter for details, and the client indicated that they had conducted the exercises as instructed—including genital caressing—but that Walter had failed to get an erection. "What was wrong?" he wanted to know.

Dr. Rostow explained that there was nothing at all wrong. She had urged Walter in the previous session not to focus on getting an erection. However, as often happens, these words can lose their meaning once a man is introduced to the sexual situation. The sex therapist went on to acknowledge that Walter's situation in treatment was somewhat contradictory: He was being asked to avoid observing his erection during exercises, yet the whole point of the overall treatment was to promote erections.

Dr. Rostow advised repeating the same exercises for the coming week, emphasizing that the question of erections should be set aside entirely. She recommended that Walter and Cynthia just focus on giving and receiving pleasure, the same as they did with the nonsexual caresses. She also suggested that closing their eyes while receiving pleasure might help to keep it a purely touching experience. The therapist further suggested to Walter that if he found he could not rid himself of the erection preoccupation, he should think of his goal as deliberately trying to avoid getting an erection during the exercise.

Session 5 Cynthia and Walter returned in good spirits. Once again they reported a failure of sorts, only in this case, it was Walter's failure to avoid an erection during the genital caressing exercise. Apparently, Dr. Rostow's paradoxical instruction had its effect. Walter found that the strategy of deliberately trying to avoid an erection allowed him to refocus his attention on the sensations of touching. By the second exercise, when adopting the same strategy, he found that he could not avoid the erection. During the third exercise, he was erect most of the time.

Clearly pleased with these results, Walter said he was ready to go for broke, meaning skip the intervening stages and proceed directly to intercourse. The sex therapist did not want to dampen Walter's enthusiasm or rob him of his newfound sense of capability; but on other the other hand, she knew from experience that jumping prematurely to later stages can be a problem if the results prove disappointing, as the patient's anxieties will then resurface. She explained, "I understand your desire to move things along. It's very possible that you and Cynthia could go ahead and have intercourse, and it would work out fine, but I'd prefer to stick to the original game plan. We only have a few weeks longer at the current rate, and jumping ahead, in case it doesn't work out, can sometimes make things take longer overall."

Dr. Rostow then explained the next step in the sequence. In the coming week, Walter and Cynthia would perform an exercise similar to the one they were already conducting, but one that would now include genital-to-genital contact. Specifically, first Walter would give Cynthia the full body and genital caresses, and then Cynthia was to do the same for Walter. This time, however, part of Cynthia's task would include sitting astride Walter as he lay on his back and stimulating his penis by rubbing it against the exterior of her vagina. During this exercise, Walter was to remain completely passive, as before, just thinking of himself as receiving a massage, paying no attention to whether he got an erection or not. As before, the goal was simply to immerse himself in the sensations, and if trying to avoid getting an erection assisted him in this endeavor, he could use that device, too. The therapist emphasized that this exercise really differed from the previous week's only in that

Erectile disorder is highly age-dependent. The prevalence rises from approximately 2 percent for men aged 40 to 49, 6 percent for men aged 50 to 59, 17 percent for men aged 60 to 69, and 39 percent for men aged 70 and older (Inman et al., 2009).

Erectile dysfunction has been projected to continue to increase because the population is aging and is likely to have high rates of coronary heart disease, diabetes, and hypertension (Dhir, Lin, Canfield, & Wang, 2011).

Cynthia would be using her genitals in addition to her hands. Cynthia and Walter agreed to conduct the exercise at least three times in the coming week.

Session 6   Cynthia and Walter reported that they had carried out the pre-scribed exercise 4 times. The first time, Walter found that he became tense when Cynthia performed the genital-to-genital contact, and this seemed to prevent the involuntary erection that he had been getting from Cynthia's manual caresses. The second time that they tried the exercise, however, Walter felt more relaxed, and Cynthia's stimulating his penis with the exterior of her vagina did not evoke anxi-ety, nor did it prevent an erection. The third and fourth exercises similarly brought positive results. After each exercise, Walter and Cynthia stimulated one another manually to orgasm, which was now permitted under the guidelines.

Dr. Rostow:	You two have been doing wonderfully with the exercises so far. The next step is only slightly different, in physical terms, from what you have been doing up to this point. Technically, it is sometimes called vaginal containment. It means that you essentially do the same exer-cise as before, but now Cynthia is using the inside of her vagina to stimulate Walter's penis, instead of just the outside. Once again, she sits astride, and she is in charge of the stimulation. She controls the insertion, and moves her body just a little bit—without Walter thrusting on his own—to maintain the stimulation. After a few min-utes she then withdraws your penis and resumes manual stimulation.
Walter:	(pause) Well, I guess we've finally made it to the real thing.
Dr. Rostow:	Meaning?
Walter:	You know. We're finally doing it. I just hope it goes okay.
Dr. Rostow:	Okay in what sense?
Walter:	I mean, I hope I can keep the erection. I guess this will be the real test of all that we've been doing.
Dr. Roslow:	I understand your feeling. It's often hard not to look at this as a test of sorts, but in my view, it is no such thing. I'm looking at it as sim-ply the next step in a progression. It's best if you can adopt the same frame of mind that you did with the other exercises. In other words, the idea is not to see if you are maintaining your erection but once again simply to immerse yourself in the sensations. The exercises should be considered a success if you can maintain that focus.
Walter:	I see what you mean. I guess I'm just anxious to get this over with, but I'll do my best.

After this exchange, the sex therapist was not entirely confident about Walter's ability to approach the exercises in the proper frame of mind. However, there was little else to be said, and she felt it best just to wait and see how Walter fared.

Common sexual myths: (a) A man is always inter-ested in and ready for sex. (b) Sex is centered on a hard penis. (c) Sex equals intercourse.

Session 7   Unfortunately, the intervening week had borne out Dr. Rostow's concerns. Walter and Cynthia reported that they had abandoned the exercises out of frustration. They explained that they had begun the exercise as before, but that soon after Cynthia inserted Walter's erect penis into her vagina, he started to grow soft; he then tried thrusting on his own to revive the erection, but to no avail. They then stopped the exercise. After experiencing a similar failure when trying the exercise the next day, they again stopped and did not attempt any more exercises for the remainder of the week. Once again, they were very upset, particularly Walter. He was wondering if this was a sign that his problem would not respond to treatment after all. The therapist felt it important to normalize Walter and Cynthia's experience.

Dr. Rostow:	What you experienced is very common at this stage of the treatment, and you shouldn't place too much importance on it. It's difficult not to think of the moment of insertion as a momentous event and to avoid examining how you're reacting, but that's what happened this time. As a result, your ability to immerse yourself in the sensations was probably undermined, your erection was reduced, and you became overly discouraged, causing you to end the exercise prematurely.
Cynthia:	What should we have done?
Dr. Rostow:	In general, it's best to follow the exercise to its conclusion, regardless of what happens. As you may recall, I recommended that you resume manual caressing of Walter's penis after vaginal insertion ended. In this case, even though the vaginal insertion ended sooner than expected—because Walter became too soft to remain inside—you still could have resumed the manual caressing.
Cynthia:	That's what I wanted to do, but Walter was so discouraged. The idea just seemed to annoy him.
Walter:	Yes. I guess it wasn't the best reaction on my part. But as soon as I realized my erection was going down and I couldn't stay inside, I lost all interest in continuing.

> If a man is able to have an erection in certain circumstances—for example, when masturbating or with certain partners or when asleep—then it is generally concluded that psychological factors are at least partially responsible for his erectile disorder.

The therapist felt that Walter might benefit by increasing his psychological tolerance for the loss of an erection. The experience was becoming far too loaded for him, and unless he could get used to the idea that erections can come and go and then come back again, he would remain overly attentive to any decline in performance.

Dr. Rostow:	In the past, before this whole problem developed, how did you handle it when your erection went down during sex?
Walter:	I never had an erection go down before.

Cynthia:	(*Interrupting*) Actually, I beg to differ.
Walter:	What? What do you mean?
Cynthia:	Well, I don't think you ever paid much attention to it before, but there have been plenty of times during foreplay when we've been taking turns on each other that you've gone soft for a time. I just stroked you for a little while, and you'd come back.
Walter:	Really?
Cynthia:	Yes. It happened all the time. You just never seemed to notice or care about it, so it never became a problem.
Dr. Rostow:	I think Cynthia has just made an important observation. It sounds like the critical aspect is not whether you lose an erection but how you interpret it once it happens. I gather in the past you never gave it any thought, so its very occurrence didn't trigger any alarms. I think it would be useful to do some exercises to promote that mind-set again.

The therapist explained a new set of exercises that she wanted the couple to try for the coming week. They would return to the earlier exercise, involving manual caressing and genital stroking. This time, however, there would be a new feature. During the time that Cynthia was stroking Walter, if he was to achieve an erection, she was to stop stroking for a while, in a deliberate attempt to have him lose the erection. Then after Walter lost the erection, he was to focus on stroking and caressing Cynthia for while; after that, Cynthia would resume stroking Walter. Walter's guideline, as usual, was to immerse himself in the sensations, giving no mind to the question of whether he got an erection at any given stage. The point of the exercise was for Walter to learn to tolerate the loss of an erection and not see it as a signal to end the sexual episode, but rather as a typical part of the experience.

> The sex therapy technique in which a man's partner stops caressing him whenever he gets an erection and does not resume caressing until the man loses the erection is sometimes called the tease technique.

Session 8   The couple returned in a happy mood. They reported carrying out the exercise to the letter. During each of four attempts at the exercise, Walter deliberately allowed himself to lose his erection after Cynthia stopped stroking him; he then turned his attention to caressing and stroking Cynthia. After that she returned to stroking him, and he found that his erection could gradually be regained. The exercise seemed to energize him. By the fourth exercise, he had developed a complete confidence in his ability to regain the erection and in fact he and Cynthia decided to resume the previous week's vaginal containment procedure. As before, Walter began to go a little soft soon after insertion. He then withdrew and took his turn at caressing Cynthia. After that, Cynthia returned to stroking Walter and, with his erection revived, she once again tried vaginal containment. This time, his erection remained hard as Cynthia continued moving on top of him. He ended up ejaculating inside her vagina. The following day, Cynthia and Walter repeated this activity with similar results. And the next day they had regular intercourse without any difficulty.

The experiences were empowering. Now Walter and Cynthia wanted to resume normal free-form intercourse. Feeling that the couple was ready, the therapist agreed to this plan. She requested, however, that Cynthia and Walter stick to a few basic guidelines: (a) Intercourse should never be initiated as a test of sexual performance adequacy, but only out of a genuine desire for lovemaking. (b) If Walter should lose an erection during lovemaking, he should not stop but switch to an alternative lovemaking activity, for example manual stimulation instead of intercourse. (c) After switching to an alternative activity under such circumstances, intercourse could be started again, if desired, but only when a sense of comfort was restored. (d) If comfort was not restored, remain with alternative activities to complete the lovemaking.

Sessions 9 to 11   Walter and Cynthia reported making love twice in the previous week. Walter had pressed for a third encounter, but Cynthia resisted, sensing that Walter was doing it mainly to test his responsiveness. On the two lovemaking occasions, Walter was able to complete intercourse both times, although the second time he appeared to become soft as he was trying to penetrate. In this case, switching back to foreplay for a while restored his comfort level, and in turn his erection, for another penetration.

At the 10th and 11th sessions, held 2 weeks apart, Walter and Cynthia reported similar experiences: They completed intercourse four times, although there was one instance when Walter did not attempt penetration again after first losing his erection, because, as he put it, "the desire did not return." On the whole, however, the couple felt that their sex life had been restored to a very satisfactory level and that by observing the guidelines, Walter could avoid the type of performance anxiety that had been hurting him previously. They wanted to discontinue their visits to the sex therapist and just go it alone for the time being.

Dr. Rostow agreed to the plan, with the strong suggestion that they call her if any difficulties arose and that either way Walter was to text her in a month's time to provide an update on how they are doing.

> Any physical problem that reduces blood flow into the penis can contribute to erectile difficulties. Common biological causes of such difficulties are vascular problems (problems with the body's blood vessels), nervous system damage (resulting from such conditions as diabetes, spinal cord injuries, or kidney failure), the use of certain medications, and various forms of substance abuse (including cigarette smoking and alcohol abuse).

Epilogue

A text a month later confirmed that Walter and Cynthia had maintained their progress. They were making love about twice a week and were completing intercourse almost every time. As before, there had been one occasion when

Walter's erection softened too much for penetration, and switching to an alternative lovemaking activity had created a satisfactory ending to the sexual encounter. The key point, they noted, was that Walter did not get anxious or upset by the experience, so it had no carryover to the next encounter. Overall, they were both back in the pleasure business, as Walter described their progress.

About 10 months after this conversation, Walter left a message for Dr. Rostow to say that he was planning to visit his physician because his problems in maintaining erections had become more pronounced in recent weeks. He was choosing a medical route because there didn't seem to be any anxiety component to his problem and also because he had noticed that maintaining an erection, even when masturbating, was proving difficult on occasion.

Walter's physician reevaluated him with a complete battery of medical tests. They revealed that he had a mild venous leakage, which could account for his recent difficulty in maintaining erections. In this condition, which often occurs with age, blood flow to the penis is sufficient to produce an erection initially, but some of the blood then leaks out of the vessels and the erection softens. The physician noted that Walter could continue dealing with the problem as he had been doing—that is, engaging in manual and oral stimulation with Cynthia rather than intercourse during some sexual encounters—or he could try one of the available medical remedies. Given that Walter was still in excellent health, the physician recommended the use of Viagra on occasion, as a kind of boost or insurance. This time Walter agreed to Viagra.

Over the following months, both Walter and Cynthia were very pleased with the medication. It almost always helped Walter to achieve an erection that was satisfactory for intercourse. At the same time, Walter noted that he did not need the drug at least half of the time, and he preferred to do without it whenever possible. Overall, he felt that the combination of psychological and medical methods offered a perfectly fine solution for his periodic problem. Cynthia and he were once again back in the "pleasure business."

> Viagra was discovered by accident. Testing it as a possible heart medication, researchers found that the drug increased blood flow to subjects' penis more effectively than to their hearts.

Assessment Questions

1. Define sexual dysfunctions.

2. What contributed to the onset of Walter's sexual dysfunction?

3. What factors may have led to Walter's difficulty in completing sexual intercourse with Cynthia?

4. What percentage of men have erectile disorder at least some of the time?

5. What may be some physical causes of erectile dysfunctions?

6. Why did Walter initially decide that psychological therapy was a better option than Viagra?

7. What were Cynthia's concerns regarding her husband's sexual dysfunction?

8. What type of therapies did Masters and Johnson use in treating sexual dysfunctions?

9. What are the two key features from the DSM-5 criteria for erectile disorder?

10. Why did Dr. Rostow want Walter and Cynthia to abstain from sexual intercourse at the onset of therapy?

11. Describe the purpose of sensate focus.

12. What are the factors that determine whether an erectile disorder is physical or psychological?

13. What were the basic guidelines requested by Dr. Rostow once Cynthia and Walter were able to resume successful sexual intercourse?

14. Why did Walter eventually begin occasional use of Viagra?

CASE 12

Gender Dysphoria

Contributed by Brooke L. Whisenhunt, Ph.D.
Missouri State University

Table 12-1

The DSM-5 changed the name of this diagnosis from gender identity disorder to gender dysphoria to focus on the dysphoria (or distress) rather than the identity of the individual (APA, 2013).

Dx Checklist

Gender Dysphoria in Adolescents and Adults

1. For 6 months or more, individual's gender-related feelings and/or behaviors are contrary to those of his or her assigned gender, as indicated by 2 or more of the following symptoms: • Gender-related feelings and/or behaviors clearly contradict individual's primary or secondary sex characteristics • Powerful wish to eliminate one's sex characteristics • Yearning for the sex characteristics of other gender • Powerful wish to be a member of other gender • Yearning to be treated as a member of the other gender • Firm belief that one's feelings and reactions are those that characterize other gender.

2. Individual experiences significant distress or impairment.

(Based on APA, 2013.)

Renee A Lonely Childhood

Renee, age 29, was born in a small town in rural Mississippi. She had a single mother, Cheryl, who worked multiple jobs as a waitress, cashier, and housekeeper to be able to afford the rent on a small, poorly maintained two-bedroom house. Renee was one of three children in the household, with an older brother and younger half-sister. Her father was rarely around during her childhood. Her parents divorced when she was 2 years old and although her father saw Renee and her older brother, Robert, on occasional weekends for a few years, he moved away from their hometown when Renee was 5 and his contact with her became less and less frequent.

Renee attended a small school with only a few hundred students from kindergarten through high school. This meant that everyone in school knew just about everything about everyone else—including how much money their parents made and whether their family attended church and where. Renee was clearly from a family that was not among the upper tier of the community. Her mother's unskilled, low-paid employment and her parents' divorce put Renee and her siblings firmly into a lower-class category among their peers. These differences did not affect her treatment at school in the early years, but by the end of elementary school, she was clearly treated differently from the kids with families who had higher status in town. One of her favorite playmates for several years in elementary school was Thomas, the son of a local banker. From kindergarten through second grade, they spent time playing together every day on the playground. They enjoyed the same sports and their personalities were similar—competitive, but kind, and somewhat introverted. When third grade started, Renee was excited to greet Thomas on the first day of school. However, Thomas barely made eye contact with her and quickly ran off with other boys on the playground. He continued to generally ignore her until one day she ran into him after school alone in the hallway. She somehow found the courage to say something, and blurted out "What's your problem these days, Thomas? I thought you were my friend and now you never do anything with me." His face turned red and he averted his gaze. He quickly mumbled, "I just like to play with the other guys like me, and my mom and dad don't think I should hang out with a girl so much anymore." Renee was crushed but didn't want Thomas to see how much his words had affected her so she quickly retorted, "Well, that's good then because I didn't really like hanging out with you anyway."

Renee was never able to recall the moment she became aware that she felt different from other girls her age. She simply had a sense that being a girl was not right for her. She remembered being very imaginative in her play activities as a child and her role in her fantasies was always male. She didn't even like the words people would use to describe her when she was young. When other people called her "pretty" or a "little princess," she would become angry and loudly remind them that she was *not* a princess. Her mother and other adults were generally amused by her initial resentment at these nicknames or compliments. However, when Renee began to refuse to wear dresses or skirts at age 3, she and her mother engaged in a battle of wills for several years. Her mother was a member of one of the local Christian church congregations and there was an unspoken dress code for Sunday mornings. Girls *always* wore dresses and boys *always* wore pants. Although Renee's mother felt she could relent and let Renee wear pants and shorts during the weekdays, the social embarrassment of allowing Renee to wear pants to church was too much for her mother to tolerate. Beginning at age 3, Renee and her mother would begin arguing on Saturday nights about the outfit Renee would wear the next morning. Occasionally, her mother would prevail by using a threat of punishment or promise of a reward. But they often ended up skipping church when Renee could not be coaxed into wearing something "appropriate." Her mother felt that she would rather not attend services at all than face the judgment from others if Renee were to show up wearing pants to church. It was at this age when Renee began to tell her mother that she wanted to be a boy. Her mother's reaction was extremely negative and anytime Renee mentioned her desire to be a boy, her mother would punish her and tell her never to say that to anyone. After a few years, Renee stopped making these types of statements in front of her mother, but her feelings never changed.

Most children who exhibit signs of gender dysphoria do not have symptoms that reach into adulthood but in some cases like Renee's, these symptoms persist (Wallien & Cohen-Kettenis (2008).

She didn't just *wish* she were a boy, she truly felt that she *was* a boy and could not reconcile these feelings with her body.

As a preschooler, Renee showed a clear preference for toys and activities that were action-oriented. She received baby dolls and Barbie dolls for birthdays and Christmas until she was old enough to verbalize her own wish list. She asked for action figures, cars/trucks, Transformers, and building sets. The dolls she owned became targets for battle reenactments and she would create masculine outfits for the dolls and give them boy's names. She would play imaginary games with her action figures and call herself "Captain Ron," fantasizing that she was a male soldier fighting in a war. Her mother and other family members at first believed that her older brother's influence was to blame for Renee's preference for boy's toys and activities. They redoubled their efforts to encourage Renee to choose more fitting activities and toys, and invited older neighborhood girls over to play with Renee whenever possible. These playdates did not typically go well as the girls preferred very different activities. Even at such a young age, Renee remembered feeling like everyone wanted her to be someone that wasn't *right* for her.

Renee refused to let her mother style her hair with barrettes or bows or ribbons. She wore her hair in a ponytail and begged her mother for several years to cut it short. At age 8, her mother finally relented, too exhausted to fight about Renee's hair every morning. Renee went to the salon and asked for a "man cut" to the dismay of the hairdresser. She left the salon in tears because although her hair was short, the stylist had used a curling iron and hairspray to make her hair appear feminine and attractive. She was relieved to go home and realize that washing her hair and letting it dry without styling aids led to a much more suitable boyish look for her. Her mother immediately regretted letting Renee cut her hair and they fought even more over Renee's choice to wear her hair unkempt on a daily basis. Her mother would often unconsciously reach out to smooth Renee's hair and Renee would inevitably recoil. Although she had been quite close to her brother when she was a preschooler, their relationship became more distant as she progressed through elementary school. Renee was dismayed when her brother began refusing to play with her or let her use his toys. His mantras became "This is not for girls" and "This is a boy game." Robert was clearly embarrassed by his younger sister's lack of adherence to gender-stereotyped interests and he often channeled his embarrassment into teasing and taunting Renee. Their relationship became so negative that they both began to avoid contact as much as possible.

Throughout elementary school, Renee excelled on the playground in all sports. She played basketball, dodgeball, and football. She was one of the fastest kids in any race and was always picked first when choosing teams for a game. Early on, the teams were composed of boys and girls but as the elementary years

---

Natal males (gender assigned at birth) are approximately 3 times more likely to experience gender dysphoria than natal females (Meyer et al., 2001).

progressed, Renee began to notice that fewer and fewer girls were participating. Soon, she was the only girl playing with the boys at recess. She was unconcerned with the gender separation, but around 4th grade, she began to hear other girls making negative comments about her. She was not invited to any birthday parties. In such a small town, everyone knew when a child was having a birthday party and none of the girls in her class wanted to invite Renee. Likewise, none of the boys would invite her either, because no one wanted to have a *girl* at their all-boys party. By the end of elementary school, Renee felt increasingly lonely. She felt like she was a boy inside but the only thing that mattered to anyone around her was the outside. She was alienated from the girls (which was fine with her), but she was equally ostracized from the boys. There was no one in her world who understood her or accepted her.

Renee Puberty Hits

Puberty hit Renee particularly hard. With horror, at age 11 she began to notice that her breasts were developing. She was terrified that her mother would notice and make her wear a bra, so she began wearing heavy, baggy sweatshirts at all times so no one would notice her changing shape. As her development advanced, she became more and more desperate. She found ACE bandages and began to wrap them tightly around her chest in an attempt to flatten the appearance of her breasts. She felt extreme disgust when her menstrual cycle began at age 12. Her mother was hopeful that puberty would help reconcile Renee to her gender, believing that when the "hormones kick in," Renee would become interested in attracting boys and wearing cute clothes, makeup, and hairstyles. If anything, Renee's aversion to all things "girly" increased with puberty and her relationship with her mother became even more distant.

Because she lived in such a small town, Renee's extracurricular athletic options were very limited. Her mother couldn't afford for Renee to participate in any sports or activities outside of school, and the only athletic options for girls at school were cheerleading and basketball. Cheerleading was obviously out of the question, so Renee threw herself into basketball. Her participation in basketball was both problematic for her and helpful. Basketball became her salvation while she was on the court. She was extremely competitive on the court and she had natural speed and ball-handling skills. She loved the feeling of stealing the ball and running down the court at full speed for an easy lay-up. It was also the only time that she was encouraged to do something she actually loved. The cheering of the fans provided her with rare moments of acceptance. However, she came to dread the 10 minutes in the locker room before and after practice when the girls would change into and out of their practice clothes. The locker room was a large open space with wooden locker doors that would open from the walls. Renee chose

> Renee's distress associated with her cross-gender identification is important in her receiving a diagnosis of gender dysphoria. Those who are not distressed by cross-gender identification would not be given the diagnosis (APA, 2013).

the locker farthest into the room and tried to hide behind the door of her own locker while changing. She hated the idea of other girls seeing her body or realizing how much effort she put into hiding her breasts. At that time, she wore 2 layers of heavy duty sports bras over her ACE bandage wrap. Luckily, her breasts were not large, so she was able to maintain the appearance of a flat chest as long as she wore baggy shirts. She also became increasingly uncomfortable with seeing the other girls undressed. She was ashamed that she began to sneak furtive glances at the other girls when they were changing. Although the girls seemed foreign to her in so many ways, she also felt an increasing sexual interest in the girls' bodies. Renee continued to excel on the basketball court but she struggled with the off-court relationships. She was generally more aggressive on the court than the other players, which exacted a toll on her ability to bond with her teammates off the court.

After high school graduation, Renee desperately wanted to get out of her small town. She thought that her lack of close friends was due to having grown up in such a judgmental place. She packed up all of her stuff the day after graduation and headed out of town. Her mother only half-heartedly attempted to talk Renee into staying. Their relationship had reached the point that her mother experienced some relief at the notion of not having to face Renee on a daily basis. There was no hostility or conflict between them, but her mother was so confused by Renee and never felt that she could understand her. Renee had saved some money from the part-time job she had during her last 2 years of high school at the local grocery store. She used the money she had to buy an old beat-up pickup truck and pay the first month's rent on a small apartment in Jackson, Mississippi. She was able to find a job at a large chain sporting goods store within her first week of arriving in Jackson. She found herself hopeful for the first time in her life.

However, it soon became apparent that she had not left all of her troubles behind in her in hometown. She found it equally difficult to make friends at work as she had in high school. Once again, she discovered that the world seemed to divide people based on gender and she simply didn't fit into the right categories. The only difference between her new life and her old life was the fact that she lived in a larger city. But she discovered that she could feel very alone in such a large place. On her 21st birthday, she found herself alone without anything to do. Her mother and sister called to wish her a happy birthday. After the call, she found herself restlessly roaming her apartment until she finally grabbed her car keys and headed out the door. She had passed a bar near her work for several years and had always wondered what it looked like on the inside. It seemed like another one of those places full of people who "belonged" and she had felt envy and a small yearning each time she passed by. She had never had anything to drink before and the idea of being able to drink something that would make her feel less tense and awkward was becoming more and more appealing. She felt that

Like Renee, almost all adults who have had persistent gender dysphoria since childhood are sexually attracted to individuals of their natal sex (Lawrence, 2010; APA, 2013).

she had never had any "normal" social experiences and she suddenly found that she could not tolerate letting her own 21st birthday pass without at least having one drink. She gathered up all of her courage and walked into the bar. She almost walked back out as she believed that every person in the room turned to look at her. But, she somehow made her way to the bar and ordered a drink. She found the taste pretty awful but having a drink in her hand gave her an excuse to be there, so she slowly nursed one drink after another. Several hours later, she felt lightheaded and relaxed. She had never felt so at ease in a public setting before and she found herself engaged in small talk conversations with the bartender and several of the men at the bar. The experience was so liberating that she found herself at the bar again several nights later. She no longer disliked the taste of beer and she quickly acquired a fondness for vodka. Alcohol became a social crutch for her and she was able to meet new people occasionally. She never developed any real "friendships," but she was at least able to have brief discussions about sports with other men who came to the bar to watch their favorite game on the big-screen televisions. She ventured further out of her comfort zone by visiting a bar known to be frequented by lesbians. She had known since her high school days that she was sexually attracted to women but she never used the term *lesbian* to describe herself because she didn't see herself as a woman in any way.

For several years, Renee established a pattern of drinking regularly, engaging in one-night stands with women she met at bars, and keeping minimal contact with her family. Her older brother, Robert, was married now and living in their hometown working as a local mechanic. Her younger sister, Ella, had actually gone to college and Renee was proud of her even though she didn't feel like she really knew her. When Renee was arrested for DUI, she realized that she was likely drinking too much. But she felt dependent on alcohol to provide her with the courage to interact with people in social and sexual settings. However, she never felt truly fulfilled by any of her sexual encounters and still found herself lonely and depressed. One night, as Renee was surfing online, an advertisement on the side of her Facebook feed caught her attention. The advertisement was for a clinic specializing in the treatment of gender identity. The clinic was in Chicago and the term *gender identity* triggered her curiosity. She quickly did a Google search using those terms and was astonished to find thousands of hits. She started clicking on the links, and as she quickly read the information, her heart began to pound. She read about the symptoms of gender dysphoria and her own life experiences flashed before her eyes. Given her mother's response to her as a child, she had been reluctant to ever discuss her internal feelings. She could not believe that her lifetime of distress and confusion was not something unique to her. The idea that other people—lots of other people—experienced the exact same thoughts and feelings as she had was not only shocking, it was the biggest relief of her life. She stayed up the entire night reading Web site after Web site full of information and

Individuals with gender dysphoria often have a high rate of comorbidity with other psychiatric conditions. One study found that 45 percent of patients with gender dysphoria also had a history of substance abuse (Hepp, Kraemer, Schnyder, Miller, & Delsignore, 2005).

personal stories about gender dysphoria. She even found an online support group for people with gender dysphoria. She read story after story and found the tears running down her face uncontrollably. It was like waking up from a nightmare in which you thought you were completely alone in the world to find yourself surrounded by people who understood exactly what your life was like. For weeks, she would rush home from work and search for more information. She slowly found the courage to create an online profile on the support group Web site and wrote her first tentative post. She only wrote a few brief sentences describing her situation and history. She waited anxiously to see if anyone would respond or if the responses would be judgmental or critical. To her amazement, the responses to her post came pouring in from all kinds of people. Everyone expressed support and understanding, and for the very first time in her life, Renee felt totally welcome and accepted.

Renee spent several more weeks posting and responding on the online support group. She learned about possible treatment options. At first, she experienced a surge of hope that she might be able to find treatment and finally feel a peace in her life. However, it became clear that the treatments she read about were incredibly expensive and her minimal health insurance would probably not cover any of the costs. Her hope was quickly shattered and she tried to reconcile herself with the fact that at least she had found a support group. One day, one of her online friends in the support group posted a link to a notice about a new research study on the treatment of gender dysphoria for transgendered individuals at the University of Mississippi Medical Center in Jackson, Mississippi. She lived in Jackson and excitedly clicked on the link. The link led her to an advertisement on the medical center Web site seeking volunteers for a treatment study on gender dysphoria. Participants of either sex between the ages of 18 and 50 were eligible for the study, and there would be no costs associated with the treatment. Renee sat back from the computer screen with her mind reeling. She felt like she didn't breathe for over a minute but she was able to slowly reach in her pocket, pull out her cell phone, and call the number on the screen.

> Fewer than 1 percent of adults experience gender dysphoria (Zucker, 2010).

> The term *transgendered* refers to individuals who identify with a gender different from their gender at birth (APA, 2013).

Treatment Stage 1 (Psychotherapy)

Renee sat in the waiting room at the counseling center with significant trepidation. The waiting room was full of children and their parents, a couple, and several individuals and she felt as if every eye in the room was on her. To normalize her feelings, she tried to tell herself that everyone there was waiting to see a therapist but the seconds ticked by slowly. When a woman finally called her name, she found it ironic to experience relief in leaving the waiting room when her true anxiety should be focused on what would happen in the actual office. She was surprised to be greeted by a woman who smiled warmly and said, "Hello, I'm

Dr. Rodriguez, make yourself comfortable—you can sit anywhere. Would you like a cup of coffee or decaf?" She chose a seat on the leather couch and noticed that the office was very nicely decorated—the perfect combination of homey and professional. She spent the next hour telling the therapist about her history. At first, she found it very difficult to discuss her childhood and the events leading her to the clinic, but Dr. Rodriguez was very skilled at asking probing questions without being too intrusive. She found that the hour-long appointment was over quickly and the therapist requested that they set-up a follow-up appointment to discuss Renee's eligibility for the treatment study and the likely course of treatment if she were to be accepted.

The next week crawled by as Renee could think of nothing other than the treatment study. She alternated between feelings of extreme optimism and utter pessimism. She walked back into the clinic a week later having slept little and feeling as if her nerves were on end. At that point, she felt like she simply needed an answer regardless of the outcome. Dr. Rodriguez called her name and gave her a smile as they walked back to the office. Renee sat down shakily and waited to hear the verdict. Dr. Rodriguez immediately put Renee's mind at ease by simply stating: "The research team met and decided that you meet diagnostic criteria for gender dysphoria and are an ideal candidate for the treatment study if you're interested in participating." After the anxiety of the past week, Renee found herself flooded with relief. The rest of the hour-long session was focused on discussing the course of the treatment protocol. Dr. Rodriguez described the treatment team as "multidisciplinary" and defined the term by stating that Renee would work with physicians, psychologists, social workers, and nurses throughout the course of her treatment. The treatment included 4 options and Renee was informed that she could avail herself of any or all of the 4 treatment steps. These options included psychotherapy, hormone therapy, something called "real-life experience," and surgery. She would receive individual psychotherapy to address issues such as goal-setting, conflict resolution, and problematic beliefs or behaviors. Renee was able to set-up a series of appointments to begin the psychotherapy stage immediately. She was informed that the typical length of psychotherapy before progressing to hormone treatments would likely be at least 3 months. That timeframe did nothing to discourage Renee because she had already waited so long to reveal her "true" self. Indeed there were many issues to address during the psychotherapy stage and her thoughts/feelings about hormone treatment were not fully developed yet.

For the next 4 months, Renee met weekly with Dr. Rodriguez. These sessions focused on setting realistic goals for her future. They discussed Renee's goals related to relationships, including those with her family, her co-workers, and her future dating life. The therapist encouraged her to contact her mother and her siblings and invite them to a therapy session. Renee was terrified to disclose her

> The DSM-5 specifically used the term *gender* rather than *sex* to include individuals who were born with both male and female genitalia (APA, 2013).

diagnosis to her family, but she was relieved to have the opportunity to do so with the help of her therapist. She could not bring herself to complete the call after 2 weeks of picking up the phone and then putting it back down. She finally chickened out and sent a group text to her mother, sister, and brother asking if they'd be able to attend an "appointment" with her the next week. Her mother immediately called, terrified that Renee had cancer or some other terminal illness. Renee quickly clarified that she was fine but that she was seeing a therapist and really wanted her family to come with her to the next appointment. Her mother sounded hesitant and confused but promised to come herself and try to talk her brother and sister into coming.

When the whole family arrived the next week, Renee was both relieved and slightly terrified. She had no idea how the session would progress or how her family members would ultimately react. She let Dr. Rodriguez start the session by explaining about the basics of gender dysphoria to her family. Then Dr. Rodriguez asked Renee to describe her own experiences to her family. She knew her face was red and she began to sweat but she was able to haltingly describe her early experiences with feeling like she was a male trapped inside a female body. She avoided eye contact completely until she finished speaking and then looked up furtively to see her mother's face crumpled and tearful, her brother's lack of expression, and her sister's sad eyes. The silence was deafening for what seemed like hours but was probably fewer than 30 seconds.

Dr. Rodriguez:	I'm sure you can all agree that this has been very difficult for Renee throughout her life and it has also been very hard for her to talk with you about in the past. Obviously, the whole family will need time to process the information, but I was hoping you could each give Renee some initial feedback about how you're feeling after hearing her explanation of what's been going on for her.
Ella:	Renee, I guess I've always really known all of this, but I just never realized how bad it was for you and I hate that you've been so sad all your life. I just want you to be happy no matter what that means.
Robert:	You think it's OK for her to become a man?
Ella:	I think it's all been really hard for Renee, and I'm sure becoming a man will also be hard. I just want to support her as much as I can.
Dr. Rodriguez:	Ella, I am very pleased to hear you voice your support for Renee. One of the most difficult aspects of gender dysphoria has been the sense of isolation that Renee has felt most of her life. It's bound to give her some reassurance to hear a response that is both understanding and supportive. But, I realize that the rest of the family may not immediately feel so optimistic. I hope that the family can continue to explore

all of your emotions and logistical concerns as we proceed in
Renee's treatment.

The session continued with Renee's mother saying very little and her sister and
brother arguing back and forth about whether it was right or wrong for Renee
to do anything in treatment to change her "God-given gender." Robert had long
been a member of the same church that Renee grew up in, and he staunchly considered both homosexuality and gender dysphoria to be sinful. The session ended
with many unresolved issues but Renee was generally relieved that the conversation had at least started.

Renee and Dr. Rodriguez spent many sessions working through her own concerns and hopes about her future. After discussing the pros and cons and spending countless hours considering both her past and her future, Renee decided that
she wanted to live as a man. After the decision was made, she felt huge relief and
excitement. Dr. Rodriguez was always quick to address her assumptions about all
the ways her life would improve if she were finally able to fully embrace her male
gender. Dr. Rodriguez helped Renee understand that all of her problems would
not magically disappear. In fact, her alcohol use was a primary focus of their treatment and after four months of therapy without having a drop of alcohol Renee
was incredibly proud. Her family issues were not fully resolved. Robert had become even more disapproving of her choices and had stopped speaking to her
altogether. Ella's supportive reaction had definitely been a surprise and their relationship slowly became closer. Her mother avoided any discussion related to
Renee's gender dysphoria and whenever Renee tried to broach the subject of
her treatment, her mother quickly changed the subject. Dr. Rodriguez helped her
focus on accepting the current state of her relationships while continuing to make
efforts to improve them.

> Prior to gender reassign-
> ment, individuals with
> gender dysphoria are at
> increased suicide risk
> (APA, 2013).

Treatment Stage 2 (Hormone Therapy)

After 5 months, Renee and Dr. Rodriguez both agreed that she was ready to progress to the next stage of treatment. She met with an endocrinologist, Dr. Scott,
who discussed the process of hormone therapy. What seemed like an easy appointment turned out to be much more complicated than Renee had imagined.
She knew she wanted to take male hormones, but she had not realized all the issues involved with doing so. First of all, Dr. Scott wanted to discuss fertility issues
with her. One of the side effects of taking testosterone, according to Dr. Scott,
was infertility. Obviously, Renee had never had any desire to conceive and carry
a child of her own, but Dr. Scott presented an interesting alternative that she had
never considered. She could have some eggs harvested and frozen in case she
ever wanted children that were biologically related to her in the future. A part of
Renee just wanted to avoid thinking about the issue entirely and move forward,
but following the appointment, she found herself wondering if there would ever

come a time that she would regret it if she didn't act now. However, the process was very expensive and wasn't covered by the treatment study. Furthermore, she would need to take female hormones for a month in order to maximize the number of eggs that could be harvested. After a few sleepless nights, she decided not to have any eggs harvested. She discovered that she was comfortable with the idea that if she later decided to have a child he or she would not be her biological offspring. She returned the next week to start the hormone therapy.

Renee began taking testosterone that week. Renee always had a fear of needles, so she was relieved to discover that she could use a transdermal testosterone patch instead of regular injections. Renee was so eager for the testosterone to make an impact, that she started scrutinizing her body immediately. After 2 weeks, she was disappointed that very little had changed. She went back to see Dr. Scott who reassured her that it would take several months for the changes to manifest.

Over the next 3 months, Renee began to notice that her voice became deeper. She was thrilled with this outcome because strangers on the phone began to refer to her as "sir" and "Mr." She also began to notice that her breasts were slightly smaller and were less noticeable in her clothing. She continued to bind her breasts, however, and was still not entirely happy with their size. She also began to grow more hair on her body including her chest and face. She found herself in the pharmacy staring at the aisle carrying men's shaving supplies. Although the choices were a little overwhelming, she was excited to be doing something inherently masculine. The appearance of hair on her face and chest were positive for Renee, but she also began to lose some of the hair on her head. She cut her hair even shorter and saw that she was experiencing some male pattern baldness. She had a mixture of reactions to this discovery—on the one hand, she did not want to be bald, but on the other hand, she was relieved to be experiencing an issue that only affected men. To her relief, the side effects of the hormones were minimal for Renee. She had read about problems with acne, emotional lability, and increased sexual desire, but her experiences with these issues were either absent or mild. After six months of hormone therapy, Dr. Scott explained that Renee had likely maximized the benefit from the hormones and it was time to move forward with the next step of treatment.

> Natal males with gender dysphoria who seek hormone treatment are treated with estrogen (Meyer et al., 2001).

Treatment Stage 3 (Real-Life Experience)

Of all the steps in treatment thus far, this stage was simultaneously the most nerve-wracking and exhilarating one yet. During this stage, Renee planned to officially and publicly change her gender identity. From this point on, she became Ron and began to live her public life as a man.

Ron woke up the day after his therapy appointment and had to pinch himself to be sure that this was really happening. He got out of bed, took his shower, and opened his closet door. He had bought a new outfit for the occasion and was shaking a bit as he put on his new slacks, polo shirt, and dress shoes. He decided not to shave that morning, feeling that the small amount of facial fuzz would help make him feel more "real" as a man. He drove to work with great anxiety and almost turned around 3 different times. He sat in the parking lot for 15 minutes trying to find the courage to walk in. He had discussed his transition with his boss weeks ago. The look on his boss's face suggested shock and possibly disgust, but his boss's words were beyond reproach. He said he would support Ron "as long as it doesn't interfere with your performance." The sporting goods store he had worked in since moving to Jackson had always been a place where he could simply blend into the surroundings. Ron had a lot of knowledge about the equipment he sold and had been a solid employee. However, he had only been promoted once while several other co-workers had been steadily climbing the ladder. He would not describe any of his co-workers as "friends" but they were generally cordial and comfortable around one another. When Ron walked into work that day, he encountered a variety of reactions. Some of his co-workers didn't pay any attention to the change that seemed so monumental to Ron himself. Others predictably stared and left the break room soon upon his entering. He had requested a new name badge when he met with his boss previously and he felt self-conscious wearing it. Not a single employee addressed him as "Ron" for the entire first week at work—they simply went out of their way not to say his name at all. He did overhear a conversation between 2 women at work who were known gossipers. One woman stated "I'm not even sure what to call him/her. Should we now refer to him/her as 'it'?" The other woman burst out laughing before they realized that Ron was standing behind them. His face was red and he looked straight at the ground as they awkwardly walked out of the room. In some ways, Ron was actually thankful that he had never established strong relationships at work so the contrast between "before" and "after" wasn't too great in the end. He found himself generally isolated and alone at work just like he always had before. Dr. Rodriguez had certainly been right when he pointed out that changing his gender wouldn't necessary solve all of his problems.

Ron decided to meet with his sister for his first effort to come out to his family as a man. She would not be surprised given their recent discussions and he felt like it would be a morale boost to start with the easiest relationship and work his way up. He invited his sister to meet for lunch one day when she was in town for a conference. He sent her a quick text just prior to their meeting time that stated, "Didn't want to shock you but I'm now officially Ron." His sister quickly responded with "!!! ☺," which immediately put his mind at ease. Ella showed up on time and they spent the entire meal rehashing the previous weeks and how hard it had been for Ron to make the transition. Ella pointedly asked if he had told their mother, and he slumped his shoulders and shook his head in answer. She tried to give him a pep talk about talking to their mom but it was only half-hearted since Ella recognized that the conversation would not likely be positive. She did come up with a recommendation that Ron send their mom an email that included an invitation to get together personally if she was interested and ready. Ron loved the idea of avoiding a real conversation and he quickly wrote an email that very night.

> Mom, this may or may not be a shock to you at this point, but I wanted to let you know that I am now living my life as a man. My name is now Ron and I finally feel like my outside appearance now matches who I am on the inside. I know this is hard for you but I hope you realize how hard it has always been for me. I love you and I'm sorry if I'm a disappointment or embarrassment but this is something I feel I have to do to be happy. I won't force this on you if you don't want to see me, but I'm happy to visit or meet sometime when/if you're ever ready.

Ron waited anxiously for a response, and became obsessed with checking his email on his phone repeatedly throughout the day. After a week, he realized he was not likely to receive a response. He spent that night alone drinking a six-pack of beer in his apartment. It was the first thing he'd had to drink in almost a year, but he felt like he had to escape his thoughts and feelings for one night. He called Dr. Rodriguez the next morning and was able to schedule an appointment for the next day. Dr. Rodriguez helped him frame his drinking episode as a negative coping strategy, and they developed a new plan for him to deal with his mother's rejection. He left the session still sad but much more optimistic than he had been.

Despite all of the setbacks, some of Ron's happiest times were during the first 6 months living as a man. He loved walking down the street and being clearly recognized as a man. It was like everyone could finally see who he really was. He enjoyed openly shopping in the men's department and using the men's restroom. He even found the courage to develop an online profile on a transgendered dating site. Although he had still not found the perfect match, he had been on a few dates and felt his confidence increasing each day.

Treatment Stage 3 (Surgery)

After a full year of living as Ron, his treatment team began to discuss possible surgical options. Ron was ambivalent about surgery for a number of reasons. Primarily, he worried about the financial costs associated with the surgeries. The treatment study would provide only partial funding for surgical treatments, assuming that his insurance would be able to cover the rest of the costs. However, he still did not have adequate health insurance coverage so he would be responsible for at least 50 percent of the medical costs, not to mention the cost of missing work to recover from the surgery. He attended a few consultations with the surgeon and Dr. Rodriguez to discuss all of his options. He was particularly interested

Many insurance companies require a diagnosis to pay for treatment. For individuals who have transitioned to living in the preferred gender, the DSM-5 allows the diagnosis to be followed with a "Posttransition" specifier in order for treatment to be reimbursed (APA, 2013).

in having a mastectomy, but he was less optimistic about genital surgery. The long process of vaginectomy and penile reconstruction would likely take at least a year to complete. Ron decided to focus on the mastectomy for now and reconsider the genital reconstruction later. He was able to use his savings to help offset the cost of the mastectomy and despite his concerns about the surgery, he had no complications. He was able to return to work after only 4 weeks, and he had saved up enough vacation time so that he did not lose any income.

Epilogue

Six months after the surgery follow-up, Ron met with Dr. Rodriguez to check-in on his progress. Ron was excited to report that he and his mother were working toward reconciliation. His mother had finally contacted him after a year of silence and agreed to meet him for dinner in Jackson. They had since seen each other twice and were tentatively communicating on the phone. Ron felt like he had already grieved the loss of his mother's relationship so any steps toward a positive relationship at this point were simply a bonus. His brother continued to avoid Ron and was unhappy about their mother's recent compromise. Ron had maintained very limited alcohol use. Most important to Ron, he had met a woman through the transgendered dating service and they had been in a relationship for the past 3 months. Overall, Ron was very pleased with his progress during treatment and was very hopeful that his worst days were behind him.

Assessment Questions

1. What were the early signs that Renee was experiencing cross-gender identification?

2. How did Renee's mother react to Renee's gender dysphoria when she was a young child?

3. What effect did Renee's gender dysphoria have on her social life as a child?

4. During puberty, what did Renee do to try to hide her physical development?

5. What problems other than gender dysphoria did Renee need to address in psychotherapy before proceeding to hormone therapy?

6. What were the effects of the hormone therapy for Renee?

7. Why did Renee choose not to have her eggs frozen?

8. What were Ron's biggest struggles with the "real-life experience" stage of treatment?

9. Why did Ron decide not to undergo genital reconstruction surgery?

CASE 13

Schizophrenia

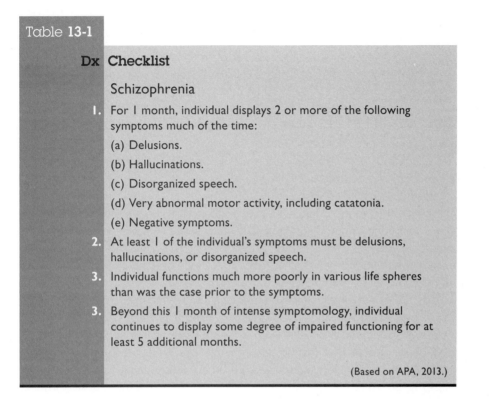

Table 13-1

Dx Checklist

Schizophrenia

1. For 1 month, individual displays 2 or more of the following symptoms much of the time:

    (a) Delusions.

    (b) Hallucinations.

    (c) Disorganized speech.

    (d) Very abnormal motor activity, including catatonia.

    (e) Negative symptoms.

2. At least 1 of the individual's symptoms must be delusions, hallucinations, or disorganized speech.

3. Individual functions much more poorly in various life spheres than was the case prior to the symptoms.

3. Beyond this 1 month of intense symptomology, individual continues to display some degree of impaired functioning for at least 5 additional months.

(Based on APA, 2013.)

Jim's parents had both been born and raised in Argentina. They met when his father was 38 and his mother was 19, and decided to marry soon after his mother became pregnant. They then immigrated to the United States where they hoped to make a better life for themselves. Their first few years on American soil were happy ones, but difficult financially. The couple went through several business failures before Jim's father started a clothing manufacturing company that did well.

After arriving in the United States, Jim's mother, Consuela, gave birth to three healthy baby boys in close succession. Jim, born in 1973, was the third boy. Her fourth child was stillborn when Jim was 13 months old. Devastated by the tragedy, Consuela soon stopped eating properly, and began drinking heavily. She eventually became so depressed that she could not function and had to be hospitalized briefly. The notion of being hospitalized for a mental disorder particularly concerned Consuela because her own mother was, at that very time, also a patient at a mental hospital back in Argentina—a hospitalization from which she was never to be discharged, as it turned out. During Consuela's hospitalization, care of the children fell to a series of nannies, as Jim's father was required to work long hours.

Schizophrenia affects approximately 1 of every 100 people in the world during his or her lifetime (Lindenmayer & Khan, 2012).

Two years after her hospitalization, Jim's mother became pregnant again. This lifted her out of her depression, and she was able to stop drinking. By the time the new baby was born, she seemed restored to her former self. She later told family members that the birth of this child had been her "salvation."

Jim Unfulfilled Promise

Throughout their childhoods, Jim and his younger brother were the better students of the 4 boys and, as such, received most of the attention from their parents. Jim was a prized pupil of his teachers, as well. He was enthusiastic, motivated, and he typically finished at the top of his class. As head of the chess club in high school, he led the school's chess team to victory in several tournaments. He was also among the top scorers on the state-wide scholastic achievement test. Everyone who knew him had high hopes for his future.

However, things began to change for Jim toward the end of high school when his father, Roberto, suffered a heart attack. Jim could no longer concentrate on his studies, and spent almost all his time praying for his father's recovery. His father did recover eventually, and Jim became convinced that it was due to his prayers.

Despite poor grades in his final semester, Jim graduated from high school; however, he seemed to have lost his bearings. He registered at a community college in the fall, but after a few weeks became lax about attending classes. Eventually, he stopped going to classes altogether and spent more and more time in front of the television set in his room at home. The extended television time, however, was not due to laziness, or lack of ambition, or lack of interest in people. Rather, Jim was starting to believe that he had special powers. He would closely observe the movements of every character on the screen, trying to determine the extent of his influence. The more he watched, the more his suspicions were confirmed. His effect on the characters was just too obvious to deny.

At first, this belief was just a feeling, but eventually Jim concluded that a specific change had occurred: He had acquired the capacity to control other people's emotions and behavior. He discovered this by going into restaurants and observing the patrons. He noticed that if he looked at people long enough, he could cause them to rub their eyes, scratch their noses, or make other simple gestures. At first, he thought he had to be within a close range to have this effect. However, as time went on, he concluded that he could project this influence over great distances. He discovered this one day as he watched the news on television. While watching, Jim observed that the reporter glanced down at her notes periodically. Suddenly, Jim realized that he himself was directing these movements. From that moment on, he believed that he could guide characters on television to move in ways that they ordinarily would not. Gradually, he became convinced that not only people but objects, such as traffic signals and automobiles, were responding to

If one identical twin develops schizophrenia, there is a 48 percent chance that the other twin will do the same (Gottesman, 1991). If the twins are fraternal, the second twin has a 17 percent chance of developing the disorder.

Delusions are strange, false beliefs that are firmly held despite evidence to the contrary. Delusions of persecution are the kind most commonly held by people with schizophrenia.

his influence. If he stood on a street corner, for example, and observed the flow of traffic, he found he could direct the cars' movements.

In the beginning, Jim was not sure how he controlled people and things, but one day, while pondering his situation, he had a flash of insight. He concluded that he, like God, must have a "life force" in his breath. In effect, he influenced people and objects through his breathing.

This was a momentous revelation for him. It meant that his power was not just your garden-variety black magic or wizardry. Rather, he had been selected for some sort of holy mission. This suspicion seemed to be confirmed soon afterward when Jim heard God's angels whispering that he had been chosen to be the Messiah.

With this discovery, Jim also became increasingly convinced that people were talking about him behind his back. One day, for example, he got on a bus and believed that some of the passengers were engaged in conversation about him, while others were glancing at him and pointing. This, he presumed, meant they knew about his power.

After the bus experience, Jim became extremely anxious. He was afraid that other people, particularly those with evil intent, might somehow gain control of his power and use it for destructive purposes. The best solution, as he saw it, was to stay home as much as possible. He also began to use greater and greater amounts of marijuana because, he believed, "it reduces the oxygen in the breath and that reduces its effect."

As Jim's discovery of his special powers evolved into the hearing of voices, then into his understanding that he would be the Messiah, and, finally, into his realization that others were talking about him, he became more and more confused. One day, as he emerged from his room after an intense session before the television, his mother asked him how he was feeling and he could only respond by babbling incoherently about "angels" and a "life force" in his breath. His parents, who previously had seen their son as merely withdrawn and somewhat depressed, were alarmed, and arranged the first of what turned out to be several hospitalizations.

At the hospital, Jim was given a diagnosis of schizophrenia, a label that initially meant nothing to his family but one they would eventually know all too well and hear all too often. At this hospital, Jim was treated with thorazine, an antipsychotic medication. Within a week, his speech became coherent again and he stopped hearing voices. He continued to believe in his special powers, but he became less preoccupied with them. After a 4-week hospital stay, he had improved considerably and was discharged.

At home, Jim continued to take the thorazine for a while and, as a result, was less troubled by symptoms. However, he lapsed into his previous lifestyle. Most of the time, he still watched television or slept, emerging periodically for meals.

Hallucinations are sights, sounds, and other perceptions that are experienced in the absence of external stimuli. Auditory hallucinations—hearing sounds or voices—are the kind most commonly experienced by people with schizophrenia (APA, 2013).

He had no interest in returning to school or doing anything else constructive, in spite of his parents' urgings.

As the weeks passed, he decided to stop taking the medication because it made him tired and dizzy. Within a couple of weeks, his hallucinations, intense anxiety, and confusion returned. Once more he had to be hospitalized.

This pattern was, unfortunately, to be repeated again and again over the next decade. Jim would be hospitalized periodically with a major flare-up of symptoms; he would be stabilized with antipsychotic medication; and, after a period of relief—sometimes just a few weeks, other times as long a year—he would either stop taking his medication or the medication would stop being effective. Even when his medication helped, only 2 of his symptoms disappeared: his hallucinations and incoherent speech. The delusion that he could control people and objects with his breath was only mildly lessened, and he remained isolated from normal events and activities.

At the age of 27, after 10 years of treatment disappointments, Jim was still spending most of his time in his room at home, not having done any productive work for several years. He had one friend, someone he had known since grade school, who he believed was immune to his breath's effect. Their interactions consisted largely of smoking marijuana together. Otherwise, Jim socialized only with his immediate family.

Jim's Mother Unfulfilled Dreams

Jim's parents were at first devastated and then, over the years, exhausted by his schizophrenic condition. Particularly hard-hit was his mother, Consuela. Having lived through difficult times at a very young age, she found her son's deterioration to be a last straw, of sorts. Occasionally, she would attend a support group for members of the families of people with severe mental disorders. The people in the group were nice, and the discussions sometimes helped her cope with Jim's condition. During one session, the focus was on her and she reflected on her reactions over the years to Jim's disorder.

> At first, I just didn't want to let myself believe that his problem was serious. I'd been through so much, and I basically didn't want to think about anything. Jim was one of the only things in my life that seemed truly fine. He was my hope that some day I would be able to look back on my life with a sense of pride and accomplishment
>
> Then, there was Roberto's heart attack. When Jim kept talking about how he had saved his father's life, I indulged him. For one thing, I sort of believed it. We were all terribly upset and anxious, and I really did believe that Roberto survived through our love and our prayers to God. Even when Jim started to insist that he and he alone had saved his father through prayer—a direct line of communication with God—I figured simply that he was being overly emotional about the situation.

Psychosis is a loss of contact with reality. Various disorders or conditions (for example, substance misuse) can produce psychosis; schizophrenia is one of the most common causes.

I thought that he had been overwhelmed by the horror of not knowing whether his father would die, and so he was now experiencing an unusual kind of relief and joy that Roberto had pulled through.

That was also when I first became aware of Jim's problems with marijuana. But, again, I didn't think that was too bad. I'd experimented with it myself when I was young. Then the problem with his room started. He would spend more and more of his time alone there. I guess I really didn't look into that closely enough. I never tried to stop his withdrawal, and I never really saw just how big his problems were. I think I was afraid of what I might find if I looked too closely.

Suddenly, my shining honor student was in his own world. I had wanted him to become someone important, to change the world. It sounds silly, but I thought he could one day be President, or a famous scientist. But he just seemed to give up, and nothing Roberto or I did could awaken him. At dinner, he would pull away from the conversation and stare at his food, mumbling when we asked questions, otherwise not talking or even acknowledging us. He was so moody, no longer the boy I had known. I didn't know what to think, but in our hearts we knew something was terribly wrong. It wasn't just that he was ignoring us; that would have been hard enough. But he actually seemed to be paying attention to something else, something we could not sense.

Finally, one night he came out of his room muttering gibberish about talking to the angels in the television set, or something like that. He said he could make the people on the screen move, and that the voices were confirming this power. I was just petrified. I figured, it's just like my mother—he's insane! We rushed him to the hospital, thinking that they would fix whatever was wrong with him. But it wasn't that easy. They told us Jim had schizophrenia. We didn't know exactly what it meant, but we knew it wasn't good. They told me that my precious little boy was seriously mentally ill and had to take antipsychotic medications. I hoped so much that they were wrong. I just couldn't face the idea that they might be right. At the same time, I knew that it was the only possible explanation for what had been happening.

That was almost 10 years ago, and since then, our problems have been endless. For periods of time, Jim will take his medicines, but even then he basically seems depressed and slow; and he is still, I am certain, focused somewhere else. And sometimes he has flare-ups; he gets really bad and has terrible psychotic episodes. He hears voices and may even scream back at them, which is terrifying.

We've had to spend so much money over the years, to put him in and out of hospitals, and to pay for his medications, that we've nearly gone into debt. We've never been able to get the kind of house we always wanted, or to travel to the places that we've always wanted to see. We know now that it is unlikely that he, or our lives, will ever be normal again.

After the support group session, one of the members, a man Consuela had not seen at past sessions, approached her. He said that he and his family had moved

Approximately 10 percent of the first-degree relatives of people with schizophrenia (parents, siblings, and children) manifest the same disorder (Gottesman, 1991).

to the area around a year ago, and at that time he and his wife had sought a therapist for their 25-year-old daughter, whose severe problems sounded a lot like Jim's. They made numerous calls—to their physician, to a referral service for people with severe mental disorders, to the leader of a support group, and to a university professor. The name Dr. Brian Sorkin kept coming up during these calls. Apparently, this psychiatrist had built a reputation for his successful treatment of people with schizophrenia—even individuals who had previously shown little improvement. Dr. Sorkin believed strongly that psychological interventions must supplement antipsychotic medications if people with this disorder were to make successful and lasting recoveries.

The man said that his daughter had now been seeing Dr. Sorkin for the past 6 months and had been making real progress for the first time in years. When he heard Consuela tell her story, it reminded him of his own situation, and he really believed that she should give Dr. Sorkin a try.

Consuela had just about run out of hope, and so she was inclined to ignore the man's suggestion. But something about his enthusiasm, his joy—perhaps it was his hope—called to her. That night, she discussed everything with Roberto, and they decided to gear up for yet one more try. The next day, they had a long talk with Jim, trying to persuade him to see Dr. Sorkin.

Jim was not interested in a new approach; he was certain it would be just another in a long list of disappointments. However, by now he tended to give in to his parents on such things. The disorder had worn him down quite a bit, and it was often easier, from his point of view, to go in whatever direction they pointed. He allowed his parents to make an appointment for him to see Dr. Brian Sorkin.

> It was once theorized that people with schizophrenia typically had mothers who were cold, domineering, and impervious to their children's needs—so-called schizophrenogenic mothers. Research does not, however, support this theory.

Jim in Treatment The Journey Back

As Dr. Sorkin directed his questions to his new client, Jim, the young man gave only minimal replies. Most of the time, he averted his eyes, looking miserable and frightened. Finally, however, he showed a spark of interest when the psychiatrist changed his approach and asked him what he considered to be the "real problem." In reply, Jim stated that he had been seeing therapists since age 17, and this was the first time anyone had shown an interest in his view of the situation. "Usually, they only want to know about the voices."

Jim then told Dr. Sorkin, at length, about the special powers that he possessed, and the problems that this had created for him. The client eventually stated that he didn't like secluding himself in his room at home, but felt it was his duty, given the overwhelming responsibility imposed by his special powers. It was like having the power of God, but with none of the desire or wisdom to use it. To cope with his predicament, he could emerge only for occasional meals, bathroom visits, and church services on Sunday mornings. By restricting his activities in this way, Jim said he minimized the chance of doing anyone unintentional harm; also, it kept his power from falling into the hands of evil forces.

The client admitted to Dr. Sorkin that he continued to hear the voices of angels; he also remained anxious that others were talking about him. Most recently, he said, he had been trying to understand his situation by immersing himself in Bible study, looking for scriptural evidence that he had been chosen for a special mission. He began to spend more and more time at this endeavor and, as his parents described it, his room was now strewn with biblical texts that he would study until the early hours of the morning.

Although at first skeptical about seeing another therapist, Jim was grateful that Dr. Sorkin was interested in hearing him out on the subject of his religious concerns. Perhaps, he stated, the psychiatrist would help him explain to his parents why his recent biblical studies were his own business and not "craziness," as they believed.

After talking to Jim and his parents at length and reviewing Jim's history, Dr. Sorkin was certain that the young man's condition did indeed meet the DSM-5 criteria for a diagnosis of schizophrenia. He exhibited a delusion, namely the belief that he could control others with his breath; he experienced auditory hallucinations; and he suffered from avolition, the inability to initiate or persist in normal, goal-directed activities, such as work, education, or a social life. In addition, his social and occupational functioning were far below what might have been expected on the basis of his capabilities as a child and adolescent. Finally, Jim's symptoms had lasted for a number of years.

Like many clinicians and researchers, Dr. Sorkin believed that schizophrenia is best explained by a diathesis–stress model. That is, certain individuals may have a predisposing vulnerability (a diathesis) to schizophrenia, but the risk of developing the disorder is affected by the degree of stress in their environment. Theoretically, the diathesis must exist in some degree in order for a person actually to develop the disorder; however, the diathesis can vary in severity. People who have a severe diathesis would probably develop schizophrenia regardless of the environment in which they are placed. Those with a milder diathesis, in contrast, might develop the disorder only in a less favorable environment. And those without the diathesis—the majority of the population—are incapable of developing schizophrenia, no matter how severe their environmental stress.

Given this view of the disorder, Dr. Sorkin used an approach called biobehavioral therapy. This treatment introduces protective factors into the life of each client—factors that will, it is hoped, lessen the person's vulnerability to schizophrenia or lessen the effects of stress on the client. For example, medications can lessen the person's biological vulnerability; training in social and independent living skills can lower his or her behavioral vulnerability.

"I shouldn't precisely have chosen madness if there had been any choice, but once such a thing has taken hold of you you can't very well get out of it."—Vincent van Gogh, 1889

Research suggests that people with schizophrenia have excessive activity of the neurotransmitter dopamine, or some form of imbalance between this neurotransmitter and the neurotransmitter serotonin.

Similarly, the degree of stress in the individual's life can often be lowered by family counseling or supportive services, such as case management, special group housing, and a sheltered work setting.

Phase 1: Engaging Jim as a Collaborator   Dr. Sorkin educated Jim and his parents as thoroughly as possible about schizophrenia, including the diathesis–stress model. The psychiatrist also explained that symptoms would likely recur without continued medication and stress management.

The delicate part was in getting Jim to try a medication treatment once again. Currently, the young man was not taking any medication, nor was he interested in returning to an approach that he felt had had no benefit for him in the past, only unpleasant side effects. Thus, Dr. Sorkin suggested that they work together to eliminate his "special powers," which Jim was finding so burdensome.

Dr. Sorkin: I know this has been a tremendous problem for you, and I want to help in any way I can. As you know, I'm a psychiatrist, and I've told you, as others have before me, that you have schizophrenia. I believe that the power that you've noticed in your breath is a result of this illness. If we can treat your illness properly, I believe that this power will go away, or at least be weakened. Do you feel that this would be desirable?

Jim: Yes. But I've been taking that crap the doctors prescribe for years, and it hasn't done any good. The power is as strong as ever.

Dr. Sorkin: I understand your reluctance to try again, but I'm going to take somewhat of a different approach. I think it is important that you feel that the medicine I prescribe is helping, otherwise I wouldn't blame you for not taking it. Therefore, I'm going to seek your guidance on this question, rather than just telling you what to take.

Jim: What exactly do you want me to do?

Dr. Sorkin: I'm going to ask you to take some medicine, and then to keep track of the medicine's effect on specific symptoms, using a special record-keeping form. This way, we'll both be able to tell whether the medicine is producing any benefits.

Jim: What if I don't think the medicine is working?

Dr. Sorkin: I'm going to take your opinion very seriously, and if you don't feel the medicine is working I'll accept that fact, and we'll have to consider our options. However, in return, I'm going to ask you to give the medicine a fair trial. It's going to take a little bit of trial and error. But I'd like you to bear with the process until we've had a chance to figure out how much benefit we can get from the medicine. This will mean living through a period when the medicine is not yet working to the

---

Dr. Sorkin's treatment for schizophrenia followed a biobehavioral program developed in the late 1980s (Psychiatric Rehabilitation Consultants, 1991). This program includes 5 behavioral training modules designed to teach basic skills in areas where patients with this disorder are often lacking: medication and symptom management, grooming and self-care, recreation, job finding, and basic conversational skills. The approach also engages the patient as a collaborator in the treatment program.

Brain scans indicate that many people with schizophrenia have smaller temporal lobes and frontal lobes, and larger ventricles—the brain cavities that contain cerebrospinal fluid (Lawrie & Pantelis, 2011).

maximum, or not working at all. I will tell you when I think I've got the best possible dose, and I'll seek your input about how much symptom reduction you've experienced each step of the way.

Jim: It sounds okay. But I'm warning you, I'm not going to take it if I don't notice any change.

Dr. Sorkin: Okay. But we may need a month before we can tell whether the medicine has any benefit. How about bearing with this for a month, and then I'll accept your verdict?

Jim: Okay. I'll give it a month.

Jim's parents, who were present during this early discussion, were heartened that their son had agreed to take the medication, but his mother doubted that he could take it reliably. She asked if Jim would let them monitor his medication use. After some discussion, Jim grudgingly agreed to let his father watch him take the medication at bedtime.

Phase 2: Attacking Jim's Symptoms   This phase of treatment was devoted to finding a medication dose that would relieve Jim's psychotic symptoms. There were three main kinds of symptoms that could be helped by the antipsychotic drugs: hallucinations (hearing angels talking), delusional thinking (Jim's belief that his breath could control others), and suspiciousness (his concern that others were aware of his powers and were hostile toward him). To track Jim's improvement, Dr. Sorkin and the patient would each regularly measure the severity of his symptoms on rating scales.

The medication that the psychiatrist had Jim try was risperidone (Risperdol), one of the newer, so-called atypical antipsychotic drugs. During the first 2 weeks, Dr. Sorkin slowly raised the dose of risperidone, while carefully monitoring symptoms and side effects in collaboration with Jim. By the end of this period, the client complained that not only were his powers unaffected, but he was experiencing some unpleasant side effects: dizziness and fatigue. He said he was ready to stop taking the medicine. Dr. Sorkin reminded Jim of their original plan to allow 4 weeks to decide whether the medication was producing any benefit. However, the psychiatrist also told Jim that he respected his concern about side effects, and would therefore slow the rate of drug increase, which should allow his body to get more accustomed to the drug.

By the fourth week, when Jim had reached the full target dose, the side effects were minimal. On the other hand, he had noticed only a slight change in his target symptoms. He pointed out that the 4-week mark had been reached, and he was leaning toward stopping the medicine.

Dr. Sorkin privately felt that the patient had not yet spent enough time at the target dose to determine whether that dose might eventually prove helpful. Still, he knew that he had, in effect, given his word to Jim that he would respect

---

Among their various actions, conventional antipsychotic drugs (also known as neuroleptic drugs) reduce the activity of dopamine in certain brain areas. This helps reduce the symptoms of schizophrenia but may also produce Parkinsonian symptoms (for example, uncontrollable shaking), which are known to be caused by low dopamine activity.

Risperidone and other so-called atypical antipsychotic drugs do not operate on the dopamine activity of people with schizophrenia in the same way as the conventional antipsychotic drugs, and so do not produce as many Parkinsonian symptoms.

the client's decision to stop the medication after 4 weeks. A critical juncture had been reached.

Dr. Sorkin: I know we had discussed using four weeks as the trial period for the medicine. However, it took a couple of weeks longer than I anticipated to iron out the side effects. I'm going to ask a favor, and request that you maintain this dose for another two weeks. Often it takes this long to determine a medicine's full potential once the maintenance dose is reached. I wish that the medicine had taken effect sooner, but I hate to abandon it at the point when we can finally find out if it's going to do any good.

Jim considered Dr. Sorkin's request. Reflecting their growing relationship, the patient said to the psychiatrist "I can tell you're trying your best to help me. I guess I can give it another two weeks."

Jim maintained the target dose for 2 more weeks, and by the second week, he noted a significant decrease in the symptoms on his rating scale. Correspondingly, he stated that although he believed he still had some power in his breath, it now seemed weaker, so he didn't have to think about it all the time. He also noted that the angels had stopped talking, and other people seemed to be talking less about him. Thus, he was willing to continue taking the medicine.

During this same period, Dr. Sorkin had Jim enroll in the psychosocial skills training program at a nearby mental health center. In particular, Jim was assigned to the medication self-management group and the symptom self-management group. In these groups, each of which met twice a week over a 3-month period, he learned (a) the importance of continuous medication regimens (that is, that medicine does not work from dose to dose but as a result of cumulative doses), (b) how to work out medication problems with a psychiatrist, (c) how to identify the warning signs of relapse, (d) how to intervene early to prevent relapse once these signs appear, (e) how to cope with psychotic symptoms that continue despite medication, and (f) how to avoid alcohol and drugs, which exacerbate the symptoms of the illness.

> A growing number of therapists now act as case managers when treating people with schizophrenia. Not only do they treat the patients, but they also try to coordinate available community services, guide patients through the complexities of community services, and protect patients' legal rights (Chan et al., 2000; Pickett et al., 1999).

Jim was quite responsible in attending these groups, which provided the first real structure in his life in years. More important, he learned skills there that were directly relevant to his situation. For example, he had always assumed that smoking marijuana was beneficial, both because it had a place in his delusions and because he believed that it lowered anxiety. He learned in his training that drugs and alcohol usually increase the symptoms of schizophrenia, and also further lower motivation and interest in normal activities.

Over the course of 3 months of meetings with these groups, Jim increasingly seemed to recognize the purpose and benefits of antipsychotic medication and became more responsible about his adherence; eventually, his family no longer needed to keep a careful watch over his taking of the medication. Jim also stopped using marijuana.

Phase 3: Stabilization After 3 months of taking risperidone, the young man's symptoms persisted, but at a lower level. His delusion about having a power in his breath remained, but he was much less focused on it. As a result, he had stopped looking through religious texts for a sign that he was the Messiah, although he continued reading the Bible for a large portion of the day. Perhaps most important, he had successfully avoided hospitalization during this period.

The next aim was to help him set some longer-term goals and teach him the skills to achieve them. Potential goals included: employment, financial security, adequate housing, friendships, dating, and family support. When discussing these matters with Dr. Sorkin, Jim identified 2 priorities: improving his relationships with his family and developing an ability to function independently. It was agreed that the psychiatrist would conduct behavioral family management sessions with Jim and his family, and that Jim would attend a separate individual behavioral skills training group.

Behavioral Family Management

During the early sessions devoted to behavioral family management—a set of procedures designed to improve family functioning—Dr. Sorkin had Jim and his parents discuss the problems they had been having. The parents started to discuss the problem of their son's remaining in his room continually, and things soon broke down into a shouting match. Jim explained that the time he spent in his room was necessary for his Bible reading, but Roberto was soon arguing that the main problem was his son's laziness. Consuela interrupted, saying that Roberto had no idea what went on most of the time because he was usually away at work. Roberto in turn replied that he was able to see enough to figure out that his son had become a "good-for-nothing slob" and that his wife was not doing anything to discourage it. Jim listened to most of this conversation with his eyes turned upward in the "Oh, brother!" mode. Eventually, however, he joined the fray, saying that a major reason he stayed in his room was so he didn't have to listen to "this kind of crap." Roberto yelled that "this crap" was due to their utter frustration in dealing with their son's problems. In short order, all of the family members were yelling.

Dr. Sorkin could see that family interactions were characterized by high levels of expressed emotion. Research has shown that individuals whose families display high levels of expressed emotion—frequent critical, hostile, or intrusive remarks during family communication—are more likely to experience a relapse of schizophrenia than those whose families have lower levels.

Dr. Sorkin: I can see that you all have been experiencing a lot of frustration in connection with Jim's problems, which has led to a lot of arguing. Having a family member with an illness such as Jim's is stressful for most families. It would benefit everyone if we could reduce the general

According to research, interventions that also address the social and personal difficulties of people with schizophrenia significantly improve their recovery rates and reduce their relapse rates (McGuire, 2000; Penn & Mueser, 1996). Such approaches offer practical advice; teach problem solving, decision making, and social skills; make sure patients are taking their medications properly; and help them find work, financial assistance, and proper housing.

tension and bad feeling. One thing we have learned through studies is that this kind of bad feeling in the family may interfere with recovery from schizophrenia. I would like to hold several sessions devoted to showing you how to reduce the arguing and bad feeling.

The family agreed, and the next 12 sessions with the psychiatrist were devoted to behavioral family management.

Several of the first of these sessions concentrated on education: simply inform-ing the family of the basic facts of schizophrenia. Dr. Sorkin gave the entire family some written material on the disorder, including descriptions of the deficits pro-duced by it. The psychiatrist also had the family view a DVD that explained that most people with schizophrenia have difficulty performing routine activities. On the DVD, a series of examples were given of patients who had stopped being able to work, go to school, or attend to even the most basic needs, such as eating or taking showers on a regular basis.

Jim's mother and father acknowledged their surprise at the resemblance be-tween Jim and the cases shown in the tape. They had often assumed, they said, that Jim's limitations were due either to his not trying hard enough or to a down-right refusal to face up to his responsibilities. Now they were feeling regret at having criticized him constantly for his failures, both large and small. Dr. Sorkin cautioned the couple not to blame themselves unfairly for their reactions or for Jim's illness. He reminded them of something else shown on the DVD, that fami-lies typically react with a certain degree of distress over the limitations of the dis-turbed family member, finding it difficult to understand how someone who once seemed so capable and full of promise had fallen to such a simple level. The task now, he said, was to put their new knowledge to good use, beginning with the next phase of family therapy, which would be devoted to communication skills training.

Among the communication skills that Dr. Sorkin attempted to teach the fam-ily members were: acknowledging positive actions in others, making positive re-quests of others, and expressing negative feelings constructively.

The psychiatrist explained that in many troubled families the simple art of praising one another for positive actions is lost. Criticism of a person's short-comings or mistakes becomes the sole form of providing feedback, while the per-son's positive efforts are simply taken for granted or ignored. Jim's parents, for example, found it easy to point it out whenever Jim failed to pick up his clothes, forgot to take out the trash, or spent an entire day holed up in his room. But they had given up praising any positive efforts by Jim, such as his mowing the lawn or sticking to his medications. Similarly, for his part, Jim had gotten into the habit of noting only what his parents failed to do for him, while ignoring their positive efforts.

Dr. Sorkin's approach to treating Jim included com-ponents of family therapy that focused on psycho-education, communica-tion skills training, and problem-solving skills.

Thus, Dr. Sorkin had the family members perform an exercise. Each of them had to identify something positive that one of the others had done in the past few days. Each member was then to practice stating his or her appreciation in Dr. Sorkin's presence. Jim, in particular, was coached to make better eye contact and to make his statement of appreciation with more vocal emphasis: "Mom, when you made my favorite meal the other night, I really felt good. Thanks a lot." To keep up with this task on a daily basis, the family had to record, over the next 2 weeks, all occasions when this skill was successfully practiced. With time, this kind of communication increased in frequency, and became more natural.

To learn another skill, how to make positive requests, the family was asked to cite examples of things that irked them, and how they had specifically communicated that annoyance to one another. Jim's mother volunteered that just that morning she had gotten fed up with the pile of laundry in Jim's room. When asked what she had told her son, she replied that she had said, "The laundry in your room is a disgusting mess. You simply must start shaping up." Dr. Sorkin then used this example to explain to the family how to rephrase concerns or requests in positive and specific terms rather than negative and global terms. "Positive" statements indicate what the person should do under the circumstances, as opposed to what the person should not do or should stop doing. "Specific" statements clarify what should be done; they are not just some vague demand for better performance. Consuela was asked to restate her concern in line with these guidelines. Her new statement was: "Jim, please bring the laundry from your room down to the basement at the end of the week." Again, the family members were told to record each successful practice of this skill over the next few weeks.

Similar training was carried out for expressing negative feelings constructively, that is, effectively letting persons know how their actions upset you. Often, family members neglect this piece of the communication process, keeping feelings of dissatisfaction or disappointment to themselves and then moving directly to criticism and insults. Expressing a feeling is a way of telling a person that there is a problem, but without making incorrect assumptions or accusations. Thus, for example, Jim's father was guided to say to his son, "When you look away while I'm talking, it makes me feel that you don't care what I'm saying," instead of, "You don't care about anything you're told."

Over the course of 6 sessions, the family members became more able to use the new communication skills, and the skills became a more natural part of their interactions.

Now the family was in a position to learn the final set of skills in behavioral family management: problem solving. To introduce these skills, Dr. Sorkin had Jim and his parents choose a concrete problem to solve. They decided to work on the problem of Jim's staying in his room continually. He acknowledged that it was not just his religious concerns that kept him there all day; he was also trying to avoid

---

Studies find that parents of people with schizophrenia often display more conflict, have greater communication difficulties, and are more critical and overinvolved with their children than other parents. Relapse is 4 times more likely for individuals with schizophrenia who live within these types of families (Bebbington & Kuipers, 2011). It may be that schizophrenia greatly disrupts family life and helps produce such family patterns.

According to some studies, family therapy—particularly when combined with drug therapy—helps reduce tensions within the families of people with schizophrenia and therefore helps relapse rates go down (Swartz, Frohberg, Drake, & Lauriello, 2012).

his parents' frequent arguments. If he left his room, he would usually get drawn into their quarrels. His parents agreed that there were many arguments in the home, but they believed that Jim's withdrawn behavior was the cause. If he could bring his activities more into line with those of the household in general, they felt that some of the arguing would be reduced.

Dr. Sorkin explained the principles of problem solving. All members would have a few minutes to reflect on solutions to the problem; then they would propose their specific ideas, with each member withholding judgment on any stated idea until all alternatives had been listed. Consuela suggested that Jim come down for meals 3 times a day. Roberto had the same suggestion, but also added that Jim might be allowed to leave the table if he felt anxious or uncomfortable. Jim proposed that he join the family for a dinner out once a week—he felt that his parents would be less likely to argue in public—and that he have some of his new friends (from his self-management groups at the mental health center) over for dinner on another night of the week. Several other possibilities were spun, and then the family members discussed the advantages and disadvantages of each alternative. Dr. Sorkin urged them to reach a solution by consensus. It was eventually decided that Jim would join the family every night for dinner, provided that the family would eat out on one night a week, and that Jim would have a friend come to the house for dinner on another night.

The family put this plan in action and it did eventually reduce the usual arguments about Jim's participation in household activities. Other sessions were devoted to similar problem-solving exercises following the same format. With time, the family members developed some skill at finding solutions to problems on their own.

Individual Behavioral Skills Training

As some of the stress in Jim's life became relieved through medication and behavioral family management, he developed a growing desire to function independently; inspired in part by the example of other patients he had met in his self-management classes. One friend there, David, had improved to the point where he got a paying job as a clerical assistant at a small social services agency called Helping Hands, which housed the homeless. Jim visited David at his job and was impressed to see that he had his own desk and was given respect and responsibility. Jim thought about developing his own work skills, with the hope that he could ultimately live independently. He raised this hope with Dr. Sorkin, who encouraged him and had him enroll in the mental health center's training group on personal effectiveness for successful living.

"I feel cheated by having this illness."—Individual with schizophrenia, 1996

This group was set up along the same lines as the medication- and symptom-management groups that Jim had already attended, but was geared toward individual problems. Led by a social worker, the group used behavioral techniques, such as modeling, role playing, corrective feedback, and behavioral practice exercises, to train members in various skills needed for managing in the world.

After a few sessions, Jim told Ms. Simpson, the social worker, and the other group members that his immediate goal was to go on interviews for jobs advertised online, something he had never done before and had no idea how to approach. The group broke the process down into separate skills: (a) researching online for appropriate ads, (b) telephoning or emailing for further information and requesting an interview, (c) arriving at the appropriate time and place, and (d) being interviewed. First, the group focused on telephoning or emailing for an interview. One member, who had a fair amount of interview experience, played the prospective employer, while Jim acted out his own role as applicant. The pair went over the process repeatedly, while Ms. Simpson and group members gave Jim corrective feedback on his telephone conversation. Jim also wrote several sample email requests for an interview and brought these to the group where the emails were edited and revised.

Jim's homework assignment was to make 5 telephone calls in response to ads and to report the results at the next group meeting. The point of the homework exercise was not for him to obtain actual interviews, just to practice his telephone behavior. In fact, to reduce pressure, it was understood that he would not be going on any interviews that he actually obtained. He would simply cancel them for now.

At the next session, Jim was excited to report that he had made the 5 phone calls. On 3 of them, he was told that the positions had been filled. On 2 others he was told he could complete an online application. He felt he had gotten much more comfortable with the process by the fifth call, and he decided to make 5 calls each week.

During this time, Dr. Sorkin had been continuing to work with Jim in individual therapy to find a medication level that would make a further dent in the young man's belief that he had power over others. Although Jim had certainly improved while taking risperidone, he felt that his breath still had some power to affect people. Dr. Sorkin tried increases and then decreases in the level of risperidone and added and subtracted some additional drugs as well. Perhaps it was the medication changes or perhaps it was the impact of the personal effectiveness group, or perhaps it was both. But at one point, psychiatrist and patient hit on a medication combination that made a large difference. Jim began to notice a significant drop in the intensity and frequency of his main symptom. He told Dr. Sorkin that the medicine seemed to have "neutralized" his capacity to influence other people through his breath. The patient also noticed that other people had stopped talking about him when he went out in public.

One study of people with schizophrenia revealed that 39 percent of them were receiving too low a dosage of their antipsychotic drugs, 32 percent too high a dosage, and only 29 percent an appropriate dosage (PORT, 1998).

Stabilization Phase   This change produced a sense of confidence and optimism that Jim had not felt in years. For the first time, he believed he was ready to seek paid employment. He discussed this with the members of his group, and eventually decided to try a volunteer position as a stepping-stone. He chose to pursue a lead given to him by David, his friend who worked at Helping Hands. David told him about another agency that delivered hot meals to the homebound elderly. Despite all his years of disability, Jim was able to drive and had in fact maintained his driver's license in good standing.

Once again, the various components of obtaining the job—the initial call, the interview, the first day on the job—were practiced in the group setting, with group members playing the role of phone screener, interviewer, and fellow employees.

Jim made the initial call and was accepted for an interview. At the interview itself, he was well-prepared for the various questions and asked some good questions himself. The interviewer was impressed with his sincerity and motivation, and told him that they would be glad to accept him on a trial basis as a volunteer assistant to one of the paid drivers. He could begin the following Monday, working 3 half-days a week.

The following Monday, at noon, Jim arrived at the agency to meet the driver for his assigned route. He was extremely nervous at first, but once he began working and saw how readily he took to the job, his confidence rose. Over the course of the next several weeks, he worked hard and, eventually, was offered a job as a paid driver.

Epilogue

Over the following years, Jim continued both to take medications and to attend his group meetings on a weekly basis. It would not be accurate to say that he made it all the way back to a fully functioning and productive lifestyle. In fact, he had several periods in which his notion of having power over others and his belief that others were talking about him returned to some degree. On the other hand, those ideas never again took over his life as they had in the past, and they were always temporary. Adjustments in his medications eliminated the ideas within days or, at most, weeks.

Similarly, Jim was not able to make it out of his parents' house and into his own apartment. Actually, he did try moving out once, but found life on his own too stressful. He had great difficulty keeping up with making his own meals, cleaning his clothes, and keeping things straight, and so he eventually concluded that he did indeed need the help of his parents. Furthermore, his job, although a huge improvement over years of unemployment, did not represent the level of work or responsibility that he had seemed destined for when he was young. No, he

Conventional antipsychotic drugs reduce or even eliminate the symptoms of schizophrenia in 65 percent of cases, and atypical antipsychotic drugs have demonstrated even higher levels of effectiveness by reducing both positive and negative symptoms of schizophrenia (Ellenbroek, 2011; Waddington et al., 2011).

hadn't made it all the way back, but, on the other hand, a decade of repeated hospitalizations, full-blown delusions, isolation, and confusion had apparently come to an end. He was now leading a much more normal life—and Jim and his parents were grateful for that.

Assessment Questions

1. What are the statistics for development of schizophrenia among identical twins?

2. What were 3 of Jim's initial symptoms that signaled signs of a mental disorder?

3. What was the diagnosis Jim received after he was hospitalized?

4. Why did he stop taking his medication and what symptoms returned when he stopped taking his medication?

5. Explain Dr. Sorkin's theory of the diathesis–stress model of schizophrenia.

6. Describe the biobehavioral therapy used by Dr. Sorkin.

7. What are some structural differences in the brains of individuals with schizophrenia?

8. How do neuroleptic drugs work to reduce the positive symptoms of schizophrenia? What are some of the downsides of using these medications?

9. Why are the newer atypical antipsychotic drugs preferred over the traditional neuropletic drugs?

10. What 6 factors were a part of the psychosocial skills training program for Jim in conjunction with his medication program?

11. What were the 2 long-term priorities for Jim once his medication stabilized some of his symptoms?

12. Why was it important to involve Jim's family in his rehabilitation?

13. What particular communication skills were important for Jim's family to learn?

14. What were some individual behavioral skills Jim learned in order to become more independent?

15. Why did Jim decide to continue to live with his parents rather than on his own?

Antisocial Personality Disorder

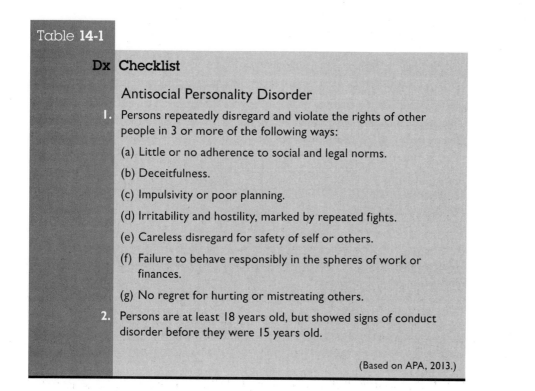

Table 14-1

Dx Checklist

Antisocial Personality Disorder

1. Persons repeatedly disregard and violate the rights of other people in 3 or more of the following ways:

   (a) Little or no adherence to social and legal norms.

   (b) Deceitfulness.

   (c) Impulsivity or poor planning.

   (d) Irritability and hostility, marked by repeated fights.

   (e) Careless disregard for safety of self or others.

   (f) Failure to behave responsibly in the spheres of work or finances.

   (g) No regret for hurting or mistreating others.

2. Persons are at least 18 years old, but showed signs of conduct disorder before they were 15 years old.

(Based on APA, 2013.)

Jack was a 22-year-old single man, admitted to a state psychiatric hospital in a large midwestern city with complaints of depression and thoughts of suicide. He was admitted to the hospital after arriving there one evening appearing completely distraught. He told the psychiatrist on call that he could not bear life any longer and was thinking of ending it all. Jack said he had spent the past hour standing on the overpass of a nearby highway, staring down at the traffic and trying to gather enough courage to jump. He eventually decided he could not do it and, realizing he was near a hospital, pulled himself together enough to "get some help instead of running away from my problems."

In relating these events, Jack seemed deeply upset. Occasionally he would stop speaking and bury his face in his hands. When the psychiatrist asked what sort of difficulty he was experiencing, Jack replied, "You name it, I've got it." He said that he had recently lost both his job and his girlfriend, and now his mother was gravely ill, among other things. He feared that unless he got some help, he was going to "go off the deep end."

Most of the individuals with antisocial personality disorder are not interested in receiving treatment. Those individuals who receive treatment typically have been forced to participate by an employer, their school, or the law (McRae, 2013).

Jack Disturbed or Disturbing?

The psychiatrist was concerned that Jack would consider suicide again, so decided to admit Jack to the psychiatric ward and place him on suicide precautions. An orderly escorted the young man to the admitting desk, where the clerk took down pertinent information. After that, Jack surrendered his valuables—a wallet with no identification, $3 in cash, and an earring—and was escorted to a locked ward. When they arrived at the door to the ward, the orderly took out an enormous skeleton key, opened the large metal door, and escorted Jack inside.

The orderly brought him to the nurses' station, a large semicircular area enclosed in safety glass, where a half-dozen staff members were busily typing patients' notes into the computers. Upon seeing Jack, a nurse exited the station, introduced herself, and took him to his room, one of 15 down a long, bare corridor reserved for male patients (female patients occupied an identical corridor on the other side of the floor). At the room, the nurse gave Jack some pajamas and a hospital-issue daytime outfit; she informed him that a relative could bring another set of his own clothes tomorrow, if he preferred. She also told Jack that she would have to take his shoelaces, since the admitting physician had ordered suicide precautions, and she gave him a pair of slippers to use as footwear.

The terms *sociopathy* and *psychopathy* denote a psychological pattern similar to antisocial personality disorder, although some distinctions have been drawn between these disorders. Typically, psychopathy is seen as a more severe form of antisocial personality disorder (Coid & Ullrich, 2010).

After the nurse left, Jack flopped down on his bed and buried his face in his pillow. An hour later, a house physician came by to give Jack a routine physical examination, which seemed to perk him up a little. Jack greeted the physician with a friendly, "Hi, Doc," and the doctor examined the young man's heart, lungs, blood pressure, and other vital signs. To make conversation, he remarked on an "interesting" tattoo that Jack had on his chest, a crude picture of a nude woman striking a pose that left nothing to the imagination. With obvious pride, the patient explained, "Yeah, I got it in honor of my girlfriend." After the physician left, Jack donned his hospital pajamas, got into bed, and slept soundly through the night.

The next morning, he joined the other patients in the day area, where breakfast was being served. As he took his place at the table, he announced that he was "hungry as a horse," and began chowing down with abandon. After he finished his own food, he glanced over at a patient across the table and noticed that the man, a patient with schizophrenia, had only nibbled at his eggs and toast. "Hey, old-timer," Jack called out, "you don't mind if I take some of your grub, do you?" The man just stared, glassy-eyed, while Jack, without waiting for a response, took his plate and started scraping its contents onto his own dish.

Another patient sitting at the table reprimanded Jack for having taken the older patient's food. "We're not supposed to share food. It's against regulations. Besides, that fellow is pretty sick. He's been throwing up for days. You wouldn't want to eat anything he's touched."

Jack was unimpressed by the patient's disapproval. "Who appointed you hall monitor?" he asked. "I guess you want all the food for yourself. Well, sorry, pal, I beat you to it."

Jack in Treatment Using Therapy to His Advantage

Later that morning, Dr. Selina Harris, a staff psychiatrist, arrived to conduct an evaluation of Jack. Dr. Harris found the young man standing at a pool table in the day area, playing a game of eight-ball with another patient. As soon as the psychiatrist approached, Jack looked up and smiled. He had an appealing, cheerful quality, and at first Dr. Harris wasn't sure she had the right patient. She was expecting someone deeply depressed, as specified in the admitting note. This patient, however, was extending the warmest, happiest greeting.

"Hey, Doc. Good to meet ya," he said. "I'm just shooting a little game of pool here."

Dr. Harris explained that she would be Jack's doctor while he was hospitalized, and had him accompany her to her office on the unit floor. Once inside, she asked Jack to take a seat and told him that she wanted to know all about the troubles he had been having and why he had been contemplating suicide. Jack confirmed that he was "real depressed" and didn't know if life was worth living. When the psychiatrist asked what he was depressed about, the patient replied, "Everything and anything." He went on to explain that it was mainly his girlfriend but, basically, he "just felt like giving up." He said, "Frankly, Doc, it's too painful to talk about." Jack didn't look particularly pained, however.

Dr. Harris told him that they would have to discuss these matters eventually, if he was to get any help. At this, Jack said he didn't think that talking would do any good. "Don't they have meds for depression?" he asked. "What's there to talk about when all you got to do is take a pill? How about giving me some Prozac?"

"Did you ever take Prozac?" Dr. Hams asked.

"Me? Oh, no."

"Did you ever take any psychiatric drugs?" she asked.

"No," Jack insisted, "This is my first time in the loony bin, or even talking to a shrink."

"How about street drugs? Did you ever try those?" the psychiatrist asked.

"To be perfectly honest with you, I have tried marijuana—but who hasn't? I stay away from the harder stuff, though."

Since Jack would not discuss his depression, Dr. Harris tried a different tack, asking the young man about his living situation, his work, and his family. Jack replied simply that he had been living with his girlfriend, but "she's real sore at me now." He explained that he had recently lost his job at a loading dock after

> Antisocial personality disorder is as much as three times more common among men than women. Women with antisocial personality disorder have been found to have more frequent parent-related adverse events in childhood, such as emotional and/or sexual abuse, and more adverse events as an adult (Alegria et al., 2013).

> People with antisocial personality disorder have higher rates of alcoholism and substance-related disorders than do the rest of the population (Brooner et al., 2010; Reese et al., 2010).

another employee had stolen some goods and then blamed the theft on Jack. Dr. Harris tried to inquire more about that matter, but Jack said he was getting tired and wanted to go lie down.

Before he departed, the psychiatrist asked him whether he was still having thoughts of suicide. Jack replied that he was feeling more secure now that he was in the hospital, and he was hopeful that Dr. Harris could help him. The psychiatrist explained that, in order for her to help him, he would have to talk more about his feelings. The patient promised that, in time, he would. He just had to develop "a little rapport" with Dr. Harris first.

Jack got up and opened the door to leave, but then paused in the doorway as if having second thoughts. He said he really appreciated the time that the psychiatrist had given him, and hoped that they could talk more. As the young man spoke, Dr. Harris observed his hand slip down the edge of the door, and push the button that unlocked the door handle, allowing entry from the outside. For a moment, she considered confronting Jack with what she had just seen, but decided to let the matter ride.

Jack said goodbye, and after he had rounded the corner, Dr. Harris pushed the button to lock the door once again. As it was getting late, she packed up her briefcase and left for the day.

The next morning she sought Jack for another interview. This time she found him seated in the television viewing area. He apparently was enjoying himself immensely, laughing loudly at a situation comedy, while the other patients stared glumly at the same set. As Dr. Harris approached, the young man looked up and greeted her with a cheery, "Hey, Doc! I'll be ready in a minute, as soon as this show is over." The psychiatrist waited for Jack in her office.

A few minutes later he ambled in, closed the door, and sat down. Then he began telling Dr. Harris that she had upset him, that she had hurt his feelings by locking her door after he had unlocked it; it showed she didn't trust him. Going even further, he told her that it was underhanded and dishonest of her. The psychiatrist was momentarily dumbstruck. Jack was accusing her of dishonesty for relocking her own door!

"What were you trying to do by unlocking my door?" she asked.

Jack replied that he just didn't like locked doors. "Speaking of which," he added, "I can't take being cooped up in here all day and night. I know I was suicidal before, but I think I'm coming out of it. Can't I have grounds privileges?" Then he went on, "Look, I'm sorry about the lock thing. It was a stupid prank I pulled. I've just been upset about having to be in a hospital—even though I know I need to be here," he quickly added.

Dr. Harris explained that in order for anything to change in Jack's hospital status—the lifting of suicide precautions, conferring grounds privileges, or whatever—he would have to discuss his situation more openly.

Twelve-month prevalence rates of antisocial personality disorder range from 0.2 percent to 3.3 percent. The prevalence is highest (up to 70 percent) among individuals with substance abuse and criminal histories (APA, 2013).

Jack's attitude then changed, and he said he was ready to speak frankly. First, he apologized profusely for any trouble he had caused. He said that if he was sometimes crude, it was a front he had developed out of fear that others might take advantage of him if he didn't act like he could take care of himself. He admitted to Dr. Harris that he had spent 6 months in prison for a "stupid petty theft"; while in prison, he was bullied constantly because of his small stature. That experience had hardened him, he said, and now he sometimes "acted like a jerk," even among people who had his best interests at heart.

Jack went on to admit that he hadn't really considered suicide; he had simply claimed that to gain admission to the hospital. In his opinion, however, it was no exaggeration to say that he was at the end of his rope. He said that since being paroled, he had had tremendous difficulty finding and keeping a job. He had tried everything, from mechanic to electrician to drill press operator, at various auto plants, but in each case he was laid off within a few weeks because of his low seniority in the union.

In addition, he explained, his mother's heart condition had worsened considerably, forcing her to be hospitalized. Because neither one of them was now working, they lost their apartment. And his girlfriend, with whom he sometimes lived, had gotten fed up with his losing jobs and his inability to contribute to the rent, and had demanded that he leave. After being kicked out, he had gone to a homeless shelter before being hounded out of there by "ruthless thugs" who stole whatever money he had left. Feeling that he was losing this daily struggle for survival, he had come to the hospital.

Jack said he was sorry if he had offended anyone with his charade for getting admitted, but he felt he was suffering as much as any patient, and his false claim of suicidal thoughts showed just how desperate he was. He said he felt he was experiencing a "crisis of confidence" and he needed some intensive therapy to help him through this period. "Look," he concluded, "I could tell you that I still want to commit suicide, but I'm trying to be honest with you now in the hope that I'll get the right kind of help."

Dr. Harris listened to Jack's story with an open mind. Although skeptical about his claims, she decided against recommending immediate discharge. Instead, she decided to proceed with a complete pretreatment evaluation, which included a mental status exam, an electroencephalogram, psychometric testing, and an occupational evaluation. His case conference would be held in 5 days, at which point the treatment team would decide whether to discharge him or proceed with treatment. In the meantime, the psychiatrist removed Jack's suicide precautions, but reminded him that he would still be restricted to the locked unit for at least the next several days.

Jack thanked her profusely for "understanding" and said he would cooperate with the evaluation procedures and make less of a pest of himself. During the next

In one study, clinical psychologists viewed videos of statements made by individuals and evaluated their truth or falsehood. The clinicians were able to identify 62 percent of the lies, a performance similar to that of federal judges (Ekman et al., 1999). Interestingly, a more recent study discovered that men, but not women, with high levels of psychopathy also performed better than chance in terms of detecting real-life emotional lies (Lyons, Healy, & Bruno, 2013).

A mental status exam is a structured interview in which the clinician asks about specific symptoms, such as anxiety or hallucinations; observes other symptoms, such as emotional expression or motor activity; and tests certain cognitive capacities, such as memory or abstract reasoning.

several days, the patient seemed true to his word. He was well-behaved and co-operated fully with all the evaluation procedures. But then, the day before his case conference, he disappeared. The building was searched, but there was no sign of Jack. A few hours later, Dr. Harris received a call from the state police saying they had picked up a patient—obviously Jack—for possession of a stolen vehicle, hers. Jack had also been charged with driving without a license, driving while intoxicated, speeding, and failure to heed a stop signal. The police said they were calling to investigate Jack's claim that the psychiatrist had lent him the car. Dr. Harris explained that she certainly had not done this, but was nevertheless willing to drop any charges. The police replied that they already had enough outstanding warrants on Jack to hold him "from here to doomsday," and he was arraigned on the other charges.

With Jack unable to return to the hospital, his next of kin—his mother—was contacted to pick up his personal articles. His mother was in perfect health, in spite of Jack's dramatic story of her grave heart condition and recent hospitalization. After picking up her son's belongings, she spoke with Dr. Harris and supplied some details about his background.

A Parent's Tale Watching Antisocial Behavior Unfold

> "In most of us, by the age of thirty, the character has set like plaster, and will never soften again."—William James (1890)

Jack's mother, Marlene, told Dr. Harris that everyone who encountered Jack as a toddler immediately fell in love with him. "He was such a sweet child, and he had a smile that could win over anyone." However, "as soon as he was old enough to go to school, the trouble started."

At about the time that Jack entered first grade, he seemed to develop a "thing" for jewelry or, more accurately, for stealing it. For example, he would take items from Marlene's jewelry case and sell them one by one to classmates or to older boys in the neighborhood, often for no more than pocket change, which he would spend on candy or trading cards. Marlene and her husband learned what Jack was doing after he tried to sell a pair of genuine pearl earrings to his second-grade teacher for $5.00. At first, his parents just scolded him. When the behavior continued, the scoldings turned into beatings. Eventually, they decided that the only way to deal with the situation was to keep their valuables—bills, coins, jewelry—under lock and key.

Jack's parents provided him with a generous allowance in an effort to reduce his desire for spending money. However, this desire could never be satisfied. By the age of 8, the boy began breaking into neighbors' houses to steal items to sell. In many ways, he became quite ingenious in these break-ins. He learned to pick locks, disable alarms, and slip into small openings. At the same time, however, the way in which he would dispose of the stolen items often seemed remarkably stupid, according to his mother. His most spectacular bungle occurred when he tried to sell jewelry to members of the very same household from which it was stolen.

This triggered his first arrest, at age 10, but he was remanded to the custody of his parents, who told the judge that they would figure out a way to control him. They did indeed try to control his antisocial ways by keeping a more careful eye on him. When Jack went to school, for example, they would actually escort him into the building to make sure that he was attending classes. But the boy was not beyond slipping out in the middle of the day, inevitably to get into some kind of trouble.

Jack's stealing soon took a more serious turn. He joined up with a group of teenagers who made a profession of shoplifting. They saw in Jack an opportunity to acquire stolen goods with a reduced risk of detection, since Jack was much younger and less likely to be suspected. Typically, one of the teenagers would case a store, locate items of interest, and then send Jack inside to remove the items according to their instructions. The gang would then sell the items to a regular fence who paid them in cash, drugs, and alcohol.

Associating with these older boys led Jack to develop more varied and sophisticated interests and a precocious sexual awareness. The turning point in his antisocial career came when, at age 12, he lured a 10-year-old neighborhood girl into some woods behind her house, undressed her, and tried to perform sex acts with her. When she started screaming, her mother came running and was confronted with the horrifying scene. Jack at first claimed that the girl had lured him into the woods. When that didn't work, he offered the girl's mother $5.00 "to keep her mouth shut." As it became apparent that the woman was not warming to the negotiations, 12-year-old Jack finally tried threats, telling the mother she had better take the money or she would get the same treatment.

With this incident, Jack entered the world of serious legal trouble and was sentenced to a year in reform school. There, he learned more advanced methods of taking advantage of others. As soon as he was released, he embarked on a career of auto theft. He could now hot-wire a car in 30 seconds, and would do so whenever he needed cash or transportation. Why take the bus, he reasoned, when there were cars all around? Jack's mother estimated that he hot-wired 50 cars before finally getting caught in the act, leading to another term in reform school, this time for 2 years.

When he was released, at almost 15 years old, his parents tried to persuade him to return to school and pay enough attention to his studies to get a high school diploma. The teenager agreed to attend a trade school to learn how to repair electrical systems and electronic components. His mother now realized that her son had probably favored this route because he had hoped to become more skilled at disabling alarm systems; also, with electronics training, he thought he might get jobs that would bring him into contact with equipment worth stealing.

Jack actually stayed with his electrical studies, and after receiving his certificate at age 17 found employment at an auto plant, assisting in the installation of

Antisocial personality disorder was called "moral insanity" during the nineteenth century.

People with antisocial personality disorder tend to respond to warnings or expectations of stress with low brain and bodily arousal, such as slow autonomic nervous system arousal and slow electroencephalogram waves (Gaynor & Baird, 2007; Perdeci et al., 2010). This may help explain the inability of many such individuals to experience constructive levels of fear or to learn from negative experiences.

A number of structural brain abnormalities have been found among individuals with antisocial personality disorder and psychopathy (for example, deficits in the frontal gray matter, amygdala, uncinate fasciculus, and hippocampus, and increased size of the corpus callosum). Although consistent differences have been difficult to find, researchers are now able to identify structural brain differences between "successful" and "unsuccessful" psychopaths (that is, the ones who don't get caught and the ones who do) (Pemment, 2013).

electrical systems. He seemed to work hard for several months, and Marlene marveled at his capacity to apply himself. But it all came to an end when he was later caught stealing electrical supplies on a massive scale. Somehow, he had gained access to the plant's supply depot where he had been removing switches, wiring, batteries, and other electrical supplies for sales to competing auto plants. He eventually got caught when, in a manner reminiscent of his childhood error, he tried selling some of these supplies back to his own plant.

Thus, at age 18, Jack was sentenced to 3 years in a state penitentiary. Not being the violent sort, he was paroled after 18 months for good behavior. Upon his release, he stunned his former colleagues by applying for employment at the very same auto plant where he had been caught stealing. He expressed outrage and hurt, seemingly sincere, when they refused to take him back. For the next several months, Jack hitchhiked around the country, bouncing from one job to the next.

As for his love life, Jack's mother reported that he had been married at least twice, although she doubted he had ever been divorced. He met his first wife at age 21, while hitchhiking around the country after his release from prison. Marlene had never met the woman, but learned from Jack that she was a 45-year-old divorcée who had picked the young man up as he was hitchhiking through her town. Jack later told his mother that this woman completely repulsed him: she was dull and unattractive, according to his description. Nevertheless, he felt a sexual stirring while riding in the car with her and proposed sexual intercourse. The woman replied, half teasingly, that he would have to marry her first. Jack immediately agreed, and they drove nonstop to a western state where they found a justice of the peace to perform the ceremony. Then they paid for a motel room where Jack got what he'd asked for hours before.

The next morning, the couple drove back to the bride's hometown, and Jack moved into her house. He resided there for a few weeks, until she started nagging him about finding work. At this, he decided he had hung around long enough, and he departed for home, hitchhiking and hot-wiring his way there.

Once back in his home state, Jack acquired several girlfriends, one of whom he married under similar circumstances. In each such involvement, Jack showed no concern about the age, appearance, or character of the woman. Rather, his interest in women seemed largely a matter of housing and, to a lesser extent, sex. No sense of love or attachment was ever involved.

At the time that Jack had sought admission to the psychiatric hospital, he was, according to his mother, in truly desperate straits. She and Jack's father—fed up with having to hide their valuables constantly—had refused to allow him entry into their home and his latest girlfriend had locked him out. Marlene suspected that in seeking hospital admission, her son was simply looking for a place to stay, although he may also have considered the prospect of obtaining psychiatric drugs, either to use or sell, as an added bonus. Typically, Jack would become bored with his schemes when they could not be executed immediately; this was probably why he ran off with Dr. Harris's car rather than continue his stay at the hospital. Marlene, an old hand at Jack's behaviors, encouraged the psychiatrist not to take the car theft personally, explaining that he probably chose her vehicle only because her name on the reserved space had caught his eye.

Jack's mother then signed for her son's belongings—the wallet, the $3, and the earring—and departed.

Jack No Success with Therapy

Marlene's departure marked the end of Dr. Harris's involvement with Jack. The young man had left the psychiatrist's professional life as suddenly as he had entered it. And the therapist was certain she had made little or no impact on him. This failure of treatment did not surprise her, although it did cause her disappointment. During her short time working with him, she had come to suspect that Jack manifested antisocial personality disorder, a pattern that is notoriously unresponsive to treatment. Based on her talks with Jack and with his mother, Dr. Harris felt that he clearly met the DSM-5 criteria for a diagnosis of this disorder. That is, he failed to conform to social norms; also, he was deceitful, impulsive, reckless, irresponsible, and remorseless. And, as the DSM-5 criteria stipulate, he would have met the criteria for conduct disorder well before the age of 15.

Although many people with this personality disorder exhibit criminal behavior, their brand of criminality is often marked by idiosyncratic qualities. For one, their criminal acts often seem to be inadequately motivated. The individual may, for example, commit a major crime for very small stakes. In this regard, Dr. Harris recalled that Jack tried to sell his mother's pearl earrings for $5. Also, the criminal acts of these individuals often seem to be committed without much sense of self-preservation. They may fail, for example, to take obvious precautions against detection when carrying out their crimes. Here, again, Dr. Harris recalled Jack's attempts to sell items to the very source from which they were stolen.

In short, Jack showed the disorder's classic overall pattern of long-standing antisocial behavior, dating from childhood, aimed at nothing higher than the immediate gratification of transient desires. His behavior did not seem to be deterred by any sense of shame, remorse, or even plain self-interest.

Clinicians have generally despaired of devising an effective treatment for antisocial personality disorder. Perhaps the main reason for this is that people with the disorder, by definition, have no recognition that their behavior pattern is problematic. They usually reject the need for or value of psychological treatment, and so they are unlikely to initiate it or adhere to it for very long. Still other factors may

The DMS-5 requires that there be evidence of conduct disorder prior to the age of 15 in order to meet the diagnostic criteria for antisocial personality disorder.

Finding an effective treatment for antisocial personality disorder has been challenging. Some short-term studies have suggested that cognitive-behavioral therapy and contingency management can help decrease substance abuse in those with antisocial personality (Messina, Wish, & Nemes, 1999). However, attempts to find value in cognitive-behavioral therapy or other forms of therapy for the treatment of antisocial personality disorder have been unsuccessful (Davidson et al., 2009).

also be at work, but the sad reality remains that the mental health field is currently unable to help most people with this personality disorder.

Unfortunately, the single greatest hope for improvement may lie with the simple passage of time. It appears that adults with this pattern, who often begin a criminal career as teenagers, significantly reduce their level of criminal activity after age 40. That is, they experience fewer convictions and serve less time in prison as they grow older. The reason for this shift remains unclear, but, for now, it is the one optimistic note in an otherwise bleak affair.

Assessment Questions

1. What is one of the most common reasons individuals with antisocial personality disorder end up in therapeutic treatment?

2. What inconsistencies did you notice as you read about Jack's complaints prior to being hospitalized and his behavior after he was admitted?

3. What other psychiatric disorders appear with patients who have antisocial personality disorder?

4. What are the statistics regarding the gender of people with this diagnosis?

5. What behaviors did Jack finally manifest that fit a diagnosis of antisocial personality disorder?

6. Give 3 examples from Jack's mother's story that suggested Jack was a candidate for a personality disorder as an adult?

7. What are some possible biological explanations for antisocial personality disorder?

8. Why is treatment usually ineffective for this personality disorder?

9. List 4 criteria that Jack exhibited that convinced Dr. Harris that Jack's diagnosis should be antisocial personality disorder.

10. What eventually happens to many individuals who have this personality disorder?

Borderline Personality Disorder

Table 15-1

Dx Checklist

Borderline Personality Disorder

1. Individuals display pronounced, wide-ranging, unstable, and impulsive patterns in their relationships, sense of self, and emotions. Such patterns begin by the time they reach their mid-20s.

2. The individuals specifically exhibit at least 5 of the following symptoms:

   (a) Desperate efforts to avoid perceived abandonment.

   (b) Fluctuations between idealizing and denigrating family members, friends, and coworkers.

   (c) Highly changeable self-concept.

   (d) Self-damaging displays of impulsivity.

   (e) Repeated self-mutilating or suicidal acts or gestures.

   (f) Significant fluctuations in moods and emotions.

   (g) Long-term sense of emptiness.

   (h) Experiences of extreme and often uncontrollable anger.

   (i) Periodic, short-term paranoid ideas or dissociation during times of stress.

(Based on APA, 2013.)

Karen, a 36-year-old woman, single and unemployed, was admitted to the West Raymond Medical Center after deliberately taking an overdose of sedatives combined with alcohol. She made this suicide attempt when the man she had been dating for 3 months told her he didn't want to see her any more. Karen lost consciousness from the overdose, and spent the next 3 days in West Raymond's intensive care unit.

Because doctors at the hospital were reluctant to discharge her until they were certain that she would receive follow-up counseling, Karen called her psychotherapist and asked him to tell the hospital staff that she was indeed in counseling. The therapist, however, did not respond as Karen expected. He pointed out that this was her third suicide attempt in the past 2 years and, as a result, he was not prepared to vouch for anything. In fact, the therapist did not think that he should continue to treat Karen. He described her suicide attempts as "manipulation," and said that she was using the suicide attempts and other forms of self-harm to draw attention to herself and to avoid confronting her underlying disturbance.

A personality disorder is a very rigid pattern of inner experience and outward behavior that differs from the expectations of one's culture and leads to dysfunctional behavior and psychological pain.

Karen had been giving herself minor injuries several times a week for years. She inflicted the injuries in a slow, deliberate fashion, typically when alone and feeling rejected or abandoned. She would sit down with a razor blade in hand and watch closely as she dragged the blade across the flesh of her arm or leg. The cuts were relatively superficial, but deep enough to draw a thin line of blood that she observed with fascination. For a brief moment, she felt reassured of her own existence. The pain was physical, real, and deserved—quite unlike the feelings of emptiness or depression she tended to experience much of the time.

The frequency of Karen's cutting, and her use of drugs and alcohol to deaden emotional pain, varied according to her relationships with men. When she had a steady boyfriend, she generally felt more positive, as though life had meaning and focus. On the other hand, the slightest hint of problems in the relationship could trigger deep emotional distress.

Karen A Typical Relationship

Karen's relationship with Gary, a 32-year-old construction worker, was in many ways typical. They met in a bar and immediately began an intense love affair; for the next 2 weeks they were together almost every night. Karen felt happy and on top of the world; after only a week, she started to fantasize about their life together, even to the point of naming their future children. She stopped drinking alone in the evenings, or doing any of the cutting that accompanied her darker moods.

As time passed, Karen and Gary stopped seeing each other every day, but her focus on him was still complete. While at work, she would check her phone and Facebook page several times an hour to see if he had left any messages. If she was home in the evening and she hadn't heard from him, she would frantically try to locate and call him, even if he had told her earlier in the week that he couldn't come over.

With time, Karen grew more and more sensitive to signs that Gary might be pulling away. She would keep asking him about his feelings for her, and she became irritated if he seemed evasive. At first, he told her he "liked her a lot"; but after a while he said he didn't understand why they had to talk about their relationship and their feelings all the time. He began texting her less and less, and Karen started feeling rejected.

On nights when she had no contact with Gary, she would sit alone in a darkened room just holding her phone in her lap. She would check his Facebook, Instagram, and Twitter pages to see if she could determine where he was and who he was with. Often, when her anxiety was especially high, she would text him. Gary sometimes would text her back, but his responses seemed distant and strained. When Karen would try to pin him down as to when they could get together, he would just reply, "I'll let you know." And if Gary did text her first, he rarely asked her to do anything special anymore. He usually texted her late at night, and his interest in seeing her seemed physical at best.

One night, Karen and Gary went to the movies together and, just as they were taking their seats, he said he wanted to get some popcorn. Karen immediately became suspicious, as she recalled seeing a cute, young woman working at the concession stand. Karen demanded that Gary stay with her. He left his seat anyway, explaining that he would be right back. Karen then reached out, grabbed his arm, and yanked him back in his seat with surprising force. Gary was momentarily shaken but, after collecting himself, he rose again and stalked out of the theater. Karen followed him out to the sidewalk; by the time she reached the curb, he was already across the street and moving briskly. She just stood on the curb screaming, "Come back, you bastard!" and finally, "I hate you!"

Karen returned home feeling miserable. She tried to call Gary, but he ignored her calls. She got out a razor blade and did some of her first cutting in weeks, making two superficial cuts on her left thigh. She tried Gary's number one more time, but still no answer.

When Karen finally got in touch with Gary the following evening, she tried apologizing, but he told her he didn't want to see her any more. She pleaded with him, declaring that she loved him and couldn't live without him. She promised to be more considerate of his need for space. Gary replied that he just didn't think it was working out and that they should part company as friends. At this, Karen became furious and threw her phone across the room. She found a bottle of wine to ease her misery, but even after drinking it all, she still couldn't bear the pain of separation. She began obsessively checking his Facebook page and sure enough, Gary had already changed his status to Single. Karen posted a nasty message on his wall and within an hour she discovered that Gary defriended her. It was then that she decided to end it all. She went to her nightstand, reached for a bottle of sedatives, looked at them for a few seconds, and then swallowed about 30 pills.

When Karen's roommate, Cecily, came home, she found Karen unconscious on the floor of her bedroom. Cecily phoned for an ambulance and Karen was rushed to the emergency room where her stomach was pumped.

Approximately 75 percent of people with borderline personality disorder attempt suicide at least once in their lives. Of the people who attempt suicide, as many as 10 percent will actually commit suicide (Gunderson, 2011; Leichsenring et al., 2011).

In some ways, Karen's stormy affair with Gary had actually been more positive than many of her relationships. Gary, for example, did not take advantage of her, whereas some of her past boyfriends were happy to maintain a sexual relationship long after losing interest in her. Several even abused her physically. She was so desperate for the sense of worth she received from being in a relationship—any relationship—that she would put up with a great deal. When a relationship did end, it was almost always at the man's instigation, and Karen always felt a profound sense of emptiness, abandonment, and despair.

Unrewarding though her relationships were, she considered almost all of them preferable to being alone. When not in a relationship, she practically felt as if she didn't exist. She never really developed any personal interests or work ambitions, and seemed to go from low-level job to low-level job.

A Roommate's Perspective "Two Years of Hell"

After finding Karen near death and finally getting her to the hospital, her room-mate, Cecily, was shaken and drained. At first, she thought that she would feel better within a few days, but a week later she took stock and realized that she was feeling, if anything, worse. Cecily's family persuaded her to make an appointment with a counselor to discuss the ordeal and her reactions. During her session, the shaken woman declared that finding Karen on the bedroom floor was, in fact, the culmination of "two years of hell."

Cecily explained to her therapist that she had met Karen 2 years earlier, after posting an ad on Craigslist for a new roommate. At the time, Karen did not re-ally confide in Cecily about her emotional problems. She did say that she was "in therapy" and described herself as "really crazy, totally neurotic." However, since Cecily herself had been in therapy, she thought little of it, and even believed that their common neurotic tendencies might be a bonding issue. As it turned out, the 2 years that followed were far from a bonding experience.

As Cecily told the therapist:

At first Karen was a lot of fun, but then she would become really depressed off and on, and . . . well, weird. For the first month, I thought that we were having fun living together, discovering that we liked a lot of the same movies and music and things. Then one night, about 2 months after she moved in, I was getting ready to go out with a friend, and Karen demanded to know where I was going. I told her I was going out. That wasn't good enough for her. Where was I going? Who was I seeing? What was I doing?

Then she tried to make me feel guilty for going. "Fine, just leave," she pouted. She complained that we were no longer spending any time together, which was ri-diculous because we had just spent a whole day at an art museum together. When I pointed that out to her, she got hysterical, yelling at me, telling me that I only cared about myself and that I was leaving her with nothing to do. By then, I was mad, and I told her in no uncertain terms that I did not plan to spend every waking moment of my life with her just because we were roommates. I stormed out.

When I came home that night, it was really scary. There was a little blood on the floor, and it made a trail that led to her bedroom door. When I banged on the door to see if she was all right, she said that she'd accidentally cut herself making a sandwich and everything was fine. I wasn't sure I believed her, but I preferred to

Prevalence rates of bor-derline personality dis-order in the general population range from 1.6 percent to 5.9 per-cent. Up to 20 percent of psychiatric inpatients may be given a diagnosis of borderline personality disorder (APA, 2013).

go along with that, rather than consider the possibility that she might be seriously disturbed.

After that evening, she was distant from me for a while. She seemed very angry, and I must admit that I was really put off. The last thing I needed was to be living with someone who wanted all my attention, who was so high-maintenance. I wasn't so much scared as annoyed. Dealing with her was starting to take a lot out of me. Eventually, she got over being angry with me and went back to her old ways: constantly draining my attention and making me feel guilty about not spending more time with her. No matter how much time I did give her, it was never enough.

Then she started dating this guy, Eric, and I thought that things were getting better. I didn't know much about him, but Karen was spending almost no time at home and that was just fine with me. When I did see her, she would gush about how incredibly happy she was—I mean, this was just weeks after she met him—how deep their relationship was and how perfect everything was. She was sure he was "the one." Of course, by now I knew how unbalanced she was and I suspected she was probably being crazy like always, but I didn't want to look a gift horse in the mouth. She was no longer my problem for the moment.

I should have seen what was coming next but, like an idiot, I didn't. Eric left her, and she was totally my problem again. She stayed home and cried for days at a time. She made me take care of her, telling me she was too depressed to do anything for herself. She even fantasized about the violent things she would do to Eric when she felt up to it, and cursed a blue streak while talking about him. And that's pretty much how it's been ever since.

After Eric, there was Ahmad, then James, then Stefan. Always the same story, always the same ending. And always with me in the middle—having to smile while she gushed endlessly about the latest relationship and having to pick up the pieces when the relationship would end.

Karen The Early Years

Karen grew up in a family that seemed stable and loving on the outside. Her father was a prominent local businessman who was also the lay minister of a church. Her mother worked at a small law office in town and volunteered in the church day care. Karen also had two older brothers who were considered model students.

In private, however, the family was violent and abusive. Even as a toddler, Karen was frequently beaten with a belt by both parents. Some of the beatings were inspired by misbehavior. Others were carried out on general principle, to "keep the devil out of her," in her father's words.

Her parents were extremely unpredictable. Her father might hold her on his lap and tell her she was a "darling girl" and how much he loved her, but minutes later he would once again be "beating the devil out of her." Nor was the abuse

Studies have often found instances of great trauma in the early lives of people who develop borderline personality disorder (Huang, Yang, & Wu, 2010).

Karen suffered at the hands of her family limited to beatings or words. Beginning at about age 6, her father began abusing her sexually, by fondling her genitals and engaging in oral-genital contact. This occurred about a dozen times and continued until Karen reached the age of 12. After molesting her, her father would call her a "cheap whore" who was "going to hell." Then he would beat her severely and make her kneel in prayer to confess her "sins."

Starting at age 6, she was also sexually abused on a weekly basis by her oldest brother, John, who was 13 years old and favored by her parents. This abuse involved both oral-genital contact and intercourse. When she was 9 years old, two of John's friends also participated in the abuse. When the young victim told her mother what was happening, the woman responded by beating her daughter for using "sexual language" and for being "seduced by the devil."

Even after John left for college, he would continue to abuse Karen during visits back home. Finally, when she was 16 years old, she told her other brother, Ted—who was 18 years old at the time and a senior in high school—what was happening. Ted, who had been Karen's only source of comfort throughout her childhood, confronted John and said he would kill him if he ever touched their sister again. This put an end to the abuse.

Two years later, on the day Karen graduated from high school, she left her family and moved to a small studio apartment in the next county. She found work as a waitress in a local diner, started dating a man whom she met there, and married him just a few weeks later. Her new husband, George, a car salesman who was 15 years her elder, began dominating Karen in short order. In many respects, their life together was a replay of Karen's upbringing.

George suspected, without basis, that Karen was flirting with other men and carrying on affairs behind his back. He made her quit her waitressing job and kept her a prisoner in their home. He demanded that his wife leave the house only with him or to do necessary food shopping; he also forbade her to buy any new clothes. On one occasion, Karen visited her former coworkers at the diner, despite George's house rules. When word of that visit got back to her husband, he confronted her with her "deceitfulness" and beat her when she defended herself.

When not in a jealous mood, George could be very nice to Karen. Often, he would take her out for dinner or dancing, tell her she was "the prettiest girl in town," and apologize for any of the hurtful things he had done. He would describe his hopes of making "a pile of money" someday and his desire to then treat Karen "like a queen." Such affection was typically short-lived, however. The next day he might very well return home from work and beat her for cheating on him.

Karen's family background made it extremely difficult for her to accurately assess her life with George. Of course, she hated the beatings, but she could not judge whether they were undeserved or whether she might be able to find better treatment elsewhere. As it happened, she never had to leave George, because he was killed in a car accident 3 years into their marriage.

After George's death, Karen went through a period of utter confusion, in which feelings of both devastation and relief rose to the surface. She was now free of his cruelty, but Karen had nevertheless become completely dependent on him. She felt lost and developed clinical depression, leading to a psychiatric hospitalization.

Karen underwent at least 10 more psychiatric hospitalizations over the next 15 years. She received a wide range of diagnoses during this period, and dozens of different drugs were prescribed for her without much benefit. When not hospitalized, she would support herself with waitressing or secretarial positions. Work was of little importance to her, however. It was relationships with men that filled her thoughts or her dreams, as she moved from one intense and unrealistic attachment to another.

Karen feared abandonment more than anything else in life. She tried to kill herself three times during this period, and indeed, all three of the attempts were direct responses to being jilted by men to whom she had formed passionate attachments.

During those 15 years, in addition to her hospitalizations, she saw at least nine different psychotherapists—psychiatrists, psychologists, and social workers—on an outpatient basis. She even had a sexual relationship with one of her male therapists, who later lost his license after two other women filed charges against him for sexual misconduct.

> Close to 75 percent of the people who receive a diagnosis of borderline personality disorder are women (APA, 2013; Grilo et al., 1996).

Karen in Treatment "The Break of a Lifetime"

After Karen's third suicide attempt and her therapist's refusal to continue working with her, the hospital discharged the troubled woman to the local community mental health system, where she received once-a-month medication management and weekly group therapy. After a while, she concluded that her treatment there was only "maintaining [her] misery" and she was about to stop when, without warning, her life took a very positive turn. In what she would later describe as "the break of a lifetime," a staff member at the mental health center recognized Karen's broad pattern for what it was, and referred her to Dr. Dierdra Banks, a psychologist specializing in dialectical behavior therapy.

During a lengthy initial session, in which Karen described her problems and history, Dr. Banks grew confident that the woman's condition met the DSM-5 criteria for a diagnosis of borderline personality disorder. Karen repeatedly engaged in frantic efforts to avoid abandonment; she exhibited a pattern of unstable and intense interpersonal relationships; she had a markedly unstable self-image, or sense of herself; she engaged in recurrent suicidal behavior and self-mutilation; her moods were unstable; she had chronic feelings of emptiness; and she frequently displayed inappropriate anger.

For years, borderline personality disorder seemed almost untreatable, as various approaches brought little or no change to the emotional turmoil and self-destructive lifestyles of those afflicted. However, by the early 1990s, an increasing number of therapists were applying dialectical behavior therapy in cases of borderline personality disorder. Dr. Banks was one such therapist.

Karen in Treatment Dialectical Behavior Therapy

Like other practitioners of dialectical behavior therapy, Dr. Banks believed that people with borderline personality disorder primarily experience emotional dysregulation, a reduced capacity to regulate their emotions, particularly negative emotions such as sadness, anger, and anxiety. Because of a biological vulnerability, the individuals have a high sensitivity to emotional stimuli, an intense response to such stimuli, and a slow rate of recovery from their emotional arousal. And because of a skills deficit, the individuals cannot hold back inappropriate behaviors or consider constructive behaviors when they experience strong emotions. In short, people with borderline personality disorder have a dual handicap. Not only are their emotions stronger than the average person's, their skills for managing emotions are deficient. The result is a lifelong pattern of emotional and behavioral instability.

According to dialectical behavior theory, the failure to acquire adequate skills for managing emotions arises from an invalidating environment during childhood. In such an environment, a child's thoughts and feelings are not taken seriously or supported. One of the most harmful kinds of invalidating environments is one in which a child is repeatedly victimized. Children who grow up in this situation may learn to not trust their own feelings or thoughts. In addition, they may develop little sense of who they are. They must depend on other people for direction, support, and meaning.

Like other dialectical behavior therapists, Dr. Banks would typically address such problems in stages throughout treatment. During a pretreatment stage, she would explain the principles of dialectical behavior therapy and ask clients with borderline personality disorder to commit themselves to the treatment program for a minimum period. Then she would move on to three treatment stages. In the first stage, she would address issues fundamental to survival and functioning, such as decreasing suicidal behaviors, decreasing therapy-interfering behaviors, decreasing behaviors that were interfering with the quality of a client's life, and increasing behavioral skills. In the second stage, the psychologist would work to reduce distress due to past trauma, such as sexual abuse. And in the final stage, she would address longer-term issues, such as increasing self-respect and achieving career, social, and interpersonal goals.

Also, like other dialectical behavior therapists, Dr. Banks would typically conduct treatment on two fronts. She would have clients participate in behavioral

Research indicates that individuals with borderline personality disorder often improve markedly during treatment with dialectical behavior therapy (Kliem, Kröger, & Kosfelder, 2010; Linehan et al., 1991, 1993; Panos, Jackson, Hasan, & Panos, 2013).

The theory and techniques followed by Dr. Banks and other dialectical behavior therapists are based largely on the work of Marsha Linehan (1993).

skills training groups, where they would develop needed behavioral skills. At the same time, she would conduct individual psychotherapy sessions with her clients, focusing on what was happening at the moment. The goal of individual therapy was to soothe clients, help them through crises, and guide them in the application of their new behavioral skills. The relationship between client and therapist was a key part of treatment; Dr. Banks would strive to create a validating environment that had been, according to the dialectical behavior therapy model, missing in the client's past.

In addition, Dr. Banks would encourage clients with borderline personality disorder to contact her, either by texting or calling, between visits. She considered such contacts opportunities for her to provide immediate help in a crisis; to guide clients in problem solving at the time the problem arose; and to deal with any strong, negative emotions that the clients might develop about therapy between sessions. The active use of consultations in dialectical behavior therapy differs from most other approaches in treating this disorder. In fact, other approaches typically view between-session contacts from borderline clients as attention-seeking, manipulative, or maladaptive, and most therapists discourage such efforts.

> The term *dialectical* is meant to suggest that the goals and methods in dialectical behavior therapy often involve achieving a balance between two opposing forces, especially a balance between self-acceptance and making changes for the better.

Pretreatment Stage   Dr. Banks's primary goal during the pretreatment sessions was to obtain a commitment from Karen to stay with therapy for a minimum period. She considered such a commitment essential in cases of borderline personality disorder, in light of most such clients' disappointing past experiences in therapy and their explosive reactions, which could lead to impulsive, premature terminations of therapy.

At the same time, Dr. Banks recognized that, prior to obtaining any sort of commitment, it was important first to discuss Karen's history fully and gain a proper appreciation of her experiences, both in therapy and out. Only then could Karen feel that the therapist's recommendations were well considered. Accordingly, Dr. Banks spent two full sessions with Karen before asking for a commitment to treatment. During these sessions, she empathized with how much fear and mistrust of the treatment process Karen must have developed because of her unsuccessful past therapies. She also expressed empathy for Karen's own attempts to handle her feelings, through the use of self-harm, dependent relationships, and, occasionally, alcohol. Finally, the psychologist expressed admiration for Karen's persistence in trying to improve her situation, despite a long history of invalidation and abuse.

Karen expressed surprise at the psychologist's recognition of her strengths, noting that more typically therapists would shake their heads over how "messed up" she was. Dr. Banks replied that she recognized Karen indeed had problems, but that she also recognized Karen was probably coping with them in the best way she knew how.

To help her client decide whether to commit herself to this therapy, the psychologist described the principles and techniques of dialectical behavior therapy. To begin, she explained that Karen's problems fit a pattern known as borderline personality disorder, a term that Karen said she recognized from some of her previous treatments. The therapist explained that the term *borderline* was unfortunate, being a holdover from days when clinicians mistakenly thought that people with the condition were "on the border" between neurosis and schizophrenia. She said that current thinking on this disorder was that it primarily involved difficulty in managing strong emotional feelings; many of the behavior problems—self-harm, impulsive behavior, interpersonal difficulties—were now seen as stemming from the individual's understandable need to cope with these feelings. The treatment, Dr. Banks explained, would involve learning more effective ways of coping with emotions. She then described the various stages of treatment and the two formats of treatment group behavioral skills training and individual psychotherapy.

Karen said she was impressed with the organization of the treatment approach. In all her previous therapies, a systematic plan had never been laid out for her. She said the approach made sense to her, but she was wary of her ability to succeed. Dr. Banks expressed sympathy for her wariness, and also tried to shift some of the burden of success, explaining that success was dependent not only on Karen's efforts but on the psychologist's ability to apply the treatment appropriately.

Moreover, she suggested that Karen define treatment success by how well she was sticking to the treatment plan, and let the symptom improvements take care of themselves.

The psychologist and Karen agreed to work together for at least 6 months. Dr. Banks estimated that the total treatment time might be 2 years.

First-Stage Treatment: Addressing Issues of Survival and Basic Functioning

In the first stage of treatment Dr. Banks focused on issues critical to survival and functioning: increasing behavioral skills, decreasing suicidal behaviors, decreasing behaviors that interfered with therapy, and decreasing behaviors that reduced the quality of one's life.

Increasing behavioral skills (group training)

Karen began attending a weekly dialectical behavior therapy behavioral skills training group, designed to teach behavioral skills in a systematic fashion, using lecture material, group practice exercises, and homework assignments. Five specific skill areas were covered: (a) mindfulness skills, (b) interpersonal effectiveness skills, (c) emotion regulation skills, (d) distress tolerance skills, and (e) self-management skills.

Mindfulness skills refer to the ability to step back from and look at one's emotions, while at the same time not being judgmental about them. Interpersonal

Although termed *behavioral*, the techniques of dialectical behavior therapy also draw from such sources as psychodynamic therapy, meditation practices, Zen Buddhism, and feminism.

effectiveness skills involve being able to make and decline requests, while at the same time maintaining self-respect and sound interpersonal relationships. Training in these skills resembles the social skills or assertiveness training techniques used with other patients who have social skills deficits. Emotion regulation skills involve being aware of intense and inappropriate emotional arousal, and behaving rationally in spite of inappropriate arousal. Distress tolerance skills refer to the ability to cope with negative emotional arousal, by employing such techniques as distracting oneself during a crisis, soothing oneself, or considering various responses. Finally, clients in the group were taught self-management skills, including how to set and achieve realistic goals.

At first, Karen was reluctant to participate in the behavioral skills training group, asking why she couldn't just see Dr. Banks for the individual sessions and forget about the "group thing." The psychologist, however, explained the importance of learning the skills; she also pointed out that if the individual sessions were spent entirely on skills training, there would be no time to deal with Karen's day-to-day concerns. The client agreed to attend as part of her commitment, and, after a few weeks, began to feel that the group training was worthwhile. In addition to gaining mastery in certain skill areas, she came to feel comfort in the emotional support supplied by the group, and a sense of gratification in providing support to others. She continued to attend the group for close to a year.

Decreasing suicidal behaviors

In the first individual therapy session, Dr. Banks explained that she would like to focus on Karen's tendency to harm herself. She invited Karen to join a file-hosting service that contained a folder full of various forms and handouts she had created. Dr. Banks began by having the client keep a daily record detailing her level of suicidal thinking, her misery level, her self-harm urges, her self-harm actions, what she did to cope with any self-harm urges, and her use of new skills.

Dr. Banks was able to access Karen's records at any time via Dropbox and then at the next session, Karen and the psychologist would review the records of the past week. In the second session, the records revealed that the client was cutting her upper arms or inner thighs with a razor blade approximately five times a week. The injuries, which she bandaged herself, were visible to others only if she wore shorts or a tank top. Unlike Karen's previous therapists, Dr. Banks was careful not to criticize her for creating these injuries, label them as "manipulation," or threaten to stop treatment if the behavior continued. Instead, she responded to each instance with a behavioral analysis, trying to get Karen to see how the cutting was serving a function. In one case during the week, a man whom Karen had met at a party took her phone number, then failed to call her the next day as promised. Karen's misery level rose as the hours passed without a phone call, and she eventually made two superficial

Because people with borderline personality disorder are more emotional than analytic, dialectical behavior therapists teach clients how to make a behavioral analysis of problems. The therapists help them to see a larger context; that their problems—emotional, behavioral, or interpersonal—are usually just one element in a chain of events.

cuts on her upper thigh, which briefly reduced her emotional pain. At that point in time, Karen had called Dr. Banks to tell her what she had done and to receive support.

During the next session, when reviewing the incident and Karen's reactions, the psychologist validated the woman's sense of disappointment, but also recommended that she start coping differently with her urges to cut. Dr. Banks explained that she wanted Karen to begin managing her emotions with a different device, by contacting the therapist and discussing her feelings *prior* to doing any cutting. In fact, they put a "24-hour rule" into effect. Karen would be prohibited from contacting the therapist for at least 24 hours following any cutting. The rationale was twofold. First, calls or texts to the therapist immediately after cutting have no problem-solving value, because the cutting has already taken place by then. Second, the rule against speaking with Dr. Banks until 24 hours after any cutting behavior would create an incentive to use the new problem-solving procedure of calling the therapist before the cutting happened..

In the early morning following this session, at about 3:00 A.M., Karen called Dr. Banks. Breathing heavily and almost sobbing, the client said that she had not yet cut herself, but desperately wanted to do so. She was afraid, on one hand, that the therapist would reject her if she carried out the cutting and, on the other, that Dr. Banks would be angered by her calling so late at night.

Though desperately tired, Dr. Banks made it clear to Karen that it was "absolutely wonderful" that she had taken this step, and was glad she had taken the risk of calling rather than doing the cutting. These words alone had a very calming effect on the client. The psychologist reminded Karen of some of the distraction, self-soothing, and distress tolerance strategies she had learned at the behavioral skills-training group. The client, in turn, decided to make herself a cup of hot cocoa, take a warm bath, and read her favorite magazine.

Karen made a similar call 2 days later, and the day after that. In both cases, Dr. Banks encouraged her to use distress tolerance strategies, and Karen was able to resist the urge to cut herself.

At the next session, her records revealed no instances of self-harm for the week. Dr. Banks devoted most of the session to analyzing this achievement, noting how Karen had successfully replaced cutting with more constructive coping strategies. Still, Karen's misery level had remained high during the week: a 10 on a scale of 10 on most days.

Over the next 3 months, she contacted the therapist an average of three times a week and succeeded in avoiding all self-harm during this period. Correspondingly, her misery level began to improve. Then she started dating a man to whom she was strongly attracted. They had sex on their second date. At her therapy session the next day, Karen announced that she had found the perfect man and felt certain she was in love. She was brimming with enthusiasm—more than

According to dialectical behavior theorists, the self-mutilation of people with borderline personality disorder serves to produce physical pain that competes with—and, hence, partially reduces—the much more painful experience of negative emotions. Other impulsive behaviors, such as gambling, substance abuse, irresponsible spending, reckless driving, binge eating, or unsafe sex, may similarly help reduce negative emotions (Muehlenkamp, Brausch, Quigley, & Whitlock, 2013).

Dr. Banks had ever seen in her. The psychologist supported her feelings, noting how wonderful it was to be in love.

Unfortunately, the man didn't share Karen's enthusiasm and failed to call the following evening as promised. When Karen finally reached him and suggested they make plans for the weekend, he said he really didn't feel like "getting involved." Karen was devastated and, over the next several days, cut herself multiple times before calling Dr. Banks. When she did call to tell the therapist what had happened, she felt certain that Dr. Banks would reject her for having regressed. She begged her not to end the treatment.

Dr. Banks: Why would I want to end treatment?

Karen: I started cutting again, and I didn't even try to call you to get help.

Dr. Banks: What kept you from calling?

Karen: I just felt so ashamed.

Dr. Banks: But you're calling now, and that's great! I understand your reluctance to call. It's perfectly natural. No one likes to bring bad news. But try not to think of this as such bad news. You were under a lot of stress for the first time since our therapy began; it's understandable that you might not be able to manage it perfectly. But, look at what you did do. You did stop the cutting eventually, and you did call me. I think it's best to look at this as a temporary slip, as opposed to a complete relapse. I think you'll find that you can get back on track again and avoid the cutting once the distress from this experience subsides.

Karen: I think I can stop cutting now. Just hearing you tell me that it was natural to get upset helps. But I feel so miserable.

Dr. Banks: I know. Let's discuss some concrete things you can do now to cope with that feeling.

Dr. Banks then reviewed some concrete problem-solving strategies. Karen agreed to make out a schedule of things to do for the rest of the day, including three errands and one recreational activity, so as to reduce her thoughts about being rejected. In the evening, she would go to a movie rather than waiting around in her apartment to see if anyone else would call her.

At the next session, Karen said she had carried out the scheduled activities the day before, and this had helped reduce her focus on the dating situation. However, now she was feeling "completely hopeless" about the progress of therapy itself. She said there was no point in continuing with something that just didn't work. She demanded that the psychologist admit that she was a hopeless case who could never live a normal life.

Dr. Banks was momentarily at a loss for words. But before she could speak, Karen herself came to her assistance. "Don't be upset," the client said, smiling. "Sometimes I say these things. If you don't overreact, if you believe in me, it's

Psychotropic medications, particularly mood stabilizers and antipsychotics, have helped calm the emotional and aggressive reactions of some people with borderline personality disorder (Haw & Stubbs, 2011; Lieb, Völlm, Rücker, Timmer, & Stoffers, 2010). However, given the heightened risk of suicide by these individuals, the use of medication on an outpatient basis can be quite risky.

easier for me to believe in myself, and not in the hopeless part." The psychologist replied that she certainly did believe in Karen, and then offered the client a parable. She said that the way out of misery is like finding your way out of the desert; you walk and walk, and often things look just the same: dirt, sagebrush, rocks, no water, no shade, no relief. However, if you follow a fairly straight path for a long time, even though things look and feel the same, you're in a very different place, much closer to getting out of the desert.

A number of times after this exchange, Karen expressed the same kind of hopelessness and claimed to be giving up. However, such claims were typically followed by her working even harder, and achieving new goals the next day or week. She gradually came to appreciate that she had a tendency to experience hopelessness, and that she should not believe the thoughts that often intruded.

Over the next year, Karen had only two episodes of self-injury, which she described as mainly due to habit. She then remained injury-free for the remainder of treatment.

Decreasing therapy-interfering behaviors   Karen frequently displayed two kinds of therapy-interfering behavior. She would repeatedly express extreme hopelessness and insist that she could not follow the treatment plan any longer, and she would experience extreme anger toward the therapist.

Although Karen seemed, overall, to have warm feelings toward Dr. Banks, there were many occasions when feelings of fear, hopelessness, shame, or depression caused her to lash out. She would turn bright red and criticize the psychologist or call her names. For example, on one occasion, she said, "Thanks for your brilliant suggestion. You know, other therapists I've had were stupid, too, but at least they cared about me."

Although at first taken aback by comments such as this, Dr. Banks recognized that they were signs that she had unwittingly invalidated some aspect of Karen's experience. Unlike her client's friends, the psychologist knew that it was important not to respond defensively to an attack or an insulting remark from her. Indeed, the most therapeutic reaction, for Karen's sake, was for Dr. Banks to admit right away that she might indeed have said something unwise. During the initial stages of therapy, for example, she would respond to Karen's outbursts by saying something like, "Boy, I must have really messed up for you to be this angry. What am I missing? I really want to know what's going on." As therapy progressed, Karen was able to exercise more and more self-restraint in her angry reactions. Instead of criticizing or attacking the psychologist, she would say something like, "Hey, I don't think you're understanding me."

Other times, the anger that Karen expressed toward Dr. Banks actually had more to do with people she had encountered and had been upset by outside of therapy. With time, she was able to distinguish between these reactions and the

Because therapists are continually confronted with the emotional crises, self-destructive acts, and intense anger of, and even insults from, clients with borderline personality disorder, treatment is emotionally demanding for the practitioners. Thus, dialectical behavior therapists often consult with other therapists to help them remain professional and stay on track with the principles of dialectical behavior therapy.

feelings produced by Dr. Banks's words. At later points in therapy, she was able to simply tell the psychologist, "I'm in a bad mood. It has nothing to do with you, just some idiot in the parking lot. It's okay. I'll get over it." Ultimately, Karen was able to apply such skills to her interactions with friends, as well.

Decreasing behaviors interfering with quality of life   When Karen began therapy with Dr. Banks, she was unemployed and dependent on disability benefits. However, as therapy progressed and Karen developed greater control over her feelings and actions, she was in a position to consider improving the quality of her life. Accordingly, about 9 months into therapy, she decided to obtain some job training, and enrolled in a training program for medical assistants at a local college. The specific job skills that were taught included answering doctors' phone calls, making appointments, retrieving and filing medical records, and filling out insurance forms.

Karen did not find the training easy. Although a bright woman, it had been 18 years since she had been in school, and sticking to a curriculum was an unfamiliar experience. The skills training that she had already received in the dialectical behavior therapy group helped her to keep up with the course work. At one point in the training, Karen temporarily stopped attending classes after becoming depressed over a broken date. However, when faced with the prospect of not obtaining her certificate and remaining stuck in her current living situation, she eventually pulled herself together and resumed the work, making up for the missed classes.

During this stage of therapy, Dr. Banks also helped Karen to see that sometimes her difficulties in relationships were not due to her own interpersonal ineffectiveness, but to a lack of compatibility between herself and the people she chose. Accordingly, Karen worked hard not only on increasing her personal effectiveness but also on choosing more stable and trustworthy friends, including romantic partners.

In spite of her efforts, she endured several failed relationships over the course of her treatment, which often brought back suicidal feelings. As she and Dr. Banks worked on managing these feelings, they became less intense. The process was helped along by a truly supportive and mutual friendship that Karen developed with another trainee in her medical assistants' training program. This friend, Ann, was a divorcee who lived not far from Karen. In response to a suggestion from Dr. Banks, Karen asked Ann to join her for coffee one day after class, and it soon became a regular event. In the past, the client had been so single-mindedly focused on her relations with men that she sometimes entirely overlooked friendships with women. And the relationships that she did develop with women were often one-sided, with Karen so completely absorbed in her own problems that other women viewed her as unbearably self-centered. With

During their 30s and 40s, most individuals with borderline personality disorder obtain somewhat greater stability in their relationships and jobs (APA, 2013).

Ann, however, she showed some of the consideration and emotional restraint that she had developed in her relationship with the therapist. Ultimately, they became close friends.

Second-Stage Treatment: Reducing Distress Due to Past Traumas

The focus of the second treatment stage was to help Karen overcome lingering feelings of distress due to past traumas, such as her sexual abuse. In fact, her abuse history had been addressed to some degree from the beginning of treatment. Indeed, in the first stage of therapy, Karen had developed skills to help her tolerate her abuse memories. She had learned, for example, to soothe herself—to do especially nice things for herself, such as eat favorite foods, dress in favorite clothes, or go for a walk in her favorite park; and to distract herself, which involved finding constructive and engaging projects to work on, such as repairing her bicycle.

At the second stage of treatment, however, the goal was not only to manage the emotional distress that would result from abuse memories, but to reduce the capacity of the memories to produce distress. Dr. Banks used exposure techniques similar to those used in the treatment of posttraumatic stress disorder, in which clients undergo repeated, controlled exposures to stimuli—external or internal—that have been linked to past traumas.

Initially, the psychologist asked Karen to describe her past abuse experiences in general terms only. As the client described the same experiences over and over again as a regular exercise, the exposure seemed to result in reductions in her distress levels. Thus, after repeatedly describing her father's molestation of her in general terms—three times per session for three sessions—Karen's distress level was relatively mild by the ninth description. The procedure was then repeated using greater and greater levels of detail, until even the most detailed descriptions of her traumatic experiences produced only moderate distress. The same procedure was applied to Karen's other traumatic memories, with similar results.

People with borderline personality disorder often have another mental disorder, as well. Common ones are mood disorders, substance-related disorders, bulimia nervosa, posttraumatic stress disorder, and other personality disorders (APA, 2013).

Third-Stage Treatment: Addressing Longer-Term Issues

The focus of the third stage of treatment was to help Karen gain greater self-respect and achieve career, social, and interpersonal goals. In fact, in her case, the achievement of these goals had been occurring naturally, as a result of the gains she had been making during the first and second stages of treatment. As Karen had stopped injuring herself, developed stable behavior patterns, increased her interpersonal effectiveness, and pursued career training, she was in fact valuing herself increasingly and providing a more dignified existence for herself. Thus, sessions with the therapist at this stage of treatment tended to solidify a process that was already well under way.

Epilogue

Karen remained in individual therapy once a week for a total of 2 years, and now continues with periodic follow-up sessions or phone calls every month or two. Overall, her life has improved greatly, especially compared with what it was prior to beginning dialectical behavior therapy with Dr. Banks.

Above all, she no longer hurts herself, even when extremely upset. She also rarely uses alcohol to deal with feelings of distress, and has not been hospitalized since her final suicide attempt, a month before her therapy began. She works part-time as an assistant in the medical records department of a local hospital, and takes courses at a nearby college, with the goal of obtaining a bachelor's degree. Once a week, she coleads a dialectical behavior therapy support group.

Most important, Karen has regained control over her mental and emotional life. As she puts it, "I get to have my feelings, and nobody has the right to control me anymore." In addition, she feels that a major achievement of therapy has been "my recognition, deep down inside, that, like other people, I am an acceptable human being and that life can be safe. My life is my own now."

Assessment Questions

1. What led to Karen's admission to West Raymond Medical Center?

2. Why did Karen's therapist decide to discontinue treatment with her at that time?

3. How many individuals with borderline personality disorder attempt suicide?

4. Describe Karen's typical relationships with men.

5. What was Karen's "greatest fear" that led to her frequent suicide attempts?

6. How did Karen's behavior meet the DSM-5 criteria for borderline personality disorder?

7. Describe the concept of dialectical behavior therapy. Be sure to describe the six main points of this type of treatment.

8. What is Dr. Banks's primary goal during the pretreatment stage? How did Dr. Banks relate this to Karen in her initial therapy sessions?

9. How did the term *borderline* originate and how accurate is it in describing Karen's problems?

10. What were the two basic formats Dr. Banks told Karen would be part of her treatment program?

11. List the five specific skill areas covered in the first-stage of treatment with Karen.

12. Why is it common for individuals to use self-destructive behaviors when they are disappointed by life events?

13. How did Dr. Banks handle Karen's cutting behaviors both to help her prevent the behaviors but also support her when she relapsed?

14. What were two therapy-interfering behaviors frequently displayed by Karen?

15. What was the focus of the second treatment stage? What types of therapeutic interventions did Dr. Banks use with Karen during this time?

16. Describe some other comorbid disorders that individuals with borderline personality disorder may develop.

17. Describe the third stage of treatment for Karen.

18. What is the ultimate achievement Karen feels she has realized from her treatment?

Attention-Deficit/Hyperactivity Disorder

Table **16-1**

Dx Checklist

Attention-Deficit/Hyperactivity Disorder

1. Individual presents 1 or both of the following patterns:

   (a) For 6 months or more, individual frequently displays at least 6 of the following symptoms of inattention, to a degree that is maladaptive and beyond that shown by most similarly aged persons: • Unable to properly attend to details, or frequently makes careless errors • Finds it hard to maintain attention • Fails to listen when spoken to by others • Fails to carry out instructions and finish work • Disorganized • Dislikes or avoids mentally effortful work • Loses items that are needed for successful work • Easily distracted by irrelevant stimuli • Forgets to do many everyday activities.

   (b) For 6 months or more, individual frequently displays at least 6 of the following symptoms of *hyperactivity* and *impulsivity,* to a degree that is maladaptive and beyond that shown by most similarly aged persons: • Fidgets, taps hands or feet, or squirms • Inappropriately wanders from seat • Inappropriately runs or climbs • Unable to play quietly • In constant motion • Talks excessively • Interrupts questioners during discussions • Unable to wait for turn • Barges in on others' activities or conversations

2. Individual displayed some of the symptoms before 12 years of age.

3. Individual shows symptoms in more than 1 setting.

4. Individual experiences impaired functioning.

(Based on APA, 2013.)

Although very low birth weight (less than 1,500 grams) presents a twofold to threefold risk for developing ADHD, most children with low birth weight do not develop the disorder (APA, 2013).

Billy was his parents' first child. He was born after a normal, uncomplicated pregnancy, an especially healthy baby who grew rapidly and reached the standard developmental milestones—sitting, crawling, standing, walking, and so forth—either at or before the expected ages. His parents marveled at his exuberance and his drive to be independent at an early age. He was sitting by the age of 5 months and walking at 11 months. Once mobile, he was a veritable dynamo (in fact, they called him "the Dynamo") who raced around the house, filled with a curiosity that led him to grab, examine, and frequently destroy almost anything that wasn't nailed down.

Billy From "Dynamo" to "Dynamite"

During his toddler period, Billy's parents had no inkling that his activity level was at all unusual and, in truth, in many ways it was just an exaggeration of tendencies that most toddlers exhibit. Still, his parents found it exhausting to cope with his behavior. Just watching over him was a full-time job. Billy's mother, Marie, had contemplated doing some freelance accounting at home to earn extra money. However, with her very first project she realized that this was completely unrealistic. Marie had hoped that she could contain Billy by keeping him in a playpen while she worked, but she found that he wouldn't tolerate such confinement for more than 2 minutes before he was yelling to get out. Once out, he was a roving accident scene. Within minutes, Marie would hear a crash or some other noise that demanded investigation.

When Billy's mother became pregnant with his sister, Billy was well into the "terrible twos" and his mother and his father, Stan, were beginning to doubt their suitability as parents. Of course, other new parents often remarked on how demanding children were, but Marie and Stan could tell that the other parents felt nowhere near the same sense of desperation.

With the arrival of Billy's sister, Jennifer, Marie and Stan developed a budding awareness that their problems in handling their son might not be due entirely to their inadequacy. As an infant Jennifer—unlike Billy—did not try to squirm and break free every time she was held. Later, there were other differences. As a toddler, she was content to sit quietly for long periods just playing with her toys, and she listened until the end of the entire story when Marie read to her, whereas Billy would get restless and run off within a couple of minutes.

When Billy reached school age, and Marie and Stan received more objective feedback about his situation, their sense of his difficulties became more defined. After his first day of school, his kindergarten teacher described him as "quite a handful"; then, at the parent-teacher conference, the teacher informed Billy's parents that his activity level was well above that of the other children. In the first and second grades, as the academic component of the curriculum increased and the demands on the children for behavioral control increased correspondingly, Marie and Stan started to get yet stronger complaints from his teachers. In addition, Billy's academic progress was slowed because of his problems with attention. Although he eventually learned to read, he didn't really begin to master the skill until the second grade. Now 8 years old and in the third grade, Billy was falling behind the other children in a wide range of academic tasks. With encouragement—actually, insistence—from his teacher, Mrs. Pease, his parents decided to seek help for him at the Child Development Center.

Half the children with ADHD also have learning or communication problems, many perform poorly in school, a number have social difficulties, and about 80 percent misbehave (Goldstein, 2011; Mash & Wolfe, 2010).

Billy at Home A Parent's Perspective

By age 8, Billy rarely carried out his parents' requests or instructions, or he carried them out only partially before becoming caught up in some other activity. One evening in November was illustrative: Billy's mother had just finished preparing dinner when she went to her son's room and asked him to stop playing his video game, wash his hands, and take his place at the dining room table. "Okay, Mom," Billy answered.

"Thank you, Billy," Marie said as she went back down to the kitchen to do some final preparations. However, 5 minutes later she realized she still had not seen Billy. She went back up to his room and found he had never turned off the video game.

"Billy, I mean it. Stop playing now!" she told him.

"Oh, all right." he said, and turned the game off.

Although this was Marie's second effort, for once Billy was coming without too much of a struggle, so his mother was relieved. "Go wash your hands," she reminded him.

"Okay," Billy replied. He headed down the hall toward the bathroom, but caught a glimpse of his 5-year-old sister already seated at the dining room table, holding a new doll. Jennifer was pulling a string that made the doll talk.

"Hey, neat!" Billy exclaimed. "Let me try." He ran over, grabbed the doll from Jennifer's hands and pulled the string. The doll spoke in a squeaky voice, while Billy's sister complained that she wanted her toy back. "Does the doll say anything else?" Billy asked, ignoring Jennifer's protests. He began to pull the string over and over in rapid succession until, finally, it broke off.

"Uh, oh," Billy observed.

"Mommy, he broke my doll!" Jennifer cried.

Billy's mother emerged from the kitchen to find him holding the broken doll while his sister wailed. What had begun as a simple attempt to get Billy to wash his hands and seat himself at the dinner table had ended in a tumultuous scene.

And so it would go. Unless Billy was escorted through every task of the day, he'd get sidetracked, and it usually ended with an argument or something getting broken. Consequently, his parents often found it easier just to do things for Billy—wash his hands, clean his room, get him dressed—because getting him to do the tasks himself was the greater effort.

When left to his own devices, Billy's behavior was disruptive in other ways. He jumped on the beds, ran through the house, or played shrill games of hide-and-seek under the dinner table with his unwilling parents or sister. If his mother was on the phone, he would think nothing of yelling out demands for a drink, a snack, or help in finding some lost toy, despite Marie's numerous warnings not to interrupt her.

> Twice as many boys as girls have ADHD. This ratio decreases to 1.6:1 when examining ADHD in adults. Females are more likely to present primarily with inattentive features (APA, 2013).

Even playing out in the yard was not a solution, because if Billy wasn't watched closely, in a flash he might run out into the street after a ball, without any regard for traffic. When playing indoors with neighborhood children, Billy was bossy, continually grabbing their toys or refusing to share his own. Thus, his play dates had to be closely supervised by his parents to avoid squabbles. Because of these problems, Billy had few friends. Instead, most of his leisure time was spent watching television or playing video games, activities that Marie and Stan were reluctant to encourage, but which they felt forced to accept since the 8-year-old could do little else without supervision.

Billy at School A Teacher's Perspective

Billy's third-grade teacher, Mrs. Pease, found his behavior intolerably disruptive in school. She was also concerned that Billy's behavior problems were interfering with his ability to learn. She believed he was a bright child, but his attention and behavior problems were causing him to fail to complete his lessons and hampering the other children's ability to complete theirs.

One day at school in mid-April Mrs. Pease had called the class to attention to begin an oral exercise: reciting a multiplication table on the blackboard. The first child had just begun her recitation when, suddenly, Billy exclaimed, "Look!" The class turned to see Billy running to the window.

"Look," he exclaimed again, "an airplane!"

A couple of children ran to the window with Billy to see the airplane, but Mrs. Pease called them back, and they returned to their seats. Billy, however, remained at the window, pointing at the sky. Mrs. Pease called him back, too.

"Billy, please return to your desk," Mrs. Pease said firmly. But Billy acted as though he hadn't heard her.

"Look, Mrs. Pease," he exclaimed, "the airplane is blowing smoke!" A couple of other children started from their desks.

"Billy," Mrs. Pease tried once more, "if you don't return to your desk this instant, I'm going to send you to Miss Warren's office." Billy seemed oblivious to her threats and remained at the window, staring excitedly up at the sky.

Mrs. Pease, her patience wearing thin, addressed Billy through gritted teeth. "Billy, come with me back to your seat." She took him by the hand and led him there. She also considered making good on her threat to send him to Miss Warren, the principal, but she glanced at the clock and realized Miss Warren would not be in her office now. Finding someone else to supervise Billy would probably be more disruptive than disciplining him within the class, so she settled for getting him back in his seat, then took her place once more in front of the class. By now she was almost 10 minutes into the lesson period and still had not finished a single multiplication table.

Approximately 5 percent of children and 2.5 percent of adults have ADHD (APA, 2013).

Mrs. Pease tried to resume the lesson. "Who can tell me the answer to 3 times 6?" she asked. Fifteen children raised their hands, but before she could call on anyone, Billy blurted out the correct answer. "Thank you, Billy," she said, barely able to contain her exasperation, "but please raise your hand like the others."

Mrs. Pease tried again. "Who knows 3 times 7?" This time Billy raised his hand, but he still couldn't resist creating a disruption.

"I know, I know!" Billy pleaded, jumping up and down in his seat with his hand raised high.

"That will do, Billy," Mrs. Pease admonished him. She deliberately called on another child. The child responded with the correct answer.

"I knew that!" Billy exclaimed.

"Billy," Mrs. Pease told him, "I don't want you to say one more word for the rest of this class period."

Billy looked down at his desk sulkily, ignoring the rest of the lesson. He began to fiddle with a couple of rubber bands, trying to see how far they would stretch before they broke. He looped the rubber bands around his index fingers and pulled his hands farther and farther apart. This kept him quiet for a while; by this point, Mrs. Pease didn't care what he did, as long as he was quiet. She continued conducting the multiplication lesson while Billy stretched the rubber bands until finally they snapped, flying off and hitting two children, one on each side of him. All three children let out yelps of surprise, and the class turned toward them.

"That's it, Billy," Mrs. Pease told him, "You're going to sit outside the classroom until the period is over."

"No!" Billy protested. "I'm not going. I didn't do anything!"

"You shot those rubber bands at Bonnie and Julian," Mrs. Pease said.

"But it was an accident."

"I don't care. Out you go!"

Billy stalked out of the classroom to sit on a chair in the hall. Before exiting, however, he turned to Mrs. Pease. "I'll sue you for this," he yelled, not really knowing what it meant.

Soon, the school bell rang, signaling the end of the period and the beginning of recess. Mrs. Pease was thankful to get some relief from the obligation of controlling Billy, but was frustrated that almost the entire math period had been wasted due to his disruptions.

Out in the schoolyard during recess, Billy's difficulties continued. As the children lined up for turns on the slide, Billy pushed to the head of the line, almost knocking one child off the ladder as he elbowed his way up. After going down the slide, Billy barged into a dodgeball game that some younger children were playing; he grabbed the ball away from one child and began dribbling it like a basketball, while the other child cried in frustration. The supervising teacher told Billy to give

---

The number of children ever given a diagnosis of ADHD increased from 7 percent in 2000 to 9 percent in 2009 (Akinbami, Liu, Pastor, & Reuben, 2011).

Symptoms of ADHD, particularly the hyperactive symptoms, are typically most pronounced during the elementary school years. They become less conspicuous by late childhood and early adolescence (APA, 2013).

the ball back, but Billy kept dribbling, oblivious to her demands. Finally, she took the ball away from him, and Billy wailed in protest.

"Hey, give that back!" he insisted.

"You took this ball from someone else," the teacher explained.

"But you took it from me. That's not fair!" Billy argued.

The teacher sent Billy to sit on a bench, where he remained sulking and feeling mistreated for the rest of the recess period.

This was an average day for Billy at school. On some of his better days, he was less physically disruptive, but he still had his problems, particularly in attending to and completing his schoolwork. In a typical case, Mrs. Pease would give the class an assignment to work on, such as completing a couple of pages of arithmetic problems. While most of the children worked without supervision until the assignment was completed, Billy was easily distracted. When he got to the end of the first page, he would lose his momentum and, rather than continuing, would begin fiddling with some object on his desk. Other times, if another child asked the teacher a question, Billy would stop his own work to investigate the situation, getting up to view the other child's work and failing to complete his own.

Finally, at a parent-teacher conference, Mrs. Pease told Billy's parents that she thought Billy's problems might be attributable to an attention-deficit disorder. Concerned about Billy's growing academic and social problems—not to mention feeling exhausted from continually having to remind, encourage, and threaten their son to get him to do the most elemental things—Marie and Stan decided to seek professional assistance. They arranged for a consultation at the Child Development Center.

Billy in Treatment The Therapist in Action

After repeatedly observing a child's tornadoes of activity, inattention, and recklessness, teachers or parents often conclude that he or she suffers from attention-deficit/hyperactivity disorder (ADHD). However, 25 years of practice had taught child psychiatrist Dr. Sharon Remoc that such a conclusion is often premature and inaccurate, leading to incorrect and even harmful interventions. Thus, when Billy's parents brought him to the Child Development Center, Dr. Remoc was careful to conduct lengthy interviews with the child, his parents, and his teacher; to arrange for Billy to be observed at home and at school by an intern; to set up a physical examination by a pediatrician to detect any medical conditions (for example, lead poisoning) that might be causing the child's symptoms; and to administer a battery of psychological tests. In addition to obtaining a description of Billy's current problems and his history from his parents, Dr. Remoc had Billy's mother respond to questions from 2 different assessment instruments: the Swanson, Nolan, and Pelham Checklist, which contains questions pertaining specifically to disruptive

Only approximately one-third of children who receive a diagnosis of ADHD from pediatricians actually undergo psychological or educational testing to support the diagnosis (Hoagwood, Kelleher, Feil, & Comer, 2000; Millichap, 2010).

In a 2007 national study of children with and without ADHD, parents reported that 46 percent of children with ADHD had a learning disability compared with 5 percent of children without ADHD who had a learning disability. In addition, 27 percent of children with ADHD versus 2 percent of those children without ADHD were reported to have conduct disorder (Larson, Russ, Kahn & Halfon, 2011).

An estimated 3.5 percent of U.S. children received stimulant medication in 2008 compared with 2.4 percent in 1996 (Zuvekas & Vitiello, 2012).

behavior problems, and the Conners Parent Rating Scale, which contains questions specifically for assessing ADHD. Similarly, Dr. Remoc sent the teacher's versions of the Swanson, Nolan, and Pelham Checklist and the Conners scale to Mrs. Pease.

Billy's battery of tests included the Wechsler Intelligence Scale for Children and the Wechsler Individual Achievement Tests (to provide scores in reading, mathematics, language, and written achievement). The results of these tests confirmed the impression already supplied by Billy's parents and Mrs. Pease: Billy's intelligence was above average, and his academic achievement was lower than his intelligence scores would predict. These findings established that Billy's academic problems were not due to intellectual limitations.

After completing this comprehensive assessment, Dr. Remoc was confident that Billy's difficulties met the criteria in DSM-5 for a diagnosis of attention-deficit/hyperactivity disorder, combined type. He exhibited a majority of the symptoms listed both for inattention (for example, difficulty sustaining attention, failure to follow instructions, oblivious to verbal commands, easily distracted) and for hyperactivity-impulsivity (for example, difficulty remaining seated, excessive motor activity in inappropriate situations, difficulty waiting his turn). The symptoms were apparent before the age of 12, occurred both at home and school, and caused significant impairments in both the social and academic spheres.

Over the years, research has indicated that many children with ADHD respond well to either stimulant drugs or systematic behavioral treatment. Although some therapists prefer one of these approaches over the other, Dr. Remoc had come to believe that a combination of the interventions increases a child's chances of recovery. By helping the child to focus better and slow down, the medications may help him or her to profit from the procedures and rewards used in the behavioral program.

Stimulant drugs, which include amphetamine/dextroamphetamine mixed salts (Adderall), methylphenidate (Ritalin), methylphenidate extended-release (Concerta), dextroamphetamine (Dexedrine), and pemoline (Cylert), were first used to treat ADHD decades ago, when clinicians noted that the drugs seemed to have a "paradoxical" tranquilizing, quieting effect on these children. Subsequent research has shown that all children—both those with and those without ADHD—experience an increase in attentional capacity when taking stimulant drugs, resulting in behavior that is more focused and controlled. This may create the appearance of sedation, but the children are actually not sedated at all.

Unfortunately, the drugs are not effective for all children, and only partially effective for others. And even when a drug is optimally effective, other areas of behavioral adjustment may still need to be addressed, because the ADHD child may have little practice in the more appropriate behaviors that he or she now is theoretically capable of producing. This is where behavioral programs may come into play.

In the ideal case, both parents and teachers are involved in implementing a behavior modification program, which is based on the ABC model of behavior. The A in the model denotes *antecedents,* the conditions that provide the occasion for a particular behavior; the B denotes the *behavior* itself; and the C denotes the *consequences* of the behavior. Thus, a given behavior is seen as prompted by certain antecedents, and maintained by its consequences. For example, Billy's sprint to the window was prompted by the antecedent condition of a boring classroom exercise and the appearance of an exciting stimulus (the airplane). It was maintained, according to the model, by the rewarding effect of viewing the airplane, which was much greater than the punishing effect of Mrs. Pease's warnings or even of being sent out of the room. In a behavior modification program, the usual strategy is to increase the rewards for engaging in alternative behaviors under the same antecedent conditions. Thus, if the reward for remaining seated can be made to exceed the reward for viewing the airplane, then, theoretically, the child will be more inclined to remain seated.

Learning alternative behaviors may involve more than just adjusting incentives or antecedents. Some skills may have to be taught directly. A child who has never practiced asking politely for a toy, as opposed to grabbing it, will need to learn this skill before he or she can respond to incentives to implement it. Direct behavioral skills training usually follows a standard sequence. First, the child receives an explanation of the skill; next, he observes a model demonstrating the skill; then, he practices performing the skill, first through role-playing in the training session and then through real-life behavioral practice. After the skill is learned, both parents and teachers can prompt the child to employ it in a given situation. For example, after the skill of sharing is well learned, the parent can prompt the child to "share" in a situation calling for cooperation with another child, and then praise the child appropriately for so doing. Theoretically, the more the skill is employed and reinforced in a variety of appropriate circumstances, the more the child will use the skill spontaneously, receiving naturalistic positive reinforcement from the environment in the form of friendly or gratified reactions from others.

Thus, Dr. Remoc outlined for Billy's parents four treatment components: (a) stimulant medication, (b) parental training in the use of behavioral modification principles, (c) social skills training for Billy, and (d) token economy in the school environment.

Dr. Remoc explained that stimulant medication was important for increasing Billy's attention and impulse control; this, in turn, would enhance his capacity to do what was expected of him, both in general and in response to the behavior modification plan. The parental training, she explained, would acquaint Marie and Stan with principles of behavior modification, allowing them to deal optimally with any remaining behavior problems, as well as with Billy's behavior during periods when he might not be taking medication (so-called drug holidays). Social

> Research suggests that a combination of drug therapy and behavioral therapy is often helpful to children with ADHD (Parker, Wales, Chalhoub, & Harpin, 2013).

skills training seemed necessary, Dr. Remoc said, in light of Billy's problems in getting along with other children and in cooperating at home. Finally, she explained that, since a large portion of Billy's difficulties occurred in the classroom, it would be helpful for both Billy and Mrs. Pease to have a behavioral program operating in that environment. Dr. Remoc spoke to Mrs. Pease about the matter, and the teacher was agreeable to instituting a program provided it wasn't too burdensome; but given Billy's problems up to now, Mrs. Pease said that almost anything seemed less burdensome than simply doing nothing.

Stimulant medication   After ruling out any physical problems (e.g., motor tics) that might preclude the use of stimulant medication, Dr. Remoc discussed the basic rationale for use of the medication with Billy's parents. She explained that the medication had been used for years to treat children with symptoms of inattention, impulsivity, and hyperactivity. She also explained that the medication is not a tranquilizer. On the contrary, the medication stimulates the central nervous system for 3 to 4 hours after it is ingested. This stimulant effect, she explained, seems to increase the capacity of children with ADHD to maintain their attention and to control their impulses. As a result, they are better equipped to meet the requirements of school, home, and a social life.

In addition, she informed Billy's parents that certain side effects can develop, including weight loss, slowed growth, dizziness, insomnia, and tics. Dr. Remoc noted, however, that these effects usually are not severe and often disappear after the body becomes accustomed to the drug or whenever a drug holiday is scheduled. The clinician noted that since most children with ADHD respond well to Concerta without prohibitive side effects, she was inclined to try Concerta first.

Dr. Remoc pointed out that the decision to take medication was not carved in stone. Indeed, the parents should consider the initial medication regimen as a trial period; if, during this time, they concluded that the medication was not worthwhile, then it should be discontinued. They could try a different medication or they could rely on the behavioral methods alone.

Once Billy began taking the medication, it was apparent that his behavior improved substantially, although not completely. In class, for example, Billy still blurted out some answers and turned around to talk to his neighbors during silent reading period, but he did these things only about one fourth as often as before. Most noticeable from Mrs. Pease's standpoint was that simply saying his name was often enough to get him to cease what he was doing.

Out in the schoolyard, Billy was now less inclined to barge into other children's games or push others aside. But, he still did not have a good social sense. Either he drifted off by himself or, if he did join a game, he failed to abide by the rules consistently, which ended up provoking arguments. For example, in joining a game of catch with four other children, Billy was inclined to hog the ball after he received

According to the United Nations, the United States produces and consumes approximately 85 percent of the world's methylphenidate. (*Medicating Kids. Statistics on Stimulant Use.* Retrieved March 24, 2014 from http://www.pbs.org/wgbh/pages/frontline/shows/medicating/drugs/stats.html.

The use of stimulant drugs to treat children with ADHD has increased by 57 percent since 2000 (Carlson, Maupin, & Brinkman, 2010).

it; he would then hold it and giggle, in spite of the other children's yells that he was supposed to throw the ball to the next receiver.

At home, Billy seemed less driven physically. He sat at the dinner table for the entire meal, without constant requests to be excused and without getting up repeatedly to grab things or to play under the table. Also, his passion for jumping on the beds was gone, and he became more dependable in carrying out instructions. For example, if his parents sent him to wash up and sit at the table, they now could count on his following through 75 percent of the time (as opposed to 25 percent, as before). Tendencies such as stubbornness and defiance remained a problem, however; it remained a struggle to get him to do chores, to get started on his homework, or to follow household rules in general. He continued to barge in on his mother when she was on the phone, shouting his insistent requests for snacks, toys, and videos. Overall, however, the medication seemed to have many advantages.

Parental training   To gain some knowledge of behavioral management techniques, Billy's parents enrolled in a training group for parents of children with ADHD (at about the same time that Billy began taking medication). The group, led by psychologist Dr. James Grendon, was designed to educate parents about both ADHD and the principles of behavior modification for managing it. Group sessions were held three times a month, and once a month Dr. Grendon met alone with Billy's parents to discuss the child's individual situation.

At the very first group session, Billy's parents found comfort in learning that other parents' experiences closely paralleled their own. All the parents were able to share their experiences and found that they were all dealing with very similar concerns. Many parents saw humor in some of the situations, and this helped to soften the impact of what they had all been going through.

It also helped Marie and Stan to know that some of their marital disputes were shared by the other parents. Like the others in the group, Billy's parents often argued over how to deal with their child. Although it didn't solve the problem, it helped them to know that even their arguments were "normal," given the circumstances.

In additional group sessions, Marie and Stan were progressively introduced to the ABC principles of behavior management. Among the points they found helpful was the idea that parents can become unduly focused on discouraging problem behaviors through criticism or punishments; the punishments, in turn, are often ineffective and just fuel resentment. A different approach, Dr. Grendon explained, was to think in terms of the alternative behaviors (B) that parents would like their children to perform under the same circumstances (A), and to provide praise and rewards (C) accordingly.

Billy's parents explored this principle in greater detail in individual sessions with the group leader, as they felt it applied particularly to the way they were handling

> Although family conflict is often present in families with a child with ADHD, negative family interaction patterns are unlikely to cause the development of ADHD (APA, 2013).

(or mishandling) many situations with their son. For example, a regular problem with Billy was that he interrupted his mother when she was on the phone. She had to lock herself in the bedroom in order to have a coherent conversation with a pediatrician, repairman, friend, or relative. Often, even locking herself in was not enough to insure peace and quiet, as Billy might start pounding on the door in order to convey his demands, in spite of repeated scolding.

To address the problem, the psychologist asked Billy's parents to think of specific, alternative actions they would like Billy to carry out under these conditions. At first, all Marie and Stan could think of was "not interrupt," but Dr. Grendon reminded them of the stipulation that they think of a tangible alternative behavior for Billy to carry out under the same circumstances. After some discussion, they came up with the idea of having Billy write down his requests whenever his mother was on the phone. They noted that their son loved to write notes, so this might be a tangible thing he could do to satisfy his demands temporarily, and allow him to resist interrupting. With further discussion, Billy's parents and the psychologist worked out the following procedure: Before Marie made a call or answered the phone, she would hand Billy a special message pad, reminding him to write down any questions or problems that he had while she was talking; Marie would then give prompt attention to Billy's messages as soon as she was off the phone; finally, if Billy succeeded in using the pad, instead of interrupting, for the majority of calls in a given week (his mother would keep a checklist to tabulate Billy's compliance), he would be given a special reward on the weekend (such as eating out at his favorite restaurant).

This was the first behavioral plan that Billy's parents put into effect, and after ironing out a few wrinkles, Billy was able to follow the procedure, even to the point of fetching the message pad himself whenever the phone rang. Eventually, he resisted interrupting almost entirely.

Other behavioral plans were then put into effect for other matters, such as household chores and homework completion. In both cases, Billy's parents found an effective formula by reversing antecedent conditions and behavioral consequences. For example, they saw to it that television viewing would always follow the completion of homework, rather than vice versa.

Social skills training   Marie and Stan also enrolled their son in a class where he could learn skills for getting along better with other children. The class was composed of other children receiving treatment at the center for ADHD.

During each class the focus was on learning one particular social skill, such as sharing. First, the group leader explained the concept of sharing, and then asked the children their own opinions of what it meant. Next, she demonstrated the implementation of the skill with several children in different, contrived, situations: sharing toys, sharing food, or sharing a seat. Then each child came up,

> Children whose parents or other close relatives had ADHD are more likely than others to develop the disorder (APA, 2013).

> About half of children with ADHD, combined type, also have oppositional defiant disorder. Conduct disorder is present in about 25 percent of children and adolescents with ADHD, combined type (APA, 2013).

one by one, and practiced sharing in each of these hypothetical circumstances. The group leader and the other children then gave the child corrective feedback on how well he or she had shared. Similar classes were devoted to other social skills, such as cooperating, speaking calmly, making polite requests, and following rules.

Billy's parents and Mrs. Pease received written guidelines for discussing the social skills training sessions at home and in school and for guiding Billy to use the skills in everyday situations. Many of the opportunities to prompt him arose at home in his interactions with his 5-year-old sister. With continued prompting, Billy started to share things with his sister spontaneously on many occasions, which increased the harmony in the household.

Because of these successes, and Billy's additional successes using the social skill of cooperation, Marie and Stan finally felt confident enough to invite one of Billy's schoolmates over for a play date. The last time a child had come to their house, it had been a disaster, as Billy had refused to relinquish any of his toys to his guest. Needless to say no child was likely to return after such treatment. Although this play date was far from perfect and needed Marie's constant attention, it turned out to be reasonably pleasant.

Token economy The token economy is an element of the ABC behavior modification system; it uses tokens, rather than immediate, tangible rewards, to reinforce desired behavior. The tokens are exchanged for an actual reward at a later time. Token reinforcement is particularly advantageous for ADHD children, who can get so wrapped up in the attractiveness of the actual reward that they find it difficult to remain mindful of the behaviors that the reward is designed to encourage.

Mrs. Pease thought that some form of behavior modification might assist her in regulating several of Billy's behaviors. Accordingly, she and the therapist decided to focus on encouraging three specific school behaviors in Billy: raising his hand to answer questions (instead of blurting out answers), staying in line, and finishing in-class assignments. As token reinforcers, Mrs. Pease would use dinosaur stickers affixed to a piece of paper, with the number of stickers in each of three columns reflecting Billy's compliance with the three behavioral objectives. According to the plan (explained to Billy in a meeting with his parents and Mrs. Pease), Mrs. Pease would keep track of Billy's compliance separately for the morning period and the afternoon period, and award him one sticker if he achieved full compliance with a given behavioral objective in a given period. He would receive his morning stickers at lunchtime, and his afternoon stickers upon dismissal. The stickers could then be redeemed at home for special privileges (going out to eat, going out to a movie, an extra half hour of television or a video game, and so forth).

Billy liked the idea of getting stickers so he agreed to the plan. On the first morning of the program, he received only one sticker: for finishing his assignment within the allotted time (he had blurted out a couple of answers and had wandered off the line going to art class). In the afternoon, however, he received two stickers: for staying in line and for finishing assignments. After a few more days on the program, Billy was averaging five stickers per day, a level that he was able to maintain, and which reflected a substantial improvement in all three areas.

Within 2 months of the combined treatment program, Billy had improved considerably. He was conforming to classroom rules by staying in his seat, not talking, and finishing his assignments most of the time. When he deviated, he required only gentle reminders from Mrs. Pease to get back on track. Similarly, at home, he was less frenetic. He could carry out instructions more dependably, and he usually accepted his household responsibilities without too much argument. In peer relations, Billy was still learning the culture of give and take, but with periodic guidance and further experience he was becoming increasingly effective. As a result, he was getting along well with his sister, and he now had a couple of friends who would come over regularly to play, and who invited him to their homes as well.

Unfortunately, after about 4 months of this improved functioning, Billy began to slip into some of his old patterns both at home and at school. His parents felt that the problems had to be addressed, as he seemed to be losing ground. The recurrence of problems seemed to coincide with the birth of his new baby brother. In a discussion with Dr. Remoc, Billy's parents wondered whether their total preoccupation with the birth of the baby, and their consequent inability to implement many features of the behavioral program (including not following through on redeeming Billy's dinosaur stickers), was responsible for the slippage in his progress. A renewed effort by the parents to apply the behavioral program, and an adjustment in the dosage of Billy's medication, helped him to regain his previous achievements within a few weeks.

In the DSM-II (1968), ADHD was known officially as hyperkinetic reaction of childhood, and it was commonly referred to simply as hyperactivity or hyperkinesis (the latter term from the Greek for *over* and *motion*).

Epilogue

After 18 sessions of group parental training (over a 6-month period), 6 sessions of individual parent training, 6 sessions of social skills training for Billy, and 4 meetings at school with Billy's teacher, his ADHD symptoms stabilized at an improved level.

Billy reported that he was happier at school and enjoying time at home with his family. He still took medication and saw Dr. Remoc for a checkup every 4 months. Billy's parents planned to give Billy a drug holiday in the summer and felt confident of their ability to manage his behavior during that time with just the behavioral techniques. They were a family again—sometimes laughing, sometimes crying—but, overall, enjoying their lives and activities together.

In addition to being viewed negatively by peers and parents, children with ADHD often view themselves negatively and have significantly lower self-esteem than children without ADHD (Mazzone et al., 2013; McCormick, 2000).

Assessment Questions

1. When did Billy's parents begin to suspect that Billy's "dynamo" personality might be a behavioral disorder?

2. Describe at least 3 behaviors that suggest that Billy's activity level is beyond what's normal for a child his age.

3. When did Billy's family finally receive more objective feedback about Billy's behavior?

4. How long did it take for Billy's teachers to suggest professional consultation regarding Billy's disruptive behavior?

5. Why did Dr. Remoc, the therapist at the Child Development Center, feel it was important to conduct a thorough assessment of Billy before diagnosing ADHD?

6. Describe at least 4 different assessment techniques used by Dr. Remoc to test for ADHD.

7. What were the assessment results that led Dr. Remoc to diagnose ADHD in Billy?

8. Why did Dr. Remoc decide to use both medication and behavioral therapy to treat Billy?

9. What are some potential problems with prescribing medication as the only treatment option for children with ADHD? What are some side effects of stimulant medications?

10. Describe the ABC model of behavioral therapy and give examples.

11. What were the four treatment components outlined for Billy's treatment?

12. Why is it important for Billy's parents to be a part of the treatment plan?

13. Describe the ABC plan that Billy's parents developed to control his "interrupting" behaviors.

14. What other childhood behavioral diagnoses are often comorbid with ADHD?

15. Describe the concept of a token economy.

16. What event disrupted Billy's progress?

17. What was the ultimate outcome after 18 sessions of group parental training?

CASE 17

Autism Spectrum Disorder

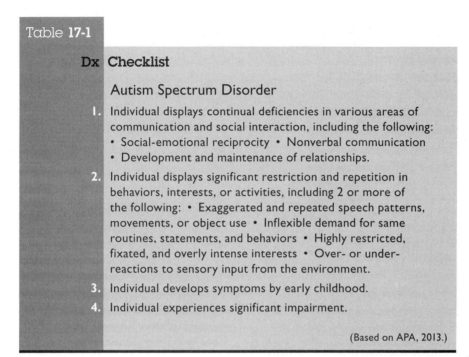

Table **17-1**

Dx Checklist

Autism Spectrum Disorder

1. Individual displays continual deficiencies in various areas of communication and social interaction, including the following:
   • Social-emotional reciprocity • Nonverbal communication
   • Development and maintenance of relationships.

2. Individual displays significant restriction and repetition in behaviors, interests, or activities, including 2 or more of the following: • Exaggerated and repeated speech patterns, movements, or object use • Inflexible demand for same routines, statements, and behaviors • Highly restricted, fixated, and overly intense interests • Over- or under-reactions to sensory input from the environment.

3. Individual develops symptoms by early childhood.

4. Individual experiences significant impairment.

(Based on APA, 2013.)

Adam was born on a beautiful sunny day, to Michelle, aged 32, and Joe, aged 39. Michelle's pregnancy was full-term, the delivery was normal, and the baby weighed 7 pounds, 15 ounces. Michelle and Joe also had another child, Jarrod, who was 6 years older than Adam. Adam was handsome, with brown hair, brown eyes, and a beautiful smile. The parents looked forward to an exciting future, filled with the dreams that having two children can inspire.

Adam's development over the first year of his life was normal. He was able to sit without support by 7 months, crawl at 10 months, and stand alone by 12 months. He took his first independent step at 15 months, and was walking everywhere within a week. All visits to the pediatrician went well, and immunizations were given at the appropriate times.

> The prevalence of autism spectrum disorder has reached 1 percent of the population (APA, 2013).

Adam Clues During the Second Year

After Adam's first birthday party, to which several young children were invited, Michelle began to pay attention to some characteristics of her son's personality that just didn't seem to match those of the other children his age. Unlike the other toddlers, or even his brother when he had been a year old, Adam was not babbling or forming any specific word sounds. Michelle thought that her son should

A 40-year longitudinal study involving normal IQ children with autism found that 75 percent of those individuals grew up with stable IQ and improved language over time. However, 25 percent of the individuals exhibited decreased intellectual functioning with severe behavioral disturbance and language impairment (Howlin, Savage, Moss, Tempier, & Rutter, 2014).

Although specific language impairment is no longer considered one of the primary diagnostic criteria for autism spectrum disorder, many individuals experience significant language delays. Some individuals with autism spectrum disorder who learn to speak show peculiarities in their speech, including *echolalia*, the exact echoing of phrases spoken by others; *pronominal reversal*, the confusion of pronouns, such as the use of "you" instead of "I"; difficulty naming objects, employing a proper tone, or speaking spontaneously; or restrictive and repetitive pattern criteria, such as obsessively repeating parts of movies or books.

have mastered at least a few words by then, especially after hearing other 1-year-olds say "mama" and "cake" and "cookie." Adam could only produce a few noises, which he would utter randomly throughout the day. Michelle also noticed that these sounds were rarely directed toward anyone or anything. The child made no attempt to label people or objects; he would just make those noises.

At first, Michelle and Joe attributed Adam's language delay to the fact that he had an older brother who would speak for him and fulfill many of his needs without Adam's ever having to ask. But they soon became suspicious that a language delay was only part of the problem. At the birthday party and in other situations, Adam seemed uninterested in playing with other children or even being around them socially. He seemed to enjoy everyone singing "Happy Birthday" to him, but he made no attempt to blow out the candles on the cake, even after others modeled this tradition for him. He was only a year old, but his indifference to the party bothered Michelle and Joe.

Upon closer examination, his parents also noticed that Adam had very few interests. He would seek out only two or three Disney figurines and their corresponding DVDs, and that was it. All other games, activities, and toy characters were rejected. And if pushed to play with something new, he would sometimes throw intense, inconsolable tantrums. Even the figurines that he enjoyed were typically not played with in an appropriate manner. Often he would line them up in a row, in the same order, and would not allow them to be removed until he decided he was finished with them. If someone attempted to rearrange or clear away the figurines, he would again have a tantrum.

As her concern grew, Michelle decided to monitor her son's play habits more closely. She was both frightened and amazed at the meticulous way in which he manipulated the Disney characters. On a few occasions, she realized that the order in which he aligned the figurines matched the order in which the characters appeared in one of his favorite Disney movies. Similarly, if Adam's figurines had movable arms and legs, he would arrange their body stances to match that movie.

He also had a marked preference for being with his mother. He had less of an interest in Joe, Jarrod, or other people. In fact, Adam might cry for hours if Michelle had to leave without him. Upon her return, he would stop crying but would not necessarily want to be with her. He would feel content knowing that she was home and go back to playing with his Disney toys by himself. In addition, when called by either parent, Adam often failed to respond to his name. And he displayed odd food preferences: he could not seem to get enough of some foods, and he simply could not tolerate the textures of others.

As the months went by and he remained unable to express his wants and needs, Adam's tantrums became more frequent. If his mother did not understand his noises and gestures, he would grow angry at not being understood. The intensity of these episodes was also growing; Adam was even beginning to hit his ears with his hands and cry for longer and longer periods. One of the most frightening aspects of this for Michelle was the fact that her misinterpretations of the episodes might sometimes endanger Adam's health; she had no way of knowing if he had an upset stomach, a headache, or some other ailment.

Finally, when Adam was 19 months old, Michelle took him to his pediatrician for some answers. The doctor agreed that there were some significant "delays" in Adam's development, and he referred the child to a neurologist for a complete evaluation. The recommendation of a neurologist greatly upset Michelle and Joe. They were now forced to confront their deepest fears. They found it extremely difficult to wait for the neurological evaluation, repeatedly dwelling on all of the terrible scenarios that the word *delay* evoked.

Prior to the appointment with the neurologist, the parents also followed up on the pediatrician's recommendation that they have Adam's hearing formally tested. His hearing was found to be within normal range, and this news caused a mixed reaction in his parents. On one hand, they were happy that serious hearing deficits could be ruled out; on the other hand, where did that leave them? The results left many questions in their minds. Also prior to the neurological evaluation, Michelle and Joe began to research the term *developmental delays* on the Internet; there, for the first time, they saw the word *disability*. When the time for Adam's appointment with the neurologist finally arrived, they were extremely frightened, but they also still held out hope that Adam's skills were just a little late in coming.

Adam Confirming His Parents' Worst Fears

The neurologist was pleasant, and very thorough. She reviewed the case history from pregnancy through birth, and then assessed Adam's milestone achievements. She also completed physical, neurological, and motor examinations. Finally, she addressed his language delays and maladaptive behaviors, by observing his lack of speech and his limited play skills. For all the weeks of waiting for this examination, it seemed to pass very quickly—almost too quickly, the parents believed, for the doctor really to get to know Adam. In fact, she was able to gather a great deal of information and she told Joe and Michelle that Adam seemed to have autism spectrum disorder.

Autism spectrum disorder is a neurodevelopmental disorder, with a range of symptoms that can occur at various levels of severity. The neurologist cited several factors that led to her tentative diagnosis of autism spectrum disorder in Adam: his deficits in social communication, including his nonverbal communication; his severely delayed receptive and expressive language skills; his lack of imaginative play with toys; and his history of repeated and rigid behaviors. In short, all

A diagnosis of autism spectrum disorder is meant to capture a range of neurodevelopmental disturbances, including symptoms that used to be an independent disorder (e.g., Asperger's disorder). The DSM-5 lists various specifiers that are meant to be used to characterize the individual clinical characteristics of the individual with autism spectrum disorder.

of the things Michelle, Joe, and several other family members had noticed were symptoms of this disorder.

A diagnosis of autism spectrum disorder had been his parents' worst fear, after having read so much about its different forms during their research. From their gathering of information, they had formed a mental image of an aggressive or self-injurious child, locked in his own world and unable to communicate. Joe began to tune out as the doctor described the typical features of the disorder. Too many questions were pounding inside his head: Should they get a second opinion? Could it possibly be as bad as she was describing? Whose fault was it? Why hadn't the pediatrician said something sooner? How would Michelle handle this? What would the rest of the family say? What was the cure?

By the time Joe was able to focus again, the visit was over, and the neurologist was talking about her forthcoming report and discussing her recommendations. He heard her explain that, with appropriate early interventions and services, the disorder was "workable," and that because Adam was starting treatment at such a young age, he had a great deal of potential for progress. Joe couldn't imagine how this devastating problem might be workable. He knew that on the long car ride home he would have to be filled in on the missing pieces of the doctor's conversation with Michelle.

Adam Seeking an Early Start

Michelle took charge and played a more active role than Joe in following up on the recommendations of the neurologist. In part, this was because she worked from home selling her handmade jewelry online, in order to be with her children. However, it was also because she felt she needed to stay busy to keep negative thoughts and mounting questions out of her mind. Joe, who was feeling overwhelmed by the weight of the diagnosis, simply followed his wife's lead.

The first course of action was to have Adam more fully and precisely evaluated and to have him begin early intervention services. And it was important that these services be provided by clinicians who specialized in the field of autism spectrum disorder. After consulting an advocacy group for individuals with developmental disabilities, Michelle learned of several prominent early intervention centers. She scheduled an evaluation with the one that would be available the soonest. Six weeks after seeing the neurologist, Adam received a comprehensive evaluation and began treatment at the Manning Child Development Center.

From this point forward, the family's lifestyle became a whirlwind of doctors' visits and a variety of therapies. The initial diagnostic evaluation itself was completed in 90 minutes. One clinician interviewed the parents, while a second took Adam to a separate room for an individual assessment. Diagnostic and rating scales were explained to the parents, including the DSM-5 criteria, the Modified

Autism spectrum disorder is four times more likely to be diagnosed in males than females. However, females tend to be more likely to having accompanying intellectual disability (APA, 2013).

Checklist for Autism in Toddlers—Revised and the Childhood Autism Rating Scale. All of Adam's delays and behaviors were specifically categorized and totaled to arrive at a detailed clinical picture and diagnosis.

Consistent with the DSM-5 criteria for autism spectrum disorder, Adam showed impairment in social communication and social interaction, including marked impairment in the use of nonverbal behaviors such as eye-to-eye gaze; failure to develop peer relationships appropriate to his developmental level; and lack of social or emotional reciprocity. He also showed the typical restricted and repetitive patterns of behavior, interests, and activities, including stereotyped motor movements (e.g., lining up toys); abnormal preoccupations and inflexible adherence to specific, nonfunctional routines or rituals; a strong attachment or preoccupation with unusual objects; and either hyperreactivity or hyporeactivity to sensory input or unusual interest in the sensory aspects of the environment (APA, 2013). His symptoms were present in early childhood, caused impairment in his life, and could not be accounted for by any other disorder.

> The pattern of autism was first identified by the American psychiatrist Leo Kanner in 1943.

Based on the Childhood Autism Rating Scale assessment, Adam's autism spectrum disorder was rated between Level I ("requiring support") and Level 2 ("requiring substantial support"), in terms of social communication and restricted, repetitive behaviors. It was also specified in his diagnosis that Adam's autism spectrum disorder was with accompanying intellectual impairment, and with accompanying language impairment. He displayed a number of symptoms from the rating scale's 15 areas of assessment, including relating to people, imitation, emotional response, object use, visual and listening response, adaptation to change, verbal and nonverbal communication, and intellectual response. Slowly, these terms were starting to have more meaning to Michelle and Joe. The diagnostic team at the center concluded that early intervention was certainly the treatment of choice at this point, and they helped the parents set up a variety of therapies for their son. Adam was enrolled in the center's early intervention program, which provided 3 hours of behavioral therapy each week: 2 hours at the center itself and 1 hour at home. The goal of these behavioral sessions was to help the child develop learning readiness skills—basic skills that one needs in order to be able to learn and acquire broader knowledge, behaviors, or skills. Adam would be taught skills such as making eye contact, sitting appropriately, and following simple directions. Again and again, in trial after trial, he would be rewarded whenever he performed these target behaviors or some approximation of them, and not rewarded if he failed to perform them. It was expected that through such efforts, the child would become increasingly able and willing to perform the behaviors across a wide range of situations and, in turn, be more ready to learn broader behaviors and skills. The sessions were to follow the principles of the applied behavior analysis model—a strict behavioral strategy that, according to research, helps many persons with autism spectrum disorder and other neurodevelopmental disorders. Adam was

In order to help children with autism spectrum disorder to speak, teachers often supplement their speech therapy with another form of communication, including sign language and simultaneous communication, a method combining sign language and speech. Applied behavior analysts will typically employ language acquisition training, which encompasses the principles of applied behavior analysis and has been effective for increasing language.

also signed up for speech therapy 2 days a week and for occupational therapy 1 day a week. Ultimately, the three therapies would all be seeking to increase his ability to engage new people.

The child's life was turned upside down by the early intervention program. Strangers were now being thrown into his world on a rotating basis, and these people were placing demands on him and changing his routines. He was also being separated from his mother in a strange place for the first time ever. During the first few therapy sessions, Michelle wanted to run from the observation room into the treatment room to "rescue" him from the therapist. Adam cried and threw tantrums throughout those sessions. The therapist continually had to reassure Michelle that the child would become less resistant as long as the sessions were carried out consistently. Otherwise, the distraught mother would have withdrawn him from the program and tried teaching him herself.

Slowly, Adam's tears and tantrums lessened as his therapy sessions became a regular part of his weekly schedule. Michelle and Joe began to notice, after 2 months, a slight increase in his eye contact and less resistance when they asked him to complete specific tasks within the home, such as clearing away his figurines after he was finished playing. Nevertheless, his progress felt unbearably slow to them, and they noticed no developments in the area of language, despite the speech therapist's positive reports. Adam also remained unreceptive to all new toys, and his play skills continued to be very limited.

Michelle and Joe decided to supplement the center's early intervention sessions by hiring therapists on a private basis to provide more learning trials at home, as well as scheduling additional speech therapy sessions. In fact, it was the speech therapy that was of most interest to the couple. They believed that if they could just help their son talk, they could better understand what he was feeling and, in turn, could more effectively resolve his other issues.

The in-home private therapy was difficult at first as Adam could not bear having his home routine disrupted even more. But the in-home therapists persevered and tried to apply their services consistently. Like the center's program, the supplemental learning trials focused on learning readiness and on teaching Adam to identify and manipulate various objects. In their work, the therapists selected objects that were particularly relevant to the child's home environment: chairs, eating utensils, and light switches, for example. When they incorporated Disney characters into the sessions, the learning tended to go even better. Nevertheless, progress continued to be slow.

The speech therapists—those at the clinic and at home—worked together on several aspects of Adam's speech. First, they did exercises with his mouth ("Open your mouth wide.") and tongue ("Stick out your tongue.") to strengthen muscles that are typically needed in speech. Second, they used imitation training to help Adam create sounds, for example, the sounds "mmm" or "babababa." Finally, they sought to develop a working communication system that would enable him to convey his wants and needs. Everyone agreed that establishing a communication system for Adam was the priority because if he could communicate better his needs could be better met and his tantrums would likely decrease. The speech therapists decided that it would be best to introduce a basic Picture Exchange Communication System—a system in which Adam could point to or select pictures to help express himself.

At first his parents were opposed to this system. Joe, in particular, feared that Adam would come to rely solely on these pictures. He believed that unless his son were required to speak or at least make sounds in order to receive items, he would have little chance of learning to speak. The therapists explained, however, that many children with language processing problems like Adam's initially learn better with a visual representation of the desired items. Eventually, the children come to appreciate that pictures of items can bring about the items themselves, and they grasp that there is a connection between their thoughts and their environment. Moreover, by helping the children to communicate their needs, the use of pictures reduces their frustrations and tantrums, thus creating a more positive environment for learning verbal skills. Although hesitant, Michelle and Joe agreed to give the picture system a try.

At the same time, though, their worries continued to grow. Adam was now 2 years old and continuing to grow physically, but was without language and with only limited cognitive understanding. Their other son had called for "mama" and "dada" long before his second birthday, and Adam could not even imitate the "m" sound. Privately, they questioned how hard the therapists were really working, and whether Adam was being given enough hours of therapy. Maybe there was more that they could do with him at home. Before long, he would be 3 years old; and if this trend continued, they would have to seek placement in a specialized full-day program.

> Speech teachers may also turn to augmentative communication systems for individuals with autism, systems in which they are taught to point to pictures, symbols, letters, or words on a communication board or computer.

Michelle and Joe Trying Everything

Michelle began to investigate other interventions that she had heard about, just to see if anything out there could make a difference. One of the most talked about treatments that she came across was diet change—eliminating certain foods from Adam's menu, foods with ingredients that some autistic children have trouble tolerating. In particular, Michelle read on the Internet that a gluten-free diet was helpful in many cases of autism spectrum disorder. Apparently, some children with autism spectrum disorder are unable to properly digest gluten (a protein found in wheat), leading many clinicians to speculate that gluten may contribute to inappropriate behaviors , perhaps by causing great discomfort. Michelle read that children like Adam who eliminated most breads, pastries, crackers, snacks,

Despite the attention from the media and some outspoken Hollywood actors, there is no scientific evidence that autism spectrum disorder is caused by the measles, mumps, rubella vaccine (Ahearn, 2010; Uchiyama et al., 2007).

and the like from their diets, sometimes showed significant improvements in their behavior. Although she knew that the outcome of this approach would be uncertain, that it would be challenging to find appropriate foods that Adam would tolerate, and that many children with autism spectrum disorder failed to respond to such diet changes, she felt that she must try everything in her power to reverse Adam's delays. Otherwise, she would be failing him and perhaps missing the one intervention that could make a difference. Michelle and Joe found a nutritionist familiar with the diet. Wanting to be as objective as possible, they decided to give the dietary changes a year, with an assessment of his skills both before and after that year's time.

The whirlwind that their lives had become was continuing. Adam's older brother, Jarrod, now 8 years old, was beginning to show signs of resentment for the amount of attention that his brother was receiving. Michelle and Joe did their best to create special activities for Jarrod, but in fact, Adam's therapies did take most of their time and energy. Time was passing, still with none of the vast improvements Michelle and Joe were hoping for.

When Adam reached 2½ years of age, the couple decided to sign him up for auditory integration training. They suspected that Adam, like a number of children with autism spectrum disorder, might be hypersensitive in the auditory sphere. That is, he might have sensory-perceptual difficulties that cause certain sounds or tones to feel particularly unpleasant making it difficult for him to listen to and process the words and noises within his environment. Auditory integration training is a procedure in which individuals wear headphones that actually alter (for example, soften) certain auditory inputs, making sounds more comfortable and, theoretically, improving the individuals' capacity to process what they are hearing. Although some children with autism spectrum disorder greatly improve their language capabilities with this training, Adam showed no such improvement. Once again, his parents were disappointed.

Some people with autism spectrum disorder seem overstimulated by sights and sounds and try to block them out, while others seem understimulated and perform behaviors that may add to their stimulation, such as flapping their arms, cupping their hands so that they can scream in their ears, or rapidly moving their fingers before their eyes.

Growing Child, Growing Problems

Even with all of his interventions at the child development center and at home, Adam continued to develop into a mystifying little boy. His fascination with the Disney characters remained strong, and was now joined by an added interest in Legos. If he were left alone, these items would occupy him for hours, but again, he didn't play with them in the usual manner. The lining up of the Disney characters continued, and the new-found Legos had to be carefully stacked according to color and then in rows, with the pattern always identical (first red, then green, then yellow, and so on). His preference for certain routines and patterns became even stronger as he grew older; increasingly, these routines were dominating the family's schedule.

For example, Adam was now in the habit of having his bath before going to sleep, and it had to be given by Michelle. For his first 2 years, this set procedure had been easy enough to carry out. But as Adam's brother, Jarrod, grew older, he often needed his mother's help with homework. Moreover, Michelle had to attend more and more parent groups or conferences regarding Adam. When someone other than Michelle had to give Adam his bath, or if a bath had to be skipped altogether, he would throw a major tantrum, followed by poor sleep throughout the night. To avoid this situation, Michelle and Joe found themselves scheduling as many activities, meetings, and outings as possible around the daily bath ritual. Recognizing that they were becoming slaves to the child's rigid routines, the couple came to realize that they needed help with their son's home behaviors every bit as much as with his educational goals.

As Adam grew older still, and encountered new milestones, he revealed delays in yet other areas—producing further difficulties at home. Michelle was uncertain how to begin toilet training him, for example, since he showed no understanding regarding how and where to go. She was also unsuccessful in teaching him to brush his teeth. The first and last time she tried, Adam became extremely upset and resistant, as his oral sensitivities to certain textures made the activity particularly uncomfortable for him. As his frustrations grew, Adam's tantrums also got worse, both in intensity and in duration. Some days he would hit his ears so hard that Michelle feared he might be damaging them.

Still another difficulty for the family was their inability to manage their growing son's behaviors out in the community. They were unsure from one outing to the next how he would behave in a grocery store, mall, or restaurant. Sometimes, accidentally leaving a Disney figurine at home would spark a tantrum so loud, upsetting, and embarrassing that Michelle and Joe would be afraid to ever return to the store or restaurant. Family outings kept decreasing, and eventually became a rarity—the very opposite of the family lifestyle the couple had always hoped for.

Adam at 3 Preparing to Enter the System

As Adam approached 3 years of age, his parents realized that a full-day program was the way to go. Once again, it fell on Michelle's shoulders to find the best such program. Joe was feeling depressed by his son's slow progress and by the position in which his family now found itself. This was not how he had envisioned his future. Since his wife seemed better able to handle everything, he decided that his role should be limited to that of breadwinner—working very hard to earn the extra income needed for all of Adam's therapies. Thankfully, they lived in a state where their insurance company was mandated to include applied behavior analysis in their health insurance plan. Still, there were many services that were not covered, and

In the 1940s and 1950s, it was believed that autism was the result of "refrigerator parents." However, research has failed to support a picture of rigid, cold, rejecting, or disturbed parents (Roazen, 1992).

Currently, 34 states have enacted laws that require insurance companies to provide coverage for the assessment and treatment of autism spectrum disorders. As a result, there has been a significant increase in the number of academic programs offering a master's degree in applied behavior analysis.

throwing himself into work also helped him to forget, at least for a few hours, that his son had a disability that would probably affect the rest of his life.

Michelle insisted, however, that Joe accompany her on tours of full-day school programs for children with autism spectrum disorder. Although they focused primarily on preschool programs, they were also provided with information about how such programs would set the stage for Adam's later years—if he were still to need services 5 years down the road. The more Joe and Michelle spoke with professionals, the better equipped they became for Adam's next few years. They started to see how the various early intervention services they had been providing would now come into play for their child as he entered a full-day program, and how the full-day services would help with later educational and vocational programs. They also learned about behavior management strategies that the family might be able to use to help deal with Adam's increasing demands and routines. In fact, the discussions with professionals at the prospective schools helped Joe emerge from his depressive state and take a few more steps toward acceptance of his son's disability.

The search for the best full-day program eventually led Joe and Michelle to two schools in two different counties. At each school, they were given a tour, an application form, and an appointment for an intake interview. The intake process was similar at each school: The director of the program would interview the parents, while three or four other professionals would take Adam into a separate area to assess his skills and behaviors.

By this point, Michelle had already contacted her school district about Adam's diagnosis and his need for specialized instruction. The district's officials had set up an appointment as well, completed their own assessment of Adam, and assigned him a case manager and a child study team. The school district's involvement was necessary because it was they who would have to provide, or pay for, any special educational services that Adam might need during his school years. The officials were supportive of Michelle's search for an appropriate outside program, as they themselves had a minimal number of preschool classrooms equipped for the special needs of students with autism spectrum disorder or other pervasive developmental disorders.

The school district's psychological and social profiles were added to the evaluations by the neurologist and the early intervention therapists to form a referral packet that Michelle took with her to interviews at the special preschool programs. She was pleased, and relieved, that this part of the process had gone so well, as she had heard many other parents describe the enormous difficulties they had encountered trying to convince their school districts' child study teams to find special programming.

The first school at which Michelle and Joe made an appointment had an exceptional reputation and had been highly recommended by several other parents

Applied behavior analysis, including early intervention, is considered the most efficacious treatment for autism spectrum disorder (Matson et al., 2012; Reichow, 2012). Applied behavior analysis uses a set of principles to guide children in diverse areas that include: social interactions, activities of daily living, and academic skills. This behavioral program also trains parents so that they can apply behavioral techniques at home.

to whom they had grown close. The school's enrollment was small—a total of 30 students—and its teaching strategies followed the applied behavior analysis principles Michelle and Joe had come to know so well from Adam's early intervention therapists. Days at this school were very structured, and there was an ongoing effort to mainstream students into less-restrictive environments.

This first interview was the most difficult, since Adam's parents had to convey all of their hopes and dreams for Adam to a complete stranger. It was also painful for them to observe while Adam had a tantrum when he was separated from them for his skills assessment. The director asked questions about Adam's history, the family's history, and how the young child was responding to the early intervention services he was receiving. Michelle and Joe tried to fit every piece of relevant information they could think of into the short hour of the interview, but left feeling as if there was much more to say.

For Adam, this was yet another set of strangers placing demands on him, in a completely new environment. The people assessing his skills at this first school included a special-education teacher, a speech therapist, and an occupational therapist. They completed a checklist of his skills, as well as his maladaptive behaviors. Their assessment agreed with previous findings that the absence of language or a formal communication system, along with Adam's problematic behaviors, would necessitate a preschool program with very special teaching techniques, including a continuation of the slow, trial-by-trial teaching program that Adam had slowly been responding to with his early intervention therapists. An opening would be available at this school in September, and Michelle and Joe were told that Adam was among several candidates applying for this opening. The parents would be contacted within the next 3 weeks.

The interview at the second school was much like the first. This school, however, was run by the Manning Child Development Center and so was closely affiliated with the early intervention program that Adam had been attending for almost a year. Michelle and Joe felt a bit more comfortable on this interview because they knew that Adam's behavioral therapist at the center would be stopping in to check on his assessment, and because they had already met the director at one of the parent training sessions offered by the center a few months earlier.

Again, the interview seemed too short to convey Adam's entire story; but Michelle and Joe made sure to express their interest in a behavioral-based program that would address every aspect of Adam's learning potential. By now, they recognized the value of learning programs in which tasks—all tasks, from toilet training to speaking—were broken down into the simplest possible steps to be learned one at a time. The consistent application of such learning programs over the past year had in fact produced some results. Adam could now maintain eye contact and sit appropriately for longer periods, as opposed to the fleeting glances and constant movements of past times. He could wave hello and goodbye on

> Mainstreaming is the placement of children with special needs and disorders in regular school classes with children who do not have those special needs.

command, a skill that helped bring him closer to his family. And his skill with the Picture Exchange Communication System was beginning to emerge; he was using pictures to convey five of his most desired items. Although the progress seemed a long time in coming, and was far behind what Michelle and Joe had expected of Adam by the age of 3, the fact remained that his improvement had begun, and they wanted to see it continue.

When asked about Adam's diet, the couple had mixed feelings. In Joe's opinion, Adam's special foods had not really brought about much change, and it was hard to keep him on these foods now that he was aware that his older brother was eating, and enjoying, different—often very tasty—foods. Food stealing had become mealtime issues at home, and Joe wondered whether they might be a problem at school lunches as well. On the opposite side, Michelle speculated that Adam's steady, if slow, progress might be due, in part, to this special diet, and so she wanted to give it more time. The school was familiar with the gluten-free diet, as several students were currently following it. Thus, Michelle and Joe's ultimate decision regarding the diet would not affect his placement at the school.

At this school, there were four candidates applying for the two openings available in September. Three of the four applicants had been receiving early intervention services at the center's associated program, and all had individual needs warranting specialized services. This decision would also be made within a few weeks, and once again Michelle and Joe were forced to wait.

While awaiting the letters of acceptance or rejection, the parents reviewed the various scenarios they might be facing. They actually preferred the second school—the one run by the Manning Child Development Center—because they were already familiar with the school's policies and staff members. They believed that the transition there would be the easiest for Adam, as well as for them. On the other hand, they felt that if he were accepted at the first school as well, they might have to accept that placement, given the sterling reputation of that program. With either school, Joe and Michelle knew that they would continue at least some of Adam's in-home therapy. They were prepared to do whatever it took to help their son reach his potential during these early years. At the same time, they understood the risk of overloading a child once full-day programming started.

They didn't even want to think of the possibility of being rejected from both schools. If Adam were not accepted by either program, the school district child study team, by law, would be responsible for finding an appropriate placement for him. Michelle and Joe feared that the team might place him in a preschool program that was designed for children less disabled than Adam. Although at the earlier meetings and evaluations, the team's case manager had seemed caring and aware of Adam's severe limitations, Michelle remained on the alert, having heard so many horror stories from other parents.

Most of today's theorists believe that autism spectrum disorder is caused by biological factors, although the precise biological causes are not yet known. One line of research has linked the disorder to abnormal development very early in life of the cerebellum, a brain area that helps to control shifts in attention (Allen, 2011; Pierce & Courchesne, 2002, 2001).

The letters from both schools came within a day of each other, a rejection from the first school and then an acceptance from the Manning Center. Michelle and Joe were overwhelmed by the emotional roller coaster ride that they experienced within a 24-hour period. If asked 5 years before how rejection from one preschool program and acceptance at another would make them feel, they would completely have underestimated the effect it would have. They found it impossible to sleep the night between the receipt of those letters. But now, with Adam's enrollment in the school that had links to his early intervention services, a school that already knew him, his parents felt a weight lifted off their shoulders.

For the first time in quite a while, they felt a sense of hope. They focused less on the many things that Adam could not do and felt more empowered by the things that he might be able to do in a proper program. With full-day, trial-by-trial learning, behavioral management strategies, and one-to-one student-to-teacher ratios, Adam was going to be given an opportunity to work through his disorder to reach his fullest potential. Although Michelle and Joe were still far from fully accepting Adam's disability, especially its lifelong implications, they were a step closer to understanding Adam and enhancing his life.

His enrollment in the new program was only 2 months away, and a number of decisions had to be made. Michelle had some transportation concerns, but was told that that responsibility fell to Adam's case manager. That is, it was the responsibility of the school district to arrange Adam's transportation to and from this school. She and Joe decided to continue with Adam's special diet for another 6 months, and to then make a further decision about it after seeing how the new school was progressing. Finally, they decided to discontinue the behavioral therapy at home for 6 months after the new school program began. The behavioral program at the school would be intense, and additional behavioral therapy at home might create burnout and hinder Adam's progress. On the other hand, they decided to continue his in-home speech therapy program, even though he would be receiving individual speech sessions four times a week at the new full-day program.

The month prior to enrollment, the school's program coordinator put together a parents' information and training session for Michelle and Joe. This meeting provided them with an introduction to the school's executive director, a review of the school's policies and procedures, and a chance to meet their son's classroom teacher and teaching assistants. There would be five other students in the class, all between the ages of 3 and 6 years old. Michelle and Joe learned that, in fact, a series of parent-training sessions would follow that at least one of them would be required to attend. The family would also be assigned a home-program consultant—a staff member who would visit their home on a regular basis to help them identify, prioritize, and manage home issues one at a time.

Adam's enrollment in this school program also had an important advantage that Joe and Michelle really didn't want to think much about at this point: the opportunity for life span services. Although students with autism spectrum disorder graduate from school at age 21, they typically have needs that last a lifetime. Recognizing these potential needs, Adam's new school had expanded its services. They offered workshop training and placement for adults with autism spectrum disorder. They also ran several group homes in which persons with autism spectrum disorder live in a house under the supervision of staff members. Their typical group home had eight residents and four supervisors. The needs of an adult Adam were a long way off, and his parents decided that they would cross that bridge when they came to it. Nevertheless, it was reassuring to know that such services would be there when the time came.

Adam at School Fully Entering the System

Adam's first day of school came, and off he went on a school van. He always enjoyed car rides, so Michelle hoped that that his enjoyment would overcome his anxiety at being separated from her. She had also provided him with a new set of his favorite Disney figurines to keep him occupied during the ride. She decided to follow the van on its 40-minute journey to the school, taking care to keep her distance so that Adam would not spot her car. Once he arrived safely at the school, Michelle watched as his teacher took him off the bus and escorted him into the building.

All day she expected a phone call saying that she would have to retrieve Adam because his tantrums were inconsolable or because he was too disruptive in the class. But no phone call came, and the van dropped Adam off at the end of the day. The note from his teacher described a typical first day—with some tears and some smiles. The note also indicated that Adam had been able to successfully carry over some of the behaviors and skills that he had acquired in the early intervention program. Michelle felt very reassured that she had underestimated her son's coping abilities; at least the first day of school was a positive experience.

The first few months were ones of transition. Adam's sleep pattern was disrupted for a while. He had to wake up an hour earlier than he was used to; this caused him to nap on the bus ride home, making it hard for him to fall asleep at the proper time later in the evening. But with the consistent application of his new schedule, and the assistance of the home-program consultant assigned to the family, he came to accept his new routine, and the family was able to move on to other issues.

The next few months of Adam's full-day school program were devoted primarily to helping him carry over gains that he had made previously in the early intervention program. The new school program also introduced several self-care skills during the early months. Adam's teacher even introduced toilet training within 2 weeks of his starting at the school, wanting to establish this skill as early as possible. He started what the school called a "5-minute schedule." He was directed to sit on a potty seat for 1 to 2 minutes, then was returned to a regular session of activity for 5 minutes, then directed back to the potty seat, and so on. Throughout the procedure, he was given extra fluids, which meant that he would have many opportunities to go to the bathroom. Whenever Adam successfully used the potty, he was rewarded with his favorite cookie. Over time, the number of toilet successes increased and the number of accidents decreased, and the teacher was able to slowly expand the length of the intervals between potty sittings. Adam was on his way to being toilet trained.

In October, Michelle and Joe met with all of the key persons in Adam's school program to discuss the goals and objectives for the coming year. The participants at the meeting included Adam's case manager, the psychologist from his school district, his special-education teacher, his speech therapist, his occupational therapist, and the director of the school. All programs and goals were reviewed, and questions from all parties were discussed. The teacher indicated that the program for the following year would center on developing a consistent communication system for Adam and on teaching him learning readiness skills and self-care skills, including maintaining eye contact; appropriate sitting; imitation skills; following simple one- and two-step directions; matching colors, shapes, and letters; pre-handwriting; waiting; appropriate play skills; hand washing; brushing his teeth; and getting dressed.

Joe asked whether mainstreaming would be included in Adam's program. The teacher indicated that at this point it was important for the child to spend a great deal of his time increasing his beginning skills through the behavioral therapy. Throughout the year there would be several community experiences and field trips for Adam's class, where he would have the opportunity to play with other children, but mainstreaming would not be a central part of his school program for this first year. At the same time, she noted, there were extracurricular activities in which other parents often enrolled their children that could provide mainstreaming experiences. Examples included toddler gymnastics sessions, music and movement classes, and specialized horseback riding lessons. More and more disciplines were becoming sensitive to working with children with special needs, and offered special sessions devoted to enhancing the socialization skills of these children.

Epilogue

As the school personnel laid out their plans and hopes for Adam, Michelle and Joe felt reassured. They sensed that he was, and they were, in good hands. It was comforting to know that they were no longer in this alone, and that Adam would have the opportunity to work every weekday with people who knew how to manage this difficult situation.

At the same time, they knew, and the staff members reminded them, that they were at the beginning, not the end, of a long and difficult and confusing journey. Although school programs such as this one were considered state-of-the-art they rarely helped children with autism spectrum disorder to reach normalcy. Nor could such programs guarantee particular gains or achievements. They could, at best help children with autism spectrum disorder reach their full potential, a potential that remained limited and somewhat unpredictable. Thus, Michelle and Joe settled in for the continued journey—with feelings of fear, depression, and also anger that this fate had befallen their child and their family. They prepared for a long journey in which their son would continue to grow and learn in his own way, with everyone involved—his teachers, his parents, and his brother—working to find the techniques and reinforcements that would challenge him and move him forward, step by step. Surely, Adam's life, and the lives of his parents, did not have to be devoid of joy, satisfaction, or accomplishment. But, just as surely, the satisfactions and accomplishments that awaited them would be very different from the ones that Michelle and Joe had envisioned just a few years ago. It was now time for Adam to become Adam.

> "No two people with autism are the same. Its precise form of expression is different in every case."—Oliver Sacks (2000)

Assessment Questions

1. What is the prevalence rate of autism spectrum disorder and what are some of the current statistics regarding the long-term prognosis of individuals diagnosed with autism spectrum disorder?

2. What were some behaviors that Adam demonstrated that concerned his mother when she compared his behavior with the behavior of the other children at his birthday party and with the development of his older brother?

3. Define the terms *echolalia* and *pronominal reversal,* and give examples.

4. List the two categories of symptoms that are hallmarks of autism spectrum disorder?

5. On the basis of the DSM-5 diagnostic criteria, the Childhood Autism Rating Scale, and the Modified Checklist for Autism for Toddlers—Revised, what level of severity was given to Adam's diagnosis and which specifiers were attached?

6. Why was it important to involve Adam in an early intervention program as soon as possible?

7. What is the preferred therapeutic intervention for children with autism spectrum disorder?

8. Why did Adam's parents decide to add home therapy to Adam's treatment program?

9. Speech therapy is an important aspect of treatment for children with autism spectrum disorder. Describe three of the techniques the speech therapists used to assist Adam in furthering his communication skills.

10. How did Adam's disorder affect the family structure? Give some examples.

11. What were the advantages of a full-day program for Adam?

12. Why might it be important for Adam's family to take advantage of individual counseling or a support group?

13. Why is the quote by Dr. Oliver Sacks important to remember in cases of autistic disorder?

CASE 18

You Decide: The Case of Julia

This case is presented in the voices of Julia and her roommate, Rebecca. Throughout the case, you are asked to consider a number of issues and to arrive at various decisions, including diagnostic and treatment decisions. Appendix A lists Julia's probable diagnosis, the DSM-5 criteria, clinical information, and possible treatment directions.

Julia Measuring Up

I grew up in a northeastern suburban town, and I've lived in the same house for my entire life. My father is a lawyer, and my mother is the assistant principal at our town's high school. My sister, Holly, is 4 years younger than I am.

My parents have been married for almost 20 years. Aside from the usual sort of disagreements, they get along well. In fact, I would say that my entire family gets along well. We're not particularly touchy-feely: It's always a little awkward when we have to hug our grandparents on holidays, because we just never do that sort of thing at home. That's not to say that my parents are uninterested or don't care about us. Far from it; even though they both have busy work schedules, one of them would almost always make it to my track and cross-country meets and to Holly's soccer games. My mother, in particular, has always tried to keep on top of what's going on in our lives.

In high school, I took advanced-level classes and earned good grades. I also got along quite well with my teachers, and ended up graduating in the top 10 percent of my class. I know this made my mother really proud, especially since she works at the school. She would get worried that I might not be doing my best and "working to my full potential." All through high school, she tried to keep on top of my homework assignments and test schedules. She liked to look over my work before I turned it in, and would make sure that I left myself plenty of time to study for tests.

In addition to schoolwork, the track and cross-country teams were a big part of high school for me. I started running in junior high school because my parents wanted me to do something athletic and I was never coordinated enough to be good at sports like soccer. I was always a little bit chubby when I was a kid. I don't know if I was actually overweight, but everyone used to tease me about my baby fat. Running seemed like a good way to lose that extra weight; it was hard at first, but I gradually got better and by high school I was one of the best runners on the team. Schoolwork and running didn't leave me much time for anything else. I got along fine with the other kids at school, but I basically hung out with just a few close friends. When I was younger, I used to get teased for being a Goody Two-Shoes, but that had died down by high school. I can't remember anyone with whom I ever had problems.

I did go to the prom, but I didn't date very much in high school. My parents didn't like me hanging out with boys unless it was in a group. Besides, the guys I had

Describe the family dynamics and school pressures experienced by Julia. Under what circumstances might such family and school factors become problematic or set the stage for psychological problems?

crushes on were never the ones who asked me out. So any free time was mostly spent with my close girlfriends. We would go shopping or to the movies, and we frequently spent the night at one another's houses. It was annoying that although I never did anything wrong, I had the earliest curfew of my friends. Also, I was the only one whose parents would text me throughout the night just to check in. I don't ever remember lying to them about what I was doing or who I was with. Although I felt like they didn't trust me, I guess they were just worried and wanted to be sure that I was safe.

Julia Coping With Stress

Now I am 17 years old and in the spring semester of my first year at college. I was awarded a scholar-athlete full scholarship at the state university. I'm not sure of the exact cause of my current problems, but I know a lot of it must have to do with college life. I have never felt so much pressure before. Because my scholarship depends both on my running and on my maintaining a 3.6 grade point average, I've been stressed out much of the time. Academic work was never a problem for me in the past, but there's just so much more expected of you in college.

It was pressure from my coach, my teammates, and myself that first led me to dieting. During the first semester, almost all my girlfriends in college experienced the "freshman 15" weight gain—it was a common joke among everyone when we were up late studying and someone ordered a pizza. For some of them it didn't really matter if they gained any weight, but for me it did. I was having trouble keeping up during cross-country practices. I even had to drop out of a couple of races because I felt so awful and out of shape. I couldn't catch my breath and I'd get terrible cramps. And my times for the races that I did finish were much worse than my high school times had been. I know that my coach was really disappointed in me. He called me aside about a month into the season. He wanted to know what I was eating, and he told me the weight I had gained was undoubtedly hurting my performance. He said that I should cut out snacks and sweets of any kind, and stick to things like salads to help me lose the extra pounds and get back into shape. He also recommended some additional workouts. I was all for a diet—I hated that my clothes were getting snug. In addition, I was feeling left out of the rest of the team. As a freshman, I didn't know any of the other runners, and I certainly wasn't proving myself worthy of being on the team. At that point, I was 5'6" and weighed 145 pounds. When I started college I had weighed 130 pounds. Both of these weights fell into the "normal" body mass index range of 18.5 to 25, but 145 pounds was on the upper end of normal.

Was the advice from Julia's coach out of line, or was it her overreaction to his suggestions that caused later problems?

Many eating disorders follow a period of intense dieting. Is dieting inevitably destructive? Are there safeguards that can be taken during dieting that can head off the development of an eating disorder?

Dieting was surprisingly easy. The dining hall food bordered on inedible anyway, so I didn't mind sticking to salads, cereal, or yogurt. Occasionally I'd allow myself pasta, but only without sauce. I completely eliminated dessert, except for fruit on occasion. If anyone commented on my small meals, I just told them that I was in training and gearing up for the big meets at the end of the season. I found ways to ignore the urge to snack between meals or late at night when I was studying. I'd go for a quick run, check Facebook and Twitter, take a nap—whatever it took to distract myself. Sometimes I'd drink water or Diet Coke and, if absolutely necessary, I'd munch on a carrot.

Once I started dieting, the incentives to continue were everywhere. My race times improved, so my coach was pleased. I felt more a part of the team and less like an outsider. My clothes were no longer snug; and when they saw me at my meets my parents said I looked great. I even received an invitation to a party given by a fraternity that only invited the most attractive first-year women. After about a month, I was back to my normal weight of 130 pounds.

At first, my plan was to get back down to 130 pounds, but it happened so quickly that I didn't have time to figure out how to change my diet to include some of the things that I had been leaving out. Things were going so well that I figured it couldn't hurt to stick to the diet a little longer. I was on a roll. I remembered all the people who I had seen on television who couldn't lose weight even after years of trying. I began to think of my frequent hunger pangs as badges of honor, symbols of my ability to control my bodily urges.

I set a new weight goal of 115 pounds. I figured if I hit the gym more often and skipped breakfast altogether, it wouldn't be hard to reach that weight in another month or so. Of course this made me even hungrier by lunchtime, but I didn't want to increase my lunch size. I found it easiest to pace myself with something like crackers. I would break them into several pieces and only allow myself to eat one piece every 15 minutes. The few times I did this in the dining hall with friends I got weird looks and comments. I finally started eating lunch alone in my room. I would simply say that I had some readings or a paper to finish before afternoon class. I also made excuses to skip dinner with people. I'd tell my friends that I was eating with my teammates, and tell my teammates that I was meeting my roommate. Then I'd go to a dining hall on the far side of campus that was usually empty, and eat by myself.

I remember worrying about how I would handle Thanksgiving. Holidays are a big deal in my family. We get together with my aunts and uncles and grandparents, and of course there is a huge meal. I couldn't bear the stress of being expected to eat such fattening foods. I felt sick just thinking about the stuffing, gravy, and pies for dessert. I told my mother that there was a team Thanksgiving dinner for those who lived too far away to go home. That much was true, but then I lied and told her that the coach thought it would be good for team morale if we all attended. I know it disappointed her, but I couldn't deal with trying to stick to my diet with my family all around me, nagging me to eat more.

Julia Spiraling Downward

I couldn't believe it when the scale said I was down to 115 pounds. I still felt that I had excess weight to lose. Some of my friends were beginning to mention that I was actually looking too thin, as if that's possible. I wasn't sure what they meant—I was still feeling chubby when they said I was too skinny. I didn't know who was right, but either way I didn't want people seeing my body. I began dressing in baggy clothes that would hide my physique. I thought about the overweight people my friends and I had snickered about in the past. I couldn't bear the thought of anyone doing that to me. In addition, even though I was running my best times ever, I knew there was still room there for improvement.

Around this time, I started to get really stressed about my schoolwork. I had been managing to keep up throughout the semester, but your final grade basically comes down to the final exam. It was never like this in high school, when you could get an A just by turning in all your homework assignments. I felt unbearably tense leading up to exams. I kept replaying scenarios of opening the test booklet and not being able to answer a single question. I studied nonstop. I brought notes with me to the gym to read on the treadmill, and I wasn't sleeping more than an hour or two at night. Even though I was exhausted, I knew I had to keep studying. I found it really hard to be around other people. Listening to my friends talk about their exam schedules only made me more frantic. I had to get back to my own studying.

The cross-country season was over, so my workouts had become less intense. Instead of practicing with the team, we were expected to create our own workout schedule. Constant studying left me little time for the amount of exercise I was used to. Yet I was afraid that cutting back on my workouts would cause me to gain weight. It seemed logical that if I couldn't keep up with my exercise, I should eat less in order to continue to lose weight. I carried several cans of Diet Coke with me to the library. Hourly trips to the lounge for coffee were the only study breaks I allowed myself. Aside from that, I might have a bran muffin or a few celery sticks, but that would be it for the day. Difficult though it was, this regimen worked out well for me. I did fine on my exams. This was what worked for me. At that point, I weighed 103 pounds and my body mass index was 16.6.

After finals, I went home for winter break for about a month. It was strange to be back home with my parents after living on my own for the semester. I had established new routines for myself and I didn't like having to answer to anyone

> Look back at Case 9, Bulimia Nervosa. How are Julia's symptoms similar to those of the individual in that case? How are her symptoms different?

> Based on your reading of either the DSM-5 or a textbook, what disorder might Julia be displaying? Which of her symptoms suggest this diagnosis?

else about them. Right away, my mother started in; she thought I spent too much time at the gym every day and that I wasn't eating enough. When I told her that I was doing the same thing as everyone else on the team, she actually called my coach and told him that she was concerned about his training policies! More than once she commented that I looked too thin, like I was a walking skeleton. She tried to get me to go to a doctor, but I refused.

Dinner at home was the worst. My mother wasn't satisfied when I only wanted a salad—she'd insist that I have a "well-balanced meal" that included some protein and carbohydrates. We had so many arguments about what I would and wouldn't eat that I started avoiding dinnertime altogether. I'd say that I was going to eat at a friend's house or at the mall. When I was at home I felt like my mother was watching my every move. Although I was worried about the upcoming semester and indoor track season, I was actually looking forward to getting away from my parents. I just wanted to be left alone—to have some privacy and not be criticized for working out to keep in shape.

> **Was there a better way for Julia's mother to intervene? Or would any intervention have brought similar results?**

Since I've returned to school, I've vowed to do a better job of keeping on top of my classes. I don't want to let things pile up for finals again. With my practice and meet schedule, I realize that the only way to devote more time to my schoolwork is to cut back on socializing with friends. So, I haven't seen much of my friends this semester. I don't go to meals at all anymore; I grab coffee or a soda and drink it on my way to class. I've stopped going out on the weekends as well. I barely even see my roommate. She's asleep when I get back late from studying at the library, and I usually get up before her to go for a morning run. Part of me misses hanging out with my friends, but they had started bugging me about not eating enough. I'd rather not see them than have to listen to that and defend myself.

> **Julia seems to be the only person who is unaware that she has lost too much weight and developed a destructive pattern of eating. Why is she so unable to look at herself accurately and objectively?**

Even though I'm running great and I'm finally able to stick to a diet, everyone thinks I'm not taking good enough care of myself. I know that my mother has called my coach and my roommate. She must have called the dean of student life, because that's who got in touch with me and suggested that I go to the health center for an evaluation. I hate that my mother is going behind my back after I told her that everything was fine. I realize that I had a rough first semester, but everyone has trouble adjusting to college life. I'm doing my best to keep in control of my life, and I wish that I could be trusted to take care of myself.

Rebecca Losing a Roommate

When I first met Julia back in August, I thought we would get along great. She seemed a little shy but like she'd be fun once you got to know her better. She was really cool when we were moving into our room. Even though she arrived first, she waited for me so that we could divide up furniture and closet space together. Early on, a bunch of us in the dorm started hanging out together, and Julia would join us for meals or parties on the weekends. She's pretty and lots of guys would hit on her, but she never seemed interested. The rest of us would sit around and gossip about guys we met and who liked who, but Julia just listened.

From day one, Julia took her academics seriously. She was sort of an inspiration to the rest of us. Even though she was busy with practices and meets, she always had her readings done for class. But I know that Julia also worried constantly about her studies and her running. She'd talk about how frustrating it was to not be able to compete at track at the level she knew she was capable of. She would get really nervous before races. Sometimes she couldn't sleep, and I'd wake up in the middle of the night and see her pacing around the room. When she told me her coach suggested a new diet and training regimen, it sounded like a good idea.

I guess I first realized that something was wrong when she started acting a lot less sociable. She stopped going out with us on weekends, and we almost never saw her in the dining hall anymore. A couple of times I even caught her eating by herself in a dining hall on the other side of campus. She explained that she had a lot of work to do and found that she could get some of it done while eating if she had meals alone. When I did see her eat, it was never anything besides vegetables. She'd take only a tiny portion and then she wouldn't even finish it. She didn't keep any food in the room except for cans of Diet Coke and a bag of baby carrots in the fridge. I also noticed that her clothes were starting to look baggy and hang off her. A couple of times I asked her if she was doing okay, but this only made her defensive. She claimed that she was running great, and since she didn't seem sick, I figured that I was overreacting.

I kept believing her until I returned from Thanksgiving. It was right before final exams, so everyone was pretty stressed out. Julia had been a hard worker before, but now she took things to new extremes. She dropped off the face of the earth. I almost never saw her, even though we shared a room. I'd get up around 8:00 or 9:00 in the morning, and she'd already be gone. When I went to bed around midnight, she still wasn't back. Her side of the room was immaculate: bed made, books and notepads stacked neatly on her desk. When I did bump into her, she looked awful. She was way too thin, with dark circles under her eyes. She seemed like she had wasted away; her skin and hair were dull and dry. I was pretty sure that something was wrong, but I told myself that it must just be the stress of the upcoming finals. I figured that if there were a problem, her parents would notice it and do something about it over winter break.

When we came back to campus in January, I was surprised to see that Julia looked even worse than during finals. When I asked her how her vacation was, she mumbled something about being sick of her mother and happy to be back at school. As the semester got under way, Julia further distanced herself from us. There were no more parties or hanging out at meals for her. She was acting the same way she had during finals, which made no sense because classes had barely

> Why was Rebecca inclined to overlook her initial suspicions about Julia's behaviors? Was there a better way for the roommate to intervene?

> How might high schools and universities better identify individuals with serious eating disorders? What procedures or mechanisms has your school put into operation?

gotten going. We were all worried, but none of us knew what to do. One time, Julia's mother sent me a message on Facebook and asked me if I had noticed anything strange going on with Julia. I wasn't sure what to write back. I felt guilty, like I was tattling on her, but I also realized that I was in over my head and that I needed to be honest.

I wrote her mother about Julia's odd eating habits, how she was exercising a lot and how she had gotten pretty antisocial. Her mother wrote me back and said she had spoken with their family doctor. Julia was extremely underweight, even though she still saw herself as chunky and was afraid of gaining weight.

A few days later, Julia approached me. Apparently she had just met with one of the deans, who told her that she'd need to undergo an evaluation at the health center before she could continue practicing with the team. She asked me point-blank if I had been talking about her to anyone. I told her how her mother had contacted me and asked me if I had noticed any changes in her over the past several months, and how I honestly told her yes. She stormed out of the room and I haven't seen her since. I know how important the team is to Julia, so I am assuming that she'll be going to the health center soon. I hope that they'll be able to convince her that she's taken things too far, and that they can help her to get better.

How might the treatment approaches used in Cases 2, 4, and 9 be applied to Julia? How should they be altered to fit Julia's problems and personality? Which aspects of these treatments would not be appropriate? Should additional interventions be applied?

You Decide: The Case of Fred

This case is presented in the voices of Fred and his wife, Margaret. Throughout the case, you are asked to consider a number of issues and to arrive at various decisions, including diagnostic and treatment decisions. You can find Fred's probable diagnosis, the DSM-5 criteria, clinical information, and possible treatment directions in Appendix B.

Margaret "My Husband's Brain Stopped Working Properly"

About 8 years ago, my life changed completely. The reason? My husband's brain stopped working properly. We had been married 34 years and Fred was 67 years old. He had worked for the same construction company in New Jersey for 32 years, first as a laborer, then as a security supervisor and union leader. He was a big strong man, a good husband, and a good father to our son, Mark. Together, we had managed to make a decent living with him in construction and me an actress in television commercials—the original Odd Couple, our friends would call us. Life was good. And then Fred's brain went downhill, taking the whole family down with it.

The problems seemed small at first, hardly noticeable really. Sometimes, when telling me about his day at work, Fred would talk about the foreman, Jimmy, driving a "tractor" when he meant "bulldozer," or he'd say that he had made a "revision" instead of "decision." Little stuff. And he'd catch himself. I didn't worry too much about it, but it was odd. It doesn't sound like much, but it wasn't like him. I even thought, "Oh, well, the old boy's slipping," and would laugh to myself. But when he forgot the anniversary of our first date, well. . . I knew something was wrong. I gave him all kinds of hell for that—I accused him of having an affair, I cried, I really let him have it. But I was also scared. I mean, maybe an anniversary like that doesn't mean much to other people, but for us—well, over the years, he'd taken me to Atlantic City for shows and to dinners in expensive restaurants. Once, after Mark was grown, he even got us a hotel room in the Catskills for a weekend. There was always some sort of surprise. So, 8 years ago, in anticipation of a special evening, I got all dressed up. When he got home from work that night and sat down on the sofa, I knew he'd forgotten; and when he saw the disappointment in my eyes, he realized the same thing pretty quickly. In fact, he felt terrible about it, and took me out to a very fancy Italian restaurant after I calmed down. But it was a bad sign. That year turned out to be a rough one.

It wasn't as if he suddenly forgot everything, but it seemed like he was forgetting a bunch of things that he'd never forgotten before. I had always been the one with my head in the clouds, forgetting dates and losing car keys. Fred would be the one telling me, "Maggie, you've got to stay more on the ball. If you forget to pay the bills, they're gonna shut off our electricity." Or he'd chew me out about forgetting to make a doctor's appointment for Mark. Of course, I'd joke, "Why don't we switch

> Forgetfulness is universal, and increases in forgetfulness are a normal part of aging. How might we distinguish normal forgetting or normal aging from the symptoms of a clinical disorder?

jobs and you'll see who's got it tougher," but he definitely had a sharper head, no denying that. Now, suddenly, he was losing his wallet and we'd find it later in the study, where he'd sworn he hadn't been in days. Or he would leave half-full glasses of juice on the floor of the living room, and when I'd chide him about it he'd say, "Oh, I'm sorry," and change the subject. This was Mr. Neat Freak who, in the past, couldn't stand it if a dirty dish sat on the kitchen table more than a half hour after dinner.

He also had little accidents, spilling food on himself, or knocking over a pile of papers or the jar of pencils from the counter. Then he started asking me to drive him to work all the time. He said that he'd caught himself veering off the road a few times and had just barely avoided an accident. "It's all the stress," he'd tell me. "We've got a new contract coming up and I don't think it's gonna go our way. I've just got too much on my mind."

As the forgetfulness and unusual behavior mounted, it couldn't be ignored any more. Yet somehow I found a way to do just that. I wanted to believe that he was fine. Then, one day, he missed a meeting with an important contractor—just didn't show up. Instead, he went to his office like it was any other day. The company lost the contract and a lot of money, and it also was bad for their image. Actually, by that point in time, I wasn't all that surprised by his error. This strong and organized man, who had taken care of everything for so many years, was by then becoming a different person, and I was now taking care of him. That's when I told him that he must see a doctor. And Fred did something I'd never seen him do: He burst into tears.

Despite his emotional outpouring that evening, Fred managed to put off medical treatment for nearly a year. Eventually, however, the incidents caught up with him— for example, leaving his glasses in the mailbox or mowing only half the lawn—and he went for a neuropsychological exam. The results of a battery of tests revealed some significant problems, and the neuropsychologist, Dr. Schoenfeld, broke the news to us that he was suffering from a neurocognitive disorder. He explained to us that we would be facing a very difficult battle—that Fred would become less and less able to take care of himself. He also told us that very little could be done to stem the progress of Fred's condition. Fred was going to have to rely on the support of his loved ones, particularly me, to see him through this.

Fred had already planned to retire, as his position in the company had been scaled down drastically after the contract debacle. The doctor's diagnosis simply made it official in our minds. Within 3 months, he was thrown a retirement party by his coworkers, many of whom he had mentored. By then he was having trouble remembering people's names, but that party meant a lot to him. He knew just how lucky he was to have so many caring friends and colleagues. He was still embarrassed about having lost that contract, but everybody tried their best to show him that they had nothing but gratitude for his years of service. He wasn't walking too well by then, either, so I helped him to a chair, where he sat for most of the

What might be the most difficult aspects of observing a spouse, parent, or other close relative gradually lose their memory or other cognitive faculties?

Neurocognitive disorders include a group of organic syndromes, marked by major problems in cognitive functioning, such as memory and learning, attention, visual perception, planning and decision making, language ability, or social awareness. Based on your reading of either the DSM-5 or your textbook, what form of neurocognitive disorder might Fred be displaying? Which of his symptoms suggest this diagnosis?

party, sometimes crying quietly to himself because he no longer had full control of his emotions. I think that was really his last great experience, the last time he had a really special night out.

At the party, Fred gave a short talk to his coworkers, thanking them for the event. He had been worried about this speech for days. He feared attempting to reminisce or trying to be too specific, because he'd been having so much trouble remembering things. But he didn't want to read a written speech, so he just kept it short. It broke my heart when I heard him say, "This is really a special night. I want to thank you all for this and for helping me out the way you've done the last few months. I'm not the kinda guy who talks a lot and makes big speeches to his friends. And that's what you are—my friends. That's why I've had a great time all these years. That's why I've loved my job, and going to work in the morning. We've had a lot of good times, and I'll miss you, my friends."

It was more than a retirement speech; it was a farewell speech. But, as painful as that was, the impromptu speech that he gave to me alone just 2 days later hurt even more. He was lucid that day. He was clear and organized and sharp as a tack, just like the old Fred. And he was hurting.

Fred "Preparing for a Trip to Nowhere"

I'm mad, I'm frustrated, I'm everything in between. It sure is embarrassing, Maggie, it sure is. Can you imagine what it's like to have to think for 2 whole minutes before remembering our own grandchild's name? A child I held in my arms when he was born, and said, "This boy is a perfect child." I watched him grow and played ball with him, and I can see his face in front of me as if he was in the room with me, but when I reach for his name, there's nothing there. Blank. How do I convince an 8-year-old child that his grandpa loves him and cares about him when I can't even be bothered to know his name?

I spend my whole life trying to be sharp, but I end up a failure. I'm a 69-year-old man who needs a woman to take care of him like he's 90. What use am I? I provided for my family. I earned money. I did my job to help keep Wellstone Construction running. And now that's all gone. All gone. I can't do any of it anymore. Lying in bed or sitting in a chair all day. My wife and son provide for me. The company takes care of me. I'm a drain. No one will ever again think of trusting me with anything. Anything. "No, it would be too taxing for the poor guy." That's what they'll say, but what they'll mean is, "He'll just screw it up, like he screws everything up."

Sometimes, all of a sudden, I don't know what time of day it is, or even what day of the week it is. I don't even know what I had for breakfast this morning. If I want to go over there to pick up that book off that table, I have to ask you if you can help me walk. I can't walk without leaning on someone. Otherwise, I'll fall or have to stop and sit down.

In 2012, more than 15 million family members and friends volunteered 17.5 billion hours to care for individuals with dementia, which can lead to a range of psychological problems for caregivers. What kinds of problems would you expect caregivers to develop?

Consider Case 5, Major Depressive Disorder. Did Fred show any symptoms of clinical depression as his disorder unfolded? Did Margaret? Would any of the treatment techniques described in Case 5 be helpful to either of them?

Why should I even want to get up in the morning? Being up isn't all that different from being asleep, only a bit more confusing. Nothing in the world is more infuriating than knowing that you know the thing you can't remember. Knowing that you're not stupid, but that everything you once knew is being stripped away from you, little by little. God knows how long I'll even know who you are, Maggie. How long will it be before it's all just shapes and colors? How long before everyone else is making plans for me. Putting me in a home, putting me out to pasture, putting me to sleep. I feel like I'm preparing for a trip to nowhere.

I don't even know if I'll mind that so much. When I don't remember anything, it won't be so hard. Probably then I won't feel so stupid. I won't realize how much I am forgetting. That's what gets me—the forgetting. It gets me mad, but it gets me scared, too. I reach for a pen that I thought I was just writing with and I realize that it's not there. I look for it and then I realize that I'm not writing anything. Now I can't find the pen, and I don't even remember why I'm looking for it, and nothing makes any damned sense. It's like this dream that's real upsetting because I don't know what's going on, but I know I should know. Oh, God!

When this all started, you know, I didn't believe it. A man can get used to a lot if he can convince himself that nothing is wrong. Every time I'd forget something, or lose something, or drive off the road, it bothered me for exactly 5 minutes. I'd be scared for 5 minutes and I'd admit to myself for those 5 minutes that there was a serious problem—that these things were happening more and more and that something was very wrong and that I should get this taken care of somehow. But after those 5 minutes, I would laugh it off and decide that everything was fine—everyone forgets things, everyone loses concentration driving, everyone misplaces things—and I'd be fine. I'd come home, and I wouldn't think about it until the next thing happened. Then I'd be upset for another 5 minutes.

I want you to put me away, Maggie—you know what I mean—let me go, if I ever don't remember who you are. I don't want to forget my beautiful wife, and if I don't know who you are anymore, have them just inject me or give me whatever is necessary in order to get this life over with. Don't worry about whether it's the right thing, because it is. I'm afraid that you won't do this, that you'll let me go on when I'm not myself anymore. I don't want you to have to see me and not know that I love you and need you with me. I don't want you to doubt my love for you because of this damned disease. Please, Maggie, don't let that happen. Please promise me.

Margaret "A Long Goodbye"

I heard that speech from Fred several other times during the next 2 years. But of course I couldn't make that promise. Eventually, he became less clear and less interested, and less able, and he stopped saying those things. The last 4 years really have been a long goodbye for us. As the years have passed, Fred has been

> If you were to lose your memory and cognitive faculties, bit by bit, how would you feel? What fears and worries do you think you would experience?

> Why would Fred and Margaret have tried to overlook his symptoms, even as they were worsening?

> Unlike most of the other disorders in this casebook, Fred's problem was organic, progressive, and largely irreversible. What role might psychological treatments play in disorders of this kind?

less and less able to do for himself. He has been increasingly unsteady on his feet. Furthermore, he lost control of his motor functions and is now unable to feed or clothe himself, or to use the bathroom on his own. At first, this was very upsetting to Fred; he was still aware enough to feel that his incapacitation made him ridiculous in some way, and he often lashed out at me in anger—even accusing me at times of trying to drug him so that he couldn't take care of himself. Later, he would tearfully apologize after these outbursts.

About 4 years ago, I bought him a walker to make it easier for him to get around. But a year later, he fell while trying to walk across the hall to take a bath. He broke his hip and couldn't leave his bed for 4 months. Fred became more and more depressed and began spending days staring at the wall or the bed sheets, refusing to talk even when I tried to speak to him. After his hip had healed, he still remained in bed, refusing to try to walk. He even began hearing voices and seeing people who weren't really in the room. Sometimes he would believe that long-gone relatives were in front of him and talking to him. Eventually, it seemed like it was just too taxing for him to try to distinguish the real from the imagined, and Fred began to treat everyone and everything around him with indifference or doubt. He treated real people who were talking to him as though they might be figments of his imagination and just turned away.

Our son, Mark, visited regularly, at least once every other weekend, from his New Hampshire home. Even so, Mark was always surprised by the speed of his deterioration. After breaking his hip, Fred, who had always looked so forward to Mark's visits, often failed to get out of bed to greet our son, sometimes sleeping through the entire visit. Mark noticed that his father appeared to get less pleasure from the visits. He tried to prepare himself for the ravages of Fred's condition, but as his father deteriorated more and more, he became very shaken.

During one visit, Fred looked Mark in the eye, then turned to me and asked, "Who is this, Maggie? Who's he? Is that your brother Jimmy? What's he doin' here?" Mark faced his father and said in a quiet voice, "Dad, it's me. Your son, Mark. And I love you." As he said this, however, Fred fell asleep, and Mark left the room feeling dejected. Later, after Mark and I ate lunch, Fred awoke again, and called out. When Mark entered the room and stood over his father's bed, Fred touched his hand to Mark's face and after a minute said, quietly and hoarsely, "Son . . ." And they held hands without saying a word for an hour. I almost couldn't bear it.

Also, about 3 years ago, Fred started having violent nightmares, and he would sometimes wake me with his screaming. During and after some of the nightmares, he seemed like a completely different person, with a crazed passion behind his frightened eyes. He was growing more and more convinced that I was plotting against him. During one of our visits to the neuropsychologist, he complained, "She's stealing things from me. She steals my clothes so that she can make me feel

---

What role might psychotherapists play in helping close relatives cope with the deterioration of a loved one? What therapy approaches described throughout this casebook might be particularly helpful to such relatives?

People with a disorder such as Fred's often become angry, suspicious, and accusatory. What are some of the potential reasons for such reactions and personality changes?

foolish when I can't find them. I was eating a banana, and she wanted the banana. I put it down and turned my back for a minute, and that banana was gone. She's taking my food. This is all her fault. I know it is."

It's now been 8 years of taking care of him. At this point, I have to feed him and help him use the bathroom. I bathe him and I take him to the doctor. Thanks to his retirement package, we're okay financially. Still, I need to spend every penny we have on Fred's care. I can't work myself, since I have to be with him. The worst part is when he looks at me and I know he doesn't know who I am, yells at me as if I'm an enemy, and accuses me of stealing his things. At other times, however, he looks at me and his eyes say, "Thanks, Maggie," and I know he hasn't forgotten—even if he's remembering for only a moment.

Fred's decline seemed to reach a new level beginning around 6 months ago. Since then, he has been completely incontinent and barely able to speak. He has also been unable to leave our bedroom. He hasn't shown any recognition of Mark during his visits, and has barely even acknowledged me. About 3 weeks ago, he developed a cold that would not go away, and last week I took him to the hospital. He's still there, with a respiratory infection, using a ventilator to breathe. He is in such a weakened condition that doctors are not sure that he will live out the week.

I suspect that Mark and I each privately hope that the doctors' prognoses are accurate and Fred will die within the week. Neither of us has dared express this to the other, but I think we will both be relieved when Fred is gone—that is, the bedridden Fred whose true spirit has already left us. When he is gone, we will all finally be delivered from this long ordeal. And Mark and I will be able to remember our beloved Fred again as he once was—strong of mind and body.

After a long ordeal such as Fred's, it is common for close relatives to find themselves almost wishing for or looking forward to the person's death. What factors might explain such feelings and reactions?

You Decide: The Case of Suzanne

This case is presented in the voices of Suzanne and her mother, Sherry. Throughout the case, you will be asked to consider a number of issues and to arrive at various decisions, including diagnostic and treatment decisions. Appendix C reveals Suzanne's probable diagnosis, the DSM-5 criteria, clinical information, and possible treatment directions.

Suzanne A Sign of Things to Come

I don't know when I started doing it. I guess I've always hated school and I've always been really nervous about things. A lot of the time, even before college, I used to play with my hair a lot and pull on it; the more nervous I became, the tighter I pulled. But I didn't think there was anything unusual about it. You know, everyone has nervous habits that they turn to when they get stressed out, right?

My parents were . . . let's say "difficult." They were always making me feel like I didn't do well enough. "Couldn't you have gotten an A? Couldn't you play basketball or soccer? Couldn't you have won the game? What could you have done to prepare for the test better? What can we learn from this? Why don't you have a boyfriend? Maybe if you dressed differently? You know, we just want you to be happy."

I guess this whole thing really started a long time ago. When I was in seventh grade, I used to pluck out my eyelashes. I can't remember how it started, but I remember that it used to relax me when I was tense. I also got the idea in my head that my eyelashes and my eyes were really irritated. I thought that maybe I had some dirt caught in there, and it was stuck between my eyelashes. So I would loosen it and stop the irritation by pulling the eyelash out. I actually remember thinking that there were microscopic bacteria—like I had seen in a science film—living on the end of the eyelash, wiggling around under my skin, and the bad eyelashes needed to be pulled out. The little pain of pulling the lash out was something I actually looked forward to, like when you have a hanging fingernail that hurts and you need to pull it out: a second of pain and instant relief. Once I started noticing that I was doing it, I would be really nervous right before I would pull it, and I would think that maybe I shouldn't pull this one. Then, when I was pulling it out, I imagined I could feel the irritating part coming out. After it was over, I felt relieved, all the nervousness gone. I would look at the lash I had pulled, almost trying to see the little bacteria wiggling like a worm on a fishhook.

Soon, my eyelids were running out of hair, but no one seemed to notice, so I thought it wasn't a big deal. Maybe I wasn't really plucking them all out, I thought. Maybe I was just plucking out the bad ones, and the eyelashes now looked exactly the way they were supposed to. Maybe, I thought, I'm just sensitive to the way it looks because I keep thinking about it so much. Of course, I couldn't help but notice that I wasn't able to pluck any long eyelashes anymore, only little stubby ones. Also, my eyelids were hurting all the time.

Many loving parents are described as being "over-concerned" about their children, or "overcontrolling" or "overinvolved." Where do such patterns of behavior come from? What can parents do to avoid crossing the line in their efforts to guide and protect their maturing children?

One night at dinner, my mom just turned to me after we'd been sitting together the whole dinner, and screamed out, "What happened to your eyelashes?" That was so embarrassing! I wanted my parents to just go away. They wouldn't understand why I had to do it. I just wanted to crawl into a hole and die. I promised my mom that I would stop, but it was easier said than done. I'd catch myself—or should I say Mom would catch me—doing it, reaching for the eyelashes even when there wasn't anything there. Eventually, my embarrassment became so great that it helped me to stop. Whenever I would reach for my eyelashes, I was able to catch myself before I touched them.

My lashes grew back, and the eyelids weren't as irritated all the time. After about 6 months, I didn't even have to think about it anymore. When I did think back on my behavior, I couldn't believe that I had plucked out every eyelash. It didn't make sense anymore, and it seemed so unnatural. I was glad I had stopped, but I didn't want to think about it too much because I didn't want to consider the possibility that I wasn't "normal."

After my victory over eyelash plucking, I found myself trying to cope with school and other stresses in other ways. Throughout high school, I bit my nails and often stayed up all night worrying myself to the point of tears, and walking around with a headache, half asleep, during the day. During my junior and senior years, I was always concerned about whether I would get into a good college. Then, after I was accepted, there were all these preparations to make, while at the same time trying to finish my senior year in good standing. And then I had to get ready to move away from home. All the while, in the back of my mind, I was worried that there was something different about me from everyone else. I really didn't get along that well with most people; I just got too nervous around them, and relationships with boys never seemed to go anywhere.

Suzanne Entering the Big Leagues

Entering college is a major life stress that seems to trigger or exacerbate psychological difficulties for many persons. Why might this be such a difficult period in life?

When I first got to college, I was really scared. I'd never been away from home for more than a couple of weeks, and never so far from my parents. Even though I couldn't wait to get away from them, I didn't know how I was going to get through life without them telling me how to do everything and how to get by in the real world. My next-door neighbor in the dorm suite, Jon, was a big help. He was from New York, so he was independent and sure of himself. He taught me how to take care of things like bills and spending money, how to get through classes, and how to get food for myself. It was really a lot of fun; we made a little family out of our suite. Jon and I spent tons of time together and I was happy that I had wound up with him; it seemed like a stroke of luck.

Then one day he kissed me. Gosh, it seems so simple just to say it like that: "*He kissed me.*" But that was how it happened. And I didn't think twice; I just kissed him back, even though I had never really kissed a boy before. Not like that. We moved on from there and had sex. I had always wondered what that would be like. How would it feel? But it felt wonderful—so right, so natural. I was so very happy with Jon, and I was feeling things that I had never felt for anyone.

One day, after we had been going together for about a month, Jon suddenly told me he thought we shouldn't be doing what we were doing anymore. He said it just like that, and just like that it was all over. He talked about expanding our horizons, exploring other relationships, and other such things. None of it made much sense or comforted me. I was totally devastated. And I was shocked by the suddenness with which the relationship ended. That alone would have been enough to crush me, but there was more. Jon wouldn't even talk to me or hang out with me anymore. It was a nightmare. I knew he was having girls come over and he was sleeping with them—each of them was a reminder of how undesirable I was, of my failure at love, of my loss. I felt terrible about myself because Jon didn't love me like I loved him, and terrible because I had loved him in the first place. I was so depressed that I started failing two of my classes.

I think it was around this time, about midway through that first semester, that I first became aware that I was pulling my hair out. I say "first became aware," because I have no idea how long I'd actually been doing it. I just suddenly noticed, while in the middle of pulling my hair one time, that there were already a few strands of blond hair on the floor. This time it wasn't my eyelashes, but actual hair from my scalp.

I realized immediately that the hair pulling was the same kind of thing that my eyelashes had been. I didn't feel so much the itchy, irritated feeling, but I would feel very uncomfortable. If I tried not to do it, I'd get really nervous and tense. I'd get this cramped, tight feeling in my stomach, and I'd worry that something bad was going to happen. By pulling out a hair, I would feel instant relief. When the hair came out, the knot in my stomach would pass and my heart would stop pumping so heavily. I could lean back in my chair or bed, and breathe much more easily. Unfortunately, this feeling of relief wouldn't last for long. In fact, as I said, the hair pulling would happen so often that I usually didn't know I was doing it—I would sometimes simply catch myself in the act.

Recalling the eyelash thing, I'd say to myself, "Remember that was just a phase. You didn't have any trouble stopping," and I'd feel reassured. But of course I had had trouble stopping the eyelash plucking; it had just faded from my memory. As I paid more attention to my hair pulling, I observed that I tended to pull it from my right temple, on the side of my head, with my right hand. But I honestly couldn't be sure that that was the only hand I ever used.

A month or two after I first noticed what I was doing, I was in the shower and felt a little patch of skin exposed around my favorite plucking spot. I think I was running the shampoo through my hair and I was rubbing it through my scalp.

> Everyone has certain habits that they exhibit when they are under stress. Only occasionally do such habits blossom into a disorder such as Suzanne's. Are there ways of distinguishing innocent bad habits from signs of problems to come?

> Based on your reading of either the DSM-5 or your textbook, what disorder might Suzanne be displaying? Which of her symptoms suggest this disorder?

When I felt the patch where there was less hair, I panicked immediately. I could feel my face turn bright red, and I think I was more embarrassed than anything else, even though I was alone. I thought, here I am doing this bizarre and perverse thing that no one else does, and now I must look like a freak. It occurred to me that everyone must know, and I just wanted to run and hide. In those first few moments of shock, I started breathing heavily, and I silently promised myself that I would never do this horrible thing again, that I was immature and stupid and disgusting, and I had to stop. I rinsed out my hair, toweled it off, then, terrified, I moved to the mirror to see just how bad I looked. Peeking from between squinted eyelids, I couldn't see a difference at first. Then I opened my eyes wide, and saw that there was definitely a bald patch, although not as bad as it had felt to my fingers in the shower.

Good, I thought, with a feeling of relief. It seems silly in retrospect, but I remember thinking that if I just combed my hair over a certain way, everything would look fine. It relieved me enough that I went right back to my routine. Time and again, I'd catch myself plucking hair from the same spot. Eventually, I could no longer pretend that I didn't have a noticeable bald patch. I invented newer, more elaborate hairstyles to cover it, while always thinking to myself, "Oh, I'm never going to do this again," or "I'm phasing it out." The truth was I hadn't slowed down a bit. It was probably becoming apparent to the people around me that there was something peculiar going on with my hair. But I kept on going.

When I went home for the winter break, I was terrified. I didn't want to risk my parents seeing this ugly bald spot on their "perfect" little daughter. For the entire month before winter break, I kept thinking, "Okay, stop pulling the hair. It needs to grow back." Then I'd think, when the urge had its grip on me, "Well, break is still 3 weeks away." And so I'd pull out the hair. And pull. And pull. And 3 weeks became 2, and 2 became 1, and the problem was as bad as ever when I had to fly home. I bit my nails the whole flight home, trying not to give in to the urge to pull my hair. I also didn't want to mess up the deceptive hairdo I had worked on so hard. Of course, there was Mom at the terminal waiting area, screaming, "Oh, my God! What kind of a hairstyle is that? You look terrible!" I told her to mind her own business and leave my hairdo alone. It was all I could do to stop her from touching it.

I was only kidding myself that I could keep this a secret for 4 weeks. Within 1 week, Mom noticed the bald spot that I'd tried so hard to hide. In her typical way, she made me feel as if I had cut off an arm, and I turned bright red and cried. I didn't want to talk to her about it, both because she was horrible and because I didn't want to face it myself. So I left the room and said, "I won't talk about this now." But I knew that the damage had been done, and later I went down and told her that, as she could see, I had been pulling out my hair. I explained that I didn't know why, but I was going into therapy (to get her off my back) and I wanted to

Suzanne's disorder is listed with the obsessive-compulsive and related disorders in the DSM-5, but it is considered a separate disorder from obsessive-compulsive disorder. Yet some clinicians believe that problems like hers are really a kind of compulsion. How are her symptoms similar to those displayed by the individual in Case 2, Obsessive-Compulsive Disorder? How are they different?

deal with it on my own. And then I refused to discuss it further. I was surprised at how well I had handled my mother, but I knew that I had yet to handle my hair problem.

I went back to school, and continued to pull my hair out. My hair looked so bad I wasn't even trying to date. It wasn't until 2 more years passed that I decided to actually try the therapy that I'd told my mom about. I've been in counseling for 8 months now. I've come to appreciate that I have a lot of anxiety issues and problems with myself and my parents, and that's probably why I do this—at least in part. At the same time, my therapist has explained that many people have this disorder. I couldn't believe that at first; I really thought I was the only one.

I'm going to graduate this coming spring, and I'm doing very well at school and in basketball. Mom and Dad are so happy! I haven't pulled any hair out in, I think, close to 4 months, and I'm not feeling the urge much anymore, which is great. I feel better about the way I look. I've also started seeing a really nice guy named Mark. It's going great, although, after the disaster with Jon, I'm trying to take it slow. All in all, things are pretty good, but I do wonder whether I am prone to pulling my hair. Will I revert to this whenever I face a crisis? That worries me, and for now that's why I am continuing to attend therapy.

> How might the treatment approaches used in Cases 2 and 5 be applied to Suzanne? Which aspects of these approaches would not be appropriate for her? Should additional interventions be applied?

A Mother's View "You've Got to Stop This"

I think Suzanne was about 13 when I first noticed the problem with her eyelashes. We were sitting at the dinner table—this was about, oh, 8 years ago—and talking about her cheerleading practice. She was excited that she'd been picked to be the top of the pyramid. Tom and I were also happy about that. We'd been encouraging Suzie to try out for this cheerleading team because she had seemed unhappy. Sometimes she'd cry, and when we'd ask her what was wrong, she'd say, "I don't know," or "School is really hard." Tom and I talked about it and thought she might want to get involved in an extracurricular activity. We gently tried to get her to go out for a sport, like basketball, which she was so good at, but she insisted she didn't like playing sports. Finally, in desperation, I suggested that since she really liked gymnastics, she might want to try cheerleading. Suzie loved the idea. Apparently, she had thought about cheerleading, but she had been afraid to ask us if she could be a part of the team. She was concerned that we'd be disappointed; she thought we might look down on it compared with basketball, soccer, or field hockey. Can you imagine that?

Anyway, the eyelashes. . . . She was telling us about this pyramid thing at the table, and I wanted to give my little girl a big hug. When I leaned in, I thought something looked peculiar about her face. At first, it seemed like she looked really sad, and her eyes were bigger than usual. I hugged her and told her that I was so proud of my little girl. Tom looked up from the paper and said he thought it was

> Are the family, school, and social pressures described by Suzanne particularly unusual? Why might they have led to dysfunction in Suzanne's case, but not in the lives of other persons?

just great. Later, during dessert, when I was passing out the ice cream, I looked at her again. We were talking about her test the next day in social studies and how much studying she should do after dinner. At one point, she looked up, and that's when I noticed it.

"What happened to your eyelashes?" I exclaimed, before I could stop myself. Suzie tried to turn her head away and look outside the room, in the opposite direction. She muttered, "I don't know." But I said, "Tom, look at this! She doesn't have any eyelashes."

He looked over, leaned in, and said, "You're right, Sherry. What's going on here, Suze?" Suzie took a deep breath and just said she sometimes plucked her eyelashes out. She didn't know why she did it. She said she just did—they itched her, maybe. I figured it was some sort of nervous habit, and I told her she had to stop. I told her it wasn't normal. She got upset, but finally promised she would try to stop doing it. I tried to give her some more incentive. "You're so beautiful," I told her, "but you look terrible without your eyelashes. You could look so much better. You've got to stop this, okay?"

For a while after that, I'd see her rubbing her eyelids where the lashes used to be. Tom and I tried to help out by stopping her whenever we saw her playing with her eyelids or eyelashes. After a while, and with some effort, it seemed to pay off. Her eyelashes eventually grew back, and she didn't seem to be plucking them anymore. Tom and I forgot all about it after a few years.

When Suzanne went off to college in Florida, the last thing on my mind was the way she had plucked out her eyelashes at the age of 13. Tom and I had been hoping she would go to a good school, with a strong girls' basketball team, but she didn't do very well on her SATs, and never did well enough in basketball to interest the scouts from the big schools. Anyway, the school she went to was fine, and we were proud that Suzie was going to college.

She never called us when she first went away. I guess it was the excitement of being somewhere new. Anyway, girls are like that at that age. When we would call her to see how she was doing in her classes, she never seemed to want to talk—she would talk very softly, say things were fine, and yes, she was making friends. She would then rush off the phone; once, I was sure that she was holding back tears.

When she came home for her first winter break, she had the most ridiculous hairdo I'd ever seen: a weird type of beehive combed over from the left. It was just horrible. I asked her why she did that to her hair, and she just said she liked it that way. After she'd been home a few days, she literally let her hair down, and when she tilted her head back once, right before she quickly brushed the hair back over, I saw it—her scalp! A horrifying, huge bald spot. I asked her what was wrong. "Are you sick?" But she just got really serious and said she didn't want to talk about it. Then she left the room.

> On the surface, Suzanne and her mother had a close and loving relationship, but they also had some serious problems in their interactions. What were some of these problems, and how might they have contributed to Suzanne's disorder?

Later, she admitted that she had started pulling her hair out. She said she didn't know why she did it, but she was going into therapy, for that and for a lot of other things. She explained that it was somehow connected to the eyelash thing from years ago, and I thought. "Of course, it all makes sense now." This is really strange, but she told me that it wasn't my problem, and I should just let her try to work on it herself.

After that, once she was back at school, whenever I would ask her on the phone how she was doing with the hair problem, she would mumble a short answer like "Fine." Sometimes she wouldn't come home at all on vacations. But I guess now that she's a senior, she's made things right and put it all behind her. She was home just last month and she certainly seemed to have a full head of lovely blond hair. We had a great visit and she's looking forward to graduating. And guess who's the starting guard on the girls' basketball team?

What defense mechanisms did Suzanne and her mother seem to use in order to cope with her eyelash problem and, later, her hair-pulling problem? How did such mechanisms help Suzanne? How did they hurt her?

Appendix A
You Decide: The Case of Julia

The individual in *Case 18: The Case of Julia* would receive a diagnosis of *anorexia nervosa*.

Dx	**Checklist**
	Anorexia Nervosa
1.	Individual purposely takes in too little nourishment, resulting in body weight that is very low and below that of other people of similar age and gender.
2.	Individual is very fearful of gaining weight, or repeatedly seeks to prevent weight gain despite low body weight.
3.	Individual has a distorted body perception, places inappropriate emphasis on weight or shape in judgments of herself or himself, or fails to appreciate the serious implications of her or his low weight.
	(Based on APA, 2013.)

Clinical Information

1. Research investigating risk factors for eating disorders have reliably identified body dissatisfaction as a significant factor in the future development of eating disorders. Some prospective studies have also found a history of depression and critical comments from teachers/coaches/siblings to be important predictors (Jacobi et al., 2011). Stice, Marti, and Durant (2011) identified two separate risk-factor pathways based on whether the individual experienced high levels of body dissatisfaction. For adolescent girls with high body dissatisfaction, their risk for developing an eating disorder was amplified by the presence of depressive symptoms. However, among girls with lower levels of body dissatisfaction, those reporting significant dieting behaviors were at the highest risk for developing a future eating disorder.

2. Individuals with anorexia typically struggle with comorbid conditions such as depression and/or anxiety disorders (Von Lojewski, Boyd, Abraham, & Russell, 2012). In addition, people with anorexia nervosa may experience low self-esteem, substance abuse, and clinical perfectionism (Cooper & Fairburn, 2011; Fairburn, Cooper, & Shafran, 2003).

3. Although anorexia nervosa can occur at any age, the peak age of onset is between 14 years and 18 years.

4. Prevalence: The lifetime prevalence estimates range from 0.5 percent to 3.5 percent. The DSM-5 reports the 12-month prevalence rate as 0.4 percent. Approximately 90 percent of all cases occur among females.

5. Surveys suggest that approximately 2 percent to 5 percent of female college athletes may suffer from an eating disorder (Greenleaf, Petrie, Carter, & Reel, 2009), with the highest rates among college gymnasts, swimmers, and divers (Anderson & Petrie, 2012).

6. The mothers of individuals with eating disorders are more likely to diet and have perfectionistic tendencies compared with mothers without a child with an eating disorder (Lombardo, Battagliese, Lucidi, & Frost, 2012; Mushquash & Sherry, 2013).

7. Anorexia nervosa has a particularly high mortality rate (up to 6 percent). A 20-year longitudinal study found that a long duration of illness, substance abuse, low weight status, and poor psychosocial functioning increased the risk for mortality among individuals with anorexia (Franko et al., 2013).

Common Treatment Strategies

The following treatment strategies are based on "enhanced" cognitive-behavioral therapy (CBT-E) proposed by Fairburn and colleagues (2008). Although empirical support is still lacking for any treatment for adults with anorexia nervosa, CBT-E appears to have the most support and promising future for immediate and long-term recovery (Cooper & Fairburn, 2011; Grave, Calugi, Conti, Doll, & Fairburn, 2013; Fairburn et al., 2013).

For patients who are underweight, treatment includes three phases:

1. First step: Help to increase the individual's readiness and motivation for change.

2. Second step: When the patients are ready, increase caloric intake to regain weight while simultaneously addressing the underlying eating disorder psychopathology, particularly extreme shape and weight concerns.

3. Third step: Focus on relapse prevention by helping patients develop personalized strategies for identifying and immediately correcting any setbacks.

Appendix B
You Decide: The Case of Fred

The individual in *Case 19: The Case of Fred* would receive a diagnosis of major neurocognitive disorder, probable Alzheimer disease.

Dx Checklist

Major Neurocognitive Disorder Due to Alzheimer Disease

1. Individual displays substantial and gradual decline and impairment in memory and learning and at least 1 other area of cognitive function as well, such as attention, planning and decision-making, perceptual-motor skills, language ability, and social awareness.

2. Cognitive deficits interfere with individual's everyday independence.

3. Genetic indications or family history of Alzheimer disease underscore diagnosis, but are not essential to diagnosis.

4. Symptoms are not due to other types of disorders or medical problems.

(Based on APA, 2013.)

Clinical Information

1. Alzheimer disease is the most common form of dementia, accounting for approximately two-thirds of all cases of dementia (Burke, 2011).

2. The disease sometimes appears in middle age, but most often occurs after the age of 65, particularly among people in their late 70s and early 80s.

3. After its onset, the disease progresses gradually, ranging in duration from 2 years to as many as 20 years with most people surviving only 10 years after diagnosis (APA, 2013; Soukup, 2006).

4. Patients with Alzheimer disease may at first deny that they have a problem, but may soon become anxious or depressed; many also become agitated.

5. Approximately 1 percent to 2 percent of the world's adult population suffer from some form of dementia, including up to 80 percent of all people older than 85 (APA, 2013).

6. Structural changes in the brains of people with Alzheimer disease include an excessive number of neurofibrillary tangles (twisted protein fibers found within the cells of the hippocampus and certain other brain areas) and of senile plaques (deposits of a small molecule known as the beta-amyloid protein that form between cells in the hippocampus, cerebral cortex, and certain other brain regions) (Fandrich, Schmidt, & Grigorieff, 2011; Selkoe, 2011).

7. The disease often has a genetic basis (Hollingsworth, Harold, Jones, Owen, & Williams, 2011).

8. Victims of the disorder usually remain in fairly good health until the later stages of the disease when they may become less active. With less activity, they may become prone to illnesses such as pneumonia, which can result in death (Ames, Chiu, Lindesay, & Schulman, 2010).

9. According to the Alzheimer's Association, Alzheimer disease is the sixth leading cause of death in the United States overall, and deaths from Alzheimer disease increased 68 percent between 2000 and 2010.

Common Treatments

1. No single approach or set of approaches is highly effective in all cases of Alzheimer disease.

2. Two types of medications have been approved to treat patients with memory loss and confusion: cholinesterase inhibitors (Aricept, Exelon, Razadyne, and Cognex) and *memantine* (Namenda). Such drugs prevent the breakdown of acetylcholine in the brain, a neurotransmitter essential to memory (Alzheimer's Association, 2013).

3. Behavioral interventions may help change everyday patient behaviors that are stressful for the family, such as wandering at night or urinary incontinence.

4. The needs of the caregivers must also be met via psychoeducation, psychotherapy, support groups, and regular time-outs.

5. Alzheimer disease day-care facilities (providing outpatient treatment programs and activities during the day) are becoming common. In addition, many assisted-living facilities are being built—apartments that provide supervision and are tailored to the needs and limitations of people with diseases such as Alzheimer disease.

Appendix C
You Decide: The Case of Suzanne

The individual in *Case 20: The Case of Suzanne* would receive a diagnosis of trichotillomania (hair-pulling disorder).

Dx **Checklist**

Trichotillomania (Hair-Pulling Disorder)

1. Individuals repeatedly pull out their hair.
2. Despite attempts to stop, individuals are unable to stop this practice.
3. Significant distress or impairment.

(Based on APA, 2013.)

Clinical Information

1. Trichotillomania is listed as one of the obsessive-compulsive and related disorders in the DSM-5, a group of disorders marked by excessive preoccupations and rituals (APA, 2013).

2. Some clinicians believe that the disorder is actually a form of obsessive-compulsive disorder, because the hair-pulling, like the compulsions found in obsessive-compulsive disorder, is compulsive in nature, feels involuntary, and is recognized as senseless (Grant, Odlaug, & Potenza, 2007).

3. Contrasts between trichotillomania and the compulsions of obsessive-compulsive disorder: Compulsions are most often performed in response to obsessions, performed in a rigid or even ritualistic way, aimed at preventing some dreaded event, done with full awareness by the patient, and span beyond a single behavior (Grant, Odlaug, & Potenza, 2007).

4. Research on trichotillomania and its treatments is very limited.

5. The disorder often first appears during early adolescence at the onset of puberty (APA, 2013).

6. The disorder may last only weeks or months, or may be chronic (lasting years or even decades).

7. Approximately 1 percent of adults exhibit the disorder. Females seem to heavily outnumber males by a ratio of 10:1 (APA, 2013).

8. In children, self-limited periods of hair-pulling are a common, temporary habit. In addition, as many as 10 percent to 15 percent of college students pull their hair regularly, but do not meet the clinical criteria of trichotillomania (Christenson et al., 1991; Tay, Levy, & Metry, 2004).

9. Often, people with trichotillomania also exhibit another psychological disorder, either concurrently or at another point in their lives. Major depressive disorder and excoriation (skin-picking) disorder are the most common co-morbidities (APA, 2013).

Common Treatments

1. Self-help groups

2. Certain antidepressant medications, such as sertraline (Zoloft) (Dougherty, Loh, Jenike, & Keuthen, 2006)

3. Cognitive-behavioral therapy, featuring :

    a. Self-monitoring of hair-pulling behaviors

    b. Exposure to situations that trigger hair-pulling

    c. Performance of alternative or competing behavior during exposure, until the urge to pull hair passes

    d. Identification and alteration of beliefs about the appearance of one's hair that may be contributing to the behavior (Rothbaum & Ninan, 1999).

4. Psychotherapy for any feelings of depression that may accompany trichotillomania

5. Relapse-prevention strategies

References

AA World Services (2011). AA fact file. New York: Author.

Abramowitz, J. S. (2006). The psychological treatment of obsessive-compulsive disorder. *Canadian Journal of Psychiatry, 51,* 407–416.

Abramowitz, J. S., & Braddock, A. E. (2011). *Hypochondriasis and health anxiety. Advances in psychotherapy—Evidence-based practice.* Cambridge, MA: Hogrefe.

Abramowitz, J. S., Whiteside, S., Lynam, D., & Kalsy, S. (2003). Is thought–action fusion specific to obsessive-compulsive disorder? A mediating role of negative affect. *Behaviour Research and Therapy, 41*(9), 1069–1079.

Ackerman, M. D., & Carey, M. P. (1995). Psychology's role in the assessment of erectile dysfunction: Historical precedents, current knowledge, and methods. *Journal of Consulting Clinical Psychology, 63*(6), 862–876.

Adler, J. (1998, May 4). Take a pill and call me tonight. *Newsweek,* p. 48.

Ahearn, W. H. (2010). What every behavior analyst should know about the "MMR causes autism" hypothesis. *Behavior Analysis in Practice, 3*(1), 46–50.

Akinbami, L. J., Liu, X., Pastor, P. N., & Reuben, C. A. (2011). Attention deficit hyperactivity disorder among children aged 5–17 Years in the United States, 1998–2009. NCHS Data Brief. No. 70. Atlanta, GA: Centers for Disease Control and Prevention.

Alegria, A. A., Blanco, C., Petry, N. M., Skodol, A. E., Liu, S. M., Grant, B., & Hasin, D. (2013). Sex differences in antisocial personality disorder: Results from the National Epidemiological Survey on Alcohol and Related Conditions. *Personality Disorders: Theory, Research, and Treatment, 4*(3), 214.

Allan, C., Smith, I., & Mellin, M. (2000). Detoxification from alcohol: A comparison of home detoxification and hospital-based day patient care. *Alcohol and Alcoholism, 35*(1), 66–69.

Allen, G. (2011). The cerebellum in autism spectrum disorders. In E. Hollander, A. Kolevzon, & J. T. Coyle (Eds.), *Textbook of autism spectrum disorders* (pp. 375–381). Arlington, VA: American Psychiatric Publishing.

Alzheimer's Association (1997, February 17). Survey: Stress on Alzheimer's care givers. Cited in *USA Today*, p. 1 D.

Alzheimer's Association (2013). 2013 Facts and Figures. *Alzheimer's & Dementia, 9(2)*, 1–68.

American Psychological Association (1994). *Diagnostic and statistical manual of mental disorders* (4th ed.). Washington, DC: Author.

American Psychological Association (1996). Interim report of the working group on investigation of memories of childhood abuse. In K. Pezdek & W. P Banks (Eds.), *The recovered memory/false memory debate*. San Diego, CA: Academic Press.

American Psychological Association (2000). DSM-IV text revision. Washington, DC: Author.

American Psychiatric Association (2013). Diagnostic and statistical manual of mental disorders (5th ed.). Arlington, VA: American Psychiatric Publishing.

Ames, D., Chiu, E., Lindesay, J., & Schulman, K. I. (2010). *Guide to the psychiatry of old age*. New York: Cambridge University Press.

Andersen, A. E. (1995). Sequencing treatment decisions: Cooperation or conflict between therapist and patient. In G. Szmukler, C. Dare, & J. Treasure (Eds.), *Handbook of eating disorders: Theory, treatment, and research*. Chichester, UK: Wiley.

Anderson, C., & Petrie, T. A. (2012). Prevalence of disordered eating and pathogenic weight control behaviors among NCAA Division I female collegiate gymnasts and swimmers. *Research Quarterly for Exercise and Sport, 83*(1), 120–124.

Andersson, E., Enander, J., Andrén, P., Hedman, E., Ljótsson, B., Hursti, T., et al. (2012). Internet-based cognitive behaviour therapy for obsessive-compulsive disorder: A randomized controlled trial. *Psychological Medicine, 21*, 1–11.

Angst, J. (1995). The epidemiology of depressive disorders. *European Neuropsychopharmacology, 5*(Suppl.), 95–98.

Angst, J. (1999). Major depression in 1998: Are we providing optimal therapy? *Journal of Clinical Psychiatry, 60*(Suppl. 6), 5–9.

Ash, R. (1999). Fantastic book of 1001 facts. New York: DK Publishing.

Atlas, J. A. (1995). Association between history of abuse and borderline personality disorder for hospitalized adolescent girls. *Psychological Reports, 77,* 1346.

Awad, A. G., & Voruganti, L. N. (1999). Quality of life and new antipsychotics in schizophrenia: Are patients better off? *International Journal of Social Psychiatry, 45*(4), 268–275.

Azrin, N. H., Nunn, R. G., & Frantz, S. E. (1980). Treatment of hairpulling: A comparative study of habit reversal and negative practice training. *Journal of Behavioral Therapy and Experimental Psychiatry, 11,* 13–20.

Baldessarini, R. J., Tondo, L., & Hennen, J. (1999). Effects of lithium treatment and its discontinuation on suicidal behavior in bipolar manic-depressive disorders. *Journal of Clinical Psychiatry, 60*(Suppl. 2), 77–84.

Ballas, C., Benton, T. D., & Evans, D. L. (2010). Pharmacotherapy and relapse prevention for depression. In C. S. Richards & J. G. Perri (Eds.), *Relapse prevention for depression* (pp. 131–153). Washington, DC: American Psychological Association.

Bandelow, B., Sher, L., Bunevicius, R., Hollander, E., Kasper, S., Zohar, J., et al. (2012). Guidelines for the pharmacological treatment of anxiety disorders, obsessive-compulsive disorder and posttraumatic stress disorder in primary care. *International Journal of Psychiatry in Clinical Practice, 16*(2), 77–84.

Barak, Y., Kimhi, R., & Weizman, R. (2000). Is selectivity for serotonin uptake associated with a reduced emergence of manic episodes in depressed patients? *International Clinical Psychopharmacology, 15*(1), 53–56.

Baron, M. (2002). Manic-depression genes and the new millennium: Poised for discovery. *Molecular Psychiatry, 7*(4), 342–358.

Bastiani, A. M., Aitemus, M., Pigott, T. A., Rubenstein, C., et al. (1996). Comparison of obsessions and compulsions in patients with anorexia nervosa and obsessive-compulsive disorder. *Biological Psychiatry, 39,* 966–969.

Bastiani, A. M., Rao, R., Weltzin, T., & Kaye, W. H. (1995). Perfectionism in anorexia nervosa. *International Journal of Eating Disorders, 17*(2), 147–152.

Bates, G. W., Thompson, J. C., & Flanagan, C. (1999). The effectiveness of individual versus group induction of depressed mood. *Journal of Psychology, 133*(3), 245–252.

Baucom, D. H., Shoham, V., Mueser, K. T., Diauto, A. D., & Stickle, T. R. (1998). Empirically supported couple and family interventions for marital distress and adult mental health problems. *Journal of Consulting Clinical Psychology, 66*(1), 53–88.

Bauer, M., Glenn, T., Rasgon, N., Marsh, W., Sagduyu, K., Munoz, R., et al. (2011). Association between median family income and self-reported mood symptoms in bipolar disorder. *Comprehensive Psychiatry, 52*(1), 17–25.

Bebbington, P. E., & Kuipers, E. (2011). Schizophrenia and psychosocial stresses. In D. R. Weinberg & P. Harrison (Eds.), *Schizophrenia* (pp. 599–624). Hoboken, NJ: Wiley-Blackwell.

Berrettini, W. (2006). Genetics of bipolar and unipolar disorders. In D. J. Stein, D. J. Kupfer, & A. F. Schatzberg (Eds.), *The American Psychiatric Publishing textbook of mood disorders*. Washington, DC: American Psychiatric Publishing.

Berrettini, W. H. (2000). Susceptibility loci for bipolar disorder: Overlap with inherited vulnerability to schizophrenia. *Biological Psychiatry, 47*(3), 245–251.

Bowden, C. L. (1995). Treatment of bipolar disorder. In A. F. Schatzberg & C. B. Nemeroff (Eds.), *Textbook of psychopharmacology* (pp. 603–614). Washington, DC: American Psychiatric Press.

Brooner, R. K., Disney, E. R., Neufeld, K. J., King, V. L., Kidorf, M., & Stoller, K. B. (2010). Antisocial personality disorder in patients with substance use disorders. In E. V. Nunes, J. Selzer, P. Levounis, & C. A. Davies (Eds.), *Substance dependence and co-occurring psychiatric disorders: Best practices for diagnosis and treatment* (pp. 1–26). Kingston, NJ: Civic Research Institute.

Brown, R. J., Schrag, A., & Trimble, M. R. (2005). Dissociation, childhood interpersonal trauma, and family functioning in patients with somatization disorder. *American Journal of Psychiatry, 162*(5), 899–905.

Burke, A. (2011). Pathophysiology of behavioral and psychological disturbances in dementia, In P. McNamara (Ed.), *Dementia, Vols 1–3: History and incidence, science and biology, treatments and developments* (pp. 135–158). Santa Barbara, CA: Praeger/ABC-CLIO.

Burnette, E., & Murray, B. (1996). Conduct disorders need early treatment. *APA Monitor, 27*(10), 40.

Burney, J., & Irwin, H. J. (2000). Shame and guilt in women with eating-disorder symptomatology. *Journal of Clinical Psychology, 56*(1), 51–61.

Bushman, B. J., Baumeister, R. F., & Stack, A. D. (1999). Catharsis, aggression, and persuasive influence: Self-fulfilling or self-defeating prophecies? *Journal of Personality and Social Psychology, 76*(3), 367–376.

Button, E. (1993). *Eating disorders: Personal construct therapy and change.* Chichester, UK: Wiley.

Bystritsky, A., Khalsa, S. S., Cameron, M. E., & Schiffman, J. (2013). Current diagnosis and treatment of anxiety disorders. *Pharmacy and Therapeutics, 38*(1), 30.

Cahill, S. P., Carrigan, M. H., & Frueh, B. C. (1999). Does EMDR work? and if so, why? A critical review of controlled outcome and dismantling research. *Journal of Anxiety Disorders, 13*(1–2), 5–33.

Cameron, P. M., Leszcz, M., Bebchuk, W., Swinson, R. P., Antony, M. M., Azim, H. F., et al. (1999). The practice and roles of the psychotherapies: A discussion paper. *Canadian Journal of Psychiatry, 44*(Suppl. 1), 18S–31S.

Canty, G. F. (1996). A heart to heart on depression. *The Institute Notebook, 5*(3), 1, 4.

Canty, G. F. (1996). Therapists at work. *The Institute Notebook, 5*(2), 1, 4.

Carek, P. J., Laibstain, S. E., & Carek, S. M. (2011). Exercise for the treatment of depression and anxiety. *International Journal of Psychiatry in Medicine, 41*(1), 15–28.

Carlson, J. S., Maupin, A., & Brinkman, T. (2010). Recent advances in the medical management of children with attention deficit/hyperactivity disorder. In P. C. McCabe & S. R. Shaw (Eds.), *Psychiatric disorders: Current topics and interventions for educators* (pp. 71–80). Thousand Oaks, CA: Corwin Press.

Centers for Disease Control and Prevention: National Center for Health Statistics. (2012). *Health, United States, 2012.* Retrieved from http://www.cdc.gov/nchs/fastats/drugs.htm.

Chan, S., MacKenzie, A., Ng, D. T., & Leung, J. K. (2000). An evaluation of the implementation of case management in the community psychiatric nursing service. *Journal of Advanced Nursing, 31*(1), 144–156.

Christenson, G. A., Mackenzie, T. B., & Mitchell, J. E. (1991). Characteristics of 60 adult chronic hair pullers. *American Journal of Psychiatry, 148*, 365–370.

Christenson, G. A., Pyle, R. L., & Mitchell, J. E. (1991). Estimated lifetime prevalence of trichotillomania in college students. *Journal of Clinical Psychiatry, 52*, 415–417.

Clark, D. M., & Wells, A. (1997). Cognitive therapy for anxiety disorders. In L. J. Dickstein, M. B. Riba, & J. M. Oldham (Eds.), *Review of Psychiatry* (Vol. 16). Washington, DC: American Psychiatric Press.

Clarke, J., Stein, M. D., Sobota, M., Marisi, M., & Hanna, L. (1999). Victims as victimizers: Physical aggression by persons with a history of childhood abuse. *Archives of Internal Medicine, 159*(16), 1920–1924.

Cloninger, C. R., Bohman, M., & Sigvardsson, S. (1981). Inheritance of alcohol abuse: Cross fostering analysis of adopted men. *Archives of General Psychiatry, 30*, 861–868.

Clyburn, L. D., Stones, M. J., Hadjistavropoulos, T., & Tuokko, H. (2000). Predicting caregiver burden and depression in Alzheimer's disease. *The Journals of Gerontology: Series B: Psychological Sciences and Social Sciences, 55*(1), S2–13.

Coid, J., & Ullrich, S. (2010). Antisocial personality disorder is on a continuum with psychopathy. *Comprehensive Psychiatry, 51*(4), 426–433.

Cole, D. A., & Turner, J. E., Jr. (1993). Models of cognitive mediation and moderation in child depression. *Journal of Abnormal Psychology, 102*(2), 271–281.

Compas, B. E., Haaga, D. A. F., Keefe, F. J., Leitenberg, H., & Williams, D. A. (1998) . Sampling of empirically supported psychological treatments from health psychology: Smoking, chronic pain, cancer, and bulimia nervosa. *Journal of Consulting Clinical Psychology, 66*(1), 89–112.

Connolly, K. R., & Thase, M. E. (2011). The clinical management of bipolar disorder: A review of evidence-based guidelines. *The Primary Care Companion to CNS Disorders, 13*(4), 1–34.

Cooper, Z., & Fairburn, C. G. (2011). The evolution of "enhanced" cognitive behavior therapy for eating disorders: Learning from treatment nonresponse. *Cognitive and Behavioral Practice, 18*(3), 394–402.

Corty, E. W., & Guardiani, J. M. (2008). Canadian and American sex therapists' perceptions of normal and abnormal ejaculatory latencies: How long should intercourse last? *The Journal of Sexual Medicine, 5*(5), 1251–1256.

Courchesne, R., & Courchesne, E. (1997). From impasse to insight in autism research: From behavioral symptoms to biological explanations. *Development and Psychopathology,* special issue.

Cowley, G. (2000). Alzheimer's: Unlocking the mystery. *Newsweek,* pp. 46–51.

Craddock, N., & Jones, I. (1999). Genetics of bipolar disorder. *Journal of Medical Genetics, 36*(8), 585–594.

Craske, M. G., & Barlow, D. H. (1993). Panic disorder and agoraphobia. In D. H. Barlow (Ed.), *Clinical handbook of psychological disorders* (2nd ed., pp. 1–47). New York: Guilford Press.

Cuijpers, P., Berking, M., Andersson, G., Quigley, L., Kleiboer, A., & Dobson, K. S. (2013). A meta-analysis of cognitive-behavioural therapy for adult depression, alone and in comparison with other treatments. *Canadian Journal of Psychiatry, 58*(7), 376–385.

Cuijpers, P., Sijbrandij, M., Koole, S. L., Andersson, G., Beekman, A. T., & Reynolds, C. F. (2013). The efficacy of psychotherapy and pharmacotherapy in treating depressive and anxiety disorders: A meta-analysis of direct comparisons. *World Psychiatry, 12*(2), 137–148.

Davidson, K. M., Tyrer, P., Tata, P., Cooke, D., Gumley, A., Ford, I., et al. (2009). Cognitive behaviour therapy for violent men with antisocial personality disorder in the community: An exploratory randomized controlled trial. *Psychological Medicine, 39*(4), 569.

Davis, L. L., Ryan, W., Adinoff, B., & Petty, F. (2000). Comprehensive review of the psychiatric uses of valproate. *Journal of Clinical Psychopharmacology, 20*(Suppl. I), 1S–17S.

Davis, T., Gunderson, J. G., & Myers, M. (1999). Borderline personality disorder. In D. G. Jacobs (Ed.), *The Harvard Medical School guide to suicide assessment and intervention.* San Francisco: Jossey-Bass.

Dawson, G., & Castelloe, P. (1992). Autism. In C. E. Walker (Ed.), *Clinical psychology: Historical and research foundations.* New York: Plenum Press.

Delinsky, S. S. (2011). Body image and anorexia nervosa. In T. F. Cash & L. Smolak (Eds.), *Body image: A handbook of science, practice, and prevention.* New York: Guilford Press, 279–287.

DeRubeis, R. J., Tang, T. Z., Gelfand, L. A., & Feeley, M. (2000). Recent findings concerning the processes and outcomes of cognitive therapy for depression. In S. L. Johnson, A. M. Hayes, et al. (Eds.), *Stress, coping, and depression.* Mahwah, NJ: Erlbaum.

DeSilva, P. (1995). Cognitive-behavioural models of eating disorders. In G. Szmukler, C. Dare, & J. Treasure (Eds.), *Handbook of eating disorders: Theory, treatment and research.* Chichester, UK: Wiley.

Dhir, R. R., Lin, H. C., Canfield, S. E., & Wang, R. (2011). Combination therapy for erectile dysfunction: An update review. *Asian Journal of Andrology, 13*(3), 382–390.

DiGrande, L., Perrin, M. A., Thorpe, L. E., Thalji, L., Murphy, J., Wu, D., et al. (2008). Posttraumatic stress symptoms, PTSD, and risk factors among lower Manhattan residents 2–3 years after the September 11, 2001 terrorist attacks. *Journal of Traumatic Stress, 21*(3), 264–273. doi:10.1002/jts.20345

Dougherty, D. D., Loh, R., Jenike, M. A., & Keuthen, N. J. (2006). Single modality versus dual modality treatment for trichotillomania: Sertraline, behavioral therapy, or both? *Journal of Clinical Psychiatry, 67,* 1086–1092.

Ekman, P., O'Sullivan, M., & Frank, M. G. (1999). A few can catch a liar. *Psychological Science, 10*(3), 263–266.

Ellenbroek, B. A. (2011). Psychopharmacological treatment of schizophrenia: What do we have and what could we get? *Neuropharmacology, 62*(3), 1371–1380.

Everson, S. A., Goldberg, D. E., Kaplan, G. A., Cohen, R. D., et al. (1996). Hopelessness and risk of mortality and incidence of myocardial infarction and cancer. *Psychosomatic Medicine, 58,* 113–121.

Express Scripts, Inc. (1999, June 29). *1998 Express Scripts Trend Report.* St. Louis, MO: Author.

Fairburn, C. G. (2008). Eating disorders: The transdiagnostic view and the cognitive behavioral theory. In Fairburn, C. G. (Ed.), *Cognitive behavior therapy and eating disorders.* New York: Guilford Press, 7–22.

Fairburn, C. G. (2008). *Cognitive behavior therapy and eating disorders.* New York: Guilford Press.

Fairburn, C. G., Cooper, Z., & Cooper, P. J. (1986). The clinical features and maintenance of bulimia nervosa. In K. D. Brownell & J. P. Foreyt (Eds.), *Handbook of eating disorders* (pp. 389–404). New York: Basic Books.

Fairburn, C. G., Cooper, Z., Doll, H. A., O'Connor, M. E., Palmer, R. L., & Dalle Grave, R. (2013). Enhanced cognitive behaviour therapy for adults with anorexia nervosa: A UK–Italy study. *Behaviour Research and Therapy, 51*(1), R2–R8.

Fairburn, C. G., Cooper, Z., & Shafran, R. (2003). Cognitive behaviour therapy for eating disorders: A "transdiagnostic" theory and treatment. *Behaviour Research and Therapy, 41*(5), 509–528.

Fairburn, C. G., Cooper, Z., Shafran, R., & Wilson, G. T. (2008). Eating disorders: A "transdiagnostic" protocol. In D. H. Barlow (Ed.), *Clinical handbook of psychological disorders: A step-by-step treatment manual* (4th ed.). New York: Guilford Press.

Fairburn, C. G., Jones, R., Peveler, R. C., Hope, R. A., & O'Connor, M. (1993). Psychotherapy and bulimia nervosa: Longer-term effects of interpersonal psychotherapy behavior therapy, and cognitive behavior therapy. *Archives of General Psychiatry, 50,* 419–428.

Fairburn, C. G., Marcus, M. D., & Wilson, G. T. (1993). Cognitive-behavioral therapy for binge eating and bulimia nervosa: A comprehensive manual. In C. G. Fairburn & G. T. Wilson (Eds.), *Binge eating: Nature, assessments, and treatment* (pp. 361–404). New York: Guilford Press.

Fairburn, C. G., Peveler, R. C., Jones, R., Hope, R. A., & Doll, H. A. (1993). Predictors of 12-month outcome in bulimia nervosa and the influence of attitudes to shape and weight. *Journal of Consulting Clinical Psychology, 61,* 696–698.

Falloon, I. R. H., & Liberman, R. P. (1983). Behavioral family interventions in the management of chronic schizophrenia. In W. McFarlane (Ed.), *Family therapy of schizophrenia* (pp. 325–380). New York: Guilford Press.

Fandrich, M., Schmidt, M., & Grigorieff, N. (2011). Recent progress in understanding Alzheimer's β-amyloid structures. *Trends in Biomedical Sciences, 36*(6), 338–345.

Farrell, C., Lee, M., & Shafran, R. (2005). Assessment of body size estimation: A review. *European Eating Disorders Review, 13*(2), 75–88.

Fava, M., Rankin, M. A., Wright, E. C., Aipert, J. E., Nierenberg, A. A., Pava, J., et al. (2000). Anxiety disorders in major depression. *Comprehensive Psychiatry, 41*(2), 97–102.

Feldman, H. A., Goldstein, I., Hatzichristou, D. G., Krane, R. J., & McKinlay, J. B. (1994). Impotence and its medical and psychosocial correlates: Results of the Massachusetts Male Aging Study. *Journal of Urology, 151,* 54–61.

Fichter, N. M., & Pirke, K. M. (1995). Starvation models and eating disorders. In G. Szmukler, C. Dare, & J. Treasure (Eds.), *Handbook of eating disorders: Theory, treatment, and research.* Chichester, UK: Wiley.

Fisher, J. E., & Carstensen, L. L. (1990). Behavior management of the dementias. *Clinical Psychology Review, 10,* 611–629.

Foa, E. B., & Kozak, M. J. (1995). Field trial: Obsessive-compulsive disorder. *American Journal of Psychiatry, 152*(1), 90–96.

Foreyt, J. P., Poston, W. S. C., & Goodrick, G. K. (1996). Future directions in obesity and eating disorders. *Addictive Behaviors, 21*(6), 767–778.

Fournier, J. C., DeRubeis, R. J., Hollon, S. D., Dimidjian, S., Amsterdam, J. D., Shelton, R. C., et al. (2010). Antidepressant drug effects and depression severity. *JAMA: The Journal of the American Medical Association, 303*(1), 47–53.

Frank, E., Grochocinski, V. J., Spanier, C. A., Buysse, D. J., Cherry, C. R., Houck, P. R., et al. (2000). Interpersonal psychotherapy and antidepressant medication: Evaluation of a sequential treatment strategy in women with recurrent major depression. *Journal of Clinical Psychiatry, 61*(1), 51–57.

Franko, D. L., Keshaviah, A., Eddy, K. T., Krishna, M., Davis, M. C., Keel, P. K., et al. (2013). A longitudinal investigation of mortality in anorexia nervosa and bulimia nervosa. *American Journal of Psychiatry, 170*(8), 917–925.

Friedman, M. (1984). Alteration of type A behavior and reduction in cardiac recurrences in postmyocardial infarction patients. *American Heart Journal, 108,* 237–248.

Friedman, M., & Rosenman, R. (1974). Type A behavior and your heart. New York: Knopf.

Friedman, M. J. (1999) Pharmacotherapy for post-traumatic stress disorder. In M. J. Horowitz (Ed.), *Essential papers on posttraumatic stress disorder.* Essential papers in psychoanalysis. New York: New York University Press.

Friman, P. C., Finney, J. W., & Christophersen, E. R. (1984). Behavioral treatment of trichotillomania: An evaluative review. *Behavior Therapy, 15,* 249–265.

Frost, R. O., Pekareva-Kochergina, A., & Maxner, S. (2011). The effectiveness of a biblio-based support group for hoarding disorder. *Behaviour Research and Therapy, 49*(10), 628–634.

Frost, R. O., Steketee, G., & Tolin, D. F. (2011). Comorbidity in hoarding disorder. *Depression and Anxiety, 28*(10), 876–884.

Frost, R. O., Tolin, D. F., & Maltby, N. (2010). Insight-related challenges in the treatment of hoarding. *Cognitive and Behavioral Practice, 17*(4), 404–413.

Fulwiler, C., & Pope, H. G., Jr. (1987). Depression in personality disorder. In O. G. Cameron (Ed.), *Presentations of depression: Depressive symptoms in medical and other psychiatric disorders.* New York: Wiley.

Gallagher, M. W., Payne, L. A., White, K. S., Shear, K. M., Woods, S. W., Gorman, J. M., et al. (2013). Mechanisms of change in cognitive behavioral therapy for panic disorder: The unique effects of self-efficacy and anxiety sensitivity. *Behaviour Research and Therapy, 51*(11), 767–777.

Gao, K., Kemp, D. E., Wang, Z., Ganocy, S. J., Conroy, C., Serrano, M. B., et al. (2010). Predictors of non-stabilization during the combination therapy of lithium and divalproex in rapid cycling bipolar disorder: A post-hoc analysis of two studies. *Psychopharmacology Bulletin, 43*(1), 23–38.

Garfinkle, K., & Redd, W. H. (1993). Behavioral control of anxiety, distress, and learned aversions in pediatric oncology. In J. C. Holland & W. Breitbart (Eds.), *Psychiatric aspects of symptom management in cancer patients* (pp. 129–146). Washington, DC: American Psychiatric Press.

Garner, D. M., Garfinkel, P. E., & O'Shaughnessy, M. (1985). The validity of the distinction between bulimia with and without anorexia nervosa. *American Journal of Psychiatry, 142,* 581–587.

Garssen, B., & Goodkin, K. (1999). On the role of immunological factors as mediators between psychosocial factors and cancer progression. *Psychiatry Research, 85*(1), 51–61.

Gaynor, S. T., & Baird, S. C. (2007). Personality disorders. In D. W. Woods & J. W. Kanter (Eds.), *Understanding behavior disorders: A contemporary behavioral perspective.* Reno, NV: Context Press.

George, E. L., Friedman, J. C., & Miklowitz, D. J. (2000). Integrated family and individual therapy for bipolar disorder. In S. L. Johnson, A. M. Hayes, et al. (Eds.), *Stress, coping, and depression.* Mahwah, NJ: Erlbaum.

Gifford, M., Friedman, S., & Majerus, R. (2010) *Alcoholism*. Santa Barbara, CA: Greenwood Press/ABC-CLIO.

Gili, M., Magallón, R., López-Navarro, E., Roca, M., Moreno, S., Bauzá, N., et al. (2013). Health related quality of life changes in somatising patients after individual versus group cognitive behavioural therapy: A randomized clinical trial. *Journal of Psychosomatic Research, 76*(2), 89–93.

Gilliam, C. M., Norberg, M. M., Villavicencio, A., Morrison, S., Hannan, S. E., & Tolin, D. F. (2011). Group cognitive-behavioral therapy for hoarding disorder: An open trial. *Behaviour Research and Therapy, 49*(11), 802–807.

Goetzel, R. Z., Anderson, D. R., Whitmer, R. W., Ozminkowski, R. J., Dunn, R. L., & Wasserman, J. (1998). The relationship between modifiable health risks and health care expenditures: An analysis of the multi-employer HERO health risk and cost database. The Health Enhancement Research Organization (HERO) Research Committee. *Journal of Occupational and Environmental Medicine, 40*(10), 843–854.

Goldstein, S. (2011). Attention-deficit/hyperactivity disorder. In S. Goldstein & C. R. Reynolds (Eds.), *Handbook of neurodevelopmental and genetic disorders in children* (2nd ed., pp. 131–150). New York: Guilford Press.

González, H. M., Tarraf, W., Whitfield, K. E., & Vega, W. A. (2010). The epidemiology of major depression and ethnicity in the United States. *Journal of Psychiatric Research, 44,* 1043–1051.

Gotlib, I. H., & Joormann, J. (2010). Cognition and depression: Current status and future directions. *Annual Review of Clinical Psychology, 6,* 285–312.

Gottesman, I. I. (1991). *Schizophrenia genesis*. New York: Freeman.

Grant, B. F., & Dawson, D. A. (1997). Age at onset of alcohol use and its association with DSM-IV alcohol abuse and dependence: Results from the National Longitudinal Alcohol Epidemiologic Survey. *Journal of Substance Abuse, 9,* 103–110.

Grant, J. E., Odlaug, B. L., & Potenza, M. N. (2007). Addicted to hair pulling? How an alternate model of trichotillomania may improve treatment outcome. *Harvard Review of Psychiatry, 15*(2), 80–85.

Grave, R., Calugi, S., Conti, M., Doll, H., & Fairburn, C. G. (2013). Inpatient cognitive behaviour therapy for anorexia nervosa: A randomized controlled trial. *Psychotherapy and Psychosomatics, 82*(6), 390–398.

Greenleaf, C., Petrie, T. A., Carter, J., & Reel, J. (2009). Female collegiate athletes: Prevalence of eating disorders and disordered eating behaviors. *Journal of American College Health, 57,* 489–495.

Grilo, C. M., Becker, D. F., Fehon, D. C., Walker, M. L., et al. (1996). Gender differences in personality disorders in psychiatrically hospitalized adolescents. *American Journal of Psychiatry, 153*(8), 1089–1091.

Gunderson, J. G. (2011). Borderline personality disorder. *New England Journal of Medicine, 364*(21), 2037–2042.

Halmi, K. A. (1995). Current concepts and definitions. In G. Szmukler, C. Dare, & J. Treasure (Eds.), *Handbook of eating disorders: Theory, treatment, and research.* Chichester, UK: Wiley.

Hardy, J. D., & Smith, T. W. (1988). Cynical hostility and vulnerability to disease: Social support, life stress, and physiological response to conflict. *Health Psychology, 7,* 447–459.

Harrington, R. C., Fudge, H., Rutter, M. L., Bredenkamp, D., Groothues, C., & Pridham, J. (1993). Child and adult depression: A test of continuities with data from a family study. *British Journal of Psychiatry, 162,* 627–633.

Hassett, A. L., & Gevirtz, R. N. (2009). Nonpharmacologic treatment for fibromyalgia: Patient education, cognitive-behavioral therapy, relaxation techniques, and complementary and alternative medicine. *Rheumatic Diseases Clinics of North America, 35*(2), 393.

Haw, C., & Stubbs, J. (2011). Medication for borderline personality disorder: A survey at a secure hospital. *International Journal of Psychiatry in Clinical Practice, 15*(4), 270–274.

Hepp, U., Kraemer, B., Schnyder, U., Miller, N., & Delsignore, A. (2005). Psychiatric comorbidity in gender identity disorder. *Journal of Psychosomatic Research, 58,* 259–261.

Hermann, C., Kim, M., & Blanchard, E. B. (1995). Behavioral and prophylactic pharmacological intervention studies of pediatric migraine: An exploratory meta-analysis. *Pain, 60*(3), 239–255.

Herzog, D. B., Dorer, D. J., Keel, P. K., Selwin, S. E., Ekeblad, E. R., Flores, A. T., et al. (1999). Recovery and relapse in anorexia and bulimia nervosa: A 7.5-year follow-up study. *Journal of the American Academy of Child and Adolescent Psychiatry, 38*(7), 829–837.

Hill, A. J. (2006). Body dissatisfaction and dieting in children. In P. J. Cooper & A. Stein (Eds.), *Childhood feeding problems and adolescent eating disorders.* London: Routledge/Taylor & Francis, 123–149.

Hill, H. E., Kornetsky, C. H., Flanary, H. G., & Wikler, A. (1952). Effects of anxiety and morphine on discrimination of intensities of painful stimuli. *Journal of Clinical Investigation, 31,* 473–480.

Hill, H. E., Kornetsky, C. H., Flanary, H. G., & Wikler, A. (1952). Studies on anxiety associated with anticipation of pain. I. Effects of morphine. *Archives of Neurology & Psychiatry, 67,* 612–619.

Hirschfeld, R. M. (1999). Efficacy of SSRIs and newer antidepressants in severe depression: Comparison with TCAs. *Journal of Clinical Psychiatry, 60*(5), 326–335.

Hoagwood, K., Kelleher, K. J., Feil, M., & Comer, D. M. (2000). Treatment services for children with ADHD: A national perspective. *Journal of the American Academy of Child and Adolescent Psychiatry, 39*(2), 198–206.

Hoedeman, R., Blankenstein, A. H., van der Feltz-Cornelis, C. M., Krol, B., Stewart, R., & Groothoff, J. W. (2010). Consultation letters for medically unexplained physical symptoms in primary care. *Cochrane Database of Systematic Reviews, 12,* 1–57.

Hollingworth, P., Harold, D., Jones, L., Owen, M. J., & Williams, J. (2011). Alzheimer's disease genetics: Current knowledge and future challenges. *International Journal of Geriatric Psychiatry, 26,* 793–802.

Howlin, P., Savage, S., Moss, P., Tempier, A., & Rutter, M. (2014). Cognitive and language skills in adults with autism: A 40-year follow-up. *Journal of Child Psychology and Psychiatry, 55*(1), 49–58.

Huang, J-J., Yang, Y-P., & Wu, J. (2010). Relationships of borderline personality disorder and childhood trauma. *Chinese Journal of Clinical Psychology, 18*(6), 769–771.

Hurwitz, T. A. (2004). Somatization and conversion disorder. *Canadian Journal of Psychiatry. Revue canadienne de psychiatrie, 49*(3), 172.

Imbierowicz, K., & Egle, U. T. (2003). Childhood adversities in patients with fibromyalgia and somatoform pain disorder. *European Journal of Pain, 7*(2), 113–119.

Inman, B. A., Sauver, J. L., Jacobson, D. J., McGree, M. E., Nehra, A., Lieber, M. M., et al. (2009). A population-based, longitudinal study of erectile dysfunction and future coronary artery disease. *Mayo Clinic Proceedings, 84*(2), 108–113.

Inskip, H. M., Harris, E. C., & Barraclough, B. (1998). Lifetime risk of suicide for affective disorder, alcoholism and schizophrenia. *British Journal of Psychiatry, 172,* 35–37.

Jacobi, C., Fittig, E., Bryson, S. W., Wilfley, D., Kraemer, H. C., & Taylor, C. B. (2011). Who is really at risk? Identifying risk factors for subthreshold and full syndrome eating disorders in a high-risk sample. *Psychological Medicine, 41*(9), 1939–1949.

James, W. M. (1890). *Principles of psychology* (Vol. I). New York: Holt, Rinehart & Winston.

Jay, S. M. (1988). Invasive medical procedures. In D. K. Routh (Ed.). *Handbook of pediatric psychology* (pp. 401–426). New York: Guilford Press.

Johnson, W. G., Schlundt, D. G., Barclay, D. R., Carr-Nangle, R. E., et al. (1995). A naturalistic functional analysis of binge eating. Special series: Body dissatisfaction, binge eating, and dieting as interlocking issues in eating disorders research. *Behavior Therapy, 26*(1), 101–118.

Johnston, L. D., O'Malley, P. M., Bachman, J. G., & Schulenberg, J. E. (2011). *Monitoring the future national results on adolescent drug use* (NIH Publication No. 07–6202). Bethesda, MD: National Institute on Drug Abuse.

Julien, R. M., Advokat, C. D., & Comaty, J. (2011). *Primer of drug action* (12th ed.). New York: Bedford, Freeman, & Worth.

Kalb, C. (2000, January 31). Coping with the darkness: Revolutionary new approaches in providing care for helping people with Alzheimer's stay active and feel productive. *Newsweek,* pp. 52–54.

Kamali, M., & McInnis, M. G. (2011). Genetics of mood disorders: General principles and potential applications for treatment resistant depression. In J. F. Greden, M. B. Riba, & M. G. McInnis (Eds.), *Treatment resistant depression: A roadmap for effective care* (pp. 293–308). Arlington, VA: American Psychiatric Publishing.

Kanner, B. (1995). *Are you normal? Do you behave like everyone else?* New York: St. Martin's Press.

Kanner, B. (1998, February). Are you normal? Turning the other cheek. *American Demographics.*

Kanner, L. (1943). Autistic disturbances of affective contact. *Nervous Child, 2,* 217–250.

Kaplan, H. S. (1987). *The illustrated manual of sex therapy* (2nd ed.). New York: Brunner/Mazel.

Kashner, T. M., Rost, K., Smith, G. R., & Lewis, S. (1992). An analysis of panel data: The impact of a psychiatric consultation letter on the expenditures and outcomes of care for patients with somatization disorder. *Medical Care, 30*(9), 811–821.

Kate, N. T. (1998, April). Two careers, one marriage. *American Demographics, 20,* 28.

Katon, W. J., & Walker, E. A. (1998). Medically unexplained symptoms in primary care. *Journal of Clinical Psychiatry, 59*(Suppl. 20), 15–21.

Kazdin, A. E., & Wassell, G. (1999). Barriers to treatment participation and therapeutic change among children referred for conduct disorder. *Journal of Clinical Child Psychology, 28*(2), 160–172.

Keel, P. K., & Mitchell, J. E. (1997). Outcome in bulimia nervosa. *American Journal of Psychiatry, 154,* 313–321.

Kenny, M., & Egan, J. (2011). Somatization disorder: What clinicians need to know. *The Irish Psychologist, 37,* 93–96.

Kessler, R. C., & Zhao, S. (1999). The prevalence of mental illness. In A. V. Horwitz & T. L. Scheid (Eds.), *A handbook for the study of mental health: Social contexts, theories, and systems.* Cambridge, UK: Cambridge University Press.

Kessler, R. C., Demier, O., Frank, R. G., Olfson, M., Pincus, H. A., Walters, E. E., et al. (2005). Prevalence and treatment of mental disorders, 1990 to 2003. *New England Journal of Medicine, 352*(24), 2515–2523.

Kessler, R. C., Gruber, M., Hettema, J. M., Hwang, I., Sampson, N., & Yonkers, K. A. (2010). Major depression and generalized anxiety disorder in the National Comorbidity Survey follow-up survey. In D. Goldberg, K. S. Kendler, P. J. Sirovatka, & D. A. Regier (Eds.), *Diagnostic issues in depression and generalized anxiety disorder: Refining the research agenda for DSM-V* (pp. 139–170). Washington, DC: American Psychiatric Association.

Kessler, R. C., McGonagle, K. A., Zhao, S., Nelson, C. B., Hughes, M., Eshleman, S., et al. (1994). Lifetime and 12-month prevalence of DSM-III-R psychiatric disorders among persons aged 15–54 in the United States: Results from the National Comorbidity Survey. *Archives of General Psychiatry, 51*(1), 8–19.

Khare, T., Pal, M., & Petronis, A. (2011). Understanding bipolar disorder: The epigenetic perspective. In H. K. Manji & C. A. Zarate, Jr. (Eds.), *Behavioral neurobiology of bipolar disorder and its treatment: Current topics in behavioral neurosciences* (pp. 31–49). New York: Springer Science + Business Media.

Kiecolt-Glaser, J. K., Glaser, R., Gravenstein, S., Malarkey, W. B., & Sheridan, J. (1996). Chronic stress alters the immune response to influenza virus vaccine in older adults. *Proceedings of the National Academy of Sciences of the United States of America, 93,* 3043–3047.

Kiecolt-Glaser, J. K., Page, G. G., Marucha, P. T., MacCallum, R. C., & Glaser, R. (1998). Psychological influences on surgical recovery: Perspectives from psychoneuroimmunology. *American Psychologist, 53*(1), 1209–1218.

Kim, K.-H., Lee, S.-M., Paik, J.-W., & Kim, N.-S. (2011). The effects of continuous antidepressant treatment during the first 6 months on relapse or recurrence of depression. *Journal of Affective Disorders, 132*(1), 121–129.

Kirn, W. (1997, August 18). The ties that bind. *Time,* pp. 48–50.

Klassen, A., Miller, A., Raina, P., Lee, S. K., & Olsen, L. (1999). Attention-deficit hyperactivity disorder in children and youth: A quantitative systematic review of the efficacy of different management strategies. *Canadian Journal of Psychiatry, 44*(10), 1007–1016.

Kliem, S., Kröger, C., & Kosfelder, J. (2010). Dialectical behavior therapy for borderline personality disorder: A meta-analysis using mixed-effects modeling. *Journal of Consulting and Clinical Psychology, 78*(6), 936.

Kocsis, J. H., Friedman, R. A., Markowitz, J. C., Miller, N., Gniwesch, L., & Bram, J. (1995). Stability of remission during tricyclic antidepressant continuation therapy for dysthymia. *Psychopharmacology Bulletin, 31*(2), 213–216.

Krall, W. J., Sramek, J. J., & Cutler, N. R. (1999). Cholinesterase inhibitors: A therapeutic strategy for Alzheimer's disease. *Annals of Pharmacotherapy, 33*(4), 441–450.

Landau, D., Iervolino, A. C., Pertusa, A., Santo, S., Singh, S., & Mataix-Cols, D. (2011). Stressful life events and material deprivation in hoarding disorder. *Journal of Anxiety Disorders, 25*(2), 192–202.

Larson, K., Russ, S. A., Kahn, R. S., & Halfon, N. (2011). Patterns of comorbidity, functioning, and service use for US children with ADHD, 2007. *Pediatrics, 127*(3), 462–470.

Laumann, E. O., Paik, A., & Rosen, R. C. (1999). Sexual dysfunction in the United States: Prevalence and predictors. *Journal of the American Medical Association, 281*(6), 537–544.

Lawrence, A. (2003). Factors associated with satisfaction or regret following male-to-female sex reassignment surgery. *Archives of Sexual Behavior, 32*(4), 299–315.

Lawrence, A. A. (2010). Sexual orientation versus age of onset as bases for typologies (subtypes) for gender identity disorder in adolescents and adults. *Archives of Sexual Behavior, 39,* 514–545.

Lawrie, S. M., & Pantelis, C. (2011). Structural brain imaging in schizophrenia and related populations. In D. R. Weinberg & P. Harrison (Eds.), *Schizophrenia* (pp. 334–352). Hoboken, NJ: Wiley-Blackwell.

Lecrubier, Y., Bakker, A., Dunbar, G., and the collaborative paroxetine panic study investigators. (1997). A comparison of paroxetine, clomipramine, and placebo in the treatment of panic disorder. *Acta Psychiatrica Scandinavica, 95,* 145–152.

Lehoux, P. M, Steiger, H., & Jabalpurlawa, S. (2000). State/trait distinctions in bulimic syndromes. *International Journal of Eating Disorders, 27*(1), 36–42.

Leichsenring, F., Leibing, E., Kruse, J., New, A. S., & Leweke, F. (2011). Borderline personality disorder. *Lancet, 377*(9759), 74–84.

Leutwyler, K. (1996). Paying attention: The controversy over ADHD and the drug Ritalin is obscuring a real look at the disorder and its underpinnings. *Scientific American, 272*(2), 12–13.

Liberman, R. P., Kopelowicz, A., & Young, A. S. (1994). Biobehavioral treatment and rehabilitation of schizophrenia. *Behavior Therapy, 25,* 89–107.

Lieb, K., Völlm, B., Rücker, G., Timmer, A., & Stoffers, J. M. (2010). Pharmacotherapy for borderline personality disorder: Cochrane systematic review of randomised trials. *The British Journal of Psychiatry, 196*(1), 4–12.

Lieberman, J. A. (1998). Maximizing clozapine therapy: Managing side effects. *Journal of Clinical Psychiatry, 59*(Suppl. 3), 38–43.

Lindenmayer, J. P., & Khan, A. (2012). Psychopathology. In J. A. Lieberman, T. S. Stroup, & D. O. Perkins (Eds.), *Essentials of schizophrenia* (pp. 11–54). Arlington, VA: American Psychiatric Publishing.

Linehan, M. M. (1993). *Cognitive-behavioral treatment of borderline personality disorder.* New York: Guilford Press.

Linehan, M. M. (1993). *Skills training manual for treating borderline personality disorder.* New York: Guilford Press.

Linehan, M. M., Armstrong, H. E., Suarez, A., Allmon, D., & Heard, H. L. (1991). Cognitive-behavioral treatment of chronically parasuicidal borderline patients. *Archives of General Psychiatry, 48,* 1060–1064.

Linehan, M. M., Heard, H. L., & Armstrong, H. E. (1993). Naturalistic follow-up of a behavioral treatment for chronically parasuicidal borderline patients. *Archives of General Psychiatry, 50,* 971–974.

Linville, D., Stice, E., Gau, J., & O'Neil, M. (2011). Predictive effects of mother and peer influences on increases in adolescent eating disorder risk factors and symptoms: A 3-year longitudinal study. *International Journal of Eating Disorders, 44*(8), 745–751.

Lloyd, G. G., & Lishman, W. A. (1975). Effect of depression on the speed of recall of pleasant and unpleasant experiences. *Psychological Medicine, 5,* 173–180.

Lombardo, C., Battagliese, G., Lucidi, F., & Frost, R. O. (2012). Body dissatisfaction among pre-adolescent girls is predicted by their involvement in aesthetic sports and by personal characteristics of their mothers. *Eating and Weight Disorders—Studies on Anorexia, Bulimia and Obesity, 17*(2), 116–127.

Looper, K. & Kirmayer, L. (2002). Behavioural medicine approaches to somatoform disorders. *Journal of Consulting and Clinical Psychology, 70,* 810–827.

LoPiccolo, J. (1991). Post-modern sex therapy for erectile failure. In R. C. Rosen & S. R. Leiblum (Eds.), *Erectile failure: Diagnosis and treatment.* New York: Guilford Press.

Lorenzo, A., & Yankner, B. A. (1996). Amyloid fibril toxicity in Alzheimer's disease and diabetes. In R. J. Wurtman, S. Corkin, J. H. Growdon, & R. M. Nitsch (Eds.), *The neurobiology of Alzheimer's disease.* New York: New York Academy of Sciences.

Lyons, M., Healy, N., & Bruno, D. (2013). It takes one to know one: Relationship between lie detection and psychopathy. *Personality and Individual Differences, 55*(6), 676–679.

Magallón, R., Gili, M., Moreno, S., Bauzá, N., García-Campayo, J., Roca, M., et al. (2008). Cognitive-behaviour therapy for patients with abridged somatization disorder (SSI 4, 6) in primary care: A randomized, controlled study. *BMC Psychiatry, 8,* 47.

Mai, F. (2004). Somatization disorder: A practical review. *Canadian Journal of Psychiatry, 49*(10), 652–662.

Manne, S. L., Redd, W. H., Jacobsen, P. B., et al. (1990). Behavioral intervention to reduce child and parent distress during venipuncture. *Journal of Consulting Clinical Psychology, 58*, 565–572.

Mariani, M. A., & Barkley, R. A. (1997). Neuropsychological and academic functioning in preschool boys with attention-deficit/hyperactivity disorder. *Developmental Neuropsychology, 13*(1), 111–129.

Marketdata Enterprises, Inc. (2011, May 1) *U.S. Weight Loss & Diet Control Market, 11th Edition.* Retrieved February 16, 2014 from http://www.prweb.com/releases/2011/5/prweb8393658.htm.

Mash, E. J., & Wolfe, D. A. (2010). *Abnormal child psychology* (4th ed.). Stamford, CT: Wadsworth/Cengage Learning.

Masters, W. H., & Johnson, V. E. (1970). *Human sexual inadequacy.* Boston: Little, Brown.

Mataix-Cols, D., Wooderson, S., Lawrence, N., Brammer, M. J., Speckens, A., & Phillips, M. L. (2004). Distinct neural correlates of washing, checking, and hoarding symptom dimensions in obsessive-compulsive disorder. *Archives of General Psychiatry, 61*(6), 564.

Matson, J. L., Turygin, N. C., Beighley, J., Rieske, R., Tureck, K., & Matson, M. L. (2012). Applied behavior analysis in autism spectrum disorders: Recent developments, strengths, and pitfalls. *Research in Autism Spectrum Disorders, 6*(1), 144–150.

Mazzone, L., Postorino, V., Reale, L., Guarnera, M., Mannino, V., Armando, M., et al. (2013). Self-esteem evaluation in children and adolescents suffering from ADHD. *Clinical practice and epidemiology in mental health: CP & EMH, 9,* 96–102.

McCormick, L. H. (2000). Improving social adjustment in children with attention-deficit/hyperactivity disorder. *Archives of Family Medicine, 9*(2), 191–194.

McCrady, B. S. (1990). The marital relationship and alcoholism treatment. In R. L. Collins, K. E. Leonard, B. A. Miller, & J. S. Searles (Eds.), *Alcohol and the family: Research and clinical perspectives* (pp. 338–355). New York: Guilford Press.

McGuire, P. A. (2000, February). New hope for people with schizophrenia. *Monitor on Psychology, 31*(2), 24–28.

McIntosh, V. V. W., Carter, F. A., Bulik, C. M., Frampton, C. M. A., & Joyce, P. R. (2011). Five-year outcome of cognitive behavioral therapy and exposure with response prevention for bulimia nervosa. *Psychological Medicine, 41*(5), 1061.

McKenzie, S. J., Williamson, D. A., & Cubic, B. A. (1993). Stable and reactive body image disturbances in bulimia nervosa. *Behavior Therapy, 24,* 195–207.

McLaughlin, K. A., & Nolen-Hoeksema, S. (2011). Rumination as a transdiagnostic factor in depression and anxiety. *Behaviour Research and Therapy, 49*(3), 186–193.

McRae, L. (2013). Rehabilitating antisocial personalities: Treatment through self-governance strategies. *Journal of Forensic Psychiatry & Psychology, 24*(1), 48–70, DOI: 10.1080/14789949.2012.752517.

Mehler, P. S. (2011). Medical complications of bulimia nervosa and their treatments. *International Journal of Eating Disorders, 44*(2), 95–104.

Meichenbaum, D. (1977). *Cognitive-behavior modification: An integrative approach.* New York: Plenum Press.

Melzack, R., Weisz, A. Z., & Sprague, L. T. (1963). Stratagems for controlling pain: Contributions of auditory stimulation and suggestion. *Experimental Neurology, 8,* 239–247.

Merikangas, K. R., Jin, R., He, J.-P., Kessler, R. C., Lee, S., Sampson, N. A., et al. (2011). Prevalence and correlates of bipolar spectrum disorder in the World Mental Health Survey Initiative. *Archives of General Psychiatry, 68*(3), 241–251.

Messina, N. P., Wish, E. D., & Nemes, S. (1999). Therapeutic community treatment for substance abusers with antisocial personality disorder. *Journal of Substance Abuse Treatment, 17*(1), 121–128.

Meyer W., III, Bockting, W. O., Cohen-Kettenis, P., Coleman, E., DiCeglie, D., Devor, H., et al. (2001). The Harry Benjamin International Gender Dysphoria Association's Standards of Care for Gender Identity Disorders, Sixth Version. *Journal of Psychology & Human Sexuality, 13*(1), 1.

Miklowitz, D. J., Goldstein, M. J., & Nuechterlein, K. H. (1995). Verbal interactions in the families of schizophrenic and bipolar affective patients. *Journal of Abnormal Psychology, 104*(2), 268–276.

Miller, I. W., Norman, W. H., & Keitner, G. I. (1999). Combined treatment for patients with double depression. *Psychotherapy and Psychosomatics, 68*(4), 180–185.

Miller, J. W., Naimi, T. S., Brewer, R. D., & Everett Jones, S. (2007). Binge drinking and associated health risk behaviors among high school students. *Pediatrics, 119,* 76–85.

Miller, K. J., Gleaves, D. H., Hirsch, T. G., Green, B. A., Snow, A. C., & Corbett, C. C. (2000). Comparisons of body image dimensions by race-ethnicity and gender in a university population. *International Journal of Eating Disorders, 27*(3), 310–316.

Miller, L. S., Wasserman, G. A., Neugebauer, R., Gorman-Smith, D., & Kamboukos, D. (1999). Witnessed community violence and antisocial behavior in high-risk, urban boys. *Journal of Clinical Child Psychology, 28*(1), 2–11.

Millichap, J. G. (2010). *Attention deficit hyperactivity disorder handbook: A physician's guide to ADHD* (2nd ed.). New York: Springer Science + Business Media.

Mitchell, J. E., Agras, S., Crow, S., Halmi, K., Fairburn, C. G., Bryson, S., et al. (2011). Stepped care and cognitive-behavioural therapy for bulimia nervosa: Randomised trial. *British Journal of Psychiatry, 198*(5), 391–397.

Montgomery, S. A., Bebbington, P., Cowen, P., Deakin, W., et al. (1993). Guidelines for treating depressive illness with antidepressants. *Journal of Psychopharmacology, 7*(1), 19–23.

Moos, R. H., & Cronkite, R. C. (1999). Symptom-based predictors of a 10-year chronic course of treated depression. *Journal of Nervous and Mental Disease, 187*(6), 360–368.

Morris, M. E., & Aguilera, A. (2012). Mobile, social, and wearable computing and the evolution of psychological practice. *Professional Psychology: Research and Practice, 43*(6), 622.

Muehlenkamp, J., Brausch, A., Quigley, K., & Whitlock, J. (2013). Interpersonal features and functions of nonsuicidal self-injury. *Suicide and Life-Threatening Behavior, 43*(1), 67–80.

Muir, J. L. (1997). Acetylcholine, aging, and Alzheimer's disease. *Pharmacology, Biochemistry, and Behavior, 56*(4), 687–696.

Mulholland, C. (2010). Depression and suicide in men. Retrieved on June 18, 2011, from http://www.netdoctor.co.uk/menshealth/facts/depressionsuicide.htm.

Müller-Oerlinghausen, B., Bauer, M., & Grof. P. (2012). Commentary on a recent review of lithium toxicity: What are its implications for clinical practice? *BMC Medicine 10*(1) 132.

Muroff, J., Steketee, G., Frost, R. O., & Tolin, D. F. (2013). Cognitive behavior therapy for hoarding disorder: Follow-up findings and predictors of outcome. *Depression and Anxiety.* DOI: 10.1002/da.22222

Mushquash, A. R., & Sherry, S. B. (2013). Testing the perfectionism model of binge eating in mother–daughter dyads: A mixed longitudinal and daily diary study. *Eating Behaviors, 14*(2), 171–179.

Myers, M. G., Stewart, D. G., & Brown, S. A. (1998). Progression from conduct disorder to antisocial personality disorder following treatment for adolescent substance abuse. *American Journal of Psychiatry, 155*(4), 479–485.

Nakajima, S., Suzuki, T., Watanabe, K., Kashima, H., & Uchida, H. (2010). Accelerating response to antidepressant treatment in depression: A review and clinical suggestions. *Progress in Neuro-Psychopharmacology and Biological Psychiatry, 34*(2), 259–264.

Narrow, W. E., Regier, D. A., Rae, D. S., Manderscheid, R. W., & Locke, B. Z. (1993). Use of services by persons with mental and addictive disorders: Findings from the National Institute of Mental Health Epidemiologic Catchment Area Program. *Archives of General Psychiatry, 50,* 95–107.

National Center for Health Statistics (1999). *Fastats A to Z. Chronic liver disease/cirrhosis.* Washington, DC: Centers for Disease Control and Prevention.

National Center for Health Statistics (2000). *Births, marriages, divorces, and deaths: Provisional data for January 1999,* National Vital Statistics Reports, Vol. 48, No. 1. Washington, DC: Centers for Disease Control and Prevention.

National Household Survey on Drug Abuse (1998). *1998 national estimates of rates of use and other measures related to drugs, alcohol, cigarettes, and other forms of tobacco.* Washington, DC: U.S. Department of Health and Human Services.

National Survey on Drug Use and Health (2010). *Results from the 2009 National Survey on Drug Use and Health: Volume 1. Summary of national findings.* (Office of Applied Studies, NSDUH Series H-38a). Rockville, MD: Substance Abuse and Mental Health Services Administration.

Nolen-Hoeksema, S. (1995). Gender differences in coping with depression across the lifespan. *Depression, 3,* 81–90.

Nolen-Hoeksema, S. (1998). The other end of the continuum: The costs of rumination. *Psychological Inquiry, 93,* 216–219.

North, C. S., Nixon, S. J., Shariat, S., Mallonee, S., McMillen, J. C., Spitznagel, E. L., et al. (1999). Psychiatric disorders among survivors of the Oklahoma City bombing. *Journal of the American Medical Association, 282*(8), 755–762.

Novaco, R. W. (1975). *Anger control.* Lexington, MA: Lexington.

Otto, M. W., Tolin, D. F., Nations, K. R., Utschig, A. C., Rothbaum, B. O., Hofmann, S. G., et al. (2012). Five sessions and counting: Considering ultra-brief treatment for panic disorder. *Depression and Anxiety, 29*(6), 465–470.

Pankevich, D. E., Teegarden, S. L., Hedin, A. D., Jensen, C. L., & Bale, T. L. (2010). Caloric restriction experience reprograms stress and orexigenic pathways and promotes binge eating. *Journal of Neuroscience, 30*(48), 16399–16407.

Panos, P. T., Jackson, J. W., Hasan, O., & Panos, A. (2013). Meta-analysis and systematic review assessing the efficacy of dialectical behavior therapy (DBT). *Research on Social Work Practice,* DOI: 1049731513503047.

Parker, J., Wales, G., Chalhoub, N., & Harpin, V. (2013). The long-term outcomes of interventions for the management of attention-deficit hyperactivity disorder in children and adolescents: A systematic review of randomized controlled trials. *Psychology Research & Behavior Management, 6,* 87–99.

Patient Outcomes Research Team (1998). Cited in S. Barlas, Patient outcome research team study on schizophrenia offers grim indictment. *Psychiatric Times, 15*(6).

Patrick, C. J., Bradley, M. M., & Lang, P. J. (1993). Emotion in the criminal psychopath: Startle reflex modulation. *Journal of Abnormal Psychology, 102*(1), 82–92.

Patrick, C. J., Cuthbert, B. N., & Lang, P. J. (1990). Emotion in the criminal psychopath: Fear imagery. *Psychophysiology, 27*(Suppl.), 55.

Paxton, S. J., & Diggens, J. (1997). Avoidance coping, binge eating, and depression: An examination of the escape theory of binge eating. *International Journal of Eating Disorders, 22,* 83–87.

Pemment, J. (2013). The neurobiology of antisocial personality disorder: The quest for rehabilitation and treatment. *Aggression and Violent Behavior, 18*(1), 79–82.

Penn, D. L., & Mueser, K. T. (1996). Research update on the psychosocial treatment of schizophrenia. *American Journal of Psychiatry, 153,* 607–617.

Perdeci, Z., Gulsun, M., Celik, C., Erdem, M., Ozdemir, B., Ozdag, F., & Kilic, S. (2010). Aggression and the event-related potentials in antisocial personality disorder. *Bulletin of Clinical Psychopharmacology, 20*(4), 300–306.

Perry-Hunnicutt, C., & Newman, I. A. (1993). Adolescent dieting practices and nutrition knowledge: Health values. *Journal of Health Behavior, Education, & Promotion, 17*(4), 35–40.

Peterlin, B. L., Rosso, A. L., Sheftell, F. D., Libon, D. J., Mossey, J. M., Merikangas, K. R. (2011). Post-traumatic stress disorder, drug abuse and migraine: New findings from the National Comorbidity Survey Replication (NCS-R). *Cephalalgia* 2011;31(2):235–44.

Pickens, R., & Fletcher, B. (1991). Overview of treatment issues. In R. Pickens, C. Leukefeld, & C. Schuster (Eds.), *Improving drug abuse treatment.* Rockville, MD: National Institute on Drug Abuse.

Pickett, S. A., Cook, J. A., & Razzano, L. (1999). Psychiatric rehabilitation services and outcomes: An overview. In A. V. Horwitz & T. L. Scheid (Eds.), *A handbook for the study of mental health: Social contexts, theories, and systems.* Cambridge, UK: Cambridge University Press.

Pierce, K., & Courchesne, E. (2001). Evidence for a cerebellar role in reduced exploration and stereotyped behavior in autism. *Biological Psychiatry, 49*(8), 655–664.

Pierce, K., & Courchesne, E. (2002). "A further support to the hypothesis of a link between serotonin, autism and the cerebellum": Reply. *Biological Psychiatry, 52*(2), 143.

Pike, K. M., & Rodin, J. (1991). Mothers, daughters and disordered eating. *Journal of Abnormal Psychology, 100*(2), 198–204.

Pinkston, E. M., & Linsk, N. L. (1984). Behavioral family intervention with the impaired elderly. *Gerontologist, 24,* 576–583.

Poulsen, S., Lunn, S., Daniel, S. I., Folke, S., Mathiesen, B. B., Katznelson, H., et al. (2014). A randomized controlled trial of psychoanalytic psychotherapy or cognitive-behavioral therapy for bulimia nervosa. *American Journal of Psychiatry, 171*(1), 109–116.

Psychiatric Rehabilitation Consultants. (1991). *Modules for training and independent living skills for persons with serious mental disorders.* Available from Dissemination Coordinator, Camarillo-UCLA Research Center, Box 6022, Camarillo, CA 93011–6022.

Puri, P. R., & Dimsdale, J. E. (2011). Healthcare utilization and poor reassurance: Potential predictors of somatoform disorders. *Psychiatric Clinics of North America, 34*(3), 525.

Pyle, R. L. (1999). Dynamic psychotherapy. In M. Hersen & A. S. Bellack (Eds)., *Handbook of comparative interventions for adult disorders* (2nd ed.). New York: Wiley.

Rachman, S. (1993). Obsessions, responsibility and guilt. *Behaviour Research and Therapy, 31*(2), 149–154.

Redd, W. H., Jacobsen, P. B., Die-Trill, M., et al. (1987). Cognitive/attentional distraction in the control of conditioned nausea in pediatric cancer patients receiving chemotherapy. *Journal of Consulting Clinical Psychology, 55,* 391–395.

Reese, J., Kraschewski, A., Anghelescu, I., Winterer, G., Schmidt, L. G., Gallinat, J., et al. (2010). Haplotypes of dopamine and serotonin transporter genes are associated with antisocial personality disorder in alcoholics. *Psychiatric Genetics, 20*(4), 140–152.

Regehr, C., Cadell, S., & Jansen, K. (1999). Perceptions of control and long-term recovery from rape. *American Journal of Orthopsychiatry, 173*(supp.34), 24–28.

Regier, D. A., Narrow, W. E., Rae, D. S., Manderscheid, R. W., Locke, B. Z., & Goodwin, F. K. (1993). The de facto US mental and addictive disorders service system: Epidemiologic catchment area prospective 1-year prevalence rates of disorders in services. *Archives of General Psychiatry, 50,* 85–94.

Regier, D. A., Rae, D. S., Narrow, W. E., Kaelber, C. T., & Schatzberg, A. F. (1998). Prevalence of anxiety disorders and their comorbidity with mood and addictive disorders. *British Journal of Psychiatry, 173*(Suppl. 34), 24–28.

Reichow, B. (2012). Overview of meta-analyses on early intensive behavioral intervention for young children with autism spectrum disorders. *Journal of Autism and Developmental Disorders, 42*(4), 512–520.

Riggs, D. S., & Foa, E. B. (1993). Obsessive-compulsive disorder. In D. H. Barlow (Ed.), *Clinical handbook of psychological disorders: A step-by-step treatment manual* (2nd ed.). New York: Guilford.

Roazen, P. (1992). The rise and fall of Bruno Bettelheim. *Psychohistory Review, 20*(3), 221–250.

Robison, L. M., Sclar, D. A., Skaer, T. L., & Galin, R. S. (1999). National trends in the prevalence of attention-deficit/hyperactivity disorder and the prescribing of methylphenidate among school children 1990–1995. *Clinical Pediatrics, 38*(4), 209–217.

Rosen J. C., & Leitenberg, H. (1982). Bulimia nervosa: Treatment with exposure and response prevention. *Behavior Therapy, 13*(1), 117–124.

Rosen, J. C., & Leitenberg, H. (1985). Exposure plus response prevention treatment of bulimia. In D. M. Garner & P. E. Garfinkel (Eds.), *Handbook of psychotherapy for anorexia nervosa and bulimia.* New York: Guilford Press.

Rosen, R. C., & Kupelian, V. (2011). Epidemiology of erectile dysfunction and key risk factors. In K. T. McVary (Ed.), *Contemporary Treatment of Erectile Dysfunction* (pp. 39–49). New York: Humana Press.

Rossow, I., & Amundsen, A. (1995). Alcohol abuse and suicide: A 40-year prospective study of Norwegian conscripts. *Addiction, 90*(5), 685–691.

Rothbaum, B. O., & Ninan, P. T. (1999). Manual for the cognitive-behavioral treatment of trichotillomania. *Trichotillomania* (pp. 263–284). Washington, DC: American Psychiatric Publishing.

Rothbaum, B. O., Shaw, L., Morris, R., & Ninan, P. T. (1993). Prevalence of trichotillomania in a college freshman population. *Journal of Clinical Psychiatry, 54*, 72.

Sacks, O. (2000, May). *An anthropologist on Mars: Some personal perspectives on autism.* Keynote address, Eden Institute Foundation's Sixth Annual Princeton Lecture Series on Autism, Princeton, NJ.

Salkovskis, P. M., & Harrison, J. (1984). Abnormal and normal obsessions—a replication. *Behaviour Research and Therapy, 22*(5), 549–552.

Salkovskis, P. M., Wroe, A. L., Gledhill, A., Morrison, N., Forrester, E., Richards, C., et al. (2000). Responsibility attitudes and interpretations are characteristic of obsessive compulsive disorder. *Behaviour Research and Therapy, 38*(4), 347–372.

Schlaepfer, T. E., Ågren, H., Monteleone, P., Gasto, C., Pitchot, W., Rouillon, F., et al. (2012). The hidden third: Improving outcome in treatment-resistant depression. *Journal of Psychopharmacology, 26*(5), 587–602.

Schoeyen, H. K., Birkenaes, A. B., Vaaler, A. E., Auestad, B. H., Malt, U. F., Andreassen, O. A., et al. (2011). Bipolar disorder patients have similar levels of education but lower socio-economic status than the general population. *Journal of Affective Disorders, 129*(1), 68–74.

Selkoe, D. J. (1991). Amyloid protein and Alzheimer's disease. *Scientific American, 265,* 68–78.

Selkoe, D. J. (1992). Alzheimer's disease: New insights into an emerging epidemic. *Journal of Geriatric Psychiatry, 25*(2), 211–227.

Selkoe, D. J. (1998). The cell biology of beta-amyloid precursor protein and presenilin in Alzheimer's disease. *Trends in Cell Biology, 8*(11), 447–453.

Selkoe, D. J. (1999). Translating cell biology into therapeutic advances in Alzheimer's disease. *Nature, 399*(Suppl. 6738), A23–31.

Selkoe, D. J. (2000). The origins of Alzheimer's disease: A is for amyloid. *Journal of the American Medical Association, 283*(12), 1615–1617.

Selkoe, D. J. (2011). Alzheimer's disease. *Cold Spring Harbor Perspectives in Biology, 3*(7), 1–16.

Selkoe, D. J., Yamazaki, T., Citron, M., Podlisny, M. B., Koo, E. H., Teplow, D. B., et al. (1996). The role of APP processing and trafficking pathways in the formation of amyloid B-protein. In R. J. Wurtman, S. Corkin, J. H. Growdon, & R. M. Nitsch (Eds.), *The neurobiology of Alzheimer's disease.* New York: New York Academy of Sciences.

Shafran, R., Fairburn, C. G., Robinson, P., & Lask, B. (2004). Body checking and its avoidance in eating disorders. *International Journal of Eating Disorders, 35*(1), 93–101.

Shafran, R., Thordarson, D. S., & Rachman, S. (1996). Thought-action fusion in obsessive compulsive disorder. *Journal of Anxiety Disorders, 10*(5), 379–391.

Shea, T., Elkin, I., Imber, S., Sotsky, S., Watkins, J., Colins, J., et al. (1992). Course of depressive symptoms over follow-up: Findings from the National Institute of Mental Health treatment of depression collaborative research program. *Archives of General Psychiatry, 49,* 782–787.

Shelby, G. D., Shirkey, K. C., Sherman, A. L., Beck, J. E., Haman, K., Shears, A. R., et al. (2013). Functional abdominal pain in childhood and long-term vulnerability to anxiety disorders. *Pediatrics, 132*(3), 475–482.

Shisslak, C. M., Crago, M., McKnight, K. M., Estes, L. S., Gray, G., & Parnaby, O. G. (1998). Potential risk factors associated with weight control behaviors in elementary and middle school girls. *Journal of Psychosomatic Research, 44*(3/4), 301–313.

Smink, F. R., van Hoeken, D., & Hoek, H. W. (2012). Epidemiology of eating disorders: Incidence, prevalence and mortality rates. *Current Psychiatry Reports, 14*(4), 406–414.

Smith, T. W. (1992). Hostility and health: Current status of a psychosomatic hypothesis. *Health Psychology, 11,* 139–150.

Smith, Y. L, Van Goozen, S. H. M., Kuiper, A. J., & Cohen-Kettenis, P. T. (2005). Sex reassignment: Outcomes and predictors of treatment for adolescent and adult transsexuals. *Psychological Medicine, 35,* 89–99.

Soukup, J. E. (2006). Alzheimer's disease: New concepts in diagnosis, treatment, and management. In T. G. Plante (Ed.), *Mental disorders of the new millennium,* Vol. 3. Biology and Function. Westport, CT: Praeger.

Spanier, C. A., Frank, E., McEachran, A. B., Grochocinski, V. J., & Kuprer, D. J. (1999). Maintenance interpersonal psychotherapy for recurrent depression: Biological and clinical correlates and future directions. In D. S. Janowsky (Ed.), *Psychotherapy indications and outcomes.* Washington, DC: American Psychiatric Press.

Spector, I. P., & Carey, M. P. (1990). Incidence and prevalence of sexual dysfunctions: A critical review of the empirical literature. *Archives of Sexual Behavior, 19*(4), 389–408.

Spiegel, D., & Classen, C. (2000). *Group therapy for cancer patients: A research-based handbook of psychosocial care.* New York: Basic Books.

Spoont, M. R. (1996). Emotional Instability. In C. G. Costello (Ed.), *Personality characteristics of the personality disordered.* New York: Wiley.

St. George-Hyslop, P. H. (2000). Molecular genetics of Alzheimer's disease. *Biological Psychiatry, 47*(3), 183–199.

Stallard, P., Velleman, R., & Baldwin, S. (1998). Prospective study of post-traumatic stress disorder in children involved in road traffic accidents. *British Medical Journal, 317*(7173), 1619–1623.

Stanley, M. A., Borden, J. W., Bell, G. E., & Wagner, A. L. (1994). Nonclinical hair pulling: Phenomenology and related psychopathology. *Journal of Anxiety Disorders, 8,* 119–130.

Stein, D. J., Christenson, G. A., & Hollander, E. (Eds.) (1999). *Trichotillomania.* Washington, DC: American Psychiatric Press, Inc.

Steinglass, J., Albano, A. M., Simpson, H. B., Carpenter, K., Schebendach, J., & Attia, E. (2012). Fear of food as a treatment target: Exposure and response prevention for anorexia nervosa in an open series. *International Journal of Eating Disorders, 45*(4), 615–621.

Steketee, G., Frost, R. O., Tolin, D. F., Rasmussen, J., & Brown, T. A. (2010). Waitlist-controlled trial of cognitive behavior therapy for hoarding disorder. *Depression and Anxiety, 27*(5), 476–484.

Stice, E., Marti, C. N., & Durant, S. (2011). Risk factors for onset of eating disorders: Evidence of multiple risk pathways from an 8-year prospective study. *Behaviour Research and Therapy, 49*(10), 622–627.

Striegel-Moore, R. H., Silberstein, L. R., & Rodin, J. (1993). The social self in bulimia nervosa: Public self-consciousness, social anxiety, and perceived fraudulence. *Journal of Abnormal Psychology, 102*(2), 297–303.

Strober, M., Freeman, R., & Morrell, W. (1997). The long-term course of severe anorexia nervosa in adolescents: Survival analysis of recovery, relapse, and outcome predictors over 10–15 years in a prospective study. *International Journal of Eating Disorders, 22*(4), 339–360.

Swartz, M. S., Frohberg, N. R., Drake, R. E., & Lauriello, J. (2012). Psychosocial therapies. In J. A. Lieberman, T. S. Stoup, & D. O. Perkins (Eds.), *Essentials of schizophrenia* (pp. 207–224). Arlington, VA: American Psychiatric Publishing.

Swedo, S. E., Leonard, H. L., Rapoport, J. L., Lenane, M. C., Goldberger, E. L., & Cheslow, C. L. (1989). A double-blind comparison of clomipramine and desipramine in the treatment of trichotillomania (hair pulling). *New England Journal of Medicine, 321,* 497–501.

Taube-Schiff, M., & Lau, M. A. (2008). Major depressive disorder. In M. Hersen & J. Rosqvist (Eds.), *Handbook of psychological assessment, case conceptualization, and treatment: Vol. 1. Adults* (pp. 319–351). Hoboken, NJ: Wiley.

Tay, Y. K., Levy, M. L., & Metry, D. W. (2004). Trichotillomania in childhood: Case series and review. *Pediatrics, 113*(5), e494–e498.

Taylor, D. J., Walters, H. M., Vittengl, J. R., Krebaum, S., & Jarrett, R. B. (2010). Which depressive symptoms remain after response to cognitive therapy of depression and predict relapse and recurrence? *Journal of Affective Disorders, 123*(1), 181–187.

Taylor, S. (1995). Anxiety sensitivity: Theoretical perspectives and recent findings. *Behaviour Research and Therapy, 33*(3), 243–258.

Taylor, S. E., Kemeny, M. E., Reed, G. M., Bower, J. E., & Gruenewald, T. L. (2000). Psychological resources, positive illusions, and health. *American Psychology, 55*(1), 99–109.

Teich, C. F., & Agras, W. S. (1993). The effects of a very low calorie diet on binge eating. *Behavior Therapy, 24,* 177–193.

Teichman, Y., Bar-El, Z., Shor, H., Sirota, P., & Elizur, A. (1995). A comparison of two modalities of cognitive therapy (individual and marital) in treating depression. *Psychiatry: Interpersonal and Biological Processes, 58*(2), 136–148.

Tek, S., Mesite, L., Fein, D., & Naigles, L. (2014). Longitudinal analyses of expressive language development reveal two distinct language profiles among young children with autism spectrum disorders. *Journal of Autism and Developmental Disorders, 44*(1), 75–89.

Timpano, K. R., Keough, M. E., Traeger, L., & Schmidt, N. B. (2011). General life stress and hoarding: Examining the role of emotional tolerance. *International Journal of Cognitive Therapy, 4*(3), 263–279.

Tkachuk, G. A., & Martin, G. L. (1999). Exercise therapy for patients with psychiatric disorders: Research and clinical implications. *Professional Psychology: Research and Practice, 30*(3), 275–282.

Tolin, D. F., & Villavicencio, A. (2011). Inattention, but not OCD, predicts the core features of hoarding disorder. *Behaviour Research and Therapy, 49*(2), 120–125.

Tomenson, B., McBeth, J., Chew-Graham, C. A., MacFarlane, G., Davies, I., Jackson, J., et al. (2012). Somatization and health anxiety as predictors of health care use. *Psychosomatic Medicine, 74*(6), 656–664.

Treasure, J., & Szmukler, G. I. (1995). Medical complications of chronic anorexia nervosa. In G. I. Szmukler, C. Dare, & J. Treasure (Eds.), *Handbook on eating disorders: Theory, treatment and research.* Chichester, UK: Wiley.

Treasure, J., Todd, G., & Szmukler, G. (1995). The inpatient treatment of anorexia nervosa. In G. Szmukler, C. Dare, & J. Treasure (Eds.), *Handbook of eating disorders: Theory, treatment, and research.* Chichester, UK: Wiley.

U.S. Department of Justice Bureau of Justice Statistics (1994). *Violence between inmates: Domestic violence.* Annapolis Junction, MD: Bureau of Justice Statistics Clearinghouse.

Uchiyama, T., Kurosawa, M., & Inaba, Y. (2007). MMR-vaccine and regression in autism spectrum disorders: Negative results presented from Japan. *Journal of Autism and Developmental Disorders, 3*(2), 210–217.

Van Bourgondien, M. E., & Schopler, E. (1990). Critical issues in the residential care of people with autism. *Journal of Autism and Developmental Disorders, 20*(3), 391–399.

Von Lojewski, A., Boyd, C., Abraham, S., & Russell, J. (2012). Lifetime and recent DSM and ICD psychiatric comorbidity of inpatients engaging in different eating disorder behaviours. *Eating and Weight Disorders—Studies on Anorexia, Bulimia and Obesity, 17*(3), 185–193.

Waddington, J. L., O'Tuathaigh, C. M. P., & Remington, G. J. (2011). Pharmacology and neuroscience of antipsychotic drugs. In D. R. Weinberg & M. A. Harrison (Eds.), *Schizophrenia* (pp. 483–514). Hoboken, NJ: Wiley-Blackwell.

Wallien, M. S. C., & Cohen-Kettenis, P. T. (2008). Psychosexual outcome of gender-dysphoric children. *Journal of the American Academy of Child & Adolescent Psychiatry, 47,* 1413–1423.

Walsh, B. T., Wilson, G. R., Loeb, K. L., Devlin, M. J., et al. (1997). Medication and psychotherapy in the treatment of bulimia nervosa. *American Journal of Psychiatry, 154,* 523–531.

Weissman, M. M., & Olfson, M. (1995). Depression in women: Implications for health care research. *Science, 269*(5225), 799–801.

Wendland, J. R., & McMahon, F. J. (2011). Genetics of bipolar disorder. In C. A. Zarate, Jr. & H. K. Manji (Eds.), *Bipolar depression: Molecular neurobiology, clinical diagnosis and pharmacotherapy. Milestones in drug therapy* (pp. 19–30). Cambridge, MA: Birkhäuser.

Wenze, S. J., Gunthert, K. C., & German, R. E. (2012). Biases in affective forecasting and recall in individuals with depression and anxiety symptoms. *Personality and Social Psychology Bulletin, 38*(7), 895–906.

Whittal, M. L., Thordarson, D. S., & McLean, P. D. (2005). Treatment of obsessive-compulsive disorder: Cognitive behavior therapy vs. exposure and response prevention. *Behaviour Research and Therapy, 43*(12), 1559–1576.

Wiederman, M. W., & Pryor, T. (1996). Substance use and impulsive behaviors among adolescents with eating disorders. *Addictive Behaviors, 21*(2), 269–272.

Wilsnack, R. W., Vogeltanz, N. D., Wilsnack, S. C., & Harris, T. R. (2000). Gender differences in alcohol consumption and adverse drinking consequences: Cross-cultural patterns. *Addiction, 95*(2), 251–265.

Wilson, K. A., & Chambless, D. L. (1999). Inflated perceptions of responsibility and obsessive-compulsive symptoms. *Behaviour Research and Therapy, 37*(4), 325–335.

Wincze, J. P., & Carey, M. P. (2012). *Sexual dysfunction: A guide for assessment and treatment.* New York: Guilford Press.

Witthöft, M., & Hiller, W. (2010). Psychological approaches to origins and treatments of somatoform disorders. *Annual Review of Clinical Psychology, 6,* 257–283.

Wooley, S. C., & Wooley, O. W. (1985). Intensive outpatient and residential treatment for bulimia. In D. M. Garner & P. E. Garfinkel (Eds.), *Handbook of psychotherapy for anorexia nervosa and bulimia.* New York: Guilford Press.

Wright, I. C., Rabe, H. S., Woodruff, P. W. R., David, A. S., Murray, R. M., & Bullmore, E. T. (2000). Meta-analysis of regional brain volumes in schizophrenia. *American Journal of Psychiatry, 157*(1), 16–25.

Wright, S. (2000). Group work. In B. Lask & R. Bryant-Waugh (Eds.), *Anorexia nervosa and related eating disorders in childhood and adolescence* (2nd ed). Hove, UK: Psychology Press/Taylor & Francis.

Zal, H. M. (1999). Agitation in the elderly. *Psychiatric Times, 16*(1), 1–5.

Zetsche, U., D'Avanzato, C., & Joormann, J. (2012). Depression and rumination: Relation to components of inhibition. *Cognition and Emotion, 26*(4), 758–767.

Zisook, S., Goff, A., Sledge, P., Shuchter, S. R. (1994). Reported suicidal behavior and current suicidal ideation in a psychiatric outpatient clinic. *Annals of Clinical Psychiatry, 6,* 27–31.

Zucker, K. G., (2010). Gender identity and sexual orientation. In M. K. Dulcan (Ed.), *Dulcan's textbook of child and adolescent psychiatry* (pp. 543–552). Arlington, VA: American Psychiatric Publishing.

Zucker, K. J., Bradley, S. J., Owen-Anderson, A., Kibblewhite, S. J., Wood, H., Singh, D., et al. (2012). Demographics, behavior problems, and psychosexual characteristics of adolescents with gender identity disorder or transvestic fetishism. *Journal of Sex & Marital Therapy, 38*(2), 151–189.

Zuvekas, S. H., & Vitiello, B. (2012). Stimulant medication use in children: A 12-year perspective. *American Journal of Psychiatry, 169*(2), 160–166.

Name Index

Subject Index